KEI KATAOKA AND JOHN TABER

MEANING AND NON-EXISTENCE

ÖSTERREICHISCHE AKADEMIE DER WISSENSCHAFTEN

PHILOSOPHISCH-HISTORISCHE KLASSE
SITZUNGSBERICHTE, 902. BAND

BEITRÄGE ZUR KULTUR- UND
GEISTESGESCHICHTE ASIENS, NR. 102

HERAUSGEGEBEN VOM INSTITUT
FÜR KULTUR- UND GEISTESGESCHICHTE ASIENS
UNTER DER LEITUNG VON BIRGIT KELLNER

Meaning and Non-existence

Kumārila's Refutation of Dignāga's Theory of Exclusion

The Apohavāda *Chapter of Kumārila's* Ślokavārttika

Critical Edition and Annotated Translation

Kei Kataoka and John Taber

AUSTRIAN
ACADEMY
OF SCIENCES
PRESS

Angenommen durch die Publikationskommission der philosophisch-historischen Klasse der Österreichischen Akademie der Wissenschaften:

Accepted by the publication committee of the Division of Humanities and Social Sciences of the Austrian Academy of Sciences by:

Diese Publikation wurde einem anonymen,
internationalen Begutachtungsverfahren unterzogen.

This publication was subject to international
and anonymous peer review.

Peer review is an essential part of the Austrian Academy of Sciences Press evaluation process. Before any book can be accepted for publication, it is assessed by international specialists and ultimately must be approved by the Austrian Academy of Sciences Publication Committee.

Die verwendete Papiersorte in dieser Publikation ist DIN EN ISO 9706 zertifiziert und erfüllt die Voraussetzung für eine dauerhafte Archivierung von schriftlichem Kulturgut.

The paper used in this publication is DIN EN ISO 9706 certified and meets the requirements for permanent archiving of written cultural property.

ISBN 978-3-7001-8641-0

Austrian Academy of Sciences, Vienna
Druck/Printed: Prime Rate, Budapest
https://epub.oeaw.ac.at/8641-0
https://verlag.oeaw.ac.at
Made in Europe

Contents

Preface

The theory of exclusion (Apohavāda) has long been an object of fascination for philosophers and Indologists despite – perhaps even because of – lack of access to the most important sources for understanding it.[1] This is not the only time in the field of Indian philosophy when inadequate knowledge of the primary sources has bestowed an aura of mystery upon an, in principle, readily intelligible idea. The first translation of one of the early defining statements of the theory was Frauwallner's German translation of the verses of the Apoha Section of *Pramāṇavārttika* 1 (PV[SV] 1.40–185), based on the Tibetan version, together with a summary of the autocommentary.[2] Although this translation represents a pioneering achievement and holds up well even today as an international team of scholars translates PV(SV) 1.40–185 directly from the Sanskrit,[3] the fact that it is in German has limited its impact. Frauwallner also published a translation of Dharmottara's *Apohaprakaraṇa* shortly after his translation of the Apoha Section of PV 1 (Frauwallner 1937), but this too was in German.[4] In 1937 Gaṅgānātha Jhā's English translation of Śāntarakṣita's *Tattvasaṅgraha* appeared. The *Śabdārthaparīkṣā* chapter of the *Tattvasaṅgraha* contains a comprehensive defence of the Apohavāda against Brahmin criticisms, in particular those of Kumārila; sixty-seven verses of Kumārila, probably taken from his *Bṛhaṭṭīkā*, are quoted. This publication gave English-speaking scholars full access to the Apohavāda for the first time, though in a more developed form.[5]

---

[1] Influential early philosophical treatments of *apoha* include Herzberger 1975, Shaw 1978, Siderits 1982, 1985, 1991: 87–110, 1999, and Ganeri 2001: 106–114.

[2] Frauwallner 1932, 1933, 1935.

[3] Using Gnoli's edition, which came out in 1960. The first part of this three-part project appeared in November, 2018. See Eltschinger et al. 2018.

[4] See Kataoka 2014b for an updated treatment of Dharmottara on *apoha* with a critical assessment of Frauwallner's view of Dharmottara.

[5] Mark Siderits' early studies of *apoha* (1982, 1985, 1991: 87–110, and 1999),

Meanwhile, the foundational statement of the theory, the fifth chapter of Dignāga's *Pramāṇasamuccaya* (PS 5), remained in obscurity. Without a clear grasp of what Dignāga was proposing, Dharmakīrti's revision and defense of the Apohavāda in his *Pramāṇavārttika*, despite the crucial materials made available by Frauwallner, were difficult to understand and assess. Frauwallner's explanation of the central role played by the Apohavāda in Dignāga's philosophy in his seminal article "Dignāga, sein Werk und seine Entwicklung"[6] was of considerable help, but it also made scholars even more aware of the need for a translation and study of PS 5 itself. Kumārila's criticism of Dignāga's theory in his *Ślokavārttika*, as well as Uddyotakara's treatment of it in his *Nyāyavārttika* (ad NBh 2.2.66), both of which were already available in English translation in 1907 and 1919, respectively,[7] are highly polemical in tone and do not allow one to gain a clear picture of Dignāga's views in all their subtlety and complexity.[8] Richard Hayes's English translation of substantial portions of the second and fifth chapters of the *Pramāṇasamuccaya* (Hayes 1988), therefore, was a major step forward, in fact, another groundbreaking achievement. Yet, based principally on the poor-quality Tibetan translations of Dignāga's text and reliant also upon the Tibetan version of Jinendrabuddhi's commentary,[9] it still left many things in the dark. As Hayes himself confesses,

---

which did much to stimulate the interest of Anglophone philosophers, are primarily based on the *Tattvasaṅgraha*. It should be noted, however, that when quoting the TS and Kamalaśīla's commentary he provides his own translations. Siderits 1991: 87–102, moreover, tackles Dharmakīrti's discussion in PV 1. This is an important contribution because it shows that Dharmakīrti upheld a sense-reference distinction in PV 1.40ff., which most scholars now accept. Siderits 1999 also references the *Pramāṇavārttika*. Siderits revisits his earlier work in Siderits 2011.

[6] Frauwallner 1959: 98–106.

[7] Jhā 1907, 1984.

[8] Mookerjee 1935 discusses various theories of *apoha* and their historical development based on the primary sources available at the time, i.e., the works of Uddyotakara, Kumārila, Śāntarakṣita, Jayanta, Vācaspatimiśra, and Ratnakīrti. His interpretations were later critically reexamined by Akamatsu 1971.

[9] Though also critically consulting the translations of passages of *Pramāṇasamuccaya* 5 into Sanskrit from Vasudhararakṣita's Tibetan translations

"trying to piece together [Dignāga's] original thought on the basis of the Tibetan translations is like looking at a human skull and trying to imagine what the person's face looked like when alive."[10]

It was not until quite recently, more than seventy years after Frauwallner's initial contributions, with the work of Ole Holten Pind, that Dignāga's Apohavāda has finally come clearly into view. In his 2009 dissertation, published in a corrected and reorganized format in 2015 in this same series (Pind 2015), he restored most of the Sanskrit text of PS 5 together with its *Vṛtti*, using a newly discovered Sanskrit manuscript of Jinendrabuddhi's commentary. Accompanying his new English translation, based on this restored text, with extensive annotations that provide the technical linguistic and philosophical background of Dignāga's arguments (some forming appendices in the *Beiträge zur Kultur- und Geistesgeschichte Asiens* edition), along with detailed discussions of text-critical issues, he was able for the first time to enable the reader willing to work through all the materials he had assembled to get a definite idea of what Dignāga is up to: what, at each stage of the treatise, he is rejecting, what he is proposing, and how he is defending his own position. Although more work remains to be done – refinements of Pind's translations and interpretations will become possible when the critical edition of Jinendrabuddhi's commentary on the fifth chapter is completed[11] – it is as it stands a seminal work of scholarship that will undoubtedly revolutionize the field of *apoha* studies.[12]

---

by Muni Jambūvijayajī in footnotes to the second part (eighth *ara*) of NĀA, as well as citations of PS 5 in other Sanskrit sources.

[10] Hayes 1988: 230.

[11] Currently being undertaken by Birgit Kellner, Horst Lasic, and Patrick McAllister of the Institute for the Cultural and Intellectual History of Asia of the Austrian Academy of Sciences.

[12] Valuable studies of the Apohavāda that appeared in the latter decades of the twentieth century, bridging the gap, so to speak, between the work of Frauwallner and Pind, were carrried out by Japanese scholars: Akamatsu 1971, Katsura 1979 and 1991, and Hattori 1977 and 1980. Hattori 2000, meanwhile, is an English translation of the initial verses of PS 5, while Hattori 1973 and 1975 are a Japanese

It is principally Pind's achievement that has made it possible for us to offer a new, annotated translation of the *Apohavāda* chapter of Kumārila's *Ślokavārttika* (ŚV *Apohavāda*). Understanding better the theory Kumārila is criticizing, one is better able to understand his criticisms. At the same time, Kumārila's criticisms in many cases clarify Dignāga's arguments in turn. We hope that our translation, accompanied by Pind's translation of PS 5, by providing direct access to the materials that represent the earliest stage of the debate about *apoha* – which comprise the earliest version of the theory itself and the first comprehensive response to it – will put future interpretations and discussions of the Apohavāda on a firmer footing.

Equally essential for a new translation of ŚV *Apohavāda*, however, was a new, critical edition of the text. This was carried out by Kataoka at the beginning of the project using six manuscripts along with some of the existing editions; it is presented here as the first part of this volume. Also essential for our work was an edition of Sucaritamiśra's important commentary on the *Apohavāda* chapter of the *Ślokavārttika*.[13] This was also prepared and published by Kataoka in three parts.[14] Finally, a critical edition of the *apoha* section of Jayanta's *Nyāyamañjarī*, executed again by Kataoka (Kataoka 2017), contributed to a broader understanding of Kumārila's position in its historical context.[15]

---

translation of ŚV *Apohavāda*. Hattori 1982 is a critical edition of the Tibetan version of PS 5 together with Jinendrabuddhi's commentary. For a useful survey of early scholarship on Dignāga and *apoha*, including Japanese contributions, see Hayes 1988: 9–32.

[13] The Trivandrum Sanskrit Series edition of Sucarita's *Kāśikā* extends only through the *Sambandhākṣepa* chapter.

[14] Kataoka 2014a covers Sucarita's extensive commentary on ŚV *Apohavāda* 1; it also describes the manuscripts used and discusses Sucarita's philosophical and chronological relation to other authors. Kataoka 2015 covers vv. 2–94 and Kataoka 2019 vv. 95–176.

[15] See also Watson and Kataoka 2017 for a translation of Jayanta's arguments on *apoha*. Other studies in the same volume (McAllister 2017), e.g., by Pascale Hugon ("On *vyāvṛtta*"), Hideyo Ogawa ("The Qualifier-Qualificand Relation and Coreferentiality"), Kei Kataoka ("Dharmottara's Notion of *āropita*"), and McAllister ("Competing Theories of Conceptual Cognition"), expand the discussion.

This project was originally conceived in 2009 as part of a larger undertaking proposed by Dr. Helmut Krasser, Director of the Institute for the Cultural and Intellectual History of Asia (IKGA) in Vienna. When funding for the larger venture did not materialize, Kataoka and Taber decided to go ahead independently. If we had chosen a chapter of the *Ślokavārttika* to translate together for ourselves, we probably would have selected a different one; both of us had avoided the topic of *apoha* up to that point in our research, daunted by its difficulty. But encouraged by Krasser we recognized the need for a translation of ŚV *Apohavāda*; moreover, it would complement other work being done on *apoha* at the IKGA. Finally, each of us had previously translated other chapters of the *Ślokavārttika* (Taber 2005, Kataoka 2011a) according to somewhat different interests and methodologies. We were curious to see what the result would be if we joined forces. We met to work on the translation in August–September, 2012, in Albuquerque, New Mexico; December–January, 2013–14, in Fukuoka, Japan; and December–January, 2014–15, again in Albuquerque. Kataoka's travel was supported by JSPS KAKENHI (the Scientific Research Fund of the Japanese Society for the Promotion of Science, grants no. 23520067 and 15K02043), Taber's by his annual travel allotment from the Department of Philosophy of the University of New Mexico. We wish to express our sincere thanks to both of these institutions. Overall, our collaboration has been very rewarding – and this, despite the fact that there are still certain questions concerning Kumārila and Dharmakīrti about which we disagree. By combining our expertise, we feel that we have produced a translation that is better than either of us could have achieved on his own.

We also would like to express our gratitude to Birgit Kellner and Patrick McAllister of the IKGA for carefully vetting the manuscript before we submitted it to the Verlag der Österreichischen Akademie der Wissenschaften for consideration for publication. They made numerous suggestions for improvement, almost all of which we followed. The anonymous reviewers for the Verlag also offered constructive criticisms that led to significant revisions, as did our copy editor, Prof. John Bussanich. Finally, we are deeply appreciative of the IKGA for covering the subvention costs for the publication of this work.

Our main goal in translating ŚV *Apohavāda* has been to figure out what Kumārila is saying and communicate our understanding of it. Our guiding principle has been only to translate a verse, relying on all the resources at our disposal, when we were confident that we fully understood the argument being made. We present our notion of what the text means in relatively short, minimally technical explanations following individual verses or groups of verses. By "resources at our disposal" we mean, besides the existing editions and manuscripts, principally the classical Mīmāṃsā commentaries on the ŚV *Apohavāda*, i.e., those of Jayamiśra (date unknown), Sucaritamiśra (first half of the tenth century), and Pārthasārathimiśra (twelfth century),[16] along with Kamalaśīla's commentary on the verses of Kumārila cited by Śāntarakṣita in the *Śabdārthaparīkṣā* chapter of his *Tattvasaṅgraha*. Although the last was always consulted, we cite it less frequently in the footnotes, when it included information not already found in the Mīmāṃsā commentaries or was helpful in deciding between interpretations of a verse or provided a noteworthy alternative. Of course, PS 5 came into play, too, when identifying the arguments of Dignāga Kumārila is attacking. Having studied and digested these materials, we usually followed what we felt to be the most plausible construal of Kumārila's statement – in the majority of cases, of course, the commentators agree. In the footnotes we discuss some, but by no means all, of the more interesting differences of interpretation and justify our selection. "Our understanding" as expressed in the explanations, thus, to a great extent, represents a processing of the traditional exegesis of Kumārila's text.

We hope that this translation will not just be of interest to specialists of Indian philosophy, though we have not tried to make it into a popular introduction to the Indian debate about the Apohavāda or, more broadly, Indian semantics. The main hurdle to overcome in gaining access to this text is not the theory of *apoha* itself, which is really not that difficult, we think – once one understands it! It is, rather, the complexity of the debate, which relates to so many topics in Indian linguistics, philosophy of language, and metaphysics. We provide much of this context in the notes. We have, however, exercized restraint in doing so, offering only as much

[16] See Kataoka 2014a: 360(3).

background and philological analysis as we feel is necessary to meet the requirements of a scientific annotated translation, without, it is hoped, completely overwhelming the reader. Hence, we do invite non-specialists interested in acquiring a deeper knowledge of Indian philosophy to attempt to penetrate this challenging material. (Even specialists will not find it easy going!) Those who are altogether unacquainted with the Apohavāda may learn the basics by reading the lucid and still essentially accurate account in Kunjunni Raja 1963: 78–94, which references Uddyotakara and Kumārila among other authors, or else by reading Chakrabarti and Siderits's introduction to the volume they recently edited together with Tom Tillemans: *Apoha*: *Buddhist Nominalism and Human Cognition* (2011). Indian philosophy cannot, any more than Western philosophy, be summarized in a list of results. It has a distinctive methodology (or, indeed, methodologies), characterized by unique ways of developing and critiquing ideas, not to mention its own set of presuppositions. To really begin to plumb its depths one must learn, or at least get a feel for, this methodology. Here, in ŚV *Apohavāda*, we encounter one of the greatest Indian philosophers hard at work on a rather technical problem, putting the machinery of Indian philosophical analysis through its paces, so to speak. At the same time, this problem was at the heart of so many controversies concerning metaphysical and epistemological questions in classical Indian philosophy.

The translation is followed by essays by each of the co-authors. Taber's locates Kumārila's contribution to the debate about *apoha* in relation to his predecessors Dignāga and the Nyāya philosopher Uddyotakara – one of the first Brahmin philosophers to react to Dignāga's proposal – and Kumārila's successor (or, possibly, younger contemporary), the great Dharmakīrti. It attempts to convey an idea of the significance of Kumārila's achievement in ŚV *Apohavāda* – for instance, although Kumārila was clearly influenced by Uddyotakara, he went well beyond him – while also giving an overview of the problems Brahmin authors thought they saw in the theory and how Dharmakīrti, at least, addressed them. (Dharmakīrti's defense, however, in its main outlines, was upheld by his successors.) Kataoka's essay carefully analyzes Kumārila's refutation of the Apohavāda with a view to assessing how successful it is. For instance, many modern scholars, not to mention Brahmin critics of the Apohavāda after

Kumārila, believe that Kumārila's famous Circularity (or mutual presupposition) Argument (anticipated by Uddyotakara) – that the exclusion of non-cow, which is allegedly the meaning of the word "cow," already presupposes the notion of a cow and vice versa; hence, one can never acquire either concept – amounts to a decisive refutation of the theory. Kataoka shows that this argument, in particular, turns on a failure to appreciate subtleties of Dignāga's presentation, and similarly for other arguments of Kumārila. His discussion, thus, at the same time bolsters Dignāga's position. Together these essays provide a thematic introduction to ŚV *Apohavāda*. They may even be read before tackling the annotated translation, or in conjunction with it. The third part of Taber's essay ("Kumārila") contains a sufficiently detailed summary of the contents of ŚV *Apohavāda* to serve as a synopsis, while Kataoka's essay includes an analysis of ŚV *Apohavāda* 1–114 (Section 6, pp. 226–232). For these reasons, our annotated translation is not preceded by a separate introductory synopsis, as is found in other translations of Sanskrit philosophical texts. The edition, however, is accompanied by an outline in Sanskrit.

Although there exists today a considerable body of scholarly literature on the topic of *apoha*, we have not felt it necessary, or desirable, to reference it at every point where our findings imply agreement or disagreement with the work of others. The main purpose of this translation, as already explained, is to provide a new resource for the study of *apoha*. We believe it would detract from it were we, at every opportuity, to go into the ways in which a more precise understanding of Kumārila calls for the modification of existing interpretations. Moreover, we feel that much of what has been written about *apoha* concerns less the actual theories of Indian authors than reconstructions of them by inventive modern scholars.[17] What is needed at this point is not further discussion of these

[17] See, for instance, Dreyfus 2011: 208–209: "In dealing with Dharmakīrti's views, I try to remain as close as possible to his own formulations. I believe that it

reconstructions but a renewed attempt to understand the original sources. Let us return to the texts![18]

Nevertheless, it would be remiss of us not to indicate at least briefly what we think some of the consequences a deeper knowledge of Kumārila's treatment of *apoha* will have for the field of *apoha* studies. We shall, therefore, venture tentatively into this literature – not too far, lest we are unable to find our way back! – in the hope of piqueing the interest of other scholars in what we have done and encouraging them to make the effort, even if they are not Sanskritists, to work through our translation. Our apologies to the non-specialist reader for a somewhat technical discussion; at this point he or she may wish to move on to the translation or the essays.

One of the most influential proposals regarding the interpretation of the Apohavāda to have been put forward recently is Tom Tillemans's suggestion that there is a distinction to be made between "top-down" and "bottom-up" theories of *apoha*. Tillemans presents this idea in his article, "How to Talk About Ineffable Things," which is included in the anthology previously mentioned, *Apoha*: *Buddhist Nominalism and Human Cogni-*

---

is problematic to deal with the apoha theory in abstraction from any historical location. Nevertheless, historical precision has its limits, especially when dealing with the philosophical reconstruction of a theory, as is the case here. Thus, it should be clear that in dealing with Dharmakīrti's views, I do not try to capture the ways in which Dharmakīrti understood his work as a commentary on and a defense of Dignāga's apoha theory. Rather, I attempt a philosophical reconstruction of his theory, presenting it as a viable attempt to defend the nominalist project of showing how thought and language can be accounted for in a world of particulars." See also Patil 2011: 150: "What I want to do in this paper is try to develop a generic interpretation of the theory of exclusion that is based on the work of Jñānaśrīmitra and Ratnakīrti, and then use it to raise questions that *a contemporary exclusion theorist* should, but may not, have very good answers for" (our italics). See, finally, Siderits 1982: 195, which may have started this reconstruction trend: "What I propose to do is offer an attempt at a rational reconstruction of some key elements of the doctrine of *apoha*, basing this reconstruction on the view sketched above of the underlying methodology of the school."

[18] In urging this we join a movement that is already underway. Several translations of important materials relating to *apoha* in addition to Pind 2015 have recently appeared: McCrea/Patil 2010, Watson/Kataoka 2017, McAllister 2019.

tion.[19] Several other distinguished contributors to that volume embrace and elaborate this dichotomy, so that it appears to have solidified itself as an interpretive paradigm. [20] Now, the scholars who endorse it seem to understand it in slightly different ways. Let us engage Tillemans's initial formulation:

> By "top-down" I mean a position that would somehow maintain that it is because of some specific – and perhaps even very ingenious – features of the logical operators of negation in the exclusion that the apoha does pertain to particular things, even though it does not have the ontological baggage of a real universal. In short, on a top-down approach the apoha would behave like a property, a sense, or a meaning, which belongs to the conceptual scheme but nonetheless qualifies and thus serves to pick out the real particulars of the world; because of some feature of double negation, we are spared commitment to real universals in addition to real particulars. On a bottom-up approach, causal chains and error are what serve to bridge the scheme-content gap, rather than the logico-metaphysical feature of a special sort of double negation. The way words link to things is thus primarily explained through the existence of a causal chain from things to thoughts and then to the utterances of words.[21]

Both of these "approaches" are intended as ways of "bridging the scheme-content gap," according to Tillemans. "Scheme" refers to conceptual scheme, "content" to experience. Thus, the Apohavāda, in either of its versions, is according to Tillemans an attempt to explain how meanings and concepts relate to real things – which for Buddhists are unique particulars – or how thought and language are anchored in non-conceptual, non-linguistic reality.

Tillemans traces this problem back to the controversy in ancient Indian grammatical literature about whether a word expresses an individual or a general property (Tillemans 2011: 52). The word "cow" in some contexts clearly refers to a class of individuals, all cows, e.g., in the sentence, "One

---

[19] Tillemans 2011a.

[20] Dreyfus 2011: 221; Ganeri 2011: 243–244; Siderits 2011: passim.

[21] Tillemans 2011a: 53. Cf. Chakrabarti and Siderits 2011: 27–28.

should not kill a cow." Yet when someone says, "Bring the cow," it is just one particular cow that is indicated. The Nyāya tradition solved this problem by proposing that general terms – i.e., class terms like "cow," property terms like "brown," and motion terms like "is walking" – refer to both an individual and a "genus" (*jāti*) at the same time, with one of its meanings becoming primary, the other secondary depending on the context. The Mīmāṃsā tradition proposed that words directly indicate only "universals" (*ākṛti* or *sāmānya*), which in turn *imply* individuals in which they inhere, which individuals themselves therefore are not actually designated by words.

But the scheme-content problem, which originated in analytic philosophy with the work of W. V. Quine and Donald Davidson, is actually slightly different from this one. It is, rather, the problem of *how* experiences of individuals can give rise to meanings and concepts that refer to them; more specifically, how are these meanings and concepts connected with the perceptual experiences of individuals through which we encounter the world first-hand? Obviously, we are able to use words to pick out individuals. How do we arrive at such an ability, given that individuals themselves are *prima facie* distinct from each other, even unique, and our perceptual experiences grasp them *individually*, as unrelated to other things? Dignāga sought to work out a "top-down" solution to this problem, Tillemans suggests, while Dharmakīrti explored a "bottom-up" one.

Now, it is easy to see how one might think that Dharmakīrti was attempting to provide a bottom-up solution; indeed, some of the essays in the volume in question give plausible and quite interesting interpretations of what he says about *apoha* from that point of view.[22] However, if one has a precise understanding of the *Apohavāda* chapter of the *Ślokavārttika*, it will appear that he is doing something rather different. Namely, it will seem that he is developing a point-by-point response to Kumārila's critique of Dignāga's version of the Apohavāda. Since Taber's essay at the end of this monograph is in part devoted to showing this, it will not be necessary to go into detail here. But in his most extensive treatement of *apoha*, what can be called the Apoha Section of the first chapter of his *Pramāṇavārttika*

[22] Though they are also rather different in their details. See Tillemans 2011a: 54–58; Dreyfus 2011: 215–221; Siderits 2011: 286–294.

(PV[SV] 1.40–185), Dharmakīrti solves many of the problems with the Apohavāda to which Kumārila draws attention in the *Apohavāda* chapter of his *Ślokavārttika*, often by adjusting and revising the theory. To be sure, he does not mention Kumārila by name – it was his practice not to identify his opponents – and it is not always immediately obvious how a certain idea he is developing addresses an objection raised by Kumārila. But when the arguments and overall plan of the Apohavāda Section finally come into view (this does not happen immediately, as those who have grappled with the text well know), it impresses one as a brilliant, comprehensive, systematic response to Kumārila's critique.

Now, one of Kumārila's most striking criticisms of the Apohavāda in his *Apohavāda* chapter – which, once again, is directed against Dignāga's version of the theory – is that, if the meanings of words were *apoha*s, then one would not be able to learn what words mean. For *apoha*s are not perceptible; certainly, Dignāga does not say that they are. Moreover, they are not real entities (*vastu*) but merely absences (*abhāva*), which are not objects of perception either for Buddhists or Mīmāṃsakas like Kumārila. In fact, the Buddhist position, as construed by Kumārila, is that we become aware of *apoha*s through language and inference. If *apoha*s, however, are not accessible independently of language or inference, then one would never be able to establish a connection between an *apoha* and a certain word or inferential mark (*liṅga*), so that the latter could be used to designate or indicate it. The defender of the Apohavāda, therefore, must explain how we become aware of *apoha*s in the first place, independently of language and inference, so that we are able to learn that words and inferential marks refer to them. The Mīmāṃsaka, by the way, had a ready solution to this problem. Meanings and referents of inferential marks are universals, and universals for him are *directly perceptible*. When we perceive a cow, we apprehend cowness as well as the individual cow. Although the relation between word and meaning is eternal, according to the Mīmāṃsaka, children are able to learn the meanings of words by observing the linguistic practice of their elders, which reveals that certain words have the capacity (*śakti*) to designate certain universals and, vice versa, certain universals have the capacity to be designated by certain words.

It is indeed this problem – how are *apoha*s cognized independently of the words and concepts that refer to them, so that connections between *apoha*s and those words and concepts can be established? – that Dharmakīrti seems to be attempting to solve by explaining how perceptual experiences of particulars can give rise to general concepts, which are *apoha*s (i.e., shared *differences* from other kinds of things), which are then erroneously projected on those particulars as their properties.[23] Again, there is no need to go into detail; several essays in *Apoha*: *Buddhist Nominalism and Human Cognition* do an admirable job of telling the rather complicated (or convoluted?) story.[24] We would stress, however, more than other scholars have done, that the psychological process Dharmakīrti traces yields a cognitive structure, which he sometimes identifies as the "appearance" (*pratibhāsa*) of a conceptual cognition, that is suitable to being assigned as the meaning of a word.[25] In answer to the problem raised by Kumārila, then, we learn what words mean by learning conventions that relate words to general concepts (*apoha*s) formed spontaneously from the experiences of particulars (and erroneously superimposed on them as real properties). That is to say, we become aware of meanings independently of language and inference solely *via* the perception of *particulars*, not universals!

This is just *one* line of defense of the Apohavāda Dharmakīrti develops in the Apoha Section of PV 1. To be sure, it is a theory that immediately *lends itself* to being applied as a solution to the scheme-content problem. The explanation of how we become aware of meanings (*apoha*s) as a result of perceptions of particulars certainly *implies* how thought and language are anchored in non-linguistic, non-conceptual reality. Yet that was not the challenge Dharmakīrti confronted; his challenge, rather, was to save the Apohavāda. He develops several other lines of defense of the Apohavāda in the Apoha Section, including but not limited to his answer to the

---

[23] In general, we reject Dreyfus's statement, Dreyfus 1997: 515, n. 32, "The question of how language is acquired is not addressed by Buddhist epistemologists." It will be evident below that Dignāga, too, was very much concerned with how the meanings of words are learned.

[24] See especially Dunne 2011: 90–102, Tillemans 2011a: 55–56, and Dreyfus 2011: 212–215.

[25] See, e.g., PVSV 38,17–24 (cf. Eltschinger et al. 2018: 76–77); 47,14–48,17; 49,16–23; 57,8–58,18.

Circularity Argument against the Apohavāda that other scholars have noted. In short, the section amounts to an impressive, comprehensive defence of the Apohavāda by way of a thorough revision of Dignāga's theory in order to correct real flaws in it that others had drawn attention to. This comprehensive defense of the Apohavāda, moreover, is embedded in an even more expansive critique of realist metaphysical and epistemological theories, i.e., those of Nyāya-Vaiśeṣika, Sāṃkhya, and Mīmāṃsā, but especially the latter: the existence of real universals, the distinction between property-bearer and property and the possession by a property-bearer of multiple properties, the authorlessness of the Veda, the existence of permanent entities (such as the Veda and the self), and certain logical principles (or mistakes) that were employed in arguments in support of these teachings. Indeed, when one takes in the entire first chapter of the *Pramāṇavārttika* it appears as less an investigation of *svārthānumāna*, "inference for oneself," the topic of the second chapter of Dignāga's *Pramāṇasamuccaya*, which it was traditionally seen as a commentary on, than a vast, meandering polemic against the metaphysical and logico-epistemological foundations of Mīmāṃsā.

Thus, it is somewhat misleading to suggest that Dharmakīrti, in his discussion of *apoha*, is engaged in crafting a bottom-up solution to the scheme-content problem, even if *part* of what he is doing can be seen, by someone trained in twentieth-century analytic philosophy, to be related to the scheme-content problem. Is this really such a big deal, then? Can't one legitimately use Dharmakīrti's writings to *construct* a solution to the scheme-content problem if one wants to, despite the fact that that was not his intention? To this, the following needs to be said. Normally, when appropriating the ideas of another author for other purposes, one not only acknowledges their source but also explains how one is employing them differently from the author they originated from, lest one's own theory be mistaken for that of the other author. And this involves answering the question: What *was* the original author's actual intent, anyway? It is in addressing this question that one often gains an unexpected benefit: one becomes aware of theories, arguments, and philosophical projects that may never have occurred to one and are perhaps undeveloped or even unknown in one's own philosophical tradition. In other words, one's own philosophical consciousness is expanded and enriched. And in this case, we are talking about Dharmakīrti, one of the great "doctors" of Indo-Tibetan Buddhism. Surely, he had something very important to say that resulted in his being held in such high esteem in the Buddhist intellectual tradition. We ought to try to understand it, also, in his own terms, in its historical context.

Nor is providing a solution to the scheme-content problem what Dignāga is trying to do in *Pramāṇasamuccaya* 5. The question Dignāga is considering is, simply, What do words mean?, or even, How is meaning possible? He begins by examining a range of established theories: words refer to universals, to individuals, to individuals possessed of universals, and so on. He rejects all of them, chiefly on the grounds that they are inconsistent with observable linguistic practices. On the theory that words refer just to individuals, it would be impossible to learn the meanings of words, since the individuals a word can potentially be used to indicate are countless. If words referred to universals or particulars possessing universals or the *inherence* of the universal in particulars, they could not be used coreferentially (as when we say, "an existing pot"), nor could one expression be used to qualify another (as when we say, "blue lotus"). Note that Dignāga does not reject the universal and universal-possessor theories on the grounds that universals do not exist; nowhere in *Pramāṇasamuccaya* 5 does he argue against the existence of universals. Having dispensed with these and other alternatives, Dignāga introduces the Apohavāda – words refer to *apoha*s – as the only viable option.[26]

It is difficult to see in any of this a concern with anchoring language and thought in non-linguistic, non-conceptual reality. The primary concern, rather, is to devise a theory of word meaning that "saves the appearances," i.e., that accounts for actual linguistic practice. Children are able to learn what words mean; certain words can be used together with certain other words coreferentially but not with others; there is a hierarchy of meanings and concepts such that, if one hears the word "tree" one knows that the referent is earthen, a substance, an existing thing, and a knowable thing, but has doubt about what specific kind of tree it is, whether a *śiṃśapā* or a *palāśa*, etc.; and so forth. All of these phenomena, Dignāga maintains, can

[26] See Sen 2011: 173–178.

be explained only if one accepts that words refer to *apoha*s. Finally, Dignāga says nothing about how "double negation," that is to say, a combination of the two kinds of negation *prasajyapratiṣedha* and *paryudāsa*, makes it possible for an expression to extend over a whole class of individuals, without any commitment to universals – which Tillemans seems to consider as the hallmark of the top-down approach.[27]

Indeed, if one must choose one of the two approaches, top-down or bottom-up, in Dignāga's *Pramāṇasamuccaya* 5, the bottom-up approach seems a better fit. A bottom-up approach allegedly traces meanings and concepts back to perceptual experiences of particulars.[28] Although Dignāga does not tell anything like a Dharmakīrtian story of how particulars cause (distinct) cognitions that themselves yield "unitary judgments"

---

[27] Nor do Śāntarakṣita and Kamalaśīla, on whom Mark Siderits bases his "double negation" account, mention a *combination* of the negations *prasajyapratiṣedha* and *paryudāsa*. See, e.g., Siderits 1982:198–202, esp. 200; 1999: 347. What Siderits takes to be their combination, "A cow is not a non-cow," is actually what is considered *prasajyapratiṣedha* by Śāntarakṣita and Kamalaśīla (see TS[P]ś 1009). Moreover, they are clear that the image or reflection of the object (*arthapratibimba*) that appears in a conceptual cognition, which is an *apoha* in the sense of *paryudāsa*, is the primary meaning of a word, not "not a non-cow" or (in their scheme) a *prasajyapratiṣedha*. TSPś 392,14–18: *yad eva hi śābde jñāne pratibhāsate sa eva śabdārtho yuktaḥ, na cātra prasajyapratiṣedhādhyavasāyo 'sti, na cāpīndriyajñānavat svalakṣaṇapratibhāsaḥ / kiṃ tarhi bāhyārthādhyavasāyinī kevalaṃ śābdī buddhir upajāyate / tena tad evārthapratibimbakaṃ śābde jñāne sākṣāt tadātmatayā pratibhāsanāc chabdārtho yuktaḥ, nānya iti bhāvaḥ /*. "That which appears in a verbal cognition alone is suitable as a word-meaning, and in this [verbal cognition] there is not the ascertainment of a *prasajyapratiṣedha*, nor the appearance of a particular, as in perception. Rather, merely a verbal cognition arises which 'ascertains' an external object. Therefore, precisely the reflection of an object, because it appears directly in a verbal cognition as identical with that [object], is appropriate as the meaning of a word, nothing else." After the [conceptual] image or reflection of the object is directly indicated by a word, a *prasajyapratiṣedha* in the form of "the nature of that image/reflection is not the nature of another image/reflection" is cognized "by implication" (*sāmarthyena*). However, that is the meaning of a word only in a figurative sense. See TS(P)ś 1012–1013. See McAllister 2020: 220, n. 332.

[28] As Siderits 2011: 284 puts it, a bottom-up approach consists essentially in an explanation of "concept possession ... using resources derived from a world containing only unique particulars."

(*ekapratyavamarśa*), which gives the impression that those cognitions are the same, thereby engendering the belief that the particulars that cause such cognitions are the same,[29] and how the conceptual cognition of their identity is then projected onto them as something that really belongs to them – although Dignāga does not give a complex psychological account like this, he does talk about how a certain *pattern* of experiencing particulars results in an awareness of *apoha*s. This is one of the central features of Dignāga's theory that becomes much clearer from studying Kumārila's critique; Kataoka's essay at the end of this volume is devoted to explaining it. Namely, one experiences, when a word is used, only particulars that fall within its extension, but never experiences particulars that do not. It is really, however, only by becoming aware of the latter that one learns what a word means. That is to say, the meaning of a word cannot be established or learned by observing a positive correlation (*anvaya*) between the use of the word and the individuals it refers to, maintains Dignāga; for a general term has infinitely many referents: the word "cow" refers to infinitely many cows. Rather, one learns what a word means simply by ascertaining what it is *not* used for, i.e., by negative correlation (*vyatireka*): one becomes aware that the word "cow" is *never* used for something that is other than a cow. In fact, however, as Dignāga will clarify, one does not do this by *observing* that "cow" is not used for this thing that is other than a cow and that thing that is other than a cow, and so on *ad infinitum*; for that would be as impossible as observing, positively, that it is used for all cows. Rather, one simply *does not observe* that it is used for non-cows.[30] Since this is primarily the way meanings are learned, the meanings we learn are exclusions. Given the predominantly negative way we come to comprehend what a word refers to, a word means, for one who has mastered the language, what is *not* other than the individuals it applies to; "cow" refers to what is *not* other than a cow.

---

[29] PV(SV) 1.109.

[30] Exactly why Dignāga believes that the relation between a word and its meaning is more "easily" established by not observing it to be employed for other things than by observing a positive correlation, is a subtle matter that Kataoka investigates in his essay.

Thus, for Dignāga just as much as for Dharmakīrti, *apoha*s are derived from experiences of particulars. In Dignāga's case, however, the aspect of the experience of particulars that is of the most significance is just when they *are* experienced and when they *are not* experienced. An *apoha* is what we are aware of as a result of a pattern of *not* experiencing certain particulars under certain conditions; at such times, however, one must of course be experiencing *other* particulars. According to Dignāga's version of the Apohavāda, then, *apoha*s can be said to be "grounded" on our experiences of particulars, and this would make it closer to a bottom-up approach to the scheme-content problem than a top-down approach – if one must view it from the standpoint of these alternatives.[31]

These are some of the implications we believe a new translation of Kumārila's *Apohavāda* chapter will have for contemporary scholarship on *apoha*. For those primarily focused on the Buddhist position, we believe it will sharpen their grasp of what the Buddhist authors were trying to accomplish. Other prominent interpretations of Dharmakīrti, on which he is offering a "naturalized account of concept formation"[32] or a "causal account of intentionality,"[33] stand subject to revision or at least qualification in the same way as the interpretation that he is bridging the scheme-content gap. Nevertheless, there will remain much room for debate about these issues.

---

[31] Thus, we would also disagree with Arnold 2012: 125: "While we see that Dharmakīrti is concerned to offer an explanation of how conceptual mental content is constructed just from the causally describable inputs to awareness, Dignāga's elaboration of *apoha* doctrine, in contrast, evinces little concern with how linguistic items 'make contact' with the world of really existent particulars. Instead, his arguments address only the relative determinacy of conceptual content – the conceptual scope or richness of terms only insofar as they are relative to the other terms in a system."

[32] See Dunne 2011: 85–88 and Dreyfus 2011: 215–221.

[33] Arnold 2012: 133–157.

Part One

Critical Edition of *Ślokavārttika*, *Apohavāda* Chapter

Kei Kataoka

Introduction

Previous editions of ŚV *Apohavāda*

For the portion of the *Ślokavārttika* edited in this book, i.e., ŚV *Apohavāda*, I have consulted five editions published so far, including the Sanskrit text adopted by Hattori attached to his Japanese translation of the same section.

C[1] Tailaṅga Rāmaśāstrī: *Mīmāṃsāślokavārtikam Śrīmatkumārilabhaṭṭapādaviracitam Nikhilatantrāparatantraśrīmatpārthasārathimiśrapraṇītayā Nyāyaratnākarākhyayā Vyākhyayā 'nugatam.* Caukhambā-Saṃskṛta-Granthamālā, No. 3. Kāśī, 1898.

D Svāmī Dvārikadāsa Śāstrī: *Ślokavārttika of Śrī Kumārila Bhaṭṭa, with the Commentary Nyāyaratnākara of Śrī Pārthasārathi Miśra.* Varanasi: Tara Publications, 1978.

H Masaaki Hattori: "Mīmāṃsāślokavārttika, Apohavāda shō no Kenkyū (Jō)." *Kyōto Daigaku Bungakubu Kenkyū Kiyō* (Kyoto University), 14 (1973), 1–44; "Mīmāṃsāślokavārttika, Apohavāda shō no Kenkyū (Ge)." *Kyōto Daigaku Bungakubu Kenkyū Kiyō* (Kyoto University), 15 (1975), 1–63.

M S.K. Ramanatha Sastri: *Ślokavārtikavyākhyā Tātparyaṭīkā of Uṃveka Bhaṭṭa.* Madras 1971: University of Madras (Madras University Sanskrit Series 13).

P *The Pandit (New Series),* Vol. III, 1879, 459–469, 513–517.

Manuscripts consulted for the present edition of ŚV *Apohavāda*

For editing this section, I consult, in addition to the previous five editions, the following six manuscripts.

A$_1$ A manuscript preserved in the Adyar Library, Chennai, No. 67593 (=20. N. 4). Malayālam. Palm leaf. Incomplete. 34 cm × 4 cm. See V. Krishnamacharya: *Descriptive Catalogue of Sanskrit Manuscripts in the Adyar Library.* Vol. IX. Madras: The Adyar

Library and Research Centre, 1952. See also Ōmae 1998 for the details.

B$_1$ A manuscript preserved in the Bodleian Library, Oxford, No. 520, Ms. Wilson 325. Devanāgarī. Paper. Complete. 30 cm × 9.5 cm. 111 folios.

B$_2$ A manuscript preserved in the Bodleian Library, Oxford, No. 521, Ms. Wilson 277a. Devanāgarī. Paper. Incomplete. 33 cm × 9 cm. 38 folios. Folios are missing in B$_2$ from the part that corresponds to ŚV *Apohavāda* v. 32b7.

I$_1$ A manuscript preserved in the British Library, London, San Ms I.O. 3739 (=No. 7976). Devanāgarī. Paper. Complete. 21.5 cm × 17.5 cm. 89 folios.

I$_2$ A manuscript preserved in the British Library, London, San Ms I.O. 1449b (=No. 2149). Devanāgarī. Paper. Complete. 24 cm × 8 cm. 139 folios.

K$_1$ A manuscript preserved in the Asiatic Society, Calcutta (Kolkata), G. 8854. Devanāgarī. Paper. Complete. Dated saṃvat 1642 (=1585 AD). 28 cm × 12.5 cm. 79 folios.

For details of editions and manuscripts, see Kataoka 2011a. H and A$_1$ are newly added for the present edition.

Abbreviations and conventions

Abbreviations and conventions follow Kataoka 2011a. The format of this critical edition is as follows. Each page is divided into four layers, except for the pages on which the third layer is not necessary. The first layer gives the edited text. The division into sections and paragraphs is mine. Numbers and Sanskrit headings in brackets, which are also mine, are given at the beginning of each section, subsection and so on, according to the structure of the text. The punctuation, using *daṇḍa*s and commas, is mine.

The second layer shows quoted or parallel passages; cross-references inside the text are also reported here as are testimonia found in commentaries. The third layer shows lacunae in the manuscripts.

The fourth layer is the critical apparatus for variants. The critical apparatus is positive: the critical text is repeated after the line number in the edition and followed by a lemma sign ']'. In case the critical text is a reading accepted in manuscripts and editions, it is then followed by the sigla of those manuscripts/editions where it is accepted.

I have not reported the punctuation and non-substantive variants of the editions and manuscripts, e.g., the non-application of *sandhi* or common orthographic variants such as gemination or degemination of consonants after or before semi-vowels, and the exchange of *anusvāra* and homorganic nasals. However I reproduce such peculiarities when a reading of an edition or a manuscript is reported as a substantive variant.

I insert commas (,) in the middle of sentences whenever I find them helpful for interpretation. In doing so, I leave *sandhi* unchanged within the verses.

ac	Readings before correction (*ante correctionem*).
pc	Readings after correction (*post correctionem*).
(eyeskip)	The reading is caused by eyeskip.
(unmetrical)	The reading is unmetrical.
ed.	Published edition.
em.	Emendation by the present editor.
ms.	Manuscript.
om.	Omission of the reading.
=	Identical passage.
≈	Similar passage.
+	Lacuna (in particular in A_1) of approximately one letter.
—	The manuscript in question intentionally leaves a space with a mark, as is often the case for Devanāgarī manuscripts.

Acknowledgments

I am indebted to the following libraries and institutes for giving me permission to consult manuscripts: the Adyar Library, Chennai; the British

Library, London; the Bodleian Library, Oxford; and the Asiatic Society, Kolkata. I also thank T. Shida for his help in acquiring a manuscript.

Sanskrit Synopsis

3.2 *buddhyākāra eva sāmānyam* 36cd-41

4 *paryāyatvadoṣaḥ* 42

4.1 *nāpohabhedāt* 43-46

4.2 *nāpohyabhedāt*

4.2.1 *apohyā bahiḥsaṃsthāḥ* 47-52

4.2.2 *ekāpohyamātrātirekaḥ* 53-57

4.2.3 *sarvāpohaḥ* 58ab

4.2.3.1 *pratyekarūpeṇa* 58cd-60

4.2.3.2 *samudāyātmanā* 61-63ab

4.2.3.3 *sāmānyarūpeṇa*

4.2.3.3.1 *nābhāsyāpohanam* 63cd-64

4.2.3.3.2 *anyonyasaṃśrayam* 65-66

4.2.3.4 *agāvo 'śvādayaḥ* 67-68ab

4.2.4 *antyaviśeṣāḥ* 68cd-70

4.2.5 *sāmānyaṃ vināviśeṣato jñātum aśaktiḥ* 71-72

5 *vasturūpasāmānyaniṣedhe doṣāḥ*

5.1 *saṃbandhānubhavānupapattiḥ*

5.1.1 *vyāptigrahaḥ*

5.1.1.1 *anvayaḥ* 73-74

5.1.1.2 *vyatirekaḥ* 75

5.1.2 *sāmānyaṃ vināpohasyātikalpanā* 76-77

5.1.3 *apohānubhavapramāṇam*

5.1.3.1 *pratyakṣam* 78

5.1.3.2 *anumānam* 79ab

5.1.4 *upasaṃhāraḥ* 79cd

5.2 *agor asiddhiḥ*

5.2.1 *agovyutpattyasaṃbhavaḥ* 80-82

Ślokavārttika, *Apohavāda* Chapter

मीमांसाश्लोकवार्त्तिके
अपोहवादः

[1 अगोनिवृत्तिस्वरूपनिरूपणम्]

[1.1 अगोनिवृत्तिर्गोत्वमेव]

अगोनिवृत्तिः सामान्यं वाच्यं यैः परिकल्पितम्।
गोत्वं वस्त्वेव तैरुक्तम् अगोऽपोहगिरा स्फुटम्॥ १॥

[1.2 अगोनिवृत्त्यात्माभावस्य बन्धनम्]

भावान्तरमभावो हि पुरस्तात्प्रतिपादितः।

1b यैः परिकल्पितम्] PS 5.1: न प्रमाणान्तरं शाब्दमनुमानात्, तथा हि सः। कृतकत्वादिवत्स्वार्थमन्यापोहेन भाषते॥; cf. also PSV 5.36d (Pind 2015: I.45,2–3): शब्दो ऽर्थान्तरनिवृत्तिविशिष्टानेव भावानाह।
1c गोत्वं वस्त्वेव] ŚVN 400,15: तैर्गोत्वं वस्त्वेव शब्दान्तरेणाभिहितम्।; but cf. *Kāśikā* (Kataoka 2014a: 309(54),6–7) and PVSVṬ (111,19): गोत्ववस्त्वेव तैरुक्तम्।
1 =$TS_Ś$ 914, PKM 433,7–8; but the GOS edition (TS) reads: अगोनिवृत्तिः सामान्यं वाच्यं यै(रुररीकृतम्।) (गोत्वं) वस्त्वेव तैरुक्त(मेतया हि गिरा स्फुटम्)॥
2a भावान्तरमभावो] ŚV *Abhāva* 11–12: प्रत्यक्षादेरनुत्पत्तिः प्रमाणाभाव उच्यते। सात्मनः परिणामो वा विज्ञानं वान्यवस्तुनि॥ स्वरूपपररूपाभ्यां नित्यं सदसदात्मके। वस्तुनि ज्ञायते कैश्चिद्रूपं किंचित् कदाचन॥ (see Kellner 1999 for interpretation); cf. PV 1.40: सर्वे भावाः स्वभावेन स्वस्वभावव्यवस्थितेः। स्वभावपरभावाभ्यां यस्माद्व्यावृत्तिभागिनः॥; *Kāśikā* (ŚVKā$ś_K$ 459(46),5): न च परेषां मते भावान्तरमपोहाश्रयतया शक्यं दर्शयितुम्।; ŚVŚar 27,12: अवश्यं भावाश्रित एव ग्रहीतव्यः।
2b पुरस्तात्प्रतिपादितः] ŚV *Abhāva* 2cd–4, 8ab (these verses are quoted by Kamalaśīla); cf. *Kāśikā* (ŚVKā$ś_K$ 459(46),2–3): स्वतन्त्राभावप्रतीतिस्तावन्नास्तीति; ŚVŚar 27,12–13: स चायमभावो ऽभाववादस्थानके प्रतिपादितः—न स्वतन्त्राभावबुद्धिरुदेतीति।; $TSP_Ś$ 915 (360,21–22): प्रागभावादिलक्षणश्चतुर्विधः सर्व एवाभावो भावान्तरात्मको व्यवस्थितः।

1c गोत्वं] $C^1DHMPB_1B_2I_2K_1$; गोत्व॰ A_1I_1 **2b** ॰पादितः] $C^1DHMPA_1B_2I_1I_2K_1$; ॰पादितं B_1

तत्राश्वादिनिवृत्त्यात्माभावः क इति कथ्यताम् ॥ २॥

[1.2.1 नासाधारणो विषयः]

नेष्टो ऽसाधारणस्तावद्विषयो निर्विकल्पनात्।

---

2 cd °त्माभावः] cf. ŚVN 400,19: न चागोनिवृत्तिरूपस्याभावस्य; *Kāśikā* (ŚVKāś$_{K}$ 459(46),6–9): न तावद् भवत्सिद्धान्ते ऽभावो नाम किमपि तत्त्वान्तरमस्ति यो ऽपोहापरनामा शब्दानामर्थो भवेत्। यदि त्वस्मत्सिद्धान्तानुसारेणाभावस्तत्त्वान्तरमवसीयते, ततो ··· ।
2 cd Cf. NV 2.2.66 (314,8–9): यश्चायमन्यापोहः "अगौर्न भवति" इति गोशब्दस्यार्थः, स किं भावो ऽथाभाव इति।; PSV 5.36c (Pind 2015: I.44,4–5): अव्यापकत्वाच्चासामान्यदोषो ऽपि नास्ति, अर्थान्तरापोहमात्रस्याभिन्नत्वात्, अद्रव्यत्वाच्च।; NĀA 733,17–18 (quoted in Pind 2015: II.134, n. 451): नापि भेदानवस्थानादनभिधानदोषः। कस्मात्। अभेदात्। न ह्यर्थान्तरापोहो भेदेषु भिद्यते, अभावात्। तन्मात्रं च शब्देनोच्यते, न भेदाः।; MHK 5.62, 64 (quoted in Pind 2015: II.137, n. 457): विजातीयेन शून्यत्वं तुल्यधीवृत्तिहेतुतः। सामान्यात्तुल्यजातीये सामान्यमिति निश्चितम्॥ अभेदाद्रव्यसत्त्वाभ्यामेकमनेकवृत्त्यपि। तद्विनाशे ऽविनाशाच्च नान्यस्मिन् तन्मतिर्न च॥; PVSV 85,21–23 (quoted in Pind 2015: II.135, n. 454): निवृत्तेर्निःस्वभावत्वान्न स्थानास्थानकल्पना (PV 1.169ab)। न ह्यन्यापोहो नाम किंचित्, तस्य च स्वभावानुषङ्गिण्यः स्वभावस्थितिप्रच्युतिकल्पना न कल्पन्ते।
2 ≈TS$_{Ś}$ 915: भावान्तरात्मको ऽभावो येन सर्वो व्यवस्थितः। तत्राश्वादिनिवृत्तात्माभावः क इति कथ्यताम्॥ (=PKM 433,9–10)
3 b °द्विषयो] *Kāśikā* (ŚVKāś$_{K}$ 458(47),2): असाधारण एवार्थात्माश्वादिनिवृत्त्यात्मना प्रतीयत इति।; In the commentaries there is no clear indication of विशेष which TS$_{Ś}$ 916 has and which Kamalaśīla clearly presupposes. See also Kumārila's reference to someone's interpretation in TV 1.3.30 (296,7): केचिदाहुः—असाधारणा विशेषा एव व्यक्तिः।; and NV 2.2.66 (308,3–4): असाधारणविशेषाभिधायको भविष्यतीति न युक्तम्, अन्यत्र प्रत्ययाभावप्रसङ्गात्।; cf. also Kumārila's usage of अपोहविषय in 71b.
3 ab ≈TS$_{Ś}$ 916ab: नेष्टो ऽसाधारणस्तावद् विशेषो निर्विकल्पनात्। (=PKM 433,11)

---

2 d क इति क°] $C^1DHMPA_1B_1B_2I_1K_1$; कः I_2^{ac}; कः इति क° I_2^{pc} **3 a** ऽसाधारण°] $C^1DHMPB_1B_2I_1I_2K_1$; साधाराण° A_1 **3 b** °द्विषयो] $C^1DMPB_1B_2I_1I_2K_1$; °द्विशेषो HA_1

[1.2.2 न शाबलेयादिः]

तथा च शाबलेयादिरसामान्यप्रसंगतः॥ ३॥
शाबलेयादिरूपं हि न सामान्यं परस्परम्।
न चैकमितरेषां, वस् तत्रानन्तार्थता भवेत्॥ ४॥
न च साक्षाद्विशेषस्य ते ऽपोह्या इति युक्तिमत्।
न शाबलेयविज्ञानमगोव्यावृत्तिबन्धनम्॥ ५॥
निवृत्त्या बाहुलेयादेस्तद्विज्ञानं प्रवर्तते।
कुर्यादगोनिवृत्तिं चेन्, नापोहेतात्मवद्धि तान्॥ ६॥
तेनांशेनानपोहश्च स्वरूपेणाप्यपोहनम्।
कल्प्यते चेद्, विरोधः स्यात्सममाक्षेपवारणे ॥ ७॥

3c च] Only M has न. The $TS_{Ś}$ also supports च.
3cd =$TS_{Ś}$ 916cd, PKM 433,12.
4c चैक॰] supported by ŚVN 400,32–401,1: न च शाबलेयबाहुलेयरूपाणि; *Kāśikā* (ŚVKāś$_{K}$ 458(47),17): इत्याह—न चैकमितरेषामिति।; but ŚVŚar seems to presuppose वा and not च when it says (27,23–24): यदि ··· यदि वा।
4c Sucarita (ŚVKāś$_{K}$ 458(47),16) glosses इतरेषां as बौद्धानाम्; he puts a pause before वस् and not after that.
5 ते] Cf. *Kāśikā* (ŚVKāś$_{K}$ 457(48),8–9): अगावो ऽश्वादयो ऽपोह्याः ··· त इत्यश्वादय इत्यर्थः।
7d ॰त्सममाक्षेपवारणे] कथम् in M seems secondary. Jayamiśra seems to presuppose समम्. ŚVŚar 28,19–20: विरुद्धमेवेदम् "आक्षिपति प्रतिक्षिपति च" इति।; *Kāśikā* (ŚVKāś$_{K}$ 456(49),7–8): युगपदेव गोशब्दाद् बाहुलेयादीनामाक्षेपो वारणं च भवेत्।

3c च] $C^{1}DHPA_{1}B_{1}B_{2}I_{1}I_{2}K_{1}$; न M **3c** शाबलेयादिर॰] $HPA_{1}B_{1}B_{2}I_{1}K_{1}$; शाबलेयादेर॰ $C^{1}DM$; शाबलेयादियत् I_{2}^{ac}; शाबलेयादिरत् I_{2}^{pc} **4c** चैकमितरेषां] $HMPA_{1}B_{1}I_{2}K_{1}$; वैकमितरेषां $C^{1}DB_{2}$; न चाव्यतममेषां I_{1} **4c** वस्] $C^{1}DHMPA_{1}B_{1}I_{1}I_{2}K_{1}$; च B_{2} **5b** इति युक्तिमत्] $C^{1}DHMPA_{1}I_{1}I_{2}K_{1}$; युक्तिमान् B_{1}^{ac}; इति युक्तिमान् B_{1}^{pc}; इति युक्तता B_{2} **6b** प्रवर्तते] $C^{1}DHMPB_{1}B_{2}I_{1}I_{2}K_{1}$; प्रवृत्तते A_{1} **6d** ॰तात्मवद्धि तान्] $C^{1}DHMPA_{1}B_{1}B_{2}I_{1}K_{1}$; ॰तात्मबुद्धिना I_{2} **7a** ॰श्च] $C^{1}DHMPA_{1}B_{1}I_{1}I_{2}K_{1}$; ॰श्चेत् B_{2} **7d** ॰त्सममाक्षेपवारणे] $C^{1}DHPA_{1}B_{1}B_{2}I_{1}I_{2}K_{1}$; त्कथमाक्षेपवारणम् M

तस्मात्प्रात्यात्मिकै रूपैरगोऽपोहो न युज्यते ।

[1.2.3 न समुदायः]

समुदायो ऽपि नैतेषामगोव्यावृत्तिबन्धनम् ॥ ८ ॥
सर्वोपलब्धौ तद्बुद्धिर्व्यासज्यैवं प्रसज्यते ।
न प्रत्येकं भवेदेषा, न समस्तेष्वशक्तितः ॥ ९ ॥

[1.3 गोत्वमेव सामान्यम्]

तस्मात्सर्वेषु यद्रूपं प्रत्येकं परिनिष्ठितम् ।
गोबुद्धिस्तन्निमित्ता स्याद्, गोत्वादन्यच्च नास्ति तत् ॥ १० ॥

---

8 a °त्प्रात्यात्मिकै] The more regular form प्रत्यात्मकैः seems to be a secondary regularization. Kumārila often uses प्रात्यात्मिक instead. See e.g. TV 2.1.5 (399,6); 3.4.15 (948,13).
8 cd समुदायो ··· °बन्धनम्] Two commentaries support this reading. ŚVN 401,23: अथ शाबलेयादिसमुदायो ऽगोव्यावृत्त्यात्मना गोविकल्पावलम्बनम् ।; ŚVŚar 29,4–5: यदि तु शाबलेयादिस्वलक्षणसमुदाय एवागोव्यावृत्त्याश्रयो भण्यते ।; cf. *Kāśikā* (ŚVKāś$_K$ 455(50),3–4): न च वाच्यं शाबलेयादिसमुदाय एवागोव्यावृत्त्यात्मना गृह्यत इत्याह ।
9 b °यैवं] Probably presupposing एवं, Sucarita (ŚVKāś$_K$ 455(50),6) glosses it as समुदायालंबनत्वे. Similarly Jayamiśra probably presupposes एवं when he uses the construction यदि ··· ततः. Neither of them seems to presuppose एव.
9 b प्रसज्यते] Jayamiśra's gloss स्यात् possibly supports प्रसज्यते.
9 d °ष्वशक्तितः] Cf. PSV 5.2b: आनन्त्ये हि भेदानामशक्यः संबन्धः कर्तुम् ।
10 ab Cf. PSV 5.36d (Pind 2015: I.44,11–45,1): जातिधर्माश्चैकत्वनित्यत्वप्रत्येकपरिसमाप्तिलक्षणा अत्रैव व्यवतिष्ठन्ते, अभेदाद् आश्रयाविच्छेदात् कृत्स्नार्थप्रतीतेः ।; see also 163ab.
10 = PKM 433,14–15; ≈ TS$_Ś$ 917: तस्मात् सर्वेषु (सर्वेषु] TS; सर्वेष्व°

---

8 a °त्प्रात्यात्मिकै] $C^1DB_1I_1K_1$; °त्प्रत्यात्मकै $HMPB_2I_2$; °त्प्रत्यामरैक A_1 (unmetrical) **8 b** युज्यते] $C^1DHMA_1B_1I_1I_2K_1$; कल्पते PB_2 **8 c** समुदायो] $HMPA_1B_1I_1I_2$; समुदाये $C^1DB_2K_1$ **8 d** °बन्धनम् PB_2I_1 ; °संभवः C^1DK_1 ; °संमतः HMA_1B_1 ; °बंधनः I_2 **9 b** °ज्यैवं] $C^1DPA_1B_1B_2I_1I_2K_1$; °ज्यैव HM **9 b** प्रसज्यते] $PMA_1B_2I_1I_2K_1$; प्रवर्तते C^1DHB_1 **9 c** भवेदेषा] $C^1DHMPA_1I_1$; भवत्येषा B_2 ; भवेदेषां $B_1I_2K_1$ **10 d** °न्यच्च] $C^1DHMPA_1B_1B_2I_1I_2$; °न्यस्य K_1

[2 अभावरूपसामान्यनिरासः]

[2.1 प्रागभावादौ सामान्यम्]

ननु च प्रागभावादौ सामान्यं वस्तु नेष्यते।
सत्तैव ह्यत्र सामान्यमनुत्पत्त्यादिरूषिता॥ ११॥
तामुत्पत्त्याद्यनुस्यूतां सत्तेति प्रतिजानते।
अन्यापोहानुविद्धा तु सैवाभावः प्रतीयते॥ १२॥

[2.2 अनित्यत्वम्]

अनित्यत्वं विनाशाख्यक्रियासामान्यमिष्यते।

[2.3 अब्राह्मणत्वनिरूपणम्]

[2.3.1 नन्वब्राह्मणत्वं ब्राह्मणाभावो ऽवस्त्वेव]

अब्राह्मणत्वं किं नु स्याद् भिन्नेषु क्षत्रियादिषु॥ १३॥
पुरुषत्वं चतुःसंस्थं, विशेषेषु च नास्ति धीः।
सामान्यप्रत्ययश्चैषु प्रत्येकमुपजायते॥ १४॥
तेनात्र ब्राह्मणाभावः सामान्यं स्याद्, अवस्तु तत्।
गोत्वादावपि तेनैवं सामान्यप्रत्ययो भवेत्॥ १५॥

[2.3.2 एकशब्दत्वम्]

$TS_{Ś}$) यद्रूपं प्रत्येकं प्रतिनिष्ठितम्। गोबुद्धिस्तन्निमित्ता स्याद् गोत्वादन्यच्च नास्ति तत्॥

11d °रूषिता] This reading is supported by Sucarita and Pārthasārathi.
15c तेनैवं] cf. ŚVN 403,5: एवं गवादावप्यभावात्मकमेव; ŚVŚar 31,2: एवमेव।

11d °मनुत्पत्त्या°] $C^1DHMPB_1B_2I_1I_2K_1$; °मनुत्प्रत्त्या° A_1 **11d** °रूषिता] $C^1DHMPA_1I_1I_2K_1$; °रूषितं B_1; °दूषिता B_2 **13b** °मिष्यते] $A_1B_1I_1I_2K_1$; °मुच्यते C^1DHMPB_2 **13c** नु] $HMA_1B_1B_2I_1I_2K_1$; तु C^1DP **14a** चतुःसंस्थं] $C^1DHA_1B_1I_1I_2K_1$; चतुस्संख्यं M; च तुष्टं (?) हि P; दनुस्थ्यं हि B_2 **14b** च] $C^1DHMPA_1B_2I_1$; हि $B_1I_2K_1$ **15c** तेनैवं] MI_1K_1; तेनैव $C^1DHPB_1B_2I_2$; तेनैववएं A_1

कैश्चित्त्वत्रैकशब्दत्वमक्षादिष्विव कल्पितम्।
जातित्रयस्य, नैवं तु संभवत्यघटादिषु॥ १६॥
नात्र ह्यनन्तके भेदे साधारण्यं निरूप्यते।

[2.3.3 क्रियागुणाः]

तस्मात्क्रियागुणाः केचिद्धेतवो ऽनन्यवर्तिनः॥ १७॥

[2.3.4 अब्राह्मणत्वं पुरुषत्वम्]

[2.3.4.1 ब्राह्मणेभ्यो निवर्तितं पुरुषत्वम्]

पुरुषत्वं नञा चैतद् ब्राह्मणेभ्यो निवर्तितम्।
चातुर्वर्ण्यप्रसक्तं सद् गम्यते ऽर्थादिभिर्यथा॥ १८॥
यद्यप्यवान्तरा नास्ति त्रिषु जातिर्व्यवस्थिता।
नञ्सामार्थ्यान्नरत्वं तु त्र्याधारं संप्रतीयते॥ १९॥
शब्दसामर्थ्यभेदेन वर्णेषु मतिभिन्नता।
पुंस्त्वे त्रिचतुराधारे पर्युदासस्वरूपतः॥ २०॥
दूरान्तिकेक्षणे शक्तिर्गृध्रवायसचक्षुषोः।
यथा रूपे, तथा पुंस्त्वे पुमब्राह्मणशब्दयोः॥ २१॥
ब्राह्मणव्यतिरिक्तार्थवृत्ति पुंस्त्वमितीदृशम्।

16a °त्त्वत्रै°] ŚVŚar 31,5: अत्र समाधिः।; *Kāśikā* (ŚVKāś$_{\mathrm{K}}$ 451(54),14): अत्रैकेषां मतेन परिहारमाह—कैश्चिदिति।
16d °क्षादिष्विव] ŚVŚar 31,9: अक्षादिष्विव।
16 c नैवं] Three manuscripts of the *Kāśikā* read नैवमिति and one manuscript reads नैतत्तु संभवत्यघटादिषु।
18c °प्रसक्तं] *Kāśikā* (ŚVKāś$_{\mathrm{K}}$ 449(56),2): चातुर्वर्ण्यप्रसक्तम्।

---

16 a कैश्चित्त्व°] $\mathrm{C^{1}DP}$; कैश्चित्त° $\mathrm{HMA_{1}B_{1}B_{2}I_{1}I_{2}K_{1}}$ **16 b** °क्षादिष्विव] $\mathrm{MA_{1}B_{1}B_{2}I_{1}^{pc}I_{2}K_{1}}$; °क्षादाविव $\mathrm{C^{1}DHP}$; °क्षादिष्वेव $\mathrm{I_{1}^{ac}}$ **16c** नैवं तु] $\mathrm{C^{1}DHMB_{2}}$; नैतत्तु $\mathrm{PA_{1}B_{1}I_{1}I_{2}}$; नैवं तत् $\mathrm{K_{1}}$ **17a** नात्र] $\mathrm{C^{1}DHMPB_{1}B_{2}I_{1}I_{2}K_{1}}$; तेनात्र $\mathrm{A_{1}}$(unmetrical) **17d** °वर्तिनः] $\mathrm{C^{1}DHMPB_{1}B_{2}I_{1}I_{2}K_{1}}$; °वर्तिनः नः $\mathrm{A_{1}}$(unmetrical) **18a** नञा] $\mathrm{C^{1}DHMPA_{1}B_{1}I_{1}I_{2}K_{1}}$; न वा $\mathrm{B_{2}}$ **18c** °सक्तं] $\mathrm{C^{1}DHMPA_{1}B_{1}B_{2}I_{1}I_{2}}$; °युक्तं $\mathrm{K_{1}}$ **19a** यद्य°] $\mathrm{C^{1}DHMPA_{1}B_{1}I_{1}I_{2}K_{1}}$; तद्य° $\mathrm{B_{2}}$ **19a** नास्ति] $\mathrm{C^{1}DHMPA_{1}B_{1}B_{2}I_{2}}$; नात्र $\mathrm{I_{1}K_{1}}$ **19c** °र्थ्यान्न°] $\mathrm{C^{1}DHMA_{1}B_{1}B_{2}I_{1}I_{2}K_{1}}$; °र्थ्यान्त° P **21 d** पुम°] $\mathrm{C^{1}DHMPA_{1}B_{1}I_{1}I_{2}K_{1}}$; पुंम° $\mathrm{B_{2}}$ **22b** °वृत्ति] $\mathrm{C^{1}DHMPB_{1}B_{2}I_{1}I_{2}K_{1}}$; °व्यत्ति $\mathrm{A_{1}}$

वाक्यं यत्र प्रवर्तेत, तत्राब्राह्मणधीपदे॥ २२॥
पार्थिवत्वादिसामान्यमेवमेवाघटादिषु।
घटत्वादिविनिर्मुक्तं विषयः संप्रतीयते॥ २३॥
असाधारणभावाच्च नञा शब्दो विशेषितः।
तावन्मात्रेण रहिते सामान्ये व्यवतिष्ठते॥ २४॥
विशेषे प्रतिषिद्धे च सामान्यं यदनन्तरम्।
सामान्याकाङ्क्षिणं शब्दं निरुणद्धि तदात्मनि॥ २५॥

[2.3.4.2 अनन्तरसामान्यानतिक्रमः]

प्रथमातिक्रमे चास्य कारणं नैव विद्यते।
ब्राह्मणत्वादतो ऽपेतं नरत्वमवशिष्यते॥ २६॥
व्युदस्य ब्राह्मणत्वं तु नञि जाते विशेषणे।
नरत्वोदसनं यत्तु कल्प्येताश्रुतमेव तत्॥ २७॥

[2.3.4.3 भेदान्तरस्थं सामान्यम्]

तस्माद्यस्यैव ते भेदा निषिद्धेरंस्तदर्थतः।
भेदान्तरस्थं सामान्यं, लोके ऽप्येवं प्रतीयते॥ २८॥
प्रसङ्गिन्यां च तद्बुद्धौ निषेधो ऽर्थादपीष्यते।

27d कल्प्येता°] *Kāśikā* (ŚVKāś$_K$ 443(62),9–10): नरत्वस्यापि व्युदसनं कल्प्येत।

22d तत्राब्राह्मण°] $C^1DHMA_1B_1B_2I_1I_2$; तत्र ब्राह्मण° PK_1 **22d** °धीपदे] $C^1DHMA_1B_1B_2I_2K_1$; °धीः पदे PI_1 **23b** °मेवाघटा°] $C^1DHMPA_1B_1I_1I_2K_1$; °मेव घटा° B_2 **23c** घटत्वादि°] $C^1DHMPA_1B_1B_2^{pc}I_1I_2K_1$; घटादित्वा° B_2^{ac} **23c** °निर्मुक्तं] $C^1DHMPA_1B_1I_1I_2$; °निर्युक्तं B_2 ; °निर्मुक्त° K_1 **23d** विषयः] $C^1DHMPA_1B_1B_2I_1I_2$; °विषयं K_1 **24b** नञा शब्दो] $C^1DHMA_1B_1I_1I_2K_1$; न भा शब्दो P ; तत्राशब्दो B_2 **25a** च] $HMA_1B_1I_1I_2K_1$; हि C^1DPB_2 **25c** शब्दं] $C^1DHMPB_1B_2I_1I_2K_1$; वाक्यशब्दन् A_1 (unmetrical) **25d** निरुण°] $C^1DHMPA_1B_1I_1I_2K_1$; तिरुण° B_2 **26a** चास्य] $MA_1B_1I_1I_2K_1$; तस्य C^1DHP ; वास्य B_2 **26d** °वशिष्यते] $C^1DHPA_1B_1B_2I_1I_2K_1$; °वतिष्ठते M **27a** तु] $A_1B_1I_1I_2K_1$; च $DMPB_2$; न C^1H **27b** जाते] $C^1DHMPA_1B_2I_1I_2K_1$; ज्ञाते B_1 **27d** कल्प्येता°] $MA_1B_1B_2I_1K_1$; कल्पेता° C^1DHPI_2 **29a** तद्बुद्धौ] $C^1DHMPA_1B_1B_2I_2K_1$; तद्बुद्धो I_1

तन्मात्ररहिते चार्थे सादृश्यात्तन्मतिर्भवेत्॥ २९ ॥

[2.3.5 अब्राह्मणत्वं सादृश्यमेव]

सादृश्यमेव वा वाच्यमिष्टमब्राह्मणादिषु।
तच्चावयवसामान्याद्, विनाप्येतेन लक्ष्यते॥ ३० ॥

[2.3.6 अब्राह्मणत्वं साहचर्यादिकम्]

क्वचिद्विनापि सादृश्यात् साहचर्यादिहेतुका।
नञ्युक्तशब्दवृत्तिः स्याद् यथा वक्ष्यत्यनीक्षणे॥ ३१ ॥
ईक्षणव्यतिरिक्ता हि क्रिया तत्राप्यपेक्षिता।
प्रत्यासत्तेर्न संकल्पमतिक्रम्य प्रतीयते॥ ३२ ॥

[2.4 नञ्योगाद् वस्तुप्रतीतिः]

नामधात्वर्थयोगी च नैव नञ् प्रतिषेधकः।
वदतो ऽब्राह्मणाधर्मावन्यमात्रविरोधिनौ॥ ३३ ॥
यत्राप्याख्यातसंबन्धात्प्रतिषेधः प्रतीयते।
तत्रौदासीन्यवस्त्वेव प्रतिपत्तावलम्बते॥ ३४ ॥

---

30 c तच्चावयवसामान्याद्] ŚV *Upamāna* 18: सादृश्यस्यापि वस्तुत्वं न शक्यमपबाधितुम्। भूयोऽवयवसामान्ययोगो जात्यन्तरस्य तत्।
31 d वक्ष्यत्यनीक्षणे] MSBh 4.1.3 (1198,9–10): इह प्रजापतिव्रतान्युदाहरणम्। नोद्यन्तमादित्यमीक्षेत नास्तंयन्तमित्यादीनि।; ṬṬ 4.1.3 (1199,23–25): आदित्यस्यानीक्षणं कर्तव्यमिति मनसा संकल्पयति। अतो ऽनीक्षणस्य मानसो व्यापारो ऽविनाभूतः। तस्याविनाभावाच्छक्नोति लक्षयितुम्, यथाकृतिर्व्यक्तिम्।; cf. TV 3.4.13 (911,22–23): प्रजापतिव्रतस्थत्वात्तत्रानीक्षणयुक्तितः। पर्युदासेन सत्यस्य विधिरित्यवगम्यते।
33 ab Cf. ŚV *Vākya* 301cd–302ab: नामधात्वर्थयोगी च निषेधो ऽन्यार्थभाग्भवेत्॥ तत्र वस्त्वन्तरोन्मुक्तं वस्त्वेवानुगुणं च तत्।
33 d Cf. PSV 2.5cd (Lasic 2009: 19): असत्येव नास्तिता, नान्यत्र न विरुद्धे।

---

32 Folios are missing in B_2 from 32b7.

---

29 c चार्थे] $C^1DHMPA_1B_1I_1I_2K_1$; वार्थे B_2 **30 ab** वाच्यमिष्टम°] $C^1DHMPA_1B_1I_1I_2K_1$; वाच्यंमिष्टक° B_2 **30 d** विना°] $C^1DHPA_1B_1B_2I_1I_2K_1$; ऋते ऽ° M **31 c** नञ्युक्त°] $C^1DHMPA_1B_1I_1I_2K_1$; नञ्यु° B_2(unmetrical) **32 d** प्रतीयते] $C^1DHPB_1I_1I_2K_1$; प्रवर्तते MA_1^{pc}; प्रवप्रवर्त्तते A_1^{ac}(unmetrical)

[2.5 वस्तुन्यपोहः]

तस्माद्वस्तुन्यपोहाः स्युर्,

[3 वस्तुरूपसामान्यनिषेधे शून्यतापत्तिः]

[3.1 अन्त्यविशेषा एवावशिष्यन्ते]

अपि चावस्तुकल्पने।
प्रागन्त्येभ्यो विशेषेभ्यो न किंचिद्वस्तु लभ्यते॥ ३५॥
न चान्त्यैर्व्यवहारो ऽस्ति, शक्यं नैषां निरूपणम्।

[3.2 बुद्ध्याकार एव सामान्यम्]

अपोहशब्दवाच्या च शून्यतान्यप्रकारिका॥ ३६॥
तस्यां चाश्वादिबुद्धीनामात्मांशग्रहणं भवेत्।
तत्रान्यापोहवाच्यत्वं मुधैवाभ्युपगम्यते॥ ३७॥
सामान्यं वस्तुरूपं हि बुद्ध्याकारो भविष्यति।

35cd–36ab Cf. ŚV *Apohavāda* 68cd–69ab.
35d लभ्यते] *Kāśikā* (ŚVKāś$_K$ 434(71),10): न किञ्चिद्वस्तु लभ्येत।
36c च] *Kāśikā* (ŚVKāś$_K$ 433(72),6): एवं चान्त्यानामपि विशेषाणामभावाद् … ।; ŚVN 407,18: एवं च … ।
36cd ≈TS$_Ś$ 918: निषेधमात्ररूपश्च शब्दार्थो यदि कल्प्यते। अभावशब्दवाच्या स्याच्छून्यतान्यप्रकारिका॥; also quoted in PVSVṬ 1.48 (129,10–11) (a. °रूपश्च] °रूपं च)
37 =TS$_Ś$ 919; Śāntarakṣita's reply in 1025.
38ab Cf. PVSV 1.71cd (40,3–6): एवं तर्हि बुद्धेरेव प्रतिभासो ज्ञानरूपत्वात् सन्नेव सामान्यम्। तन्न। यस्मात्—ज्ञानादव्यतिरिक्तं च कथमर्थान्तरं व्रजेत्॥ 71cd॥ ज्ञानस्य रूपं कथमर्थानां सामान्यम्, तस्य तेष्वभावात्।; TS$_Ś$ 1024: सामान्यवस्तुरूपत्वं न युक्तं त्वस्य भाविकम्। बुद्धेरनन्यरूपं हि यायादर्थान्तरं

35b चा°] $C^1DHMA_1B_1I_1I_2$; वा° PK_1 **35d** लभ्यते] $C^1DHPA_1B_1$; गम्यते MI_1K_1; लक्ष्यते I_2 **36c** चान्त्यै°] $C^1DHMB_1I_1I_2K_1$; चान्यै° P; चान्तै° A_1 **36c** °च्या च] $MA_1B_1I_1I_2K_1$; °च्याथ C^1DH; °च्या या P **36d** °प्रकारिका] $C^1DHMA_1B_1I_1I_2K_1$; °प्रकाशिका P **37a** तस्यां चा°] $C^1DHMA_1B_1I_1I_2K_1$; तस्या वा° P **37c** तत्रान्या°] $C^1DHMA_1B_1I_1I_2$; तत्रान्यो° P; अत्रान्या° K_1

शब्दार्थो ऽर्थानपेक्षो हि, वृथापोहः प्रकल्पितः॥ ३८॥
वस्तुरूपा च सा बुद्धिः शब्दार्थेषूपजायते।
तेन वस्त्वेव कल्प्येत वाच्यं बुद्ध्यनपोहकम्॥ ३९॥
असत्यपि च बाह्ये ऽर्थे वाक्यार्थः प्रतिभा यथा।
पदार्थो ऽपि तथैव स्यात्किमपोहः प्रकल्प्यते॥ ४०॥
बुद्ध्यन्तराद्व्यवच्छेदो न च बुद्धेः प्रतीयते।
स्वरूपोत्पादमात्राच्च नान्यमंशं बिभर्ति सा॥ ४१॥

कथम्॥

38 =TS$_{Ś}$ 920, PVSVṬ 1.71 (175,10–11); Śāntarakṣita's reply in 1026ab.
39 ab quoted in PVSVṬ 1.71 (175,12)
39 c कल्प्येत] *Kāśikā* (ŚVKāś$_{K}$ 432(73),7–8): तेन वस्तुरूप एव बुध्याकारः शब्दार्थ इति वरं कल्पितम्, किमपोहवाच्यत्वपरिकल्पनया।
39 =TS$_{Ś}$ 921: वस्तुरूपा च सा बुद्धिः शब्दार्थेषूपजायते। तेन (तेन] TS$_{Ś}$; तेषु TS) वस्त्वेव कल्प्येत वाच्यं बुद्ध्यनपोहकम्॥; Śāntarakṣita's reply in 1026cd.
40 b वाक्यार्थः प्रतिभा] PS 5.46cd: वाक्यार्थः प्रतिभाख्यो ऽयं तेनादावुपजन्यते॥; ŚVŚar 37,24: प्रतिभा बुद्धिरेव विशिष्टार्थाकारा वाक्यार्थः; *Kāśikā* (ŚVKāś$_{K}$ 432(73),12–14): वाक्यार्थो न बहिरस्तीति वाक्याधिकरणपूर्वपक्षे वक्ष्यते। तदभावाच्च प्रतिभैव संसर्गविच्छेदप्रतिभासा वाक्यार्थ इत्याक्षिप्तम्।; ŚVN 408,8: वाक्यार्थो हि यथा बाह्यार्थासंभवाद् बुद्ध्याकारः कल्पितो नापोहरूपः।; TSP$_{Ś}$ 922 (363,21–364,8): वाक्यार्थस्तु प्रतिभालक्षण एव। ··· वाक्यार्थो भवद्भिः प्रतिभालक्षण एव वर्ण्यते नापोहलक्षणः।
40 = TS$_{Ś}$ 922: असत्यपि च बाह्ये ऽर्थे वाक्यार्थः प्रतिभा यथा (वाक्यार्थः प्रतिभा यथा] TS; प्रतिभालक्षणो यथा TS$_{Ś}$)। पदार्थो ऽपि तथैव स्यात् किमपोहः प्रकल्प्यते॥; Śāntarakṣita's reply in 1027.
41 = TS$_{Ś}$ 923: बुद्ध्यन्तराद् व्यवच्छेदो न च बुद्धेः (बुद्धेः] TS$_{Ś}$; बुद्धौ TS) प्रतीयते। स्वरूपोत्पादमात्राच्च नान्यमंशं (°मंशं] TS; °संज्ञं TS$_{Ś}$) बिभर्ति सा॥; Śāntarakṣita's reply in 1028.

---

38 d वृथा°] C^{1}DHPA$_{1}$B$_{1}$I$_{1}$I$_{2}$K$_{1}$; मृसा° M **38 d** प्रकल्पितः] C^{1}DHMPB$_{1}$I$_{1}$I$_{2}$K$_{1}$; प्रकल्प्यते A$_{1}$ **39 c** कल्प्येत] MA$_{1}$B$_{1}$I$_{1}$K$_{1}$; कल्पेत C^{1}DHPI$_{2}$ **40 a** च] C^{1}DHPA$_{1}$B$_{1}$I$_{2}$; हि M; तु I$_{1}$K$_{1}$ **40 a** बाह्ये ऽर्थे] C^{1}DHPA$_{1}$B$_{1}$I$_{1}$I$_{2}$; बाह्यार्थे MK$_{1}$ **40 b** वाक्यार्थः प्रतिभा] H; वाक्यार्थप्रतिभा C^{1}DMPA$_{1}$B$_{1}$I$_{1}$I$_{2}$K$_{1}$ **40 b** यथा] C^{1}HMPA$_{1}$B$_{1}$I$_{1}$I$_{2}$K$_{1}$; तथा D **40 c** पदार्थो ऽपि] HMA$_{1}$B$_{1}$I$_{1}$I$_{2}$K$_{1}$; पदार्थे ऽपि C^{1}D; पदादपि P **41 c** °मात्राच्च] C^{1}DPA$_{1}$I$_{1}$I$_{2}$K$_{1}$; °मात्राद्धि HM; °मात्राच B$_{1}$

[4 पर्यायत्वदोषः]

भिन्नसामान्यवचना विशेषवचनाश्च ये।
सर्वे भवेयुः पर्याया यद्यपोहस्य वाच्यता॥ ४२॥

[4.1 नापोहभेदात्]

ननु भेदादपोहानां प्रसङ्गो ऽयं न युज्यते।
सामान्यापोहक्लृप्त्या चेद्वस्तुमात्रे समं तव॥ ४३॥
भिद्यन्ते मम वस्तुत्वात्सामान्यानि परस्परम्।
असंकीर्णस्वभावानि न चैकत्वं वितन्वते॥ ४४॥
संसृष्टैकत्वनानात्वविकल्परहितात्मनाम्।
अवस्तुत्वादपोहानां तव स्याद् भिन्नता कथम्॥ ४५॥
यदि वा भिद्यमानत्वाद्वस्त्वसाधारणांशवत्।
अवस्तुत्वे त्वनानात्वात्पर्यायत्वान्न मुच्यते॥ ४६॥

[4.2 नापोह्यभेदात्]
[4.2.1 अपोह्या बहिःसंस्थाः]

---

42 =$TS_Ś$ 924; also quoted in PVSVṬ 1.48 (129,12–13) (°नाश्च ये] °नाश्रये); Śāntarakṣita's reply in 1029; cf. PVSV 1.42 (25,24–26): तस्मात् स्वभावाभेदे ऽपि येन येन धर्मेण नाम्ना यो विशेषो भेदः प्रतीयते, न स शक्यो ऽन्येन प्रत्याययितुमिति नैकार्थाः सर्वशब्दाः।

45a संसृष्टै°] *Kāśikā* (ŚVKāś$_K$ 429(76),9): संसृष्टेति।

45 ≈$TS_Ś$ 925: संसृष्टैकत्वनानात्वविकल्परहितात्मनाम्। अवस्तुत्वादपोहानां नैव भेदो ऽपि विद्यते॥; cf. PV 1.41: तस्माद् यतो यतो ऽर्थानां व्यावृत्तिस् तन्निबन्धनाः। जातिभेदाः प्रकल्प्यन्ते तद्विशेषावगाहिनः॥

46 =$TS_Ś$ 926; cf. PSV 5.36c (Pind 2015: I.44,4–5): अव्यापकत्वाच्चासामान्यदोषो ऽपि नास्ति, अर्थान्तरापोहमात्रस्याभिन्नत्वात्, अद्रव्यत्वाच्च।

43a ननु] $C^1DHMA_1B_1I_1I_2K_1$; न तु P **43d** तव] $C^1DHMPA_1B_1I_1I_2$; भवेत् K_1 **44c** °स्वभावानि] $C^1DHMPA_1I_1I_2K_1$; °स्वभावानानि B_1(unmetrical) **44d** वितन्वते] $C^1DHMA_1B_1I_1I_2K_1$; वितन्यते P **45a** संसृष्टै°] $C^1DHMPA_1B_1K_1$; संस्पृष्टै° I_1I_2 **46c** त्वनाना°] $C^1DHMPA_1B_1I_2K_1$; त्वनामा° I_1 **46d** मुच्यते] $C^1DHMPB_1I_2K_1$; मुच्यसे A_1 ; युज्यते I_1(eyeskip)

ननु चापोह्यभेदेन भेदो ऽपोहस्य सेत्स्यति।
स्वतस्तावदभेदः स्यात् परतस्त्वौपचारिकः॥ ४७॥
तेनैवाधारभेदेनाप्यस्य भेदो न युज्यते।
न हि संबन्धिभेदेन भेदो वस्तुन्यपीष्यते॥ ४८॥
किमुतावस्त्वसंसृष्टमन्यतश्चानिवर्तितम्।
अनवाप्तविशेषांशं यत्किमित्यनिरूपितम्॥ ४९॥
तस्माद्यथैव भेदे ऽपि पिण्डानां नैव भिद्यते।
तथैवापोह्यभेदे ऽपि नानेको ऽयं भविष्यति॥ ५०॥
भेदे वा प्रतिपिण्डं स्यादगोऽपोहस्, तथा सति।
सामान्यं शाबलेयादेरिति नेष्टं प्रसिध्यति॥ ५१॥
संसर्गिणो ऽपि चाधारा यं न भिन्दन्ति रूपतः।

---

47 ab Cf. PS 5.14: अपोह्यभेदाद् भिन्नार्थाः स्वार्थभेदगतौ जडाः। एकत्राभिन्नकार्यत्वाद् विशेषणविशेष्यकाः॥; 5.14ab is quoted in $TSP_{\acute{S}}$ 927 (365,15).
47 cd *Kāśikā* ($ŚVKāś_{K}$ 427(78),1–2): स्वत इति। स्वाभाविकस्तावदपोहानां भेदो नास्ति। परतस्तु भवन्नौपचारिको भवेत्।; cf. PS 5.4ab: तद्वतो नास्वतन्त्रत्वाद्, उपचारात्।; PSV 5.36c (Pind 2015: I.44,2–3): न ह्यर्थान्तरमुपादाय शब्दः स्वभेदेषु वर्तते। तस्मात् पारतन्त्र्येण स्वभेदानाक्षेपदोषो नास्ति। भाक्तदोषो ऽपि नास्ति।
47 ≈$TS_{\acute{S}}$ 927: ननु चापोह्यभेदेन भेदो ऽपोहस्य सेत्स्यति। न विशेषः स्वतस्तस्य परतश्चौपचारिकः॥; also quoted in PVSVṬ 1.48 (129,16–17) (**a.** चापोह्यभेदेन] चापोहभेदेन); Śāntarakṣita's reply in 1045.
48 ≈$TS_{\acute{S}}$ 929: तथैवाधारभेदेनाप्यस्य भेदो न युज्यते। न हि संबन्धिभेदेन भेदो वस्तुन्यपीष्यते॥
49 d यत्किमित्य°] *Kāśikā* ($ŚVKāś_{K}$ 426(79),9): यत्किमित्यनेन स्वरूपेणानिरूपितं।
49 =$TS_{\acute{S}}$ 930.

47–48ab ननु ··· युज्यते] $C^1DHMPA_1B_1I_2K_1$; *om.* I_1(eyeskip) **47c** स्वतस्तावदभेदः स्यात्] $B_1I_2K_1$; न विशेषः स्वतस्तस्य C^1DH; न विशेषः स्वतश्चास्य M; न विशेषः स्वतः स्तस्य P; स्वतस्तावन्न भेद स्यात् A_1 **47d** परतस्त्वौ°] $A_1I_2K_1$; परतश्चौ° C^1DHMPB_1 **49a** °स्त्वसंसृष्ट°] $C^1DHPA_1B_1B_2I_1K_1$; °स्तुसंसृष्ट° M **49d** °त्किमित्य°] $MA_1B_1I_1I_2K_1$; °त्किमप्य° C^1DHP **50b** नैव भिद्यते] $DPA_1I_1I_2K_1$; नैव विद्यते C^1; नैष भिद्यते HMB_1 **51a** भेदे] $C^1DHMPB_1I_1I_2K_1$; भेदो A_1 **52a** चा°] $C^1DHMPA_1B_1K_1$; वा I_1I_2 **52a** °धारा] $C^1DHMPA_1I_1I_2K_1$; °कारा B_1

अपोह्यैः स बहिःसंस्थैर्भिद्येतेत्यतिकल्पना॥ ५२॥

[4.2.2 एकापोह्यमात्रातिरेकः]

अगव्यश्वातिरेकः स्यादनश्वश्च गवाधिकः।
शेषं हस्त्याद्यपोह्यं तु द्वयोरपि न भिद्यते॥ ५३॥
तत्रैकभेदाद् भेदो ऽस्तु बह्वभेदादभिन्नता।
भूयसां स्यात्सधर्मत्वमित्यभेदः प्रसज्यते॥ ५४॥
गौश्च हस्त्याद्यपोहेन नाश्वरूपाद्विशिष्यते।
करोति तदपोहं चेद्, ऐकरूप्यं विरुध्यते॥ ५५॥
सर्वशब्देषु चैकैकमपोह्यमतिरिच्यते।
तत्रासाधारणत्वेन तन्मात्रापोह्यता भवेत्॥ ५६॥
ततो ऽश्वापोहरूपत्वात्सिंहादिः सर्व एव ते।
तन्निमित्तमगोऽपोहं बिभ्रदुच्येत गौरिति॥ ५७॥

[4.2.3 सर्वापोहः]

सर्वापोहो यदीष्येत, स वक्तव्यः कथं पुनः।

---

52 =$TS_{ś}$ 928: संसर्गिणो ऽपि चाधारा (चाधारा] $TS_{ś}$; ह्याधारा TS) ये न भिन्दन्ति रूपतः। अपोहैः स बहिःसंस्थैर् (अपोहैः स बहिःसंस्थैर्] $TS_{ś}$; अपोह्यैर्बहिरङ्गैस्स TS) भिद्येतेत्यतिकल्पना॥; also quoted in PVSVṬ 1.48 (129,18–19) (**b.** रूपतः] भावतः)
54 c MS 12.2.22: विप्रतिषिद्धधर्माणां समवाये भूयसां स्यात् सधर्मत्वम्॥; MSBh 12.2.22 (2246,22–2247,3): विप्रतिषिद्धधर्माणामेतेषामग्निष्टुतश्चैकादशानां चाह्नां समवाय एतस्मिन् पञ्चदशरात्रे भूयसामेकादशानामह्नां सधर्मत्वं स्यात्, तदीयो धर्मः कर्तव्यः। को हेतुः। भूयस्त्वमेव। बहुषु गुणसंपन्नेषु महत्फलं भवति। एकस्मिन्नल्पं फलम्। एष हि लोके दृष्टान्तः। लोक एकादशसु प्रदीपेषु तैलवर्तिसंपन्नेष्वेकस्मिन् गृहे महान् प्रकाशो भवति। विपर्यये ऽल्पः।
57 quoted in PVSVṬ 1.59 (144,19–20).

---

52 c बहिःसंस्थै॰] $HMA_1B_1I_1I_2K_1$; बहिर्भूतै॰ C^1DP **52 d** ॰त्यतिकल्पना] $C^1DHMA_1B_1I_1I_2K_1$; ॰त्यपि कल्पना P **55 b** ॰द्विशिष्यते] $HMA_1I_1I_2K_1$; ॰द्विशेष्यते C^1DP; ॰द्विशिते B_1(unmetrical) **55 d** विरुध्यते] $C^1DHMPA_1^{pc}B_1I_1I_2K_1$; विशिष्यते A_1^{ac} **56 c** तत्रा॰] $DHMA_1B_1I_1I_2K_1$; तत्र C^1P **57 a** ततो ऽश्वा॰] $C^1DHMPA_1B_1I_1I_2$; ततश्व॰ K_1 **58 a** यदीष्येत] $C^1DHMPB_1I_1I_2K_1$; यदीष्येते A_1

[4.2.3.1 प्रत्येकरूपेण]

यदि प्रत्येकरूपेण नापोह्यानन्त्यतो भवेत्॥ ५८॥
भिन्नत्वाच्चाप्यपोह्यानां भिन्नो ऽपोहः प्रसज्यते।
तत्रैकस्मिन् भवेत्पिण्डे ऽनन्तजातिसमन्वयः॥ ५९॥
ततो गौरिति सामान्यं वाच्यमेकं न सिध्यति।
जात्यन्तरमतिश्चैषु भवेज्जात्यन्तरेष्विव॥ ६०॥

[4.2.3.2 समुदायात्मना]

समुदायात्मना नापि भवेदेषामपोह्यता।
समुदायो हि नैकेन विना धर्मेण जायते॥ ६१॥
नाप्येकदेशता तेषामस्ति नाप्येककालता।
व्यतिरिक्तश्च संघातस्तेषां कश्चिन्न विद्यते॥ ६२॥
यदि त्वव्यतिरेकः स्यादानन्त्यं तदवस्थितम्।

[4.2.3.3 सामान्यरूपेण]

[4.2.3.3.1 नाभावस्यापोहनम्]

यदि सामान्यरूपेण ते ऽपोह्यन्ते, न वस्तुता॥ ६३॥
कथं वावस्त्वपोह्येत, नाभावो ऽभावमृच्छति।
अपोह्यमाने चाभावे भाव एवावशिष्यते॥ ६४॥

---

60 ab quoted in PVSVṬ 1.59 (144,25)
63 a त्वव्यतिरेकः] *Kāśikā* (ŚVKāś$_K$ 419(86),14): अव्यतिरेके तु ··· ; but cf. ŚVŚar 43,16: यदि त्वव्यतिरिक्त इत्युच्यते।
64 ab Cf. ŚV *Apohavāda* 96ab.
64 b ऽभाव॰] *Kāśikā* (ŚVKāś$_K$ 418(87),10–11): भावान्तरप्रतिषेधो ह्यभावः, न तुच्छ एवाभावो ऽभावं प्राप्नोतीति।; ŚVŚar 43,21–22: न ह्यभावस्यापरो ऽभावो ऽस्ति।
64 cd Cf. ŚV *Apohavāda* 97abc and 111abc.

---

58 d ॰ह्यानन्त्यतो] HMK_1; ॰ह्यानन्तता $C^1DPA_1B_1I_1^{ac}I_2$; ॰ह्यानंत्यता I_1^{pc} **61 c** ॰यो हि] C^1DHP; ॰यो ऽपि $MA_1B_1I_1I_2$; ॰ये पि K_1 **63 a** ॰तिरेकः] $A_1B_1I_1I_2K_1$; ॰तिरिक्तः C^1DHP; ॰तिरिक्तं M **64 a** कथं वाव॰] $C^1DPA_1B_1I_1I_2$; कथं चाव॰ HMK_1 **64 b** चाभावे] $C^1DHMPA_1B_1I_1I_2$; वाभावे K_1 **64 d** ॰वशिष्यते] $C^1DHMPB_1I_1I_2K_1$; ॰वषशिष्यते A_1(unmetrical)

[4.2.3.3.2 अन्योन्यसंश्रयम्]

अपोह्यभेदक्लृप्तिश्च नाभावाभेदतो भवेत्।
तद्भेदो ऽपोहभेदाच्चेत्, प्राप्तमन्योन्यसंश्रयम्॥ ६५॥
गोसामान्यस्य भिन्नत्वादगौरित्येष भिद्यते।
अगौरित्यस्य भेदेन गोसामान्यं च भिद्यते॥ ६६॥

[4.2.3.4 अगावो ऽश्वादयः]

अगावो ऽश्वादयश्चेत् स्युस्ते ऽप्यभावात्मकाः पुनः।
कर्काद्यपेक्षया, ते ऽपि तथेत्येवं न गम्यते॥ ६७॥
किमपोह्यं क्व वापोहो, गोपिण्डेष्वेवमेव च।

[4.2.4 अन्त्यविशेषाः]

तत्र स्याद् द्वयमप्येतदन्त्येषु परमाणुषु॥ ६८॥
न चान्त्येषु द्वयोरस्ति व्यवहारो ऽभिधां प्रति।
गवाश्वपरमाणूनां विशेषश्च न विद्यते॥ ६९॥
स्वरूपजातिसंस्थानपरिमाणादिलक्षणः।
के ऽपोह्यन्तां क्व वापोहस्तत्रापि न विशिष्यते॥ ७०॥

[4.2.5 सामान्यं विनाविशेषतो ज्ञातुमशक्तिः]

न चाप्रसिद्धसारूप्यानपोहविषयात्मना।
शक्तः कश्चिदपि ज्ञातुं गवादीनविशेषतः॥ ७१॥

65ab Cf. ŚV *Apohavāda* 104cd.
70c *Kāśikā* (ŚVKāś$_K$ 413(92),2): तत्र न विद्मः—को ऽपोह्याः कुत्र वापोह इति।
71 =TS$_Ś$ 931: न चाप्रसिद्धसारूप्यान् (°रूप्यान्] TS$_Ś$; °रूप्यम् TS) अपो-

---

66d च भिद्यते] $C^1DHMPA_1I_1I_2K_1$; °स्य भिन्नता B_1 **67a** °श्चेत्] $HMA_1B_1I_1I_2K_1$; °श्च C^1DP **67b** पुनः] $C^1DHMA_1B_1I_1I_2K_1$; शुभाः P **67d** °त्येवं न गम्यते] $C^1DHMA_1B_1I_1I_2K_1$; °त्येवावगम्यते P **68a** वा°] $MA_1B_1I_1I_2K_1$; चा° C^1DHP **68c** तत्र] $C^1DHMA_1B_1I_1I_2K_1$; तस्य P **69b** ऽभिधां] $HMPA_1B_1I_1I_2K_1$; भिदां C^1D **69d** विद्यते] $C^1DHMPA_1I_1I_2K_1$; गम्यते B_1 **70c** के ऽपोह्यन्तां] $MA_1B_1I_1I_2K_1$; किमपोह्यं C^1DHP **70c** क्व वा°] $MA_1B_1I_1I_2K_1$; क्व चा° C^1DHP **70d** विशिष्यते] $C^1DHPA_1B_1I_1I_2K_1$; विशेष्यते M **71c** °दपि ज्ञातुं] $C^1DHMPA_1B_1I_2$; °दभिज्ञातुं I_1K_1

अपोह्यानपि चाश्वादीनेकधर्मान्वयाद्विना।
न निरूपयितुं शक्तिस्, तत्रापोहो न सिध्यति॥ ७२॥

[5 वस्तुरूपसामान्यनिषेधे दोषाः]

[5.1 संबन्धानुभवानुपपत्तिः]

[5.1.1 व्याप्तिग्रहः]

[5.1.1.1 अन्वयः]

न चान्वयविनिर्मुक्ता प्रवृत्तिर्लिङ्गशब्दयोः।
ताभ्यां च न विनापोहो, न चासाधारणे ऽन्वयः॥ ७३॥
अपोहश्चाप्यनिष्पन्नः, साहचर्यं क्व दृश्यताम्।
तस्मिन्नदृश्यमाने च न तयोः स्यात्प्रमाणता॥ ७४॥

हविषयात्मना। शक्तः कश्चिदपि ज्ञातुं गवादीनविशेषतः॥; also quoted in PVSVṬ 1.108 (225,23–24).

72 c शक्ति°] *Kāśikā* (ŚVKāś$_K$ 413(92),14–412(93),1): अपोह्यानिति शक्तिरन्तेन।

72 ≈TS$_Ś$ 932, PVSVṬ 1.108 (225,29–226.7): अपोह्यानपि चाश्वादीनेकधर्मान्वयादृते। न निरूपयितुं शक्तिस् (शक्तिस्] TS; शक्यस् PVSVṬ) तदपोहो न सिध्यति॥

73 a °विनिर्मुक्ता] *Kāśikā* (ŚVKāś$_K$ 412(93),7): न चान्वयविनिर्मुक्ता शब्दलिंगयोः प्रवृत्तिः संभवति।

73 Cf. PS 5.12: बहुधाप्यभिधेयस्य न शब्दात्सर्वथा गतिः। स्वसंबन्धानुरूप्यात्तु व्यवच्छेदार्थकार्यसौ॥

73 c Cf. ŚV *Apohavāda* 78ab.

73 d Cf. ŚV *Apohavāda* 78c.

73 ≈TS$_Ś$ 933: न चान्वयविनिर्मुक्ता प्रवृत्तिः शब्दलिङ्गयोः। ताभ्यां च न विनापोहो न चासाधारणे ऽन्वयः॥; also quoted in PVSVṬ 1.120–121 (241,29–242,6): न चान्वयविनिर्मुक्ता प्रवृत्तिः शब्दलिङ्गयोः। ताभ्यां न विनापोहे धीर्न चासाधारणे ऽन्वयः॥

74 ab Cf. ŚV *Apohavāda* 78d.

74 ≈TS$_Ś$ 934: अपोहश्चाप्यनिष्पन्नः साहचर्यं क्व कथ्यताम्। तस्मिन्नदृश्यमाने

---

72 b °द्विना] $B_1I_1I_2K_1$; °दृते C^1DHMPA_1 **72 cd** शक्तिस्, तत्रापोहो] $C^1DPA_1B_1I_1I_2K_1$; शक्तस्तदपोहो H; शक्तस्तत्रापोहो M **73 a** न चा°] $C^1DHMA_1B_1I_1I_2K_1$; न वा° P **73 a** °र्मुक्ता] $HMA_1B_1I_2K_1$; °र्मुक्ते C^1DPI_1 **73 d** न चासा°] $C^1DHMA_1B_1I_1I_2K_1$; न वासा° P **74 d** न तयोः] $C^1DHPA_1B_1I_1I_2K_1$; तयोर्न M

[5.1.1.2 व्यतिरेकः]

न चादर्शनमात्रेण ताभ्यां प्रत्यायनं भवेत्।
सर्वत्रैव ह्यदृष्टत्वात् प्रत्याय्यं नावशिष्यते॥ ७५॥

[5.1.2 सामान्यं विनापोहस्यातिकल्पना]

अथासत्यपि सारूप्ये स्यादपोहस्य कल्पना।
गवाश्वयोरयं कस्मादगोऽपोहो न कल्प्यते॥ ७६॥
शाबलेयाच्च भिन्नत्वं बाहुलेयाश्वयोः समम्।
सामान्यं नान्यदिष्टं चेत्, क्वागोऽपोहः प्रवर्तताम्॥ ७७॥

[5.1.3 अपोहानुभवप्रमाणम्]

[5.1.3.1 प्रत्यक्षम्]

इन्द्रियैर्नाप्यगोऽपोहः प्रथमं व्यवसीयते।
नान्यत्र शब्दवृत्तिश्च, किं दृष्ट्वा स प्रयुज्यताम्॥ ७८॥

च न तयोः स्यात् प्रमाणता॥; ≈ PVSVṬ 1.120–121 (242,7–8): अपोहश्चाप्य-प्रसिद्धो ऽव्यभिचारः क्व कथ्यताम्। तस्मिन्नविद्यमाने च न तयोः स्यात्प्रमाणता॥
75 a PS 5.34: अदृष्तेरन्यशब्दार्थे स्वार्थस्यांशे ऽपि दर्शनात्। श्रुतेः संब-न्धसौकर्यं न चास्ति व्यभिचारिता॥; PSV 5.34: अतुल्ये तु सत्यप्यानन्त्ये शक्यमदर्शनमात्रेणावृत्तेराख्यानम्। अत एव च स्वसंबन्धिभ्यो ऽन्यत्रादर्शनात् तद्व्यवच्छेदानुमानं स्वार्थाभिधानमित्युच्यते।; cf. ŚV *Apohavāda* 81cd.
75 ≈TS$_{Ś}$ 935: न चादर्शनमात्रेण ताभ्यां प्रत्यायनं भवेत्। सर्वत्रैव ह्यदृष्टत्वात् प्रत्ययो न विशिष्यते॥
75 d प्रत्याय्यं] TSP$_{Ś}$ 935 (368,16–18): ततश्च "अयं स्वार्थः" "अयं परा-र्थः" इत्येवं प्रत्ययो ज्ञानं न विशिष्येत। … क्वचित् प्रत्याय्य इति पाठः।
76 a See ŚV *Apohavāda* 71.
76 =TS$_{Ś}$ 936, PVSVṬ 1.108 (225,25–26), PKM 435,3–4
77 =TS$_{Ś}$ 937; PVSVṬ 1.108 (225,27–28) (**d.** प्रवर्तताम्] प्रवर्त्तनं), PKM 435,5–6
78 ab Cf. ŚV *Apohavāda* 73c.
78 c Cf. ŚV *Apohavāda* 73d.
78 d Cf. ŚV *Apohavāda* 74ab.
78 =TS$_{Ś}$ 938; ≈ PVSVṬ 1.119 (238,14–16): तेन यदुच्यते भट्टेन—संकेता-

---

75 b प्रत्यायनं] C^{1}DHPA$_{1}$B$_{1}$I$_{1}$I$_{2}$K$_{1}$; प्रत्ययनं M **75 c** सर्वत्रैव] C^{1}DHMP B$_{1}$I$_{1}$I$_{2}$K$_{1}$; सत्रैव A$_{1}$(unmetrical) **78 c** °वृत्तिश्च] C^{1}DHMPA$_{1}$B$_{1}$I$_{1}$I$_{2}$; °श-क्तिश्च K$_{1}$ **78 d** स प्रयुज्यताम्] C^{1}DHMPA$_{1}$B$_{1}$I$_{1}$I$_{2}$; संप्रयुज्यतां K$_{1}$

[5.1.3.2 अनुमानम्]

पूर्वोक्तेन प्रबन्धेन नानुमाप्यत्र विद्यते।

[5.1.4 उपसंहारः]

संबन्धानुभवो ऽप्यस्य तेन नैवोपपद्यते॥ ७९॥

[5.2 अगोरसिद्धिः]

[5.2.1 अगोव्युत्पत्त्यसंभवः]

निवृत्तिवाचिनः शब्दा न प्रसिद्धाश्च यान् प्रति।
तेषामगोरसिद्धत्वान्न सामान्यनिराक्रिया॥ ८०॥
अगोशब्दाभिधेयत्वं गम्यतां च कथं पुनः।
न दृष्टो यत्र गोशब्दः संबन्धानुभवक्षणे॥ ८१॥
एकस्मात्तर्हि गोपिण्डाद् यदन्यत्सर्वमेव तत्।
भवेदपोह्यमित्येवं न सामान्यस्य वाच्यता॥ ८२॥

[5.2.2 अपोहापोह्ययोरन्योन्यसंश्रयम्]

सिद्धश्चागौरपोह्येत, गोनिषेधात्मकश्च सः।

त्पूर्वमिन्द्रियैरन्यापोहो न गम्यते। नान्यत्र शब्दसंकेतः किं दृष्ट्वा स प्रयुज्यताम्॥

79 a पूर्वोक्तेन] ŚV *Apohavāda* 73–75 (cf. $TS_ś$ 939 quoted below). But Hattori 1975: 13 quotes ŚV *Abhāva* 40–41 instead.

79 =$TS_ś$ 939; ≈ PVSVṬ 1.119 (238,17–18): अन्वयेन विमुक्तत्वान्नानुमाप्यत्र विद्यते। संबन्धानुभवो ऽप्यस्य तेन नैवोपपद्यते (°पपद्यते] *em.*; °पद्यते *ed.*)

81 cd Cf. ŚV *Apohavāda* 75.

81 =$TS_ś$ 940; ≈PVSVṬ 1.120–121 (240,4–5): गोशब्दानभिधेयत्वमश्वादीनां हि ते कथम्। न दृष्टस्तत्र गोशब्दः संकेतसमये यदि॥

82 ≈$TS_ś$ 941: एकस्मात्तर्हि गोपिण्डाद् यदन्यत् सर्वमेव तत्। भवेदपोह्यमित्येतन् न सामान्यस्य वाच्यता॥; also quoted in PVSVṬ 1.120–121 (240,6–7): एकस्मात्तर्हि ते पिण्डाद्यदन्यत् सर्वमेव तत्। भवेदपोह्यमित्येवं न हि सामान्यवाच्यता॥

---

82 a गो°] $C^1DHMA_1B_1I_1I_2K_1$; ते P **82 d** वाच्यता] $C^1DHMA_1B_1I_1I_2K_1$; बाद्ध्यता P **83 b** गो°] $C^1DHMPA_1B_1I_1^{ac}I_2K_1$; यो I_1^{pc}

तत्र गौरेव वक्तव्यो नञा यः प्रतिषिध्यते॥ ८३॥
स चेदगोनिवृत्त्यात्मा, भवेदन्योन्यसंश्रयम्।
सिद्धश्चेद् गौरपोह्यार्थं, वृथापोहप्रकल्पना॥ ८४॥
गव्यसिद्धे त्वगौर्नास्ति, तदभावे च गौः कुतः।

[5.3 अपोहविशिष्टो ऽर्थः]

[5.3.1 अपोहापोहवत्संबन्धः]

[5.3.1.1 अपोहवतः सामान्यरूपत्वे]

नाधाराधेयवृत्त्यादिसंबन्धश्चाप्यभावयोः॥ ८५॥

[5.3.1.2 अपोहवतः स्वलक्षणत्वे]

न चासाधारणं वस्तु गम्यते ऽपोहवत्तया।

---

83 =TS$_Ś$ 942, PVSVṬ 1.113cd–114 (233,24–25) (नञा] नन्यो), PKM 436,9–10
84b Cf. criticism by Mādhava and Uddyotakara quoted in Pind 2015: II.157, n. 528.
84c °रपोह्यार्थं] *Kāśikā* (ŚVKāś$_K$ 405(100),3): वस्तुरूपे तु गव्यपोह्यार्थमभ्युपगते वृथागोपोहकल्पना।; but Kamalaśīla clearly presupposes अपोहार्थं. See TSP$_Ś$ 943: अपोहार्थम् अगोव्यवच्छेदलक्षणापोहसिद्ध्यर्थम्।
84 ≈TS$_Ś$ 943, PVSVṬ 1.113cd–114 (233,26–27), PKM 436,11–12: स चेदगोनिवृत्त्यात्मा भवेदन्योन्यसंश्रयः। सिद्धश्चेद् गौरपोह्यार्थं (°पोह्यार्थं] PVSVṬ; °पोहार्थं TS, PKM) वृथापोहप्रकल्पनम् (°प्रकल्पनम्] TS, PKM; °प्रवर्त्तनं PVSVṬ)॥
85ab ≈PVSVṬ 1.113cd–114 (233,28), PKM 436,13: गव्यसिद्धे त्वगौर्नास्ति तदभावे ऽपि गौः कुतः।
85 = TS$_Ś$ 944: गव्यसिद्धे त्वगौर्नास्ति तदभावे तु गौः कुतः। नाधाराधेयवृत्त्यादिसंबन्धश्चाप्यभावयोः॥; PKM 436,13–14 (**b.** च] ऽपि)

83cd–84ab तत्र ··· °न्योन्यसंश्रयम्] MA$_1$B$_1$I$_2$K$_1^{pc}$; तत्र ··· °न्योन्यसंश्रयः C^{1}DHI$_1$; तत्र गौरेव वक्तव्यो नञा यः प्रतिषिध्यते P; *om.* K$_1^{ac}$ **83d** प्रतिषिध्यते] C^{1}DHMPA$_1$B$_1$I$_2$K$_1^{pc}$; प्रतिषिद्ध्यति I$_1$ **84–85ab** स चेद° ··· गौः कुतः] C^{1}DHMA$_1$B$_1$I$_1$I$_2$K$_1^{pc}$; *om.* P **84b** भवेद°] C^{1}DHMA$_1$I$_1$I$_2$K$_1^{pc}$; प्राप्तम° B$_1$ **84b** °संश्रयम्] MA$_1$B$_1$I$_2$K$_1^{pc}$; °संश्रयः C^{1}DHI$_1$ **84c** °पोह्यार्थं] C^{1}DHA$_1$B$_1$; °पोहार्थं M; °पोह्यर्थं I$_1$I$_2$K$_1$ **84d** °कल्पना] C^{1}DA$_1$B$_1$I$_1$I$_2$K$_1$; °कल्पनम् HM **85b** च] C^{1}DMA$_1$B$_1$I$_1$I$_2$K$_1$; तु H

कथं वा परिकल्प्येत संबन्धो वस्त्ववस्तुनोः॥ ८६॥

[5.3.2 विशेषणविशेष्यभावः]

[5.3.2.1 विशेषणभूतो ऽपोहो न ज्ञायते]

स्वरूपसत्त्वमात्रेण न च किंचिद्विशेषणम्।
स्वबुद्ध्या रज्यते येन विशेष्यं तद् विशेषणम्॥ ८७॥
न चाप्यश्वादिशब्देभ्यो जायते ऽपोहबोधनम्।
विशेष्यबुद्धिरिष्टेह न चाज्ञातविशेषणा॥ ८८॥

[5.3.2.2 अज्ञातस्य विशेषणस्य कल्पनाया असंभवः]

न चान्यरूपमन्यादृक् कुर्याज्ज्ञानं विशेषणम्।
कथं चान्यादृशे ज्ञाने तदुच्येत विशेषणम्॥ ८९॥

---

86 =$TS_Ś$ 945, PVSVṬ 1.124–127 (249,27–28), PKM 438,4–5.
87 ≈$TS_Ś$ 946, PVSVṬ 1.124–127 (249,29–250,1), PKM 438,6–7: स्वरूपसत्त्वमात्रेण न स्यात् किंचिद् विशेषणम्। स्वबुद्ध्या रज्यते येन विशेष्यं तद्विशेषणम्॥
88 =$TS_Ś$ 947, PVSVṬ 1.124–127 (250,6–7), PKM 438,8–9 (**b.** °बोधनम्] °भासनम्; **c.** विशेष्य°] विशेष्ये)
88 cd MSBh 7.2.13 (1545,21–22): न चागृहीतविशेषणा विशेष्ये बुद्धिरुत्पद्यते।; TV 1.3.33 (304,19–20): व्यक्तिविशिष्टाकृतिमार्गो ऽपि "नागृहीतविशेषणा" इति न्यायाद् व्यक्तेः प्रथमग्रहणप्रसङ्गात् ··· ।; 1.4.2 (326,5–6): सर्वत्र ह्यगृहीतविशेषणा विशिष्टबुद्धिर्न दृष्टा, न त्वनभिहितविशेषणा।; 3.4.13 (915,26–916,1): विशिष्टग्रहणं नेष्टमगृहीतविशेषणम्। अभिधानभिधाने तु न केनचिदिहाश्रिते॥ अगृहीतविशेषणे तदनुरक्ता विशेष्यबुद्धिर्नोपजायत इति तद्ग्रहणमादर्तव्यम्।; 3.4.13 (919,1–2): शोणे ऽपि नैव वाजित्वमनुक्त्वा तद्गते ऽभिधा। दृष्टा हि न क्वचिद् बुद्धिरगृहीतविशेषणा॥; 3.1.13 (704,17–20): विशिष्टो हि विधिः कृत्स्नो नाप्रक्लृप्तविशेषणः। विशिष्टो विशिनष्टीति तत्पूर्वं प्रविशत्यसौ॥ गृह्णती भावनाप्येवमेकसंख्यं ग्रहं श्रुतम्। न गृह्णाति विशिष्टं तमगृहीतविशेषणम्॥
89 =$TS_Ś$ 948, PVSVṬ 1.124–127 (250,8–9) (**b.** °ज्ञानं] °ज्ञान°), PKM 438,10–11 (**c.** चा°] वा°)

---

89 lacuna A_1 89b4–90b2

87c येन] $C^1DHMPA_1^{pc}B_1I_1I_2K_1$; तेन A_1^{ac} **88c** विशेष्य°] $C^1HMA_1B_1I_1I_2$; विशिष्ट° D; विशेष° PK_1 **88d** न चाज्ञातविशेषणा] $C^1DHB_1I_1I_2K_1$; न चाज्ञाते विशेषणे MA_1; न वा ज्ञातविशेषणा P **89c** ज्ञाने] $HMB_1I_1I_2K_1$; ज्ञाते C^1DP

अथान्यथा विशेष्ये ऽपि स्याद्विशेषणकल्पना ।
तथा च सति यत्किंचित्प्रसज्येत विशेषणम् ॥ ९० ॥

[5.3.2.3 अभावविशिष्टस्यापोहवतो ऽवस्तुता]

अभावरूपगम्ये च न विशेष्ये ऽस्ति वस्तुता ।
विशेषितमपोहेन वस्तु वाच्यं न ते ऽस्त्यतः ॥ ९१ ॥

[5.3.3 सामान्यमेव विषयः]

यद्यप्यपोहनिर्मुक्ते न वृत्तिः शब्दलिङ्गयोः ।
युक्ता, तथापि बोधस्तु ज्ञातुर्वस्त्ववलम्बते ॥ ९२ ॥
न चासाधारणं वस्तु बुद्धौ विपरिवर्तते ।
न चापि निर्विकल्पत्वात्तस्य युक्ताभिधेयता ॥ ९३ ॥

---

90 ≈TS$_{Ś}$ 949: अथान्यथा विशेष्ये ऽपि स्याद् विशेषणकल्पना । तथा सति हि यत्किंचित् प्रसज्येत (प्रसज्येत] TS$_{Ś}$; प्रपद्येत TS) विशेषणम् ॥; PKM 438,12–13.
91 ≈TS$_{Ś}$ 950, PVSVṬ 1.124–127 (250,10–11), PKM 438,14–15: अभावगम्यरूपे च न विशेष्ये ऽस्ति वस्तुता । विशेषितमपोहेन वस्तु वाच्ये (वाच्ये] TS$_{Ś}$; वाच्यं TS, PVSVṬ, PKM) न ते ऽस्त्यतः ॥
92 ≈TS$_{Ś}$ 951: यद्यप्यपोहनिर्मुक्ते न वृत्तिः शब्दलिङ्गयोः । युक्ता (युक्ता] TS$_{Ś}$; युक्तस् TS) तथापि बोधस्तु ज्ञातुं वस्त्ववलम्बते ॥; also quoted in PVSVṬ 1.48 (128,27–28).
93 ≈TS$_{Ś}$ 952: न चासाधारणं वस्तु बुद्धौ विपरिवर्तते । न चापि निर्विकल्पत्वात् तस्य युक्ताधिगम्यता ॥; Pārthasārathi clearly presupposes अभिधेयता, ŚVN 417,30: न चाभिधेयत्वमपि तस्य युक्तम् ।; Śāntarakṣita reads अधिगम्यता and Kamalaśīla presupposes the same. Jayamiśra uses the word अध्यवसानम्. *Kāśikā* (ŚVKāś$_{K}$ 401(104),14–15) reads: निर्विकल्पं चासाधारणं वस्तु कथं तच्छाब्दे ज्ञाने विशेष्यतयावसीयते ।; this may support the variant reading

---

90 lacuna A$_1$ 90d6–91d7 **92** A$_1$ 92b7–93b4 **93** lacuna A$_1$ 93d4–94d3

---

90 c तथा च सति] B$_1$I$_1$I$_2$K$_1$; तथा सति हि C^{1}DHMP; तथा सति च A$_1$ **91 d** वाच्यं] C^{1}DHMPB$_1$I$_2$K$_1$; वाच्य I$_1$ **92 b** शब्दलिङ्गयोः] C^{1}DHPB$_1$I$_1$I$_2$K$_1$; लिङ्गशब्दयोः M; शब्दलि+++ A$_1$ **92 c** बोधस्तु] MB$_1$I$_1$I$_2$K$_1$; बुद्धिस्तु C^{1}DHP **93 d** °भिधेयता] B$_1$I$_1$I$_2$K$_1$; विशेष्यता C^{1}DHMP

शब्देनागम्यमानं च विशेष्यमिति साहसम्।
तेन सामान्यमेष्टव्यं विषयो बुद्धिशब्दयोः॥ ९४॥

[6 अपोह्यस्यापोहः]

[6.1 अगोऽपोहः]

[6.1.1 वस्तुन एवापोह्यता]

यदा चाशब्दवाच्यत्वान्न व्यक्तीनामपोह्यता।
तदापोह्येत सामान्यं, तस्यापोहाच्च वस्तुता॥ ९५॥
नापोह्यत्वमभावानामभावाभाववर्जनात्।
व्यक्तो ऽपोहान्तरे ऽपोहस्तस्मात्सामान्यवस्तुनः॥ ९६॥

[6.1.2 अभावस्यापोह्यत्वे प्रसङ्गः]

अभावस्य च यो ऽभावः स चेत्तस्माद्विलक्षणः।
भाव एव भवेन्, नो चेद् गौरगौस्ते प्रसज्यते॥ ९७॥

[6.2 असतो ऽपोहः]

यद्यप्यन्येषु शब्देषु वस्तुनः स्यादपोह्यता।

विशेष्यता but not necessarily. The glosses by Jayamiśra and Sucarita may suggest yet another, unrecorded reading अवसेयता.

94 PKM 438,17–18, ≈$TS_{\acute{s}}$ 953: शब्देनागम्यमानं च विशेष्यमिति साहसम्। तेन सामान्यमेष्टव्यं विषयो बुद्धिशब्दयोः॥

95 ab But cf. Dignāga's own view at PS 5.34: अतुल्ये तु सत्यप्यानन्त्ये शक्यमदर्शनमात्रेणावृत्तेराख्यानम्। अत एव च स्वसंबन्धिभ्यो ऽन्यत्रादर्शनात् तद्व्यवच्छेदानुमानं स्वार्थाभिधानमित्युच्यते।; cf. also ŚV *Apohavāda* 75 and 81.

95 =$TS_{\acute{s}}$ 954, PKM 439,16–7.

96 ab Cf. ŚV *Apohavāda* 64ab.

96 = $TS_{\acute{s}}$ 955, PKM 439,8–9: नापोह्यत्वमभावानामभावाभाववर्जनात्। व्यक्तो ऽपोहान्तरे ऽपोहस् (°रे ऽपोहस्] supported by $TSP_{\acute{s}}$, PKM; °रो ऽपोहस् $TS_{\acute{s}}$; °रापोहस् TS) तस्मात् सामान्यवस्तुनः॥

97 =$TS_{\acute{s}}$ 956; cf. ŚV *Apohavāda* 64cd and 111abc.

---

95 lacuna A_1 95a5–96a4 **96** A_1 96c2–97b8 **98** A folio is missing in A_1 for 98–117.

---

95 a यदा चा°] $C^1DHMA_1^{pc}B_1I_1I_2K_1$; यदा वा° P; तदा चा° A_1^{ac} **95 d** तस्यापोहाच्च] $C^1DMPB_1I_1I_2K_1$; तस्यापोह्याच्च H

सच्छब्दस्य त्वभावाख्यान्नापोह्यं भिन्नमिष्यते॥ ९८॥
तत्रासतो ऽपि भावत्वमिति क्लेशो महान् भवेत्।
तदसिद्धौ न सत्तास्ति, न चासत्ता प्रसिध्यति॥ ९९॥

[7 अपोहभेदः]

[7.1 न वासनाभेदात्]

[7.1.1 अर्थभेदः]

न चापि वासनाभेदाद् भेदः सद्रूपतापि वा।
अपोहानां प्रकल्प्येत, न ह्यवस्तुनि वासना॥ १००॥
स्मृतिं मुक्त्वा न चास्त्यस्याः शक्तियोगः क्रियान्तरे।
तस्मान्नान्यादृशे सार्थे करोत्यन्यादृशीं मतिम्॥ १०१॥

[7.1.2 शब्दभेदः]

भवद्भिः शब्दभेदो ऽपि तन्निमित्तो न लभ्यते।
न ह्यसाधारणः शब्दो वाचकः प्रागदृष्टितः॥ १०२॥
भिन्नत्वाच्चापि नैवैका वासना तैः प्रकल्प्यते।
न चास्ति शब्दवस्त्वेकं वासनां यत्करिष्यति॥ १०३॥

[7.2 शब्दान्तरापोहपरिकल्पने दोषाः]

तत्र शब्दान्तरापोहे सामान्ये परिकल्पिते।

---

98 $=\mathrm{TS}_{\acute{s}}$ 957; cf. ŚV *Apohavāda* 144cd for *prameya*, *jñeya*, etc.
99 $\approx\mathrm{TS}_{\acute{s}}$ 958: तत्रासतो ऽपि भावत्वमिति क्लेशो महान् भवेत्। तदसिद्धौ न सत्तास्ति न वा (वा॰] $\mathrm{TS}_{\acute{s}}$; चा॰ TS) सत्ता प्रसिध्यति॥
100 $=\mathrm{TS}_{\acute{s}}$ 959: न चापि वासनाभेदाद् भेदः सद्रूपतापि वा। अपोहानां प्रकल्प्येत न ह्यवस्तुनि वासना (वासना] $\mathrm{TS}_{\acute{s}}$; सा मता TS) ॥; cf. ŚV *Apohavāda* 145a: अपोह्यकल्पनायां वा and a passage of the *Hetumukha* quoted there.
102 $=\mathrm{TS}_{\acute{s}}$ 960.

100a ॰पि वा] C^1DHMP; ॰पि च $B_1I_1I_2K_1$ **100c** अपोहानां] C^1DHMP$I_1I_2K_1$; अपोह्यानां B_1 **100c** प्रकल्प्येत] C^1DHPI_2K_1; प्रकल्पेत MB_1I_1 **101a** चास्त्य॰] C^1DHP$B_1I_1K_1$; चाप्य॰ M; वास्त्य॰ I_2 **102d** ॰दृष्टितः] C^1DHMP$B_1I_1I_2$; ॰दृष्टतः K_1 **103b** प्रकल्प्यते] C^1DHP$B_1I_1I_2K_1$; प्रसाध्यते M **103c** चा॰] C^1DHM$B_1I_1I_2K_1$; वा॰ P **103d** वासनां] C^1DHMP$B_1I_1I_2$; वासना K_1

तथैवावस्तुरूपत्वाच्छब्दभेदो न लभ्यते॥ १०४॥
वाचकानां यथा चैवं वाच्यवाचकयोर्मिथः।
न चाप्यपोह्यभेदेन भेदो ऽस्तीत्युपपादितम्॥ १०५॥

[7.3 शब्दापोहग्रहणप्रमाणम्]

नागृहीतश्च गमकः शब्दापोहः कथंचन।

[7.3.1 न प्रत्यक्षम्]

प्रत्यक्षं च न तच्छक्तं

[7.3.2 नापि लिङ्गवाचकौ]

न च स्तो लिङ्गवाचकौ॥ १०६॥
यतः स्याद् ग्रहणं तस्य, लिङ्गादीनां च कल्पने।
न व्यवस्थेति वाच्यैवं विना प्रत्यक्षमूलतः॥ १०७॥

[7.4 गम्यगमकत्वाभावः]

न गम्यगमकत्वं स्यादवस्तुत्वादपोहयोः।
भवत्पक्षे, यथा लोके खपुष्पशशशृङ्गयोः॥ १०८॥
वृष्टिमेघासतोर्दृष्ट्या यद्यनैकान्तिकं वदेत्।

104c तथैवा॰] See ŚV *Apohavāda* 65ab.
104 ≈TS$_{\acute{s}}$ 961, PKM 440,10–11: तत्र शब्दान्तरापोहे सामान्ये परिकल्पिते। तथैवावस्तुरूपत्वाच्छब्दभेदो न कल्प्यते॥
105d ॰पपादितम्] See ŚV *Apohavāda* 47 ff.
105 ≈TS$_{\acute{s}}$ 962: वाचकानां यथा नैवं (नैवं] TS$_{\acute{s}}$; चैवं TS) वाच्यवाचकयोर्मिथः। न चाप्यपोहभेदेन भेदो ऽस्तीत्युपपादितम्॥
107a यतः] *Kāśikā* (ŚVKāś$_{K}$ 310(11),13): यतस्तस्य ग्रहणं स्यादित्याह।
108 =TS$_{\acute{s}}$ 963; also quoted in PVSVṬ 1.48 (129,8–9).

104d लभ्यते] $MB_1I_1I_2K_1$; कल्प्यते C^1DHP **105b** वाच्यवाचकयो॰] $C^1DHPB_1I_1I_2K_1$; वाच्यानां च तयो॰ M **106c** च न] $I_1I_2K_1$; न च C^1DHMPB_1 **107a** यतः] C^1DHPI_1; येन $MB_1I_2K_1$ **109a** ॰र्दृष्ट्या] MI_1K_1; ॰र्दृष्ट्वा $C^1DHPB_1I_2$ **109b** यद्य॰] $C^1DHMB_1I_1I_2K_1$; यद् घ॰ P **109b** ॰नैकान्तिकं] C^1DHMPI_1; ॰नैकांतिको B_1I_2; ॰नेकांतिकं K_1 **109b** वदेत्] $C^1DHMPB_1I_1K_1$; भवेत् I_2

वस्त्वेवात्रापि मत्पक्षे, भवत्पक्षे ऽप्यदः कुतः॥ १०९॥

[7.5 व्यतिरेकाभावः]

[7.5.1 व्यतिरेको विधिरूपपूर्वकः]

विधिरूपश्च शब्दार्थो येन नाभ्युपगम्यते।
न भवेद्व्यतिरेको ऽपि तस्य, तत्पूर्वको ह्यसौ॥ ११०॥

[7.5.2 निषेधद्वययोगित्वम्]

निषेधद्वययोगित्वादसतो याप्यभावता।
सवस्तुके भवेत्सापि न तुच्छे बुद्ध्यसंभवात्॥ १११॥

[7.5.3 अपोहवस्तुनोरभेदः]

ननु युक्त्यानयैवायं वस्तुनो ऽपि न भिद्यते।
अपोहस्, तेन दोषो ऽत्र पूर्वोक्तो न भविष्यति॥ ११२॥
सिद्धमेवं मदिष्टं स्यान्, नैवान्या गतिरस्ति हि।
अभावे वस्तुबुद्धिर्वा यद्वा वस्तुन्यभावधीः॥ ११३॥
तत्राभावात्मकत्वे स्यान्निर्निमित्तैव वस्तुधीः।

---

109 d ऽप्यदः] ŚVŚar 57,9–10: तव तदपि नास्तीति गम्यगमकत्वमपि नास्ति।; *Kāśikā* (ŚVKāś$_K$ 308(13),3–4): ततो गम्यगमकत्वमप्यदः कुतो भवताम्।; TSP$_Ś$ 964: भवतस्तु बौद्धस्य पक्षे ऽदो ऽप्येतद्वृष्टिमेघाभावयोर्गम्यगमकत्वं कुतः, नैव। अपिशब्दो भिन्नक्रमः "अदः" इत्यस्यानन्तरं संबध्यते।
109 ≈TS$_Ś$ 964: वृष्टिमेघासतोर्दृष्ट्वा यद्यनैकान्तिकं वदेत्। वस्त्वस्त्वेवात्र मत्पक्षे, भवत्पक्षे ऽप्यदः कुतः॥
110 =TS$_Ś$ 965, PVSVṬ 1.124–127 (253,28–29).
111 Cf. ŚV *Apohavāda* 64cd and 97abc.
112 d पूर्वोक्तो] ŚV *Apohavāda* 102 and 104.

---

109 ऽप्यदः] C^{1}DHP; **d** त्वदः MB$_1$I$_1$I$_2$K$_1$ **110 c** °द्व्यतिरेको] C^{1}DHMPB$_1$I$_2$K$_1$; °द्व्यतिरिक्तो I$_1$ **111 a** °योगि°] C^{1}DHMB$_1$I$_1$I$_2$K$_1$; °योग° P **112a** ननु] C^{1}DHMB$_1$I$_1$I$_2$K$_1$; न तु P **112b** वस्तुनो ऽपि] HMPB$_1$I$_1$K$_1$; वस्तुनापि C^{1}D; वस्तुतो पि I$_2$ **112 d** पूर्वोक्तो न] C^{1}DHPB$_1$I$_1$I$_2$K$_1$; न पूर्वोक्तो M **113a** °मेवं मदिष्टं] C^{1}DHPI$_1$K$_1$; °मेव मदिष्टं MB$_1$; °मेवमदृष्टं I$_2$ **113 c** अभावे] C^{1}DHMB$_1$I$_1$I$_2$K$_1$; अभाव° P **113 d** वस्तु°] C^{1}DHPB$_1$I$_1$I$_2$K$_1$; भाव° M **114ab** स्यान्निर्निमित्तैव] C^{1}DHMPB$_1$I$_2$K$_1$; स्यान्निर्मिनिमित्तैव I$_1$(unmetrical)

वस्तुन्यभावबोधस्तु सिध्यत्यन्यमपेक्ष्य तु॥ ११४ ॥

[8 अपोहमात्रवाच्यत्वे]

अपोहमात्रवाच्यत्वं यदि त्वभ्युपगम्यते।
नीलोत्पलादिशब्देषु शबलार्थाभिधायिषु॥ ११५ ॥
विशेषणविशेष्यत्वसामानाधिकरण्ययोः।
न सिद्धिर्,

[8.1 विशेषणविशेष्यत्वाभावः]

न ह्यनीलत्वव्युदासे ऽनुत्पलच्युतिः॥ ११६ ॥
नापि तत्रेतरस्, तस्मान्न विशेष्यविशेषणे।

---

115 a अपोहमात्रवाच्यत्वं] PSV 5.14: यद्यन्यापोहमात्रं शब्दार्थः, कथं नीलोत्पलादिशब्दानां सामानाधिकरण्यं स्याद् विशेषणविशेष्यभावश्च। कथं च न स्यात्। यस्माद्भिन्नमपोह्यं सामान्यविशेषशब्दानाम्। एष दोषो नास्ति।; PS 5.14: अपोह्यभेदाद् भिन्नार्थाः स्वार्थभेदगतौ जडाः। एकत्राभिन्नकार्यत्वाद् विशेषणविशेष्यकाः॥; NV 2.2.66 (316,5–6): यस्य चान्यापोहः शब्दार्थः, तेनानीलानुत्पलव्युदासौ कथं समानाधिकरणाविति वाच्यम्।
115 d शबलार्थाभिधायिषु] TSP$_\text{Ś}$ 966 quotes PS 5.15abc: न हि तत् केवलं नीलं न च केवलमुत्पलम्। समुदायाभिधेयत्वात्।
115 ≈TS$_\text{Ś}$ 966: अपोहमात्रवाच्यत्वं यदि वा(यदि वा°] TS$_\text{Ś}$; यदिहा° TS)भ्युपगम्यते। नीलोत्पलादिशब्देषु शबलार्थाभिधायिषु॥; Sucarita (ŚVKāś$_\text{K}$ 305(16),14–304(17),1) quotes PS 5.2: न जातिशब्दो भेदानामानन्त्यव्यभिचारतः। वाचको योगजात्योर्वा भेदार्थैरपृथक्श्रुतेः॥
116 =TS$_\text{Ś}$ 967.
117a तत्रेतरस्] TSP$_\text{Ś}$ 968: इतरो नीलव्युदासः। क्वचिद् इतरेति स्त्रीलिङ्गस्य पाठः।
117 PSV 5.14: नीलोत्पलादिशब्दा हि सत्यप्यपोह्यभेदे स्वार्थविशेषव्यञ्जनार्थमूर्ध्वताकाकनिलयवत् स्वमपोहार्थमेकत्रोपसंहरन्तः समानाधिकरणा भवन्ति।

114d सिध्यत्य°] $C^1DHPB_1I_1I_2K_1$; सिद्धस्त्व° M **115a** अपोहमात्र°] $C^1DHMPB_1I_2K_1$; आपोहमात्र° I_1 **115a** °वाच्यत्वं] $C^1DHPI_1I_2K_1$; °वाचित्वं MB_1 **115b** त्व°] $B_1I_1I_2K_1$; चा° C^1D; वा° HMP **115d** शबला°] $C^1DMPB_1I_1I_2K_1$; शब्ला° H(unmetrical) **116c** °नीलत्व°] $C^1DHMB_1I_1I_2K_1$; °नीलत्वं P **116d** ऽनुत्पल°] $C^1DHPB_1I_1I_2K_1$; नूत्पल° M

शब्दयोर्नापि ते स्यातामभिधेयानपेक्षयोः॥ ११७॥

[8.2 सामानाधिकरण्याभावः]

सामानाधिकरण्यं च न भिन्नत्वादपोहयोः।
अर्थतश्चेत्तदिष्येत, कीदृश्याधेयता तयोः॥ ११८॥

तथा हि ते प्रत्येकं स्वार्थविशेषे संशयहेतवः शब्दान्तरसहितव्यङ्ग्यार्थासंभवाश्च (°भवाश्च] *em.*; °भवाच्च *Pind*) विशेषणविशेष्यभूताः।; PS 5.19abc: यद्यप्येकार्थवृत्तिता जातिगुणयोस्त्वार्थयोः। न सामान्यविशेषत्वं; PSV 5.19abc: यद्यपि हि नीलगुणोत्पलजात्योरेकत्र द्रव्ये वृत्तेः सामानाधिकरण्यं स्यात्, न विशेषणविशेष्यभावः। न हि [*नीलगुणस्योत्पलजातियोगः, नाप्युत्पलजातेर्नीलगुणयोगः।]; cf. PVSVṬ 1.75 (188,8–11): अन्यनिवृत्तिमात्रमपोहं गृहीत्वा नीलादिव्यावृत्तावनुत्पलादिव्यावृत्तेरभावाद् अनुत्पलादिव्यावृत्तौ चानीलादिव्यावृत्तेरभावाच्च न विशेषणविशेष्यभावस्तयोर्धर्मयोः, तदभावाच्च न तदभिधायकयोः (तदभिधायकयोः] *em.*; तदाभिधायकयोः *ed.*) शब्दयोरपि (शब्दयोरपि] *em.*; शब्दयोः शब्दयोरपि *ed.*) विशेषणविशेष्यभावः।
117 =TS$_Ś$ 968.
117 cd Cf. PS 5.20ab: [*तथा द्रव्यजातिगुणमात्रवाचकशब्दयोः।]; PSV 5.20ab: [*यस्मान्नार्थयोर्मिथो योगः, तस्मात् तच्छब्दयोर्न विशेषणविशेष्यभावः।]
118 ab PSV 5.2cd: तथा हि "सद्द्रव्यम्" "सन्गुणः" "सत्कर्म" इति भेदार्थैर्द्रव्यादिशब्दैः सामानाधिकरण्यं न स्यात्। तच्च दृष्टम्। न हि सत्ता तद्योगो वा द्रव्यं गुणो वा भवति, किं तर्हि द्रव्यस्य गुणस्य वा।; PS 5.14a: अपोह्यभेदाद् भिन्नार्थाः।; PS 5.15abc: न च तत् केवलं नीलं न च केवलमुत्पलम्। समुदायाभिधेयत्वात्।; NV 2.2.66 (316,6–8): यस्य पुनर्विधीयमानः शब्दार्थः, तस्य जातिगुणविशिष्टं नीलोत्पलशब्दाभ्यां द्रव्यमुच्यते, जातिगुणौ च द्रव्ये वर्तेते, न पुनरनीलानुत्पलव्युदासौ। तस्मात् समानाधिकरणार्थो नास्तीति।
118 c Cf. PS 5.14c: एकत्राभिन्नकार्यत्वाद् and PSV 5.14.
118 =TS$_Ś$ 969; cf. PVSVṬ 1.75 (188,11–13): नापि सामानाधिकरण्यं शब्दवाच्ययोर्भिन्नत्वात्। नापि यत्रार्थे ऽपोहयोर्भावस् तद्द्वारकं सामानाधिकरण्यम्, अवस्तुत्वेनापोहस्याधेयत्वाभावात्।

---

118 lacuna A$_1$ 118c5–7

---

118 b न] C^{1}DHMPA$_1$B$_1$I$_2$K$_1$; *om.* I$_1$(unmetrical) **118 c** °तश्चेत्त°] HM I$_1$K$_1$; °तश्चैत° C^{1}DPB$_1$I$_2$; °तश्चे+ A$_1$ **118 d** कीदृश्याधेयता] C^{1}DHM PA$_1$B$_1$I$_2$K$_1$; कीदृशी दृश्याधेयता I$_1$(unmetrical)

न चासाधारणं वस्तु गम्यते, ऽन्यच्च नास्ति ते।
अगम्यमानमैकार्थ्यं शब्दयोः क्वोपयुज्यते॥ ११९ ॥

[9 अन्यापोहवद्वस्तुवाच्यत्वे]

[9.1 अनाक्षेपदोषः]

[9.1.1 व्याप्तिः शब्दान्न प्रतीयते]

अथान्यापोहवद्वस्तु वाच्यमित्यभिधीयते।
तत्रापि परतन्त्रत्वाद् व्याप्तिः शब्देन दुर्लभा॥ १२०॥
खण्डे भिन्नव्यपोह्यत्वाद् यथैव मधुरादिभिः।
शुक्लादिव्याप्त्यभावेन नाक्षेपो न विशेषणम्॥ १२१॥
तथैवासद्व्युदासांशविच्छिन्नार्थावधारणे।
नाघटादिनिवृत्त्यंशव्याप्तिः शब्दात्प्रतीयते॥ १२२॥

[9.1.2 अर्थरूपेण व्याप्तिः सत्तयैव]

---

119 =$TS_{ś}$ 970; cf. PVSVṬ 1.75 (188,13–14): न च स्वलक्षणं शब्दविषयः। अन्यच्चाधिकरणं नेष्यते। न च स्वलक्षणे ऽपोहयोर्भावे ऽपि शब्दयोः सामानाधिकरण्यम्, एकविषयत्वस्याप्रतीतेः।

120 ab PSV 5.36d: शब्दो ऽर्थान्तरनिवृत्तिविशिष्टानेव भावानाह।

120 c Cf. PS 5.4a: तद्वतो नास्वतन्त्रत्वात्।; PS 5.18a: पूर्वमुक्तत्वात्।; PSV 5.18a: तद्वदभिधानं हि "तद्वतो नास्वतन्त्रत्वात्" इत्येवमादिना पूर्वमेव निषिद्धम्।; PSV 5.36c: न ह्यर्थान्तरमुपादाय शब्दः स्वभेदेषु वर्तते। तस्मात्पारतन्त्र्येण स्वभेदानाक्षेपदोषो नास्ति।

120 =$TS_{ś}$ 971.

121 Cf. PSV 5.4a: एवमपि हि सच्छब्दो जातिस्वरूपमात्रोपसर्जनं द्रव्यमाह न साक्षाद् इति तद्गतघटादिभेदानाक्षेपाद् अतद्भेदत्वे सामानाधिकरण्याभावः। न ह्यसत्यां व्याप्तौ सामानाधिकरण्यभावः। तद्यथा शुक्लशब्दः स्वाभिधेयगुणमात्रविशिष्टद्रव्याभिधानात् सत्यपि द्रव्ये मधुरादीन् नाक्षिपति। ततश्चातद्भेदत्वम्। एवमत्रापि प्रसङ्गः।

120a °वद्वस्तु] $C^1DHMA_1B_1I_1I_2K_1$; °बद्धस्तु P **120d** दुर्लभा] $C^1HMA_1B_1I_1I_2K_1$; दुर्बला DP **121a** खण्डे] $C^1DHPA_1I_1I_2K_1$; खण्ड° M; ++ B_1 **121d** नाक्षेपो] $C^1DHMA_1B_1I_1I_2K_1$; नापेक्षो P **122ab** °सांशविच्छिन्ना°] $C^1HMPA_1I_1K_1$; °सांशावच्छिन्ना° DB_1 ; °सार्थविछिन्ना° I_2 **122b** °धारणे] $C^1DHMPB_1I_1I_2K_1$; °धारणात् A_1

व्याप्तिश्चेदर्थरूपेण, सत्तयैव हि सा भवेत्।
न घटत्वादिमानर्थः कश्चिन्न व्याप्यते तया॥ १२३॥
न च वस्तुतया व्याप्तिस्तया शब्दस्य वार्यते।
प्रतीतिं प्रति तुल्यस्तु व्यापारो वस्त्ववस्तुनोः॥ १२४॥

[9.1.3 शब्दैर्वस्त्वात्मा भागेन प्रतीयते]

निर्भागो ऽपि च वस्त्वात्मा शब्दैर्भागेन गम्यते।
न हि सच्छब्दविज्ञानाद् घटाद्यर्थः प्रतीयते॥ १२५॥
तेनानाक्षेपदोषो ऽस्ति,

[9.2 भाक्तदोषः]

भाक्तदोषश्च विद्यते।
विशेषणत्वान्मुख्यत्वमपोहस्य हि जातिवत्॥ १२६॥
तस्मात्तद्वृति गौणत्वान्नाभिधेयत्वसंभवः।

---

123 a For Dignāga's notion of *vyāpti*, see PSV 5.18b: यत्तर्हीदमुक्तम् "अन्तर्भूतविशेषं सामान्यम्" इति। नैतदुक्तमभिधेयत्वात्, किं तर्हि—अनपोहनात्। (PS 5.18b); for *artharūpeṇa*, see ŚV *Apohavāda* 118c: अर्थतश्चेत्तदिष्येत।
124 Cf. PS 5.11c, which will be criticized at ŚV *Apohavāda* 133–134.
125 Cf. PS 1.5: धर्मिणो ऽनेकरूपस्य नेन्द्रियात्सर्वथा गतिः। स्वसंवेद्यं ह्यनिर्देश्यं रूपमिन्द्रियगोचरः॥; PS 5.12: बहुधाप्यभिधेयस्य न शब्दात्सर्वथा गतिः। स्वसंबन्धानुरूप्यात्तु व्यवच्छेदार्थकार्यसौ॥; PV 1.43: एकस्यार्थस्वभावस्य प्रत्यक्षस्य सतः स्वयम्। को ऽन्यो न दृष्टो भागः स्याद् यः प्रमाणैः परीक्ष्यते॥
126 a PSV 5.36c: न ह्यर्थान्तरमुपादाय शब्दः स्वभेदेषु वर्तते। तस्मात्पारतन्त्र्येण स्वभेदानाक्षेपदोषो नास्ति।
126 Cf. PS 5.4b: उपचारात्।; PSV 5.4b: सच्छब्दो हि भूतार्थेन स्वरूपं वा जातिं वाह। तत्र प्रवृत्तस् तद्वृत्युपचर्यते। न तु यो यत्रोपचर्यते, स तमर्थं भूतार्थेनाह।; PSV 5.36c: भाक्तदोषो ऽपि नास्ति।

---

123 b सत्तयैव] HMA$_1$B$_1$K$_1$; सत्तयैवं C^{1}DPI$_1$; सत्तयेव I$_2$ **123 c** °मानर्थः] C^{1}DHMPA$_1$B$_1$I$_2$K$_1$; °मानार्थः I$_1$ **123 d** तया] C^{1}DHMPB$_1$I$_1$I$_2$K$_1$; नश्चा A$_1$(unmetrical) **124 a** च] C^{1}DHPA$_1$B$_1$I$_1$I$_2$K$_1$; हि M **124 c** प्रतीतिं] C^{1}DHMPA$_1$B$_1$I$_2$K$_1$; प्रतीति° I$_1$ **125 a** च] MA$_1$B$_1$I$_1$I$_2$K$_1$; हि C^{1}DHP **125 b** °र्भागेन] C^{1}DHPA$_1$B$_1$I$_1$I$_2$K$_1$; °र्भागेण M **125 c** न हि] C^{1}DHPA$_1$B$_1$I$_1$I$_2$K$_1$; तेन M **126 d** हि] C^{1}DHPI$_1$; च MA$_1$B$_1$I$_2$K$_1$

अवस्तुत्वान्न मुख्यश्चेन्, न स्यादेवं विशेषणम्॥ १२७॥

[9.3 अपोहवतामवाच्यता]

[9.3.1 भेदाः]

भेदाश्चापोहवन्तः स्युस्, तेषां चावाच्यतोदिता।
आनन्त्यव्यभिचाराभ्याम्, अन्यो नास्ति त्वपोहवान्॥ १२८॥

[9.3.2 अपोहवत्त्वम्]

नापोहवत्त्वमन्यद्धि भेदापोहान्तरे ऽस्ति ते।

[9.3.2.1 भावो वाभावो वा]

तच्चापि कल्प्यमानं स्याद् अभावो भाव एव वा॥ १२९॥
वस्तु चेज्जातिरेवासाव्, अवस्तुत्वे ऽपि पूर्ववत्।

[9.3.2.2 संबन्धः]

---

127 c PSV 5.36c: अर्थान्तरापोहमात्रस्याभिन्नत्वाददृव्यत्वाच्च।

128 ab Cf. PS 5.8cd: तद्वांश्च भेद एवेष्टः, स च पूर्वं निराकृतः।; PSV 5.36c: नापि भेदानवस्थानादनभिधानदोषः।

128 bc PS 5.2ab: न जातिशब्दो भेदानाम्, आनन्त्याद् व्यभिचारतः।

129 a PSV 5.9ab: ननु चोक्तं जातिशब्दो जातिमन्मात्रस्य वाचकः, न तु भेदरूपेणेति। ··· तद्वन्मात्रं हि तद्वत्त्वम्।

130 b पूर्ववत्] ŚV *Apohavāda* 42 ff.; cf. ŚVŚar 63,5–6: अभावरूपं चेत् सर्वेषामेवापोहवत्त्वेनाविशेषात् पर्यायत्वादिदूषणं पूर्वोक्तमापादयितव्यम्।

---

127 c मुख्यश्चेन्] $C^1DHPA_1B_1I_1I_2K_1$; मुख्यं चेन् M **128 ab** स्युस्, तेषां] $C^1DHMPA_1B_1I_1I_2$; स्युरेषां K_1 **128 d** त्वपोहवान्] $C^1DHMA_1B_1I_1I_2K_1$; त्वपोहवत् P **130 a** वस्तु चेज्जा॰] $C^1DA_1B_1I_1I_2K_1$; वस्तुत्वे जा॰ HM; वस्तुवज्जा॰ P **130ab** ॰वासाव्, अ॰] $A_1B_1I_1I_2K_1$; ॰व स्याद॰ C^1DHMP **130b** ऽपि] $C^1DHMPB_1I_1I_2K_1$; च A_1

संबन्धो वैष कल्प्येत, तस्य चेष्टा न वाच्यता॥ १३०॥

[9.3.3 एको ऽपोहवानर्थः]

न चैको ऽपोहवानर्थो वर्तते ऽर्थान्तरे क्वचित्।
तस्मादपि न सामान्यं वाच्यं, न च विशेषणम्॥ १३१॥

[9.4 आत्मन्यविद्यमानत्वम्]

---

130 cd PS 5.9ab: तद्वन्मात्रं तु संबन्धः सत्ता वेति विचारितम्।; PSṬ 5.9ab (Pind 2015: II.40–41, nn. 125–126, Ms B 201b5–7): कथं पुनस्तद्वन्मात्रं सत्ता संबन्धो वा स्यादित्याह—तद्वन्मात्रमित्यादि। मात्रशब्देन भेदनिराकरणे सामान्यं सर्वानुगतं रूपं शब्दार्थ इत्युक्तं भवति। तच्च प्रवृत्तिनिमित्तत्वाद् भावप्रत्ययेनाभिधेयं न सत्तां संबन्धं वा मुक्त्वान्यदुपलभ्यते, भावप्रत्ययस्य तत्रैव विधानात्।; PS 5.2cd: (न हि तयोरपि) वाचको योगजात्योर्वा भेदार्थैरपृथक्श्रुतेः॥

131 ab Cf. PS 5.9cd–10a: तद्वानर्थो घटादिश्चेन्, न पटादिषु वर्तते॥ सामान्यमर्थः स कथम्।

131 c The particle *api* probably implies that another reasoning shown by Dignāga in PS 5.10c is also relevant, although Kumārila omits to discuss it. But, cf. Sucarita's comment: न केवलं सामानाधिकरण्यानुपपत्त्यासामान्यवाच्यत्वम्।

131 d Cf. PSV 5.10c: *न विशेष्यविशेषणता।; PSṬ 5.10c (Pind 2015: II.48, n. 156, Ms B 203a1–2): यदि हि सच्छब्देन सामान्यमुच्येत, ततस्तद्विशेषणार्थं घट इत्युच्येतेति स्यात्सामानाधिकरण्यम्। असति तु सामान्याभिधाने किं केन विशेष्यते। ततश्चाभ्युपेतहानम्।; PSV 5.10d: अथ पुनरनन्यस्मिन् द्रव्ये वर्तते सद्गुणम्, सच्छब्दाद् घटाद्याकाङ्क्षायां विशेषणविशेष्यभावः स्यात्, नीलतरादिवत्। PS 5.10d: यद्येकत्रासितादिवत्।; PSṬ 5.10d (Pind 2015: II.49, n. 159, Ms B 203a4–7): यथा नीलगुणं द्रव्यमन्यत्र नीलतरादौ द्रव्ये ऽतद्गुणे च न वर्तत इति न तत्सामान्यम्, तथापि नीलमित्युक्ते नीलशब्दाद् भेदाकाङ्क्षा भवति—यदेतन्नीलमित्युक्तम्, तत्किं नीलतरमथ नीलतममिति। ततो भेदशब्दैर्विशेष्यते नीलतरो नीलतमो वेति। एवं सन्नित्युक्ते सत्ताया अनेकार्थवृत्तित्वाद् घटाद्याकाङ्क्षा भवति—यो ऽयं सन् स किं घटो ऽथ पट इति। ततस्तच्छब्दैर्विशेषयिष्यामः—घटः पटो वेति।

---

130 c संबन्धो वैष] $C^1DHMA_1B_1I_1I_2K_1$; संबन्ध्येवैष P **131 a** चैको ऽपोह॰] $C^1DHA_1B_1I_1$; चैकापोह॰ MI_2K_1; वैको ऽपोह॰ P **131 ab** ॰वानर्थो व॰] $C^1DHMPA_1I_1I_2K_1$; ++++ B_1

नात्मन्यविद्यमानत्वाद् विशेषापोहसूचनम् ।
तस्मान्न तैर्विशेष्यत्वं प्रकृष्टत्वेन नीलवत्॥ १३२॥

[9.5 नार्थाक्षेपः]

अर्थाक्षेपो ऽपि नास्त्येव संदेहाल्लिङ्गलिङ्गिवत् ।
न सामान्यात्मनापोहस्तैर्विना न च सिध्यति॥ १३३॥
एवमेव त्वनाक्षेपः स्यादपोहेन वस्तुनः ।
यतः शशविषाणे ऽपि तदपोहस्य संभवः॥ १३४॥

[9.6 न लिङ्गसंख्यादिसंबन्धः]

लिङ्गसंख्यादिसंबन्धो न चापोहस्य विद्यते ।
व्यक्तेरव्यपदेश्यत्वात् तद्द्वारेणापि नास्त्यसौ॥ १३५॥

132ab Cf. PS 5.11ab: उपेत्यापि नैतज्, जातेरजातितः ।; PSV 5.11ab: नैवं सज्जातिर्घटादिजातिमती यतस् तान् विशेषानुपादाय द्रव्ये वर्तमानो (वर्तमानो] *em.*; वर्तेत *Pind*) ··· ।

132 b विशेषापोहसूचनम्] *Kāśikā* (ŚVKāś$_K$ 290(31),3–4): विशेषरूपस्याघटाद्यपोहस्य सूचनं क्रियत इति ।. Sucarita must have presupposed an analysis of the compound as विशेषस्यापोहस्य सूचनम्. This reading is recorded in the Notes by Kunhan Raja on p. 190 in his edition of the ŚVŚar as the reading of its manuscript.

132 d See PSV 5.10d for the example of blue.

133ab Cf. PS 5.11c: अर्थाक्षेपो (°क्षेपो] *em.*; °क्षेपे *Pind*) ऽप्यनेकान्तः ।; PSV 5.11c: अर्थाक्षेपो हि यस्मिन्नर्थे निश्चयोत्पत्तिः। तद्यथा दिवा न भुङ्क्त इति रात्रिभोजने निश्चयः। इह पुनः सदित्युक्ते न घटादिषु निश्चय इति संशये सति नास्त्यर्थाक्षेपः।

134 d तदपोहस्य] Cf. ŚVŚar 65,5: तद्रूपस्य (=तुच्छरूपस्य); but cf. *Kāśikā* (ŚVKāś$_K$ 289(32),4–5): यथा चासदपोहो ··· तदपोहस्य ··· ।

135 ≈TS$_Ś$ 972: लिङ्गसंख्यादिसंबन्धो न चापोहस्य विद्यते। व्यक्तेश्चाव्यपदेश्यत्वात् तद्द्वारेणापि नास्त्यसौ॥

132b विशेषापोह°] $A_1I_1^{pc}$; विशेषो ऽपोह° $C^1DHMPB_1I_1^{ac}I_2K_1$ **132b** °सूचनम्] PA_1I_1; °सूचकः $C^1DHMB_1I_2K_1$ **134 b** वस्तुनः] $C^1DHMPB_1I_1I_2K_1$; वस्तुतः A_1 **135 b** चा°] $HMA_1B_1I_1I_2K_1$; वा° C^1DP

न ह्यसाधारणत्वेन सापोहेनापि गम्यते।
न चाप्यगम्यमानस्य वस्तुनः स्याद्विशेष्यता॥ १३६॥
लिङ्गसंख्याद्यपोहानां नोपकारः स्वरूपतः।
वस्तुनश्चोपकार्यत्वं कथं शब्दैः प्रतीयते॥ १३७॥

[9.7 न गोत्वादेरनुपलब्धिः]

न विनानुपलब्ध्या च स्यादभावमतिः क्वचित्।
न चाभावप्रमेयत्वं गोत्वादेरिह गम्यते॥ १३८॥

[10 अन्ये शब्दाः]

[10.1 आख्यातः]

आख्यातेषु च नान्यस्य निवृत्तिः संप्रतीयते।
न पर्युदासरूपं हि निषेध्यं तत्र विद्यते॥ १३९॥
न नेति ह्युच्यमाने ऽपि निषेधस्य निषेधनम्।
पचतीत्यनिषिद्धं तु स्वरूपेणावतिष्ठते॥ १४०॥

---

137 ab Jayamiśra (ŚVŚar 66.3) quotes PS 5.5cd: गुणोपकारात् ताद्रूप्ये प्रकर्षः स्याद्विना धिया, which is not directly relevant to what Kumārila intends here. Dignāga's verse only explains Kumārila's particular use of the term उपकारः together with स्वरूपतः.
139 a Cf. TV 1.3.30 (289,21–23): इह नामाख्यातोपसर्गनिपातानां मध्यान्नामानि परिगृह्यन्ते, तेषामपि जातिगुणक्रियाद्रव्ययदृच्छासर्वनामशब्दानां मध्याज् जातिशब्दाश्चिन्त्यन्ते। तेषामप्येकं गोशब्दमुदाहृत्य विचार्यते—किं पुनरयमाकृतेर्वाचको ऽथ व्यक्तेरिति।
139 =$TS_{Ś}$ 973.
140 ≈$TS_{Ś}$ 974: न नेति ह्युच्यमाने ऽपि निषेधस्य निषेधनम्। पचतीत्यनिषिद्धं तु स्वरूपेणैव तिष्ठति॥

---

136 b गम्यते] $C^1DHMPA_1I_1I_2K_1$; गम्यते॥ व्यक्तेरव्यपदेश्यत्वात्तद्वारेणापि नास्त्यसौ॥ न ह्यसाधारणत्वेन सापोहेनापि गम्यते॥ न ह्यसाधारणत्वेन सापोहेनापि गम्यते॥ B_1 **136 d** °द्विशेष्यता] $C^1DHMA_1B_1I_1I_2K_1$; °द्विशेषता P **137 c** °कार्यत्वं] $C^1DHMPB_1I_1I_2K_1$; °कारत्वं A_1 **138 d** °रिह गम्यते] $C^1DPA_1B_1I_1I_2K_1$; °रवगम्यते HM **139 a** च नान्यस्य] $C^1DHPI_1I_2$; न चान्यस्य MA_1K_1 ; च वाच्य° B_1(unmetrical) **140 c** °निषिद्धं तु] $C^1DHMPB_1I_1I_2K_1$; °निषेन्तुधन्तु A_1(unmetrical) **140 d** °रूपेणावतिष्ठते] $C^1DHMA_1B_1I_1I_2K_1$; °रूपेणैव तिष्ठति P

साध्यत्वप्रत्ययश्चात्र तथा भूतादिरूपणम् ।
निष्पन्नत्वादपोहस्य निर्निमित्तं प्रसज्यते ॥ १४१ ॥
विध्यादावर्थराशौ च नान्यापोहनिरूपणम् ।

[10.2 **नञ्**]

नञश्चापि नञा युक्तादपोहः कीदृशो भवेत् ॥ १४२ ॥

[10.3 **चादयः**]

चादीनामपि नञ्योगो नैवास्तीत्यनपोहनम् ।

[10.4 **वाक्यम्**]

वाक्यार्थे ऽन्यनिवृत्तिश्च व्यपदेष्टुं न शक्यते ॥ १४३ ॥

[10.5 **अनन्यापोहशब्दः**]

अनन्यापोहशब्दादौ वाच्यं न च निरूप्यते ।

---

141 a साध्यत्व°] ŚVŚar 67,4: यः पुनरयं साध्यत्वादिप्रत्ययः; but *Kāśikā* (ŚVKāś$_{\mathrm{K}}$ 285(36),4): साध्यार्थेति ।

141 =TS$_{\acute{s}}$ 975: साध्यत्वप्रत्ययश्चात्र तथा भूतादिरूपणम् । निष्पन्नत्वादपोहस्य निर्निमित्तं प्रसज्यते ॥

142 b °निरूपणम्] *Kāśikā* (ŚVKāś$_{\mathrm{K}}$ 285(36),7–8): अत्राप्यपोह्यानिरूपणादपोहो दुर्निरूप इत्याह ।; see also Kamalaśīla's gloss ad TS$_{\acute{s}}$ 976: अन्यापोहस्यान्यव्यवच्छेदस्य न निरूपणमुपलम्भो ऽस्ति ।

142 ≈TS$_{\acute{s}}$ 976: विध्यादावर्थराशौ च नान्यापोहनिरूपणम् । नञश्चापि नञा युक्तावपोहः कीदृशो भवेत् ॥

143 =TS$_{\acute{s}}$ 977.

144 ab Cf. NV 2.2.66 (315,16): इदं च तावत् प्रष्टव्यो भवान् किमयमपोहो वाच्यो ऽथावाच्य इति ।

---

141 a साध्यत्व°] $\mathrm{C^{1}DHPI_{1}K_{1}}$; साध्यार्थ° $\mathrm{MA_{1}B_{1}I_{2}}$ **142 b** °निरूपणम्] H; °निदर्शनम् $\mathrm{C^{1}DPA_{1}B_{1}I_{1}I_{2}K_{1}}$; °स्य दर्शनम् M **142 cd** युक्ताद°] $\mathrm{C^{1}DMPA_{1}B_{1}I_{1}I_{2}K_{1}}$; युक्ताव° H **143a** चादी°] $\mathrm{C^{1}DHMA_{1}B_{1}I_{1}I_{2}K_{1}}$; वादी° P **143a** नञ्योगो] $\mathrm{C^{1}DHMPA_{1}I_{1}I_{2}K_{1}}$; नञ्योयोगो $\mathrm{B_{1}}$(unmetrical) **143c** वाक्यार्थे] $\mathrm{HMB_{1}I_{1}I_{2}K_{1}}$; वाक्यार्थो $\mathrm{C^{1}DP}$; वाक्ये $\mathrm{A_{1}}$(unmetrical) **143d** °देष्टुं] $\mathrm{C^{1}DHMPA_{1}B_{1}I_{2}K_{1}}$; °देष्टं $\mathrm{I_{1}}$ **144 a** अनन्यापोह°] $\mathrm{C^{1}DHMPA_{1}I_{1}I_{2}K_{1}^{pc}}$; अन्यापोहन° $\mathrm{B_{1}K_{1}^{ac}}$ **144 b** वाच्यं] $\mathrm{C^{1}DHMA_{1}B_{1}I_{1}I_{2}K_{1}}$; वाष्पं P

[10.6 प्रमेयज्ञेयशब्दादयः]

प्रमेयज्ञेयशब्दादेरपोह्यं कुत एव तु॥ १४४॥
अपोह्यकल्पनायां वा वरं वस्त्वेव कल्पितम्।
ज्ञानाकारनिषेधाच्च नान्तरार्थाभिधेयता॥ १४५॥
न चाप्यपोह्यता, तस्मान्नापोहस्तेषु सिध्यति।

[10.7 एवमित्यादिशब्दाः]

एवमित्यादिशब्दानां न चापोह्यं निरूप्यते॥ १४६॥

[11 भेदानामपोहः]

[11.1 न विरोधित्वात्]

[11.1.1 अन्योन्याश्रयम्]

विरोधित्वेन भेदानामपोहो यदि कल्प्यते।

---

144 d कुत एव तु] PV 1.122b: विनिवर्त्य कुतश्चन।
144 =$TS_Ś$ 978.
145 a °कल्पनायां वा] The ablative कल्पनायाः seems secondary. Cf. a similar syntax in ŚV *Vākya* 210cd: स एवार्थद्विशक्तित्वे वरं क्लेशः समाश्रितः॥
145 c This refers to ŚV *Śūnyavāda*.
145 ≈$TS_Ś$ 979: अपोह्यकल्पनायां च वरं वस्त्वेव कल्पितम्। ज्ञानाकार-निषेधाच्च नान्तरार्थाभिधेयता (°र्थाभिधेयता] *em.*; °र्थाभिधेयतः $TS_Ś$; °र्थो ऽभिधीयते TS)॥; cf. *Hetumukha* quoted in $TSP_Ś$ 385,7–8 (cf. Hattori 1975: 37, n. 40): ननु हेतुमुखे निर्दिष्टम् "अज्ञेयं कल्पितं कृत्वा तद्व्यवच्छेदेन ज्ञेये ऽनुमानम्" इति।; ŚVŚar 68,6–7: नन्वेवमादिषु हि दिङ्नागेनोक्तम् "अज्ञेयं तु कल्पितं कृत्वा तदपोहेन ज्ञेयशब्दः प्रवर्तते" इति।; ŚVN 605,2–3: अज्ञेयं कल्पितं कृत्वा ज्ञेयशब्दः प्रवर्तते।; PV I 122: क्वचिन्निवेशनायार्थे विनिवर्त्य कुतश्चन। बुद्धेः प्रयुज्यते शब्दस् तदर्थस्यावधारणात्॥
146 a See ŚV *Apohavāda* 41ab: बुद्ध्यन्तराद्व्यवच्छेदो न च बुद्धेः प्रतीयते।
146 =$TS_Ś$ 980.
147 ab PSV 5.28ab: किं पुनरत्र कारणं येन भेदशब्दो भेदान्तरशब्दार्थमपोहते।; PS 5.28ab: भेदो भेदान्तरार्थं तु विरोधित्वादपोहते।

---

144 c °ज्ञेय°] $C^1DHMPB_1I_1I_2K_1$; *om.* A_1(unmetrical) **144 d** कुत एव तु] $C^1DHMPB_1I_1I_2K_1$; कुत ए तु A_1(unmetrical) **145 a** °नायां वा] $B_1I_2K_1$; °नायां तु C^1DP; °नायाश्च HMA_1; °नाया वा I_1 **146 c** एवमि°] $C^1DHMA_1B_1I_1I_2K_1$; एवं नि° P **146 d** न चा°] $HMA_1B_1I_1I_2K_1$; न वा° C^1DP **147 b** कल्प्यते] $C^1DHMPA_1B_1I_1I_2$; कल्पते K_1

विरोधो ऽपोहतस्तत्र विरोधाच्चाप्यपोहनम्॥ १४७॥
न सामान्यापहारित्वं विधिरूपेण तत्र ते।
पलाशादीनपोह्यातो वृक्षं हरति शिंशपा॥ १४८॥

[11.1.2 विरुद्धाविरुद्धताधिकरणम्]

सामान्याद्यनपोहश्च नाविरोधेन कल्पते।

[11.1.2.1 शब्दः]

न हि शब्दस्वरूपाणां स्याद्विरुद्धाविरुद्धता॥ १४९॥

[11.1.2.2 वस्तु]

न च वस्तुस्वरूपेण, तस्य शब्दैरसंगतेः।

[11.1.2.3 अपोहः]

प्राक् शब्दव्यापृतेर्नापि सापोहानां प्रतीयते॥ १५०॥

---

148 ab PSV 5.28ab: भेदार्था हि शब्दाः सामान्यार्थापहारित्वाद् राजपुत्रवत् परस्परविरोधिनः। ततश्च न परस्परार्थं क्षमन्ते। तद्यथा "अयं वृक्षः शिंशपा" इति शिंशपाशब्दो वृक्षशब्देन सह प्रयुज्यमानः खदिरादिभ्यो वृक्षत्वं व्यवच्छिद्य स्वविषये व्यवस्थापयति। तथेतरत्रापि।
149 a कल्पते] *Kāśikā* (ŚVKāś$_K$ 278(43),3): तदिदमविरोधस्यैवानन्तरोक्तेन प्रकारेण दुरधिगमत्वान्न कल्पत इति।
149 ab PS 5.25cd: अन्यत्वे ऽपि न सामान्यभेदपर्यायवाच्यनुत्।; PSV 5.25cd: तुल्ये ऽपि ह्यन्यत्वे शब्दो न सामान्यभेदपर्यायशब्दानामर्थमपोहते। कुत इति चेत्। अविरोधात्। पर्यायशब्दस्य तावत् तुल्यमपोह्यम्, युगपदप्रयोगात्। न च स्वार्थप्रतिक्षेपो युक्तः। सामान्यशब्देनापि स्वभेदेष्वर्थान्तरं व्युदस्तं भेदशब्दो ऽनुमोदते, अर्थित्वात्। यथा हि शिंशपा न पलाशादि, एवं न घटाद्यपि। एतेन सामान्यसामान्यशब्दार्थाप्रतिक्षेपो ऽप्युक्तः। तथा सामान्यशब्दः स्वार्थमभिप्रेते विषये व्यवस्थाप्यमानं विशेषशब्देन विशेषविशेषशब्देन वा कथं नोपेक्षते। एवमविरोधान्न सामान्यादिशब्दार्थापोहो युक्तः।

---

148 a °न्यापहारि°] $C^1DHMPB_1I_1I_2K_1$; °न्यापाहारि° A_1 **148 c** पलाशा°] $HMPA_1B_1I_1I_2K_1$; पलशा° C^1D **149 b** कल्पते] MB_1; कल्प्यते C^1DHPA_1; कथ्यते $I_1I_2K_1$ **149 c** °रूपाणां] $C^1DHMPB_1I_1I_2K_1$; °रूपेण A_1

अन्येनानवबुद्धे ऽर्थे यदा शब्दः प्रवर्तते।
सामान्यात्मकता तस्य केन रूपेण गम्यते॥ १५१॥

[11.1.2.3.1 न शब्दात्]

शब्दानुरूपतश्चेत्स्यादन्यापोहनिरूपणम्।
भिन्नत्वाद् वृक्षतर्वादेर् अपोहः केन वार्यते॥ १५२॥

[11.1.2.3.2 न लिङ्गात्]

शब्दस्पृष्टेर्विनापोहो न च लिङ्गेन गम्यते।
न विरुद्धाविरुद्धत्वं तस्य लिङ्गाच्च सिध्यति॥ १५३॥

[11.2 नादृष्टत्वात्]

अदृष्टत्वाद् व्युदासस्तु पुरस्तादेव वारितः।
सामान्यशब्दो भेदे च नेष्यते वाचकात्मना॥ १५४॥
व्युदासस्तत्र दुर्वारः, कथंचिद्दृष्टता पुनः।
ब्राह्मणे क्षत्रियस्यापीत्यव्युदासः प्रसज्यते॥ १५५॥

---

152 b Cf. PS 5.28ab: भेदान्तरार्थं ··· अपोहते and PSV 5.28ab: भेदान्तरशब्दार्थापोहो युक्तः।

154 a PS 5.31a: अदृष्टत्वाद्व्युदासो वा।; PSV 5.31a: अथ वा यस्माद् भेदशब्दो भेदान्तरार्थे न दृष्टः, तस्माद् अपोहते।

154 b पुरस्तादेव] ŚV *Apohavāda* 75. Cf. also 82.

154 cd PS 5.31b: सामान्यं स्यात् स्वभेदनुत्।; PSV 5.31b: यद्यदर्शनेनापोहते, सामान्यशब्दस्यापि स्वभेदेष्वदर्शनादपोहप्रसङ्गः स्यात्।

155 b PS 5.31c: नान्ययुक्तस्य दृष्टत्वात्।; PSV 5.31c: दृष्टो ह्यर्थप्रकरणादिभिः सामान्यशब्दो विशेषं प्रतिपादयन् (प्रतिपादयन्] *em.*; प्रतिपादयति *Pind*)।

---

151 a अन्येनान°] $C^1DHMB_1I_2K_1$; अन्येनाप्य° P; अन्येना° A_1(unmetrical); अन्येनांन° I_1 **151 b** यदा] $HMPA_1B_1I_1I_2K_1$; सदा C^1D **151 d** गम्यते] $C^1DHPI_1K_1$; गम्यताम् $MA_1B_1I_2$ **152–153ab.** शब्दानुरूप° ··· गम्यते] $C^1DHMA_1I_1I_2K_1$; *om.* P; शब्दानुमान° ··· गम्यते B_1 **153 c** °विरुद्धत्वं] $C^1DHMA_1B_1I_1I_2K_1$; °विरुद्धत्वे P **154 a** °स्तु] $C^1DHMA_1B_1I_1I_2K_1$; °श्च P **154 b** वारितः] $C^1DHMA_1B_1I_1I_2K_1$; वाचितः P **154 c** भेदे च] $MPA_1B_1I_1I_2K_1$; भेदेन C^1DH **155 b** कथंचिद्दृ°] $C^1DHMA_1B_1I_1I_2K_1$; कथं चिदृ° P **155 cd** °पीत्यव्युदासः] $HMPA_1B_1I_1I_2K_1$; °पि पर्युदासः C^1D

[11.3 नाकाङ्क्षणात्]

आकाङ्क्षणादथात्यागस्,

[11.3.1 नामाख्यातयोः]

तुल्यो द्रव्यक्रियादिषु।

वृक्षेणातो ऽनपोहः स्यात्तिष्ठत्यादेरसंशयम्॥ १५६॥

[11.3.2 नाम्नोः]

पुरुषस्य तथा राज्ञा, व्युदासे न विशेष्यता।
अव्युदासत्वपक्षे च स्यान्नीलोत्पलतुल्यता॥ १५७॥

[12 प्रातिलोम्यानुलोम्यम्]

वृक्षत्वपार्थिवद्रव्यसज्ज्ञेयेषु यदुच्यते।
प्रातिलोम्यानुलोम्येन विधौ सर्वार्थबोधनम्॥ १५८॥
तदयुक्तं, न सर्वो हि शब्दः सर्वत्र दृश्यते।

---

156 a PS 5.26ab: तन्मात्राकाङ्क्षणाद् भेदः स्वसामान्येन नोज्झितः।
157 a राज्ञा] *Kāśikā* (ŚVKāś$_K$ 274(47),9): पुरुषस्येति ज्ञान्तेन।
158 d Commentators gloss *sarvārtha* as *sarvātmakārtha* probably presupposing Dharmakīrti's view. ŚVŚar 72,20–21: सर्वात्मकार्थ-ग्रहणं प्राप्नोति; 73.9: सर्वात्मकवस्तुग्रहणप्रसङ्गः; *Kāśikā* (ŚVKāś$_K$ 272(49),4): सर्वात्मकार्थावबोधनमापादितम्।; cf. PV 1.52–53ab: यस्यापि नानोपाधेर्धीर्ग्राहिकार्थस्य भेदिनः। नानोपाध्युपकाराङ्गशक्त्यभिन्नात्मनो ग्रहे। सर्वात्मनोपकार्यस्य को भेदः स्यादनिश्चितः॥
158 PS 5.35: वृक्षत्वपार्थिवद्रव्यसज्ज्ञेयाः प्रातिलोम्यतः। चतुस्त्रिद्व्येकसंदेहे निमित्तं, निश्चये ऽन्यथा॥; PSV 5.34: अन्वयद्वारेण चानुमाने वृक्षशब्दादेकस्मिन्वस्तुनि शिंशपाद्याभासः संशयो न स्यात्। तत्संशयवत् पार्थिवत्वद्रव्यत्वाद्याभासो ऽपि संशयः स्यात्।

156a ॰दथा॰] C[1]DHMA$_1$B$_1$I$_1$I$_2$K$_1$; ॰दप्य॰ P **156b** ॰क्रियादिषु] C[1]DHMA$_1$B$_1$I$_1$I$_2$K$_1$; ॰क्रियोक्तिषु P **157a** राज्ञा] PA$_1$B$_1$I$_1$I$_2$K$_1$; राज्ञो C[1]DHM **157c** अव्युदास॰] C[1]DHMPI$_1$I$_2$K$_1$; अव्युदस्त॰ A$_1$B$_1$ **157a** च] C[1]DHMPA$_1$B$_1$I$_1$I$_2$; पि K$_1$ **158b** ॰सज्ज्ञेयेषु] DHP; ॰संज्ञेयेषु C[1]MA$_1$B$_1$I$_1$I$_2$K$_1$ **159a** सर्वो] C[1]DHMPB$_1$I$_1$I$_2$K$_1$; सतो A$_1$(unmetrical)

देशाविभागतो वृत्तिर्नेत्रस्यापि रसादिषु॥ १५९ ॥
ग्राहकत्वेन वृत्तिस्तु प्रतिजाति व्यवस्थिता।
चक्षुरादिवदेवात्र संकरो न भविष्यति॥ १६० ॥
निवृत्तचेष्टे शब्दे तु व्याप्त्यव्याप्तिकृतं पुनः।
सत्त्वादेर्बोधकत्वं स्यादेकन्यूनातिरेकतः॥ १६१ ॥
तवैव दोषः स्यादेष विशेषे यस्य वर्तते।
सामान्यशब्दो, वाच्यानां भेदो नाप्यस्ति वस्तुतः॥ १६२ ॥

[13 जातिधर्मव्यवस्थितिः]

---

160 b प्रतिजाति व्यवस्थिता] TV 3.4.13 (920,5–6): बालत्वादौ समाने ऽपि तद्गतैश्चेष्टितादिभिः। वयोभेदाः प्रसिद्ध्यन्ति प्रतिजाति व्यवस्थिताः॥; $TS_Ś$ 3160 (*Bṛhaṭṭīkā*, see Kataoka 2011: II.57 and 327, n. 367): प्राज्ञो ऽपि हि नरः सूक्ष्मानर्थान् द्रष्टुं क्षमो ऽपि सन्। स्वजातीरनतिक्रामन्नतिशेते परान् नरान्॥; cf. also ŚV *Codanā* 114: यत्राप्यतिशयो दृष्टः स स्वार्थानतिलङ्घनात्। दूरसूक्ष्मादिदृष्टौ स्यान्न रूपे श्रोत्रवृत्तितः॥
162 bc Cf. PSV 5.18a: द्वावपि विशेषार्थौ सामान्ये विशेषान्तर्भावात् तुल्यरूपौ सामान्यार्थेन।; 5.18b: यत्तर्हीदमुक्तम् "अन्तर्भूतविशेषं सामान्यम्" इति। नैतदुक्तमभिधेयत्वात्, किं तर्हि—अनपोहनात् (5.18b)।
162 cd ŚV *Apohavāda* 42–46, in particular 45cd: अवस्तुत्वादपोहानां तव स्याद् भिन्नता कथम्॥
162 d वस्तुतः] See ŚVŚar 74,3: न चान्ततो भिन्नाः परव्यावृत्तयः।; *Kāśikā* ($ŚVKāś_K$ 268(53),4–9): न वस्तुरूपात्स्वलक्षणाद् वाच्यानां व्यावृत्तीनां त्वन्मते भेदो ऽस्ति। … अपि चायमेवंविधो भेदो न वस्तुतो न तात्त्विक इति यावत्।; but cf. ŚVN 433,2–3: न हि वस्तुनः स्वलक्षणाख्यस्य व्यावृत्तिर्नाम कथंचिदस्ति। … वस्तुनो व्यावृत्तीनां भेदाभावः। Pārthasārathi probably reads: न ह्यस्ति वस्तुनः।

---

159 c देशावि°] $C^1DMPA_1I_1I_2K_1$; देशवि° H(unmetrical); देशादि° B_1 **160 d** संकरो] $C^1DHMPA_1B_1K_1$; सकरो I_1; संस्कारो I_2 **161 a** तु] $A_1B_1I_1I_2K_1$; च C^1DHMP **161 b** व्याप्त्य°] $C^1DHPMA_1B_1I_2^{pc}K_1$; व्याप्त्या° I_1; व्याप्तिस्त्यैस्य° I_2^{ac}(unmetrical) **161c** सत्त्वा°] $C^1DHMA_1B_1I_1I_2K_1$; सत्ता° P **162 a** तवैव] $C^1DHMA_1B_1I_1I_2K_1$; तदैव P **162 b** यस्य] $C^1DHMPB_1I_1I_2K_1$; यत्र A_1 **162 d** नाप्यस्ति वस्तुतः] D; नाप्यस्ति वस्तुनः $C^1HPI_1I_2K_1$; नास्त्येव वस्तुतः MA_1; नाप्यत्रवस्तुनः B_1(unmetrical)

अपि चैकत्वनित्यत्वप्रत्येकसमवायिताः।
निरुपाख्येष्वपोहेषु कुर्वतो ऽसूत्रकः पटः॥ १६३॥
तस्माद्येष्वेव शब्देषु नञ्योगस्तेषु केवलम्।
भवेदन्यनिवृत्त्यंशः, स्वात्मैवान्यत्र गम्यते॥ १६४॥

[14 नैयायिकानुमाननिरासः]

[14.1 अनेकान्तः]

ज्ञेयार्थान्यानपोहत्वं प्रमाङ्गत्वात्त्वगादिवत्।
येनोक्तं, तस्य नञ्युक्तैः शब्दैः स्याद्व्यभिचारिता॥ १६५॥
पक्षीकुर्याद्यदा सर्वांस्तदाप्यावीतहेतुभिः।

---

163 ≈TS$_Ś$ 1000: अपि चैकत्वनित्यत्वप्रत्येकसमवायिताः (°वायिताः] TS$_Ś$; °वायिनः TS)। निरुपाख्येष्वपोहेषु कुर्वतो ऽसूत्रकः (कुर्वतो ऽसूत्रकः] TS; कुर्वतोस्तत्र कः TS$_Ś$) पटः॥
163 PS 5.36d: जातिधर्मव्यवस्थितेः।; PSV 5.36d: जातिधर्माश्चैकत्वनित्यत्वप्रत्येकपरिसमाप्तिलक्षणा अत्रैव व्यवतिष्ठन्ते, अभेदाद् आश्रयाविच्छेदात् कृत्स्नार्थप्रतीतेः।
164 =TS$_Ś$ 1001, PVSVṬ 1.124–127 (248,23–24) (**a.** तस्माद्] यस्माद्); cf. PVSVṬ 1.40–42 (114,10–15): न त्वन्यापोहकृच्छब्दो युष्मत्पक्षे ऽनुवर्णितः। निषेधमात्रं नैवेह प्रतिभासे ऽवगम्यते॥ किं तु गौर्गवयो हस्ती वृक्ष इत्यादिशब्दतः। विधिरूपावसायेन मतिः शाब्दी प्रवर्तते॥ तस्माद्येष्वेव शब्देषु नञ्योगस् तेषु केवलम्। भवेदन्यनिवृत्त्यंशः (°त्त्यंशः] *em.*; °त्त्यङ्गः *ed.*) स्वात्मैवान्यत्र (स्वात्मैवान्यत्र] *em.*; स्वात्मेवान्यत्र *ed.*) गम्यते॥
166 b NV 1.1.5 (43,11–12): व्यतिरेकी विवक्षितव्यापित्वे सति सपक्षाभावे सति विपक्षावृत्तिः, यथा नेदं जीवच्छरीरं निरात्मकम्, अप्राणादिमत्त्वप्रसङ्गादिति।; 1.1.35 (116,10–14): नेदं निरात्मकं जीवच्छरीरमप्राणादिमत्त्वप्रसङ्गादिति। यदुभयपक्षसंप्रतिपन्नमप्राणादिमत्, तत्सर्वं निरात्मकं दृष्टम्। न चेदमप्राणादिमद्

---

163 a °नित्यत्व°] C^{1}DHMPB$_1$I$_1$I$_2$K$_1$; °नित्व° A$_1$(unmetrical) **163 cd–164** निरुपाख्ये° … गम्यते] C^{1}DHMPA$_1$B$_1$I$_1$K$_1$; *om.* I$_2$ **163 c** °ष्वपोहेषु] C^{1}DHMPB$_1$I$_1$K$_1$; °षभावेषु A$_1$ **163 d** पटः] C^{1}DHMA$_1$B$_1$I$_1$K$_1$; परः P **164 cd** °त्त्यंशः स्वात्मैवा°] C^{1}DHPA$_1$B$_1$I$_1$K$_1$; °त्त्यंशो वस्त्वेवा° M **165 b** प्रमाङ्ग°] C^{1}DHMPA$_1$B$_1$I$_2$K$_1$; प्रमाग° I$_1$ **166 ab** सर्वांस्त°] C^{1}DHMA$_1$I$_1$I$_2$K$_1$; सर्वास्त° PB$_1$ **166 b** °दाप्या°] HMPA$_1$I$_1$; °दाथा° C^{1}D; °दास्या° B$_1$I$_2$K$_1$

अनेकान्तो,

[14.2 लोकप्रसिद्धिविरोधः]

विरोधश्च सर्वलोकप्रसिद्धितः॥ १६६॥

[14.3 नापोहत इति]

[14.3.1 व्याख्यानद्वयम्]

नापोहत इतीदं च कारकत्वेन चेद्भवेत्।
केवलापोहबुद्धेर्वा, ततः स्यात् सिद्धसाध्यता॥ १६७॥

[14.3.2 अपोहवत्यर्थे न वर्तते]

अथान्यापोहवत्यर्थे वृत्तिर्नास्तीति साध्यते।
ततः प्राक्पक्षबाधः स्याद् गोत्वे ऽप्यश्वाद्यभावतः॥ १६८॥
साध्यहीनश्च दृष्टान्तश्, चक्षुराद्यपि तस्य हि।
वर्तते ऽपोहवत्यर्थे, तं यद्यपि न बुध्यते॥ १६९॥

भवति। तस्मान्नेदं निरात्मकमिति। सो ऽयमवीतः परपक्षप्रतिषेधाय भवतीति। (As Katsura 1998: 275–276 points out, the correct *udāharaṇa* should be: यन्निरात्मकं तत्सर्वमप्राणादिमत्)

166 cd ŚV *Anumāna* 61cd–62ab: त्रिधा शब्दविरोधः स्यात्प्रतिज्ञादिविभागतः॥ प्रतिज्ञापूर्वसंजल्पसर्वलोकप्रसिद्धितः।; 64cd–65ab: (सर्वलोकप्रसिद्धिविरोधः): चन्द्रशब्दाभिधेयत्वं शशिनो यो निषेधति॥ स सर्वलोकसिद्धेन चन्द्रज्ञानेन बाध्यते।

168 c ŚV *Anumāna* 64ab (पूर्वसंजल्पविरोधः): बौद्धस्य शब्दनित्यत्वं पूर्वोपेतेन बाध्यते।

169c ऽपोहवत्यर्थे] *Kāśikā* (ŚVKāś$_K$ 264(57),1): तदपि चापोहवत्यर्थे वर्तते।

---

166 c अनेकान्तो] $I_1I_2K_1$; अनैकान्तो $C^1DHMPA_1B_1$ **167 a** इतीदं च] $C^1DHMPB_1I_1I_2K_1$; इतीदन्तु A_1 **167 d** ततः स्यात्] $C^1DHMA_1B_1I_1I_2$; स्यात्ततः P; ततः सा K_1 **167 d** °साध्यता] $C^1DHMPB_1I_1I_2K_1$; °साधनं A_1 **168 b** साध्यते] $C^1DHMPB_1I_1I_2K_1$; साध्यतो A_1 **168 c** ततः] $C^1DHMPB_1I_1I_2K_1$; तस्य A_1 **168 d** गोत्वे ऽप्य°] $HMA_1B_1I_1K_1$; गोत्वे ऽथा° C^1DP; त्वे प्य° I_2(unmetrical) **168 d** °द्यभावतः] $C^1DHMPB_1I_1I_2K_1$; °दिवद्यतः भावतः A_1(unmetrical) **169 c** वर्तते ऽपोहवत्यर्थे] A_1K_1; वर्तते ऽपोहवत्येव C^1DHPB_1; वर्तते ऽपोहवत्येंव M; वर्ततपोहवत्वर्थे I_1; वर्त्तते पोहवत्त्यपि I_2 **169 d** बुध्यते] $C^1DHPA_1B_1I_1I_2K_1$; बुध्यति M

[14.3.3 अपोहनिर्भासा बुद्धिर्नास्ति]

अथान्यापोहनिर्भासा न बुद्धिः, सिद्धसाधनम्।
अपोहरूपमप्येतद्वस्त्वित्येवं हि गम्यते॥ १७०॥

[14.3.4 अपोहेन न वर्तते]

अथापोहनिमित्तास्य वृत्तिरर्थे निषिध्यते।
व्यतिरेकाङ्गतेष्टत्वात् पुनः प्राक्पक्षबाधनम्॥ १७१॥
अनुमाने तथा चैतदित्यनैकान्तिको भवेत्।
संदेहबाधजातेन प्रत्यक्षेणापि चेतसा॥ १७२॥
विरुद्धता च हेतोः स्याच्, छब्दः श्रोत्रादिवद्यतः।
आत्मान्तःकरणाकाशस्ववर्वाचित्वं जहाति च॥ १७३॥
विधिरूपप्रवृत्तिर्वा शब्दो ऽपोहेन वर्तते।
अनुमानाङ्गभूतत्वाद्यथैव प्रतिषेधकः॥ १७४॥

---

171 d पुनः] See ŚV *Apohavāda* 168.
172 cd Cf. ŚV *Anumāna* 95ab: संघाते निर्णयस्ताभ्याम् ऊर्ध्वताकाकवत्त्ववत्।; *Vākya* 363: पदार्था गमयन्त्येतं प्रत्येकं संशये सति। सामस्त्ये निर्णयोत्पादात् स्थाणुमूर्द्धस्थकाकवत्॥
173 d °स्ववर्वाचित्वं] *Kāśikā* (ŚVKāś$_{K}$ 263(58),14): आत्मान्तःकरणाकाशस्वर्गादिशब्दानां … ।
173 d च] ŚVŚar 76,24–25: तत्र चैवं वक्तुं शक्यम्—नात्मादीनां शब्दो वाचकः, प्रमाङ्गत्वात्, श्रोत्रादिवत्—इति।; *Kāśikā* (ŚVKāś$_{K}$ 263(58),14–15): आत्मान्तःकरणाकाशस्वर्गादिशब्दानां नात्मादिवादित्वम्, प्रमाङ्गत्वात्, श्रोत्रादिवद् इति च प्रयोग इति।; but cf. ŚVN 434,26–27, which supports *vaḥ*: यो हि लोकमनादृत्य नञ्योगिनामप्यपोहवाचित्वं निषेधति, तं प्रत्यात्मादिशब्दानामप्यात्मादिवाचित्वनिषेधेनायं हेतुरिष्टविघातकारीति।
174 For विरुद्धाव्यभिचारिन्, see ŚV *Anumāna* 91cd–96ab.

---

170 a अथान्या°] $C^1DHMPA_1^{pc}B_1I_1I_2K_1$; अथा° A_1^{ac}(unmetrical) **170 d** °त्येवं] $MB_1I_1I_2K_1$; °त्येव C^1DHPA_1 **171 d** °बाधनम्] $DHMPA_1B_1I_1K_1$; °साधनम् C^1 ; °बोधनं I_2 **173 b** °वद्यतः] $C^1DHMA_1B_1I_1I_2K_1$; °वायतः P **173 cd** °णाकाशस्ववर्वाचित्वं] HMA_1 ; °णाकाशैः स्ववाचित्वं C^1DK_1 ; °णाकाशस्ववाचित्वं PB_1 ; °णाकाशः स्ववर्वाचित्वं I_1I_2 **173 d** च] $HMA_1I_1K_1$; वः C^1DPB_1 ; हि I_2 **174 d** प्रतिषेधकः] $C^1DHMPB_1I_1I_2K_1$; प्रतिषेकः A_1(unmetrical)

जातिं वा न ब्रवीत्येष व्यक्तिं वा तद्विशेषिताम्।
प्रमायामङ्गभूतत्वात् त्वक्श्रोत्रादि यथैव च॥ १७५॥

[14.4 उपसंहारः]

एवं साधनमार्गेण वाच्यावाच्यनिरूपणम्।
नावतिष्ठत इत्यत्र कथ्यते लोकवर्त्मना॥ १७६॥

176 Cf. TV 1.3.30 (290,11–12): यदि शब्दार्थानामनन्यत्वं लोकवेदयोर्भवेत्, तत एतस्या व्यक्त्याकृत्यभिधानचिन्ताया वृद्धव्यवहारस्थानेकप्रयोगानुसरणद्वारेणाभिधेयानभिधेयत्वनिर्णयः शक्यते कर्तुम्।

175b ॰शेषिताम्] $C^1DHMA_1B_1I_1I_2K_1$; ॰शेषितम् P **175d** च] $C^1DHMPA_1I_1I_2K_1$; हि B_1 **176b** वाच्यावाच्य॰] $C^1DHMA_1B_1I_1I_2K_1$; वाच्यवाच्य॰ P **176b** ॰निरूपणम्] $HMA_1B_1I_1I_2K_1$; ॰निरूपणा C^1DP **176c** इत्यत्र] $C^1DHPA_1I_1I_2$; इत्येवं M; इत्येतत् B_1K_1

Part Two

Annotated Translation of *Ślokavārttika*, *Apohavāda* Chapter

Kei Kataoka and John Taber

Translation

1 What is called an "exclusion" can only be a real universal.

1 It is obvious that those who imagine the general entity which is the negation of non-cow as the denotation (*vācya*) [of words] speak of cowness, which is indeed a real thing, by means of the expression "exclusion of non-cow."[1]

2 For it was taught previously [in the *Abhāvapariccheda*] that non-existence is another entity. In that case, one must explain what the non-existence is which has the nature of the negation of horse, etc.

Kumārila begins with the assertion that a non-existence (*abhāva*) is "another entity" (*bhāvāntara*) that is to say, some real thing (e.g., a

---

[1] Dignāga, in fact, typically says that a word "denotes its referent through the exclusion of other [referents]," *svārtham anyāpohena bhāṣate* (PS 5.1c'd; Pind 2015: I.1,4), or else that it indicates "entities precisely insofar as they are qualified by the negation of other referents," *arthāntaranivṛttiviśiṣṭān eva bhāvān āha* (PSV 5.36d; Pind 2015: I.45,2–3). Thus, Kumārila's suggestion that Dignāga considers the *apoha* to be the meaning (*vācya*) is already contentious. Later Kumārila takes both possibilities into consideration: 1. *apohamātra*, a mere *apoha*, is the *vācya* (v.115ab: *apohamātravācyatvaṃ yadi tv abhyupagamyate* /); 2. *apohavad vastu*, a real thing possessing an *apoha*, is the *vācya* (v.120ab: *athānyāpohavad vastu vācyam ity abhidhīyate* /). Dignāga considers both positions but seems to prefer the *apohavat* view, as suggested by the statement of PSV 5.36d above (words indicate things *qualified* by *apohas*). However, at PSV 5.14, the *pūrvapakṣin* assumes that *anyāpohamātra* is the meaning of a word: *yady anyāpohamātraṃ śabdārthaḥ* [...] (Pind 2015: I.16,3). And at PSV 5.36c Dignāga asserts that an *apoha simpliciter* is the meaning: "Thus, because of the absence of the previous[ly mentioned] problems it is correct that the meaning of a word is indeed the exclusion of other referents." *evaṃ pūrvadoṣābhāvād arthāntarāpoha eva śabdārthaḥ sādhuḥ* (Pind 2015: I.44,7–8). Therefore, it is also not unreasonable to attribute to the Apohavādin the view that just an *apoha* (and not something qualified by an *apoha*, an *apohaviśiṣṭa*) is the meaning of a word.

cloth) that is apprehended as a non-existence (e.g., as not a pot/the absence of a pot). The defender of the view that words refer to exclusions, which are negations or non-existences – roughly, according to the Apohavāda the meaning of the word "cow" is what is not non-cow – is therefore obliged to explain what other entity is being apprehended as the non-existence of something. Kumārila will argue in this opening section, in a preliminary way, that in fact it could be nothing other than the universal cowness.

In his ŚV *Abhāvapariccheda* Kumārila argued that the non-existence of something is in fact a "real thing" (*vastu*), for several reasons: (1) We recognize different types of non-existence – prior non-existence, non-existence from destruction, mutual non-existence, and absolute non-existence – and differences must belong to something real (v. 8ab). (2) The absence of the effect, etc., is nothing other than [a property of] the cause, etc. (v. 8cd). (3) A non-existence is cognized as being of the same sort yet distinct from other non-existences, like other real things, e.g., cows (v. 9abc). And (4) a non-existence is something that can be known (*prameya*) (v. 9d).[2] It is the second reason that implies that non-existence is "another entity." Kumārila explains the situation in detail, ŚV *Abhāva* 12–17. Things have a dual nature; they are both existent and non-existent, according to their own-nature (*svarūpa*) and another nature (*pararūpa*), respectively (v. 12). One might say, things both are what they are and are not what they are not. Perception and the other four *pramāṇa*s cognize something according to its own nature, as existing; the *pramāṇa* of absence (*abhāvapramāṇa*, which Kumārila explains is the absence of the occurrence of other *pramāṇa*s, v. 11ab) cognizes something according to another nature, i.e, what it is not, as non-existent. Thus, the non-existence of, say, a cloth as a pot (the cognition of which one would express as, "This is not a pot") is just as much an "aspect" (*aṃśa*) or property of the cloth as any of its other properties, insofar as it continues to exist and function as an "assisting factor" even when the cloth is being cognized as a cloth (v. 14). Now, Kumārila also holds that a property-bearer and its properties are not

[2] Cf. Kellner 1997: 70–72, who understands the fourth reason *prameyatva* as the primary reason from which (1) and (3) are derivable.

completely different from each other, an idea which he introduces at ŚV *Pratyakṣasūtra* 141 ff., but also returns to in ŚV *Abhāva* 19–20 when refuting the Nyāya view that non-existence is apprehended by perception (so, according to the Naiyāyika, a distinct *pramāṇa* for non-existence is not required). Therefore, non-existence is "another entity," namely, that real thing of which it is an aspect – and which can be referred to as its substratum or support, *āśraya* – and from which it is not really different.

Kumārila already explicitly stated this in the conclusion of his discussion of perceptual error and the cognition of non-existent things at ŚV *Nirālambanavāda* 117cd–118: "Therefore, that [erroneous] cognition which cognizes something to be other than what it is – that is [a cognition] 'without an object.' And that has an absence as its object. Absence is another entity, nothing else, because it is not ascertained [independently]."[3]

Kumārila now proceeds to consider – and reject – various proposals for what the "other entity," the *āśraya* of the *apoha*, might be. Once again, the question in effect is: What is the positive entity that is being apprehended as the exclusion, that is, the absence, of other things?

1.1 Nothing could be the basis (*āśraya*) of an exclusion other than a universal.

3 It [i.e., that non-existence] is not considered the particular (*asādhāraṇa*) object,[4] because [the latter] is not conceptualized. Nor is it a [subtype such as] spotted cow, etc., because it would turn out not to be a universal.

4 For the natures of [subtypes such as] spotted cow, etc.,

---

[3] *tasmād yad anyathāsantam anyathā pratipadyate // tan nirālambanaṃ jñānam abhāvālambanaṃ ca tat / bhāvāntaram abhāvo 'nyo na kaścid anirūpaṇāt //*. For a discussion of this passage cf. Freschi 2010.

[4] That is, the concrete particular, *svalakṣaṇa*. Cf. ŚVŚar 27,16: *tatra yady avyapadeśyaṃ svalakṣaṇam asyāśrayatvena kalpyate* [...] /.

are not common to each other;[5] nor can one [of them] be common to [all] the others.[6] For you, then, [the word "cow"] would have unlimited meanings.

According to the Buddhist particulars are inexpressible;[7] they are not objects of conceptual awareness. A particular cow could not be what is conceived as the non-existence of non-cows and so could not be the substratum (*āśraya*) of the exclusion of non-cows. A subtype of cow, on the other hand, e.g., spotted cow, is not a particular thing but a kind of universal, and so a more likely candidate for being the substratum. If, however, the subtype spotted cow were grasped as the exclusion of non-cow, i.e., as the meaning of "cow," then "cow" would not denote a universal that includes all types of cows. For in order for a specific subtype of cow to be the positive entity that is being cognized as the universal cow, it would have to have a nature common to other types of cow, which however is not the case; the nature of one subtype of cow is not that of another, nor is the nature of one subtype that of all the other subtypes. If the word "cow," then, referred whenever it is used to

[5] The lower universal *śābaleyatva* is common to a certain group of cows. Similarly the lower universal *bāhuleyatva* is common to another group of cows. Let us consider *śābaleyatva* and *bāhuleyatva* (as well as other lower universals) as the *āśraya* of *agovyāvṛtti*. This would not work, because *śābaleyatva*, for example, is not common to the other group of cows (cow$_3$ and cow$_4$). Similarly *bāhuleyatva* is not common to the other group of cows (cow$_1$ and cow$_2$).

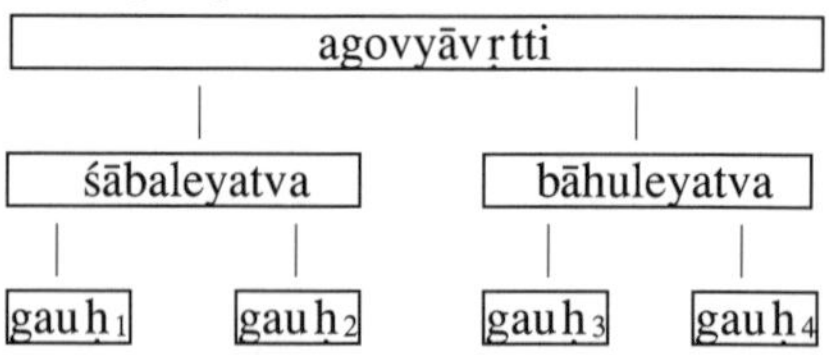

[6] Suppose one assumes that one of these, e.g., *śābaleyatva*, is common to all cows. But this is not the case, either, because *śābaleyatva* is not common to the other groups, cow$_3$ and cow$_4$.

[7] PS 1.5cd: *svasaṃvedyaṃ hy anirdeśyaṃ rūpam indriyagocaraḥ* //. "For the object of perception is a form knowable to itself and inexpressible." Cf. PSV 5.45: *anirdeśyo hi pratyakṣārthaḥ* (Pind 2015: I.55,3). "For the object of perception is inexpressible."

a certain subtype of cow, it would have as many meanings as there are subtypes.

5 And it is not logical that for a specific type [of cow, such as spotted cow] those [things which the Apohavādin believes are excluded in the case of "cow," namely, non-cows] are what are directly excluded. It is not the case that the cognition of spotted cow is the cause of the exclusion of non-cow.

6 The cognition of that [subtype, spotted cow] occurs by means of the negation of black cow, etc. [and not non-cow]. Objection: It would exclude non-cow [as well]. [Reply:] [Then] it would certainly not exclude those [black cows, etc.] as it would not exclude its own nature.

A specific type of cow, say spotted cow, does not in fact exclude all non-cows. It excludes black cows as well as non-cows, hence it would not be suitable as the *āśraya* of the *apoha* of non-cows. If one thought that "spotted cow" in fact could mean cow by virtue of the fact that it does exclude all non-cows after all, then it would lose its specific sense as referring to a particular type of cow since it would now actually include in its meaning black cows.

7 If it is postulated that through that aspect [i.e., as a cow] there is non-exclusion [of the subtype black cow, etc.], while there is exclusion by means of its specific nature [namely, as spotted cow, then] there would be a contradiction insofar as [the cognition of spotted cow, arising from hearing the word "cow," would] include and oppose [the subtype black cow] at the same time.

One might attempt to defend the idea that a subtype such as spotted cow could be the *āśraya* of the exclusion of non-cow insofar as it *both* excludes all non-cows *and* excludes other subtypes such as black cow, etc. In that case, however, the other subtypes would, paradoxically, be both included in and excluded from the meaning of the word "cow" at the same time.[8]

Kumārila concludes,

8ab Therefore, the exclusion of non-cow is not possible by specific natures [whether of individuals or subtypes].[9]

Now Kumārila turns to the proposal that the *āśraya* of the *apoha* is the collection of individuals.

8cd Nor is the collection of those [various individual cows, spotted cows, etc.] the cause of the exclusion of non-cow.

9 In this way it would follow that there would be a cogni-

---

[8] ŚVKāś$_{K}$ 456[49],7–8: *evaṃ sati yugapad eva gośabdād bāhuleyādīnām ākṣepo vāraṇaṃ ca bhavet* /. "That being the case, from the word 'cow' [with the subtype spotted cow as its basis] there would simultaneously be the implication and rejection of black cows, etc."

[9] Jayamiśra takes v. 8ab to be summarizing the discussion of the *āśraya* of the *apoha*, which goes back to v. 2cd. In v. 3ab the *svalakṣaṇa* is rejected as the *āśraya*. From vv. 3cd–7 subtypes are rejected. Thus, according to Jayamiśra, v. 8ab would be referring to the impossibility of an exclusion being based on the "specific natures" of either individuals or subtypes. Both Sucaritamiśra and Pārthasārathimiśra, on the other hand, seem to take *rūpaiḥ* in v. 8a to be referring to the nature of subtypes. However, they gloss *prātyātmikai rūpaiḥ* using the expressions *śābaleyādīnāṃ prātyātmikai rūpaiḥ* (ŚVKāś$_{K}$ 456[49],12–455[50],1) and *prātyātmikaiḥ śābaleyādirūpaiḥ* (ŚVN 401,22), which are somewhat ambiguous (since subtypes, *avāntarasāmānya/sāmānyaviśeṣa*, are not explicitly mentioned). Moreover, Kumārila's discussion goes on, vv. 8cd–9, to reject the *samudāya* as the *āśraya*. It is clear that Jayamiśra takes the *samudāya* to be the collection of *individuals* (*śābaleyādisvalakṣaṇasamudāya*, ŚVŚar 29,4). Sucarita and Pārthasārathi, however, continue to refer just to *śābaleyādi*: *sarvaśābaleyādyupalabdhau* (ŚVKāś$_{K}$ 456[49],6–7); *śābaleyādisamudāyaḥ* (ŚVN 401,23). But it seems clear from the rest of what they say (and also from the implausibility of the idea of a "collection of subtypes"), that in this case they too have in mind individuals, like Jayamiśra. Therefore, it seems possible that when they employed *śābaleyādi* previously they could have, like Jayamiśra, intended it to include individuals as well as subtypes (*avāntarasāmānya*).

tion of that [exclusion] part-by-part (*vyāsajya*)[10] when one perceives all [the cows]. [That is to say, each cow would only be cognized as a portion of cowness.]. Nor would it occur [completely] with respect to each one, nor with respect to [all of] them collected together, because one cannot [cognize them all].

If the exclusion of non-cow were based on the collection of individual cows as its *āśraya*, we could not have the idea "cow" or employ the word "cow" with respect to an isolated individual cow, since it would comprise only one part of the collection. The idea "cow" would arise only after all individuals of the collection were cognized, which is obviously not the case. In fact, each individual cow we cognize as "cow" and refer to by the word "cow." Moreover, the collection of cows being rather large, we could never cognize it entirely so that it could serve as the *āśraya* of the exclusion.

Concluding his discussion of the *āśraya* of the *apoha*, Kumārila suggests that it could only be a real universal, such as cowness in the case of the word "cow." Therefore, the Apohavāda – the theory that the word "cow" refers to the exclusion of non-cow – would just be another way of stating that the meaning of a word is the universal.

10 Therefore, that nature which is in all of them, complete in each one – the cognition "cow" must be based on that. And that is nothing other than cowness.

Now, however, Kumārila considers objections to his main assumption that non-existence is simply "another [positive] entity" (*bhāvāntara*).

---

[10] Cf. ŚV *Vanavāda* 30 and Pārthasārathimiśra's commentary thereon. The question according to him is whether a universal exists in each particular (*pratyekam*) or distributively/part-by-part (*vyāsajya*) over many particulars. He defines *vyāsajyavṛtti* as follows, ŚVN 440,13: *vyāsajyavṛttir nāma parasparasāpekṣeṣu vṛttiḥ* /. "What is called part-by-part occurrence is occurrence in mutually dependent things."

1.2 Even words such as "non-existence," "impermanence," and "non-Brahmin" must refer to real universals.

11ab [Objection:] It is not believed that there is a universal which is a real thing in the case of prior non-existence, etc.

The different kinds of absences or non-existences are mentioned by Kumārila at ŚV *Abhāva* 2cd–4, namely: prior non-existence (the non-existence of yoghurt in milk), non-existence from destruction (the non-existence of milk in yoghurt), mutual non-existence (a horse not being a cow and *vice versa*), and complete or absolute non-existence (the non-existence of horns on a rabbit's head). They are all called non-existences, yet it is difficult to see how there is one thing they have in common which is being referred to as "non-existence." Thus, it seems most plausible that it is just non-existence itself which is not an aspect of another entity that is being apprehended in each case.[11]

11cd [Reply:] Existence (*sattā*), indeed, qualified by non-arising, and so forth, is the universal in their case.

12 That [existence], insofar as it is connected to arising, etc., is declared to be existence, but, associated with exclusion of another, that very same thing is cognized as non-existence.

In fact, Kumārila replies, all non-existences have something in common. In the case of prior non-existence the *existence* of the milk is qualified by non-arising of yoghurt. In the case of the non-existence from destruction the *existence* of that which remains (yoghurt) would be qualified by the destruction of that which preceded it (milk); and so

[11] Pārthasārathimiśra suggests that the question here concerns the lack of any real universal common to all four types of non-existence. The opponent thinks that just *abhāvatva*, which is not another real entity, is common to them (ŚVN 402,6–7). Sucaritamiśra, meanwhile, takes the question to concern what is common to two prior non-existences (*prāgabhāva*). Milk is the prior non-existence of yoghurt, while fresh butter is the prior non-existence of ghee. There is no single real entity that is common to both that could be the referent (*ālambana*) of the idea of prior non-existence (ŚVKāś$_{K}$ 454 [51],3–12).

on. Thus, existence would appear to be the positive entity that is apprehended as a particular type of non-existence in each case. Nevertheless, existence and non-existence can still be distinguished: an entity connected with arising, persisting, and transformation is known as existence; an entity associated with exclusion of another is known as non-existence.[12]

One might question, however, whether a negative concept like "impermanence" does not simply refer to that which is not permanent or the exclusion of what is permanent, without there being some other positive thing common to all impermanent things that is apprehended in that way. If it does, then other expressions like "cow" could refer just to exclusions as well.

13ab Impermanence is considered the universal of the activity called ceasing to exist.

In all impermanent things there is the activity of *vināśa*, ceasing to exist. The universal of that activity is the other entity that is the referent of the idea of impermanence. Impermanence is therefore not just the absence of permanence.

13cd [Objection:] How is it possible that there is non-Brahminhood in distinct [*varṇa*s], Kṣatriyas, and so forth?

14 Humanity resides in all four [*varṇa*s], and there is no cognition [of non-Brahminhood] in regard to specific [*varṇa*s]. Moreover, the cognition of the universal [humanity] arises for each of them.

15 Therefore, in regard to these [non-Brahmin *varṇa*s] the non-existence of Brahmins should be the universal; that is not a real thing. Therefore, in the case of cowness, etc., as well, there should be a cognition of a universal in the same way.

The opponent is not ready to give up, however. Surely, the idea, "This

---

[12] ŚVKāśK 453[52],4–5: *utpattisthitipariṇāmeṣv anusyūto bhāvaḥ sattety jñāyate / anyāpohānuviddhas tv abhāvātmaneti viveka iti /.*

person is not a Brahmin," that is, the idea of non-Brahminhood (*abrāhmaṇatva*), which pertains to the three non-Brahmin *varṇa*s, Kṣatriyas, Vaiśyas, and Śūdras, refers just to an absence or non-existence and not to some other entity, as the Mīmāṃsaka holds.[13] Since humanity resides in all four *varṇa*s (i.e., Brahmins as well as the three non-Brahmin *varṇa*s), the universal humanity cannot be the referent of the idea of non-Brahminhood. Since there is the cognition of non-Brahminhood in regard to all of the non-Brahmin *varṇa*s (Kṣatriya, Vaiśya, Śūdra), a specific *varṇa* also obviously cannot be the referent. Finally, since the cognition of non-Brahminhood arises in regard to

---

[13] The term *abrāhmaṇa* is discussed extensively in grammatical literature beginning with MBh ad P 2.2.6. The problem as posed by Patañjali is, in a *tatpuruṣa* compound with *nañ* such as *abrāhmaṇa*, what is the primary factor: the meaning of the second word, the meaning of an external word in apposition (such as the word *kṣatriya* used together with *abrāhmaṇa*), or the meaning of "non-" itself? Patañjali's discussion is extended and elaborated by Bhartṛhari at VP 3.14(*Vṛttisamuddeśa*).248–315. He argues that in order for all three views to be possible in regard to a compound such as *abrāhmaṇa*, the negative particle *nañ* must be taken as indicating "the general substratum of the performance of the action [of existing]" as qualified by its own meaning of non-existence. In this way, it can be combined with the following word *brāhmaṇa*, which conveys the particular substratum of existing that is being negated. Thus, VP 3.14.255: *kriyāyāḥ sādhanādhārasāmānye nañ vyavasthitaḥ / tato viśiṣṭair ādhārair yujyate brāhmaṇādibhiḥ /*. "'non-' is used in the meaning of the general substratum of the performance of the action [of existing]. Therefore, it is combined with specific substrata [of the action of existing, namely,] Brahmin and so forth." *nañ* and *brāhmaṇa* thus stand in a qualifier-qualificand relation to each other, and depending on the speaker's intention, one or the other, or even an outside word, can be taken as primary, hence the three views considered by Patañjali. See Iyer 1974: 241–271.

Kumārila's preferred analysis of the word *abrāhmaṇa*, that it refers to "humanity [...] as excluded from Brahmins by the negative prefix ['non-']," was probably influenced by Bhartṛhari. In this case, however, it is not the substratum of the action of existing in general that is indicated by "non-," but, one could say, the substratum in general of a more specific activity, namely, being human.

Kumārila holds in general that distinctions of *varṇa* are anchored in real universals, which are available to perception. See especially TV ad MS 1.2.2 (Harikai 2007: 9,3–11,7) and Halbfass 1991: 367–377. The problem in this case, however, is that there is apparently no universal common to all three non-Brahmin *varṇa*s.

each of the non-Brahmin *varṇa*s individually, the collection of them cannot be the thing that is conceived as non-Brahmin, either. Therefore, having apparently eliminated all other possibilities, only the non-existence of Brahmins devoid of any real entity as its support must be the universal that is referred to as "non-Brahmin."[14] Similarly for other words such as "cow," and so forth: they, too, should refer just to the negation of non-cow, etc., and not some other positive entity. One may call these meanings universals, but one should understand that they are negations and not real things.

16abc [Reply:] Some, however, postulate that in this case the three classes [Kṣatriya and so forth] are referred to by the same word [used in different senses], as in the case of *akṣa*, and so forth.

One might say in response to the opponent that in the case of each non-Brahmin *varṇa* the specific *varṇa* is the referent of "non-Brahmin," so that the word does not refer to a mere negation. That is to say, a different entity is referred to as "non-Brahmin" in each case; thus it in fact means different things – it is a polysemic word. We know from other words, such as *akṣa*, which refers variously to a die for gambling, an axle, a sense faculty, etc. that this is possible.[15]

This is, however, only a preliminary answer to the opponent, which Kumārila now rejects.

16cd-17ab But it could not be like this in the case of "non-pot," and so forth. For in this case, where there are an unlimited number of kinds [of things that are not pots], sameness

---

[14] ŚVKāśK 451(54),4-5: *ato 'vaśyam abrāhmaṇādiṣu brāhmaṇābhava eva vastūpaṣṭambhaśūnya eva sāmānyam ity āpatitam* /.

[15] However, MBh I.247,14–15 (on P 1.2.64, *Vārttika* 59: *vyartheṣu ca sāmānyāt siddham*) maintains that polysemic (*vibhinnārtha*) words such as *akṣa* have a certain action – e.g., in the case of *akṣa*, the action of pervading, *aśnoti* – as the common condition for usage (*pravṛttinimitta*) (according to Śivaramendrasarasvatī). See Scharf 1996: 145–148, together with n. 91.

[of the word used for all of these different kinds] is not discerned.

The proposed solution will not work for other negative expressions such as "non-pot." "Non-pot" can be applied not just to three kinds of things but to countless kinds: books, cups, hats, and so forth. It would be impossible to learn an infinite number of connections of the word "non-pot" with the infinite kinds of things which are not pots.

17cd Therefore, there are certain actions and qualities not present in the others [i.e., Brahmins and pots],[16] which are the causes [of the employment of negative expressions like "non-Brahmin" and "non-pot"].

One might hold that all non-Brahmins share certain actions and qualities. This is another possible solution to the problem of what positive, real thing is the referent of a negative expression like "non-

---

[16] The compound *ananyavartinaḥ* can be construed in two ways: (1) residing (*vartinaḥ*) in those things that are not other (*ananya*), i.e. present only in the three *varṇa*s, and (2) not (*an-*) present (*vartinaḥ*) in the others (*anya*), e.g. not present in Brahmins (*an-anya-vartinaḥ* = *anya-avartinaḥ*). Both interpretations amount to approximately the same thing. It is difficult to tell which of the two interpretations any of the commentators holds, because they all mention both aspects, the positive (*vartinaḥ* = *anugatāḥ*) as well as the negative (*avartinaḥ* = *vyāvṛttāḥ*). Jayamiśra says that the quality or action is present in all three *varṇa*s such as Kṣatriyas and excluded from Brahmins, ŚVŚar 31,19–21: *tad idānīm ekarūpaṃ sāmānyaṃ kṣatriyādiṣu triṣv apy* ***anugataṃ*** *brāhmaṇebhyo* ***vyāvṛttam*** *kiṃcid apratigrāhakatvam anyad vā karmānveṣaṇīyaṃ sāmānyapratyayasya hetubhūtam* /. "Therefore, some universal having a single nature, common even to all three [*varṇa*s], Kṣatriya and so forth, and excluded from Brahmins, such as not being one who accepts [gifts] or some other action, is now to be sought as the cause of the cognition of a universal [pertaining to those three]." Sucaritamiśra, who glosses *ananyavartinaḥ* as *abrāhmaṇavartinaḥ*, ŚVKāśK 450(55),12, says essentially the same thing, ŚVKāśK 450(55),9–10: *brāhmaṇebhyo* ***vyāvṛttāḥ*** *kṣatriyāditraya****ānugatāḥ*** *kecit kriyāguṇā abrāhmaṇaśabdasya pravṛttau hetavaḥ* /. "Certain actions or qualities excluded from Brahmins and common to Kṣatriyas, etc., are the causes of the use of the word 'non-Brahmin.'" Similarly, ŚVN 403,21–22: *brāhmaṇ****āvartinaḥ*** *kṣatriyādiṣv* ***anugatāḥ*** [...] /.

Brahmin" or "non-pot."[17] Kumārila now seems to set this proposal aside as well in favor of the solution that such words refer, not to certain actions and qualities that all the things to which those words apply share, but rather to a common universal.

18 But it is this humanity which, though it pertains to all four *varṇa*s, is comprehended [from the word "non-Brahmin"], as excluded from Brahmins by the negative prefix ["non-"/*a*-], just as [there is exclusion] by [mentioning a particular] purpose, etc.

19 Although there is not an intermediate universal restricted to those three [*varṇa*s], nevertheless due to the capacity of the prefix "non-" humanity is cognized as contained in [just] those three.

Humanity, then, insofar as it is excluded from the class of Brahmins, is the referent of the word "non-Brahmin." The prefix "non-" functions to exclude humanity from the class of Brahmins just as the mentioning of a particular purpose would in other cases. If one were to say, for example, "Bring a Brahmin to be fed," the indication of the purpose of feeding would limit the expression "Brahmin" to just *worthy* Brahmins, even though in general "Brahmin" refers to all kinds of Brahmins. The designation of humanity as restricted to the three non-Brahmin *varṇa*s, even though they do not share a common intermediate universal that distinguishes them from other humans, is accomplished just by the prefix "non-" attached to the word "Brahmin."

---

[17] It is not clear whether this is meant as a solution to the problem of the denotation of the expression "non-pot" or the expression "non-Brahmin." Sucaritamiśra and Pārthasārathimiśra, however, take 17cd to be proposing another solution for the denotation of "non-Brahmin," which they believe would not really work for "non-pot." Perhaps one can postulate certain qualities or actions that all non-Brahmins share, for instance, "not being a recipient of gifts from others" (*pratigrahanivṛtti*) or "holding a sword." (This suggestion seems to follow Kātyāyana's and Patañjali's proposal for how to explain polysemic words like *akṣa* mentioned above, n. 15.) But it is difficult to conceive how all the things that are not pots have any common properties or actions. Thus, another solution must be sought.

One might, however, hold that if humanity is comprehended from the word "non-Brahmin," then it should refer to all four *varṇas*, since humanity resides in all four. In other words, why is there a difference in the conception of humanity as contained in three *varṇas*, from the word "non-Brahmin," and as contained in all four, from the word "man"? Kumārila explains:

20 Due to the different capacities of the words ["non-Brahmin" and "man"] there is a difference of cognition in regard to the *varṇa*s. [This difference of capacity is] in regard to humanity either as contained in just three of them or in all four, due to a *paryudāsa* or [the word] by itself (*paryudāsasvarūpataḥ*).

Words by nature have different denotative capacities (*śakti*). Although both words "non-Brahmin" and "man" refer to humanity, due to their specific capacities the former refers to it as restricted to three *varṇas*, the latter to it as included in all four. These differences in capacity are due, specifically, to the type of negation, known as term negation (*paryudāsa*),[18] effected by the prefix "non-" in the case of "non-

---

[18] *paryudāsa* or term negation is one of the two types of negation recognized by Mīmāṃsakas, the other being *pratiṣedha*, sentential negation or prohibition. These types of negation are also sometimes called "implicative negation" and "simple negation," respectively. The scope of the former is a particular term or expression, insofar as the negative particle is construed together with a word; the scope of the latter is the entire statement, insofar as the negative particle is construed together with the verbal ending (see MNP 262,4–5). Thus, one is often able to distinguish two meanings of a sentence that involves a negation according to whether it involves a *paryudāsa* or a *pratiṣedha*. For example, the sentence *na-anuyājeṣu ye yajāmahaṃ karoti* (ĀpŚS 24.13.6) is ambiguous. If the word *na*, "not," is construed as expressing a *paryudāsa*, then the scope of the negation is just the expression *anuyājeṣu*, and the sentence means, "Not at the *anuyāja*s does one say *ye yajāmahe*." This sentence actually has a positive meaning (it would in effect be an injunction), namely, one *should* utter *ye yajāmahe* at the preliminary offerings *other* than the *anuyāja*s, namely at the *prayāja*s, etc. If *na*, on the other hand, is interpreted as expressing a *pratiṣedha*, then the entire sentence is its scope. The sentence would then mean: "One does not say *ye yajāmahe* at the *anuyāja*s." It would have strictly

Brahmin," and to the word itself (without any qualifying prefix) in the case of "man."

21 Just as there is a capacity of the eye of a vulture for seeing visible form far away and of the eye of a crow for seeing it close by, so [are there different capacities] of the words "man" and "non-Brahmin" in regard to humanity.

Just as the vulture's sense of vision is suited to seeing things far away, while a crow's sense of vision is suited to seeing things up close, so the word "man" has the capacity to refer more broadly to all kinds of humanity, whereas the word "non-Brahmin" has the capacity to refer to humanity in the form of the three *varṇa*s Kṣatriya, Vaiśya, and Śūdra.

22 The cognition and word "non-Brahmin" [arise] in regard to that same thing with respect to which one would use a sentence like, "Humanity is occurring in a thing distinct from a Brahmin."

One may take the word "non-Brahmin" to refer to a complex state of affairs – that is, a sentence-meaning – namely, humanity as occurring in something distinct from a Brahmin. We find this to be the case with many other words, for instance *aupagava*, which means "one who is a descendent of Upagu."

23 In just this way, in the case of non-pot, etc., the universal earthenness etc., excluded from potness, etc., is cognized as the object.

---

a negative meaning (i.e., it would be a prohibition), limited to denying that *ye yajāmahe* is to be uttered at the *anuyājas*; it would not simultaneously imply that it should be uttered at other preliminary offerings. See MNP 263,28–265,33 (trans., pp. 170–174) and MSBh ad MS 10.8.4. The scope of the negative prefix "non-"/*a-* in "non-Brahmin" is clearly the term to which it is affixed, hence it expresses a *paryudāsa*, and the word together with the prefix implies a positive meaning.

24 Because of its being unique, the word modified by the prefix "non-" is restricted to the universal which is devoid of only that.

In the case of a word such as "non-Brahmin," because Brahminhood is the unique or uncommon meaning of the word that is being negated, i.e., "Brahmin" – among all the meanings implied as well as directly indicated by that word, such as humanity – it (i.e., the word "non-Brahmin") will refer to the universal humanity devoid of just that Brahminhood.[19] The negative prefix "non-" negates the chief or uncommon meaning of the word it is affixed to. In the case of the word "non-pot," it will refer to the universal earthenness devoid of just potness.

25 When a lower universal is negated [in a negative expression "non-X"], the next higher universal restricts the word, which is in need of some universal [as its denotation], to itself.

When for example, in the expression "non-Brahmin," the more specific universal Brahminhood is negated, then the next higher universal, namely humanity, becomes the denotation of the word; for a word always requires some universal as its denotation. The denotative function of the word does not drift to a yet higher universal, such as living-beingness, because its need for a denotation is satisfied. Thus, "non-Brahmin" refers to humanity from which Brahminhood has been excluded.

26 There is no reason at all for that [word "non-Brahmin"] to go beyond the first [universal, namely humanity]. Thus, humanity devoid of Brahminhood remains [as the meaning].

27 On the other hand, one might postulate an exclusion of

---

[19] ŚVŚar 33,8–9: *tena tad abhidhāyaiva nañā viśeṣitas tadrahitaṃ yat param arthaprāptaṃ tadaniṣiddhaṃ bodhayaty eveti* [...] /. "Therefore, indicating that [uncommon meaning], equipped (*viśeṣita*) with 'non-,' [the word 'non-Brahmin'] makes known, as devoid of that [uncommon meaning], that other [thing/universal] which is implied [by 'Brahmin'] [but] not negated by that ['non-'] [...]."

humanity once the qualifier "non-" has excluded Brahminhood. That, however, would not at all be based on what is heard (*aśruta*).

One might object that if the word excludes Brahminhood, why should it not also exclude humanity? But that would not have any linguistic basis. The function of the prefix "non-" is exhausted in excluding Brahminhood; it could not also function to exclude humanity.

28 Therefore, the universal of which those subtypes [such as Brahmin] are indeed denied will be located, by implication, in other subtypes [namely, Kṣatriya and so forth]. It is cognized in this way in ordinary discourse as well.

The humanity from which Brahminhood has been excluded will, by implication, be located in other subtypes of humanity, i.e., Kṣatriyas and so forth, since a universal must exist in particulars.

This analysis of the word "non-Brahmin" as denoting humanity from which Brahmins have been excluded is not just something scholars have invented. It is also reflected in everyday linguistic practice. Thus, in the end, what is expressed by the word "non-Brahmin" is humanity, that is, something positive, and not a mere negation.

29 Given that the cognition of X [e.g., the universal humanity] applies (*prasaṅgin*) [to all its subtypes, e.g., the *varṇa*s], a negation [of a particular type or types, e.g., other *varṇa*s] is accepted even by implication. And the meaning [of "non-X"] being something which is devoid of just that [X], there would be a notion of those [other *varṇa*s] due to their similarity [to X].

Even though the idea of humanity, which applies to all four *varṇa*s, arises from the word "Brahmin" in the expression "non-Brahmin," it can be excluded from Brahmins by the prefix "non-." In other cases, we even see humanity excluded from certain *varṇa*s by implication. Sucarita gives the example of the sentence, "Bring a man to carry liquor." Although "man" denotes the universal humanity, which includes all kinds of men, the phrase "to carry liquor" restricts it to types of men other than those of the three highest *varṇa*s, who are not allowed to come into contact with liquor. Thus, there is a negation of certain *varṇa*s by implication, even without an explicit use of "non-" in these cases. The negation of Brahmins and the restriction of the universal humanity to other *varṇa*s by the prefix "non-," therefore, is nothing unusual.

The word "non-Brahmin" strictly denoting just some thing or other which lacks Brahminhood, the meaning must somehow be specified. Due to the similarity of other *varṇa*s to Brahmins, they are the specific meaning that comes to mind.

30ab Or else, [this] similarity (*sādṛśya*) [with Brahmins] itself is accepted as the meaning of the word "non-Brahmin," etc.

That is, "non-Brahmin" could mean simply those who are similar to Brahmins, which would come to the same thing: Kṣatriyas, etc. This is another solution to the problem of what positive entity could be the referent of "non-Brahmin" that Kumārila appears to accept.

30cd And that [similarity] is due to their having the same kinds of parts (*avayavasāmānyāt*) [i.e., hands, etc.]; even without this [i.e., having the same kinds of parts, similarity] is noticed.

Two things may be similar due to having the same kinds of parts, i.e., looking the same,[20] but also for other reasons. For instance pots and non-pots may be similar because they have the same qualities (such as being earthen) or the same functions (such as holding water) or the same

[20] See ŚV *Upamāna* 18cd: *bhūyo'vayavasāmānyayogo jātyantarasya tat //*. "That [similarity] is the connection of one type of thing [e.g., a wild cow] with abundant part-universals [of another type of thing, e.g., a domestic cow]."

origin (such as being made by a potter).[21]

31 In some cases, even without similarity, the employment of a word combined with "non-" is possible on the basis of association, and so forth, as [Śabara] will say in regard to "non-looking."

At MSBh 4.1.3 Śabara discusses *Manusmṛti* 4.37a: *nekṣetodyantam ādityam* [...] /, "One should not look at the rising sun [...]."[22] He explains, this does not mean that one should not look at the sun but rather that one should form the resolution (*saṅkalpa*) not to look at it. That is to say, this is a positive injunction (*vidhi*), not a prohibition (*pratiṣedha*). Since refraining from doing something is closely associated with resolving not to do it, mentioning the former can serve as a reference to the latter.

32 In the case of that [expression "non-looking"] also, some action distinct from the looking is expected. Because of

---

[21] ŚVKāś$_{K}$ 440(65),11–439(66),3: *nāvaśyam avayavasāmānyād eva sarvatra sādṛśyam / vināpi tena kvacil lakṣyata evety uktam evaṃ jātiguṇety atra / ato 'ghaṭādīnām api śarāvādīnāṃ ghaṭenābdhāraṇādikriyāsādṛśyam utpattisādṛśyaṃ vā vācyam / samānaṃ hi kulālādikāraṇam utpattau ghaṭādīnām / anyeṣāṃ ca pārthivānāṃ kāṭhinyādiguṇasāmanyam iti* /. "It is not necessarily the case that similarity is always due to having the same kinds of parts. For it has been stated [in ŚV *Upamāna* 20ab] in regard to this that even without that [i.e., even without having the same kinds of parts,] similarity is perceived in some cases: 'In this way, [there is a variety of similarity] due to origin, quality[, etc.] [...].' Thus, even of non-pots such as a cup, etc., there can be declared similarity with a pot consisting in the holding of water, etc., or similarity of origin; for pots have a similar cause in regard to their origin, [namely,] a potter, and so forth. And of other earthen things there is sameness of the quality of hardness, etc." Jayamiśra, however, suggests that (in the case of Kṣatriyas, etc.) they could be similar by virtue of "an intermediate universal such as humanity" (*avāntarasāmānyena puruṣatvādinā*, ŚVŚar 35,7).

[22] Cf. MNP 261,31–263,26 (trans. 167–170). Manu 4.37 in its entirety reads: *nekṣetodyantam ādityaṃ nāstaṃ yāntaṃ kadācana / nopasṛṣṭaṃ na vāristhaṃ na madhyaṃ nabhaso gatam* //. "He should never look at the sun when it is rising or setting, nor when it is eclipsed, nor when it is reflected in water, nor at noon" (Doniger/Smith 1991: 78).

its proximity, one does not understand anything beyond the resolution [not to look].

Since the statement, "One should not look at the rising sun," occurs in the section which concerns the taking of vows,[23] one expects it to refer to some action or observance one should undertake. Since the intention or resolution (*saṅkalpa*) is the first thing one must do when making a vow, that is the first thing that comes to mind as the object of the injunction. There is no reason to pass beyond that, just as when one uses the expression "non-Brahmin," one need not seek something beyond the universal humanity as its meaning (see v. 26).

33 And [generally speaking] the particle "non-" when it is connected with a noun or a verbal root is never negating. [Hence] the two words "non-Brahmin" and *adharma* express something that is merely other and something that is opposite [, respectively].

The word "non-Brahmin," as we have seen, means *varṇa*s other than Brahmins. The word *adharma* means the opposite of *dharma*, i.e., the violation of *dharma*. Kumārila does not offer an example of the negation of a verbal root in this verse, but *anīkṣaṇa*, "non-looking," discussed in the previous two verses can serve as an example. Normally in Sanskrit grammar, the prefix *a-* can mean "other than X" (*anya*) and "opposite to X" (*virodhin*) as well as "the absence of X" (*abhāva*).[24]

---

[23] Manu 4.13 refers to the numerous rules to be observed by the twice-born specified in the verses that follow, as "vows" (*vratāni*): *ato 'nyatamayā vṛttyā jīvaṃs tu snātako dvijaḥ / svargyāyuṣyayaśasyāni vratānīmāni dhārayet //*. "Thus, a twice-born Vedic graduate, making a living by means of one or another of the occupations [mentioned above], should practice one of these vows, which win for him fame, long life, and a place in heaven" (adapted from Doniger/Smith 1991: 75). Cf. MNP 262,8–17 (trans. 168, esp. n. 220).

[24] Six meanings of *nañ* are mentioned by Vasu 1997: I.258 ad P 2.2.6: *sādṛśya*, *abhāva*, *bheda*, *alpatā*, *aprāśastya*, and *virodha*. In his explanations of *avidyā* in AKBh 3.39 and *Pratītyasamutpādavyākhyā* Vasubandhu gives four and seven meanings of *a-*, respectively (Mejor 2002). In explaining the logical term *asapakṣa*

34 Even in the case where negation is [normally] understood [from the word "not"] due to its relation with the finite verb [as in the prohibition, "One should not drink,"] the listener has as his object a real thing consisting in inactivity.

The commentators explain "inactivity" as one's own nature, devoid of any activity.[25] In other words, when one understands a prohibition that one should not do something, one comprehends that one should not undertake the mentioned action (killing, illicit drinking, etc.) and just remain as one is. This neutrality is a real thing (*vastv eva*), one's very self.

Summarizing the discussion that began with v. 11, Kumārila says,

35ab Therefore, there would be exclusions [i.e., negations] only in respect to something real.

A positive entity can always be identified as the referent even in the case of negative expressions such as "non-Brahmin," "impermanence," "previous non-existence," and so forth. Therefore, there could be the notion of the exclusion (i.e., absence) of non-cow, for example, only with regard to something real, namely, a real universal.

Dharmakīrti mentions specifically the three meanings *anya*, *viruddha*, and *abhāva* at NB 104.7–8, and seems to consider all of them candidates for the *a-* of *asapakṣa*. Dignāga mentions these three meanings at PSV 2.5cd as well, but implies there and argues explicitly in PSV 3.19 that only *abhāva* is possible. See Watanabe 2008: 1145(109)–46(110) and Lasic 2009: 14.

[25] ŚVKāś$_K$ 435(70),14: *niṣedhyahananādikriyārahitam udāsīnam ātmānam* [...], "the inactive self insofar as it is devoid of the negated act of killing, etc. [...]." ŚVŚar 36,11–12: *hananādivyapāre hi pravartamāno yadā viśiṣṭena vidhinā pratiṣidhyate tadātmānam eva tadvyāpāraśūnyam avagacchatīty arthaḥ* /. "The meaning is, when someone engaged in the activity of killing, etc., is prohibited by a specific injunction, then he comprehends just the self devoid of that activity."

1.3 If one rejected real universals, there would just be Emptiness.

35cd Furthermore, if one postulates an unreal thing [as a universal], then something real is not obtained prior to ultimate differences [i.e., atoms].

If one considers the "universals" which are the meanings of words to be unreal entities, i.e., exclusions, then since all universals would be non-entities, one would not obtain *real* entities until one got to ultimate differences, which are in no sense universals. But the ultimate differences, i.e., particulars, of reality are single atoms; even a dyad, an aggregate of two atoms, is common to its two constituent atoms, hence a universal. Thus, it would follow implausibly on the Buddhist theory of *apoha* that the only real things are atoms.

36ab There can be no activity [based on language] by means of ultimate [differences, i.e., atoms]. They are not capable of being ascertained [by conceptual cognition].[26]

Kumārila has stated in v. 3ab that unique particulars cannot be conceptualized. Thus, ultimate differences, having nothing in common with anything else, could not be the objects of conceptual or linguistic awareness, hence practical activity could not be based on them. If one

---

[26] Our translation follows Jayamiśra's gloss, which alludes to ŚV *Apohavāda* 3ab: the unique individual cannot be the positive entity (*bhāva*) which is apprehended as a non-existence, "because it is not conceptualized" (*nirvikalpanāt*). (He quotes, however, only the first *pāda* of 3ab: *neṣṭo 'sādhāraṇas tāvat*, ŚVŚar 36,23.) Sucaritamiśra, however, offers a different explanation, ŚVKāśK 433(72),1–4. Atoms do not appear in cognition but are only postulated in order to explain the perception of gross objects. (In Vaiśeṣika philosophy typically, however, atoms are postulated as [1] the ultimate limit of the scale of magnitude and [2] to account for differences in the size of objects. See, e.g., NKand 31,16–25.) If, however, gross objects themselves do not exist because they have the status of universals (as suggested by the preceding verse), then there would be no basis for ascertaining atoms. Being inaccessible to cognition therefore, whether as individual atoms (which, again, are imperceptible) or as the ultimate constituents of large objects, there could be no activity based on them.

embraced the *apoha* theory, practical activity would be undermined.

36cd And it is Emptiness [in the sense of the absence of external objects] stated in another way that is expressed by the word *apoha*.

If the meaning of a word were an *apoha*, it would follow from the preceding considerations that nothing real at all is referred to by words.

37 If there is that [Emptiness, i.e., if word and cognition do not refer to external objects], then for cognitions such as "horse," etc., there would be an apprehending [by the cognitions] of a portion of themselves. In that case, it is vain indeed to assume that exclusion of others is the meaning.

38 For a universal which is a real thing, [namely,] the form in the cognition, will be the meaning of the word; for it is indeed independent of [external] objects. An *apoha* is imagined in vain.

If words did not refer to real things, then a cognition of a certain type of animal, such as a horse, would just refer to the appearance of horse within the cognition itself.[27] In that case, however, the meaning – the form within the cognition, which appears as a universal – would be something real; for it is an aspect of the cognition itself, which is real.[28] There would be no need to posit an *apoha* as the meaning.

---

[27] The theory that the *buddhyākāra* could be the meaning, which came to be associated with Dharmakīrti, seems to derive from Bhartṛhari. See Ogawa 1999, Kataoka 2009: 490(9)–487(12), and Kataoka 2014.

[28] ŚVKāś$_{K}$ 433(72),15–432(73),1: *evaṃ hi varaṃ pratibhāsānuguṇyena vasturūpam eva sāmānyaṃ buddhyākaraḥ śabdavācya ity aṅgīkriyatām* /. "For in this way it is better to accept, in accordance with the way things appear, that the form in the cognition is what is expressed by a word, which is a real universal." ŚVŚar 37,12–13: *etāvad atra yuktaṃ vaktuṃ – vasturūpam idaṃ sāmānyaṃ bahirbhāvaśūnyaṃ buddhyāropitaṃ śabdenocyate – iti* /. "At least this much can be said, that this universal which is real [but] which does not exist externally and is superimposed on the cognition, is expressed by a word."

39 That cognition which has a real entity as its content arises with respect to word-meanings. Therefore, a real thing which does not exclude other cognitions would be postulated as the meaning.

The opponent might think that even on the idealist view that cognitions apprehend aspects of themselves and there are no external objects to be excluded, the meaning could still consist in the exclusion of *other cognitions*. Thus, he could insist that the meaning is still a negation. Cognitions, however, arise with their own positive content, namely, the form in the cognition which is a real universal. They do not ascertain an exclusion from other cognitions.

40 [Moreover,] just as intuitive apprehension (*pratibhā*) is accepted [by you] as the sentence-meaning even though there is no external object, so the word-meaning should be that as well [namely, a cognition]. So why is *apoha* postulated?

Dignāga at PS 5.46cd accepts that the sentence-meaning is an intuitive apprehension, that is to say, a certain type of cognition.[29] In that case, why cannot the word-meaning, too, be a cognition with a certain content? Even for the Buddhist, it seems, an *apoha* is unnecessary.

41 And the exclusion of a cognition from another cognition is not cognized [when one hears a word like "cow"]. And that [cognition] does not bear another aspect [of exclusion or negation] which is distinct from merely the arising of the nature [of the cognition itself as the awareness of a real universal].

And one will not get anywhere by insisting that the awareness of word-meaning is somehow different from that of sentence-meaning, in that it

---

[29] PS 5.46cd: *vākyārthaḥ pratibhākhyo 'yaṃ tenādāv upajāyate* // (Pind 2015: I.55,7). "The sentence-meaning, which is known as intuition, arises initially through that [word, which is in fact unreal and only imagined due the method of abstraction]" (cf. Pind 2015: II.166). Dignāga probably adopted this view from Bhartṛhari. See Kunjunni Raja 1963: 224–227, Pind 2015: II.253–255, and Hattori 1980.

presents an *apoha*. For a word does not give rise to a cognition which one ascertains as excluded from other cognitions. There is not another exclusion-aspect to the cognition it produces besides just the awareness of its content.

Now Kumārila develops a new objection against the Apohavāda: for the Apohavāda, all words would be synonymous. The development of this argument and exploration of its ramifications extend through v. 92.

2 If meanings were *apoha*s, all words would be synonyms.

42 If exclusion were the meaning, then all [words] expressing different universals [such as "cow," "horse," etc.] and those expressing specific types [such as "spotted cow," "white horse," etc.] would become synonyms.

For they would all actually express the same thing: exclusion or non-existence.

43 [Objection:] This absurd consequence is not admissible because of the difference of exclusions. If [you attribute this consequence to us] by postulating the universal "exclusion," then it would be the same for you with respect to a real thing in general.

The opponent charges against Kumārila: If you claim that on the Apohavāda all meanings would be the same insofar as every word denotes exclusion in general, you would have the same problem. For it could be said that on your theory, all words mean the same insofar as they all refer to a real thing, namely, a universal, in general.

44 [Reply:] For me, because they are real things, universals can differ from each other. And not having natures that are confused, they do not exhibit identity.

45 For you, since they are not real things, how can exclusions, which are without the possibility of being mixed, identical, or diverse, be distinct?

46 Or else if [an *apoha* is distinct,] then because it differs [from others,] it would be a real thing like a unique factor [i.e., an individual]. On the contrary, if it is not a real thing, then because it is not diverse there is no escape from synonymy.

Since exclusions are not real things, they cannot be distinct from each other; if they were distinct from each other, they would be real things. Therefore, assuming that they are not real things as the Buddhist insists, they would not be distinct from each other and, as a result, all words would be synonymous.

The Buddhist now objects that exclusions can be distinct from each other by virtue of the distinctions of the things they exclude (*apohya*s).

2.1 Differences between *apoha*s cannot be based on their *apohya*s (the things they exclude) or *ādhāra*s (bases).

47 [Objection:] But isn't it the case that there will be a difference of the exclusion due to the difference of what is excluded? [Reply:] First, there is no inherent difference. An extrinsic one, however, would be figurative.

It has been established that there is no intrinsic difference of *apoha*s, which being mere negations, lack all features. Nor could there be an extrinsic difference, i.e., a difference due to other things associated with them, such as *apohya*s, the things to be excluded.[30] For any such difference would be figurative, i.e., say the commentators, it would be imagined (*kālpanika*).[31]

---

[30] Dignāga seems to suggest this at PS 5.14a: *apohyabhedād bhinnārthāḥ* [...] (Pind 2015: I.16,7), "[words] having different meanings because of the difference of the things they exclude [...]."

[31] Thus ŚVŚar 39,25. ŚVN 409,9–10: *na hy abhinnasya sambandhibhedād vāstavo bhedo bhavati* /. "For of [an *apoha*] which is not distinct there cannot be a real difference due to a difference of what is [merely] connected with it." TSPś I.365,19–20 ad TSś 927cd (= ŚV *Apohavāda* 47cd): *parato 'py asau bhavan*

48 For the same reason, a difference of it is not possible even by virtue of a difference of the things it is based on [e.g., individual spotted cows, black cows, etc., in the case of the word "cow"]; for it is not thought that there is a difference even of a real thing by virtue of a difference of things that are connected with it.

49 How much less can something that is not real, which is not connected with [anything], which is not [really] excluded from another, which is not of a specific type, [and] which is not specified as this or that [become different by virtue of a difference of things connected with it]?

50 Therefore, just as it does not differ even if there is a difference of the individuals [upon which it is based], so even if there is a difference of what is to be excluded, this [*apoha*] will not be diverse.

Just as differences of *apoha*s cannot be based on *apohya*s, so they cannot be based on their "bases" (*ādhāra*s), that is, the individual things that fall under the *apoha* – e.g., for "cow," individual cows. A real thing does not become different from another due to something associated with it. The commentators give the example of a person, "Devadatta," who does not become different by occupying a different seat or changing his clothes. A difference in his seat or clothes, things associated with Devadatta, does not bring about a difference in Devadatta himself. How much less, then, could there be a difference in an *apoha*, which is something unreal, due to a difference of its bases, which are things associated with it? But if an *apoha* cannot differ from another due to a difference of its bases, how could it differ due to a difference of the things it excludes?

---

kālpanikaḥ syān na pāramārthikaḥ /. "[A difference] that is due even to something else would be imaginary, not real." Sucaritamiśra, however, suggests that if the difference of *apoha*s were extrinsic, "then all linguistic usage would be figurative, because in no case is there a *real* difference." *evaṃ hi sarvo 'yam śābdo vyavahāra aupacāriko bhavet, kvacid api vāstavasya bhedasyābhāvāt*, ŚVKāś$_{K}$ 427(78),4–5.

51 If there were a difference [of the *apoha* due to a difference of the individuals upon which it is based] then with respect to each individual there would be a [distinct] exclusion of non-cow. Then the desired view that [this exclusion of non-cow] is the universal of [all cows,] spotted cows, etc., is not established.

If an *apoha* were differentiated according to the individuals on which it is based, then there would ultimately be a different *apoha* for each individual; for each individual cow, being unique, excludes all things different from itself. Cow_1, cow_2, etc., then, would not share the same exclusion of non-cow: cow_1 would have the exclusion of non-cow_1, whereas cow_2 would have the exclusion of non-cow_2, etc. There would be no exclusion that includes all cows. Therefore, there would be no exclusion that functions as a universal.

52 It is a risky hypothesis (*atikalpanā*) [to suppose] that [an *apoha*,] which even its bases (*ādhāra*), which are connected with it, do not essentially differentiate, could be differentiated by the things to be excluded, which are remote [from it].

One might perhaps accept that something could be differentiated *in a figurative sense* by the differences of things connected with it. But how could it be differentiated by things which are external to it and not connected with it at all? How could an *apoha* be differentiated by the things it excludes?

53 In the case of non-cow, it is horse which is different, and non-horse has cow as what is additional. The rest of what is to be excluded, elephant, etc., does not differ for either of those two [words].

Now Kumārila develops his argument that on the Apohavāda all words would be synonymous in another way. If the differences of *apoha*s were based on the differences of what they exclude, then since there is actually very little difference between what *apoha*s exclude, they would be virtually identical. For the meaning of the word "cow" is the exclusion of non-cow. Non-cow consists of horse, elephant, lion, etc.

And the meaning of the word "horse" is the exclusion of non-horse. Non-horse consists of cow, elephant, lion, etc. In the case of the meaning of "cow," it is only horse which differs from the set of things excluded by the word "horse," and in the case of the meaning of "horse," it is only cow which is additional to the set of things excluded by the word "cow." So each word is virtually identical in what it excludes. Hence, any two words, on the *apoha* theory, are virtually identical in meaning.[32]

54 [One might suggest,] in that case, let there be a difference [of the words "cow" and "horse"] due to a difference of [just] one [of the things to be excluded or] non-difference due to the non-difference of many [things to be excluded]. [In response, we point out that according to the rule that] the greater number are what is to be performed (*sadharmatva*), non-difference [of these words] results.

If one were to suggest that the differences of the *apoha*s of words could be based on the fact that there is at least one thing that is different in what they exclude – i.e., in the case of the words "cow" and "horse," there would be a difference due to the fact that the *apoha* of "cow" excludes horse while the *apoha* of "horse" excludes cow, even though all of the other things they exclude are the same – if one were to argue in this way, then one should consider the general principle accepted in Mīmāṃsā that when presented with two conflicting procedures, the one

[32] The table below shows how what is excluded by different words would practically coincide:

word	excluded	not in common	in common
"cow"	non-cow	horse	elephant, lion, tiger ...
"horse"	non-horse	cow	elephant, lion, tiger ...

followed in the greater number of instances takes precedence.[33] By analogy, since for the *apoha*s of "cow" and "horse" *most* of things they exclude are the same (and only one of them is different), they should be considered the same.

55 And cow does not differ from the nature of horse in that it excludes elephant, etc. If it excluded that [namely, horse], then its identity [with horse] would be contradicted.

As stated in v. 53, the meaning of "cow," i.e., the exclusion of all things that are not cows, is virtually the same as that of "horse" in that almost all of the things they exclude are the same – elephants, lions, etc. Therefore, if it were thought that the one excluded the other, i.e., "cow" excluded horse and "horse" excluded cow, by virtue of just *one* thing to be excluded, then their (virtual) identity would be contradicted.

---

[33] *sadharmatva* alludes to MS 12.2.22: *vipratiṣiddhadharmāṇāṃ samavāye bhūyasāṃ syāt sadharmatvam* /. "When there is a convergence of [sacrifices] with conflicting details, those which are more numerous should be [considered as] possessing merit [i.e., as to be performed]." When in the Pañcadaśarātra the procedure of the one-day Agniṣṭut conflicts with that of the Ekādaśāha sacrifice (i.e., the Eleven-day Sacrifice), the procedure of the latter should be followed – it is *sadharma*, possesses merit – because eleven days are more numerous. To explain: The Pañcadaśarātra (Fifteen-night Sacrifice) is a type of Soma sacrifice that lasts fifteen days. On the first day, the Agniṣṭut is performed. The Ekādaśāha sacrifice (Eleven-day Sacrifice) that lasts from the fifth to fifteenth day has as its *prakṛti*, its archetype, the Dvādaśāha (Twelve-day Sacrifice). The question is, at this Pañcadaśarātra, what is to be adopted as the *subrahmaṇyā* to be recited by the Udgātṛ when the *soma* is pressed: the Āgneyī, which belongs to the Agniṣṭut, or the Aindrī, originally belonging to the Dvādaśāha? The conclusion is: the Aindrī, the element of the Ekādaśāha derived from the Dvādaśāha, should be adopted, because eleven days are "more." See Jhā 1933–36: III.2305; Sandal 1974: CCXXIV; Watson and Kataoka 2017: 47, n. 28.

Similarly, the question concerning whether two *apoha*s are different or not is this: Which is to be adopted, the *difference* which pertains to just one of the things excluded (cow or horse) or the *non-difference* which pertains to many more things to be excluded (elephant, etc.)? Kumārila is suggesting that the non-difference belonging to many *apohya*s should be adopted, because it pertains to a greater number.

56 [Objection:] But for every word individually that which is to be excluded exceeds [that of its counterpart]. In that case, due to [that element] being unique [the word] would have just that as what is to be excluded. [And that would make the word different from other words.]

The opponent objects: The meaning of "cow" may have the exclusion of elephant, lion, etc., in common with the meaning of its counterpart "horse," but the fact remains that it differs from the latter in that it excludes horse![34] So, for "cow," let that unique thing that is excluded determine its meaning.

57 [Reply:] Then for you, a lion, etc., due to its nature of being an exclusion of horse, would each without exception (*eva*) be called "cow" insofar as it for that reason [i.e., due to its also having the nature of an exclusion of horse] bears the exclusion of non-cow.

If the meaning of "cow" is different from that of "horse" just insofar as it excludes horse – which is the unique element among all the things it excludes – then the meaning of "lion," "elephant," etc., would all be the same as "cow"; for they too exclude horse. Thus, a lion, elephant, etc., would be called "cow"!

58 If it is believed that there is exclusion of all [the things that are non-X, so that there would be a difference between "cow" and "lion," then] it must be explained how that [is possible]. If [it were to be done] one-by-one, then it would not be possible because of the unlimited number of things to be excluded.

59 Furthermore, because of the difference of the things to

---

[34] ŚVN 410,15–16: *sarvaśabdeṣu śabdāntaraṃ pratiyoginaṃ gṛhītvālocyamāneṣv ekaikam apohyaṃ pratiyogyapohyāt svāpohye 'tiricyate* /. "All words being considered after one comprehends another word that is its counterpart, for each one, what is to be excluded exceeds, in regard to what is to be excluded for itself, what is to be excluded for its counterpart."

be excluded the *apoha* would be divided. In that case, there would be the conjunction of innumerable universals in one individual.

60 As a result, the single universal expressed by "cow" is not established. There would be the cognition of other universals in respect to these [innumerable meanings of the word "cow"], as in regard to other universals [like horseness, etc.].

The opponent might come back and say that the word "cow" refers not just to the exclusion of horse but to the exclusion of *all* non-cows, including lions, elephants, and so forth; and the words "lion," "elephant," etc., refer to the exclusions of *all* non-lions, etc., including cows. So the word "cow" could hardly mean the same thing as "lion," "elephant," etc. If the difference of an *apoha*, however, were based on *all* of the things to be excluded (*apohya*), then, the question arises, How are they excluded?[35] First of all, if the things to be excluded by an *apoha*

---

[35] In the background of Kumārila's discussion ŚV *Apohavāda* 58–64 (perhaps even all the way to v. 72) appears to be the exchange between Dignāga and the Sāṃkhya philosopher Mādhava that extends from PS 5.39 to 43. Mādhava is apparently defending his proof of *pradhāna* against criticisms raised by Dignāga in another work (the *Sāṃkhyaparīkṣā* or *Sāṃkhyaparīkṣāvyāsa*; see Pind 2015: II.251–252, also Yoshimizu 2017: 975–978), while also raising criticisms of his own against the *apoha* theory. At PS(V) 5.43a Dignāga considers the objection that, on the Apohavāda, there could be no "first cognition" (*ādyapratyaya*). That is to say – Jinendrabuddhi quotes from Dignāga's Sāṃkhya source – "if the cognition of something of one nature is due to observation of the non-existence of something of another nature, there is no occurrence of a first cognition. Why? Because then there is no observation of the non-existence of something of another nature." *yady ātmāntarābhāvadarśanād ātmāntare pratyayo bhavati ādyapratyayasaṃvṛttir eva nāsti. kasmāt? na hi tadātmāntarābhāvadarśanam astīti* (Pind 2015: II.157, n. 528). This objection is obviously related to the objection brought against the Apohavāda later by Uddyotakara, NV 314, 2–7, and modified by Kumārila as the mutual presupposition or circularity objection, ŚV *Apohavāda* 83–85ab. Dignāga responds with PS(V) 5.43a, maintaining that the problem does not exist for him because according to him linguistic usage is beginningless: *iṣtasiddhir anāditvāt* (Pind 2015:

were excluded one-by-one, then the *apoha* could never be comprehended, since there are an unlimited number of things to be excluded. Moreover, there would be an *apoha* for each thing excluded.[36] The word "cow," for example, excludes horse, elephant, lion, etc. If "cow" excluded all of these one-by-one, then it would mean the exclusion of horse, the exclusion of elephant, the exclusion of lion, etc. In that case, used in reference to a single individual, the word "cow" would have many exclusions – non-horse, non-elephant, non-lion, etc. – associated with it, and so would indicate many things – many universals – not just the universal cowness.

61 Nor would these [non-cows] as a collection be what is to be excluded. For a collection does not arise without one property [that all of the members of the collection share].

62 They neither occur in the same place nor at the same time. And some collection of them that is separate [from its parts] does not exist [according to you].

Could, then, the *apoha* be based on all of the things to be excluded as a

---

I.52,9). At PS(V) 5.43b he then considers the charge that "there could be no cognition at all" of the word-meaning (*pratyayavṛttir eva nāsti*), "because" – again according to Jinendrabuddhi, apparently quoting from a Sāṃkhya source – "the other [kinds of] natures of what is to be excluded are infinite; for there is no observation of the non-existence of all the other [kinds of] natures." *vyudasyātmāntarānantyāt. na hi sarvātmāntarābhāvadarśanam astīti* (Pind 2015 II.160, n.536). Kumārila may be picking up on this objection here.

[36] In an attempt to head off this objection, Dignaga says, PSV 5.43b: *na hi so 'nyāṃ jātiṃ pratidravyam apohate, kiṃ tarhi vyavacchedyavivakṣayaikena sāmānyadharmeṇa* (Pind 2015:I.53,4–54,1). "For that [word] does not exclude a different type (*jāti*) for each individual; rather, [they are all excluded] by intending to denote what is excluded by means of a single common property." See below, ŚV *Apohavāda* 61, and n. 37. Jayamiśra, ŚVŚar 42,21–22, misses the reference to Dignāga and refers in this connection to PV 1.41 instead: *tasmād yato yato 'rthānāṃ vyāvṛttis tannibandhanam / jātibhedāḥ prakalpyante tadviśeṣāvagāhinaḥ //*. "Therefore, from whatever things objects are excluded, different types (*jāti*) are conceived, based on those [exclusions], which reveal the [various] differences of these [objects]."

collection? But in order for all the things to be excluded by "cow" to be a collection, they would have to share some property, such as being located in the same place, as is the case, e.g., for the trees that comprise a forest.[37] Non-cows do not all occur in the same place, nor at the same

---

[37] In response to the objection of Mādhava that "there could be no cognition at all" (see above, n. 35) Dignāga says that all of the *apohya*s are not excluded individually but rather on the basis of the same property which is a general feature, PS 5.43b: *sāmānyena nirākṛteḥ* (Pind 2015: I.53,3). He explains in his *Vṛtti* ad loc., "For that [word] does not exclude a different type (*jāti*) for each individual; rather, [they are all excluded] by intending to denote what is excluded by means of a single common property." *na hi so 'nyāṃ jātiṃ pratidravyam apohate, kiṃ tarhi vyavacchedyavivakṣayaikena sāmānyadharmeṇa* (Pind 2015: I.53,4–54,1). The general property in question, according to Jinendrabuddhi, "has the nature of an imputed non-difference insofar as one thinks, 'This is not a tree,'" *prāpitābhedarūpeṇa vṛkṣo na bhavatīti* (Pind 2015: II.161, n. 540). This interpretation would appear to make Dignāga's position immediately vulnerable to the problem of mutual presupposition that Kumārila will go on to raise, ŚV *Apohavāda* 83–85ab. Dignāga, however, goes on in PSV 5.43b to say, "And it has been stated in regard to this that there is inference due merely to non-observation [of the word's application] in dissimilar things," *uktaṃ cātra vijātīye 'darśanamātreṇānumānam* (Pind 2015: I.54,1–2), thereby suggesting the common property in question is actually *not being observed as the referent of the word.* This is evident from the rest of PSV 5.43b. One infers the fact that something is not a horse from the fact that it has horns, Dignāga says, simply by *not* observing any horse to have horns, not by excluding separately white horses, and so forth, individually. Nor is there an inference of not being a horse in regard to each individual type of non-horse, cows, and so forth: *tasmād yathā viṣāṇitvād anaśva ity vacane 'śve viṣāṇitvādarśanena tadvyavacchedānumānam, na tu karkādīn pratyekam apohate, nāpy ekaikeṣu gavādiṣu vartate* (Pind 2015: I.54,3–5). Hence, Dignāga seems to be implying: only by *not* observing the word "cow" used for non-cows do we know that they are non-cows. See Kataoka's essay below, pp. 245–246. The problem that no cognition would arise from a word – the original objection of Mādhava – would exist only for someone who thinks that everything to which the word applies is ascertained by positive concomitance: *yadi svajātīyavyāptyā varteta, vyāpyasyānantyaṃ syāt* (Pind 2015: I.54,2–3). "If [the word] were to apply by pervasion of similar things, then what is to be pervaded would be infinite." See below, n. 41. We are not convinced by the interpretation of this passage proposed by Yoshimizu 2011: 573–576 and 2017: 984–987 in terms of "componential analysis," which however cannot be entirely discounted, either.

time. Thus, they cannot possibly constitute a collection. Moreover, the Buddhist does not really believe in collections: he denies that they are real things over and above their parts.

63 On the other hand, if it is not different, then [the problem of] an unlimited number remains. If they were excluded insofar as they are [some kind of] universal, then it [namely, that universal] would not be real.

64 Or how could something unreal be excluded? Non-existence does not become non-existent. And if non-existence were excluded, existence would remain.

If the Buddhist tried to say that there is such a thing as a collection, but it is not different from its parts, then an *apoha* would again be based on an infinite number of things to be excluded and could not possibly be cognized. (See above, v. 58d.) If the Buddhist held that a *universal* of all of the things to be excluded – e.g., in the case of "cow," the universal non-cowness – is excluded,[38] then it should be pointed out that the Buddhist does not accept real universals, so a universal is not something that could be excluded.

In general, something unreal cannot be the object of exclusion. As Jayamiśra puts it (ad v. 63cd), "[...] Since that [universal] according to your view is not real, it would be supposed that it is to be excluded as something unreal. But how could there be exclusion of what is unreal? For there is not another non-existence of a non-existence."[39] If, on the other hand, one accepted that it is unreal and is excluded, then the

---

It is evident, in any case, that Kumārila understands "one/the same property" quite differently from the way Dignāga intended it – if indeed there is any allusion to Dignāga here at all.

[38] It seems PS 5.43b *sāmānyena nirākṛteḥ* could be construed in this way.

[39] ŚVŚar 43,20-21: [...] *tasya tvanmatena vastutvaṃ nāstīty avasturūpeṇāpohyatvam aṅgīkṛtaṃ syāt / kathaṃ cāvastuno 'poho bhavati / na hy abhāvasyāparo 'bhāvo 'stīty āha /*.

exclusion of it – the non-existence of a non-existence – would be something positive!

65 And a difference of things to be excluded would not be appropriate, because of the non-distinction of non-existences. If one thought there could be a difference of those [things to be excluded] as a result of a difference of *apoha*s, then mutual dependence results.

66 [That is to say,] due to the difference of the universal cow there is a difference of this [thing to be excluded called] "non-cow." Due to the difference of this [thing to be excluded] "non-cow" there is a difference of the universal [i.e., the *apoha*] cow.

67 If [one were to say that] non-cows are [just] horses, etc., [and these taken together are different from the things that are non-horse, etc., then we would say that] they, too, however, have the nature of non-existences with respect to [their subtypes] such as white horse, etc. And those [subtypes] as well are like that [i.e., they too have the nature of non-existences].

68ab In this way one cannot understand what is to be excluded or [based] on what there is an exclusion. And it is just like this for individual cows, etc. [which are the bases of the *apoha*].

Moreover, all of the things to be excluded, non-cows, non-horses, etc., are themselves non-existences; therefore, since non-existences cannot be distinct from each other (see above, v. 45), there could be no differences between them. If one suggested that there could be a difference of *apohya*s because they are the objects of different *apoha*s, then there would obviously be a situation of mutual presupposition: a difference of *apoha*s is supposed to be based on a difference of *apohya*s and a difference of *apohya*s is supposed to be based on a difference of *apoha*s.

One might try to get around this problem by suggesting that what are excluded in the case of the word "cow," for instance, are not all non-cows construed as some universal but in fact horses, lions, elephants etc. The set of non-cows would then be really different from the set of non-horses, i.e., all those kinds of things excluded by the meaning of "horse" (i.e., cows, lions, elephants, etc.). Thus, there would a difference of the things to be excluded for different *apoha*s. However, employing reasoning already hinted at in v. 35cd, Kumārila points out that, with reference to their own subtypes, horses, etc., are universals (for horse is common to many horse subtypes) hence, according to the Buddhist, non-entities. Nor could one base the difference of things excluded on those subtypes, either, for they too are universals with respect to *their* subtypes. And so it becomes difficult ever to say what the thing to be excluded *is*. Even individual cows, which are considered the bases of the *apoha* (the things that fall under it), would have the nature of non-existences with respect to their ultimate constituents, insofar as they are common to them.

68cd-69ab In that case, these two [namely, that which is to be excluded and that upon which exclusion is based] would exist [only] in ultimate atoms. But, with respect to ultimate [atoms], you cannot talk about these two.

The differences of that which is to be excluded and the bases of *apoha*, then, would have to rest on ultimate atoms, since being unique, they cannot be considered universals, i.e., non-entities. However, as Kumārila pointed out in v. 36ab, we cannot refer to or talk about ultimate differences.

69cd-70cd And of the atoms of cows and horses there is no difference by way of essence, universal, configuration, or size, etc. [So] with regard to those [atoms] as well, one cannot differentiate which are to be excluded or [based] on which there is an exclusion.

If what is to be excluded and the bases of exclusion are ultimately reducible just to the atoms that cows and horses, etc., are made of, then, since cows and horses are actually comprised of the same kinds of atoms, they could not be differentiated on that basis, either.

71 And no one at all can know cows, etc., as the objects [i.e., bases] of *apoha* equally, insofar as their similarity is unknown.

72 Nor can anyone discern horses, etc., [equally] as what is to be excluded without continuity of the same property. In that case [since neither what is to be excluded nor the basis of *apoha* can be discerned], exclusion is not established.

Without something shared by all the individual things upon which an *apoha* is based, and by all things to be excluded by it – the Mīmāṃsaka would say that in either case it would have to be a real universal – one could not discern the various things to which an *apoha* applies, nor all the various things it excludes. Hence, one could not comprehend the *apoha*.

3 There is no way of knowing *apoha*s.

73 And there is no functioning of an inferential mark or a word without a positive concomitance [between the word or inferential mark and what it indicates]. And without those two an *apoha* is not [cognized]. But there is no positive concomitance with something unique.

74 And an *apoha* is not evident [before knowing it through a word or an inferential mark, so] with regard to what will one observe the coexistence of [a word or inferential mark with the *apoha*]? And if that [coexistence] is not observed, those two [namely, the word and inferential mark] would not be means of knowing [it].

Now a new criticism of the *apoha* theory is raised. The Buddhist holds that the means of knowing an *apoha* is a word or an inferential mark,[40]

---

[40] Jayamiśra, ŚVŚar 46,5, paraphrases in this context PV 1.47ab: *tasmād apohaviṣayam iti liṅgaṃ prakīrtitam* /. "Therefore, it is stated that the inferential mark has an exclusion for its object." Manorathanandin attributes this statement to Dignāga, PVV 305,6. Cf. PVSV 25,27–28: [...] *vyavacchedaḥ śabdaliṅgābhyāṃ*

and that means, it is known *only* through a word or an inferential mark; it cannot be known by perception. However, a word or an inferential mark can make one aware of something only if there is an established relation between them and the thing they indicate, as between smoke and fire. But if an *apoha* is known only by a word or an inferential mark, one could never grasp the relation between word or inferential mark and the *apoha* in the first place, so that the former could indicate the latter. Nor can an invariable relation between a word or an inferential mark and an individual be established – say, between the word "cow" and a particular cow – which might serve as the basis for cognizing an *apoha* by means of them.

75 And those two would not make [an *apoha*] known merely because one never observes [the word or the inferential mark being used in relation to something else]. [Since you hold that there is no positive concomitance which is the basis of a word or inferential mark making the *apoha* known, the word or inferential mark] would not be observed in regard to anything at all, so nothing is left as the thing to be made known.

One might think that an invariable relation between a word or an inferential mark and the exclusion of non-X (say, cow) could be established by never observing the word or inferential mark applied to non-X.[41] But if one also rejects any *positive* concomitance at all

---

pratipādyate [...] /. "[...] An exclusion is made known by a word or inferential mark [...]."

[41] Dignāga seems to favor this method of determining the referent of a word at PS(V) 5.34:

> *adṛṣṭer anyaśabdārthe svārthasyāṃśe 'pi darśanāt /*
> *śruteḥ sambandhasaukaryaṃ na cāsti vyabhicāritā //* [34]

anvayavyatirekau hi śabdasyārthābhidhāne dvāram, tau ca tulyātulyayor vṛttyavṛttī. tatra tu tulye nāvaśyaṃ sarvatra vṛttir ākhyeyā kvacid, ānantye 'rthasyākhyānāsambhavāt. atulye tu saty apy ānantye śakyam adarśana-mātreṇāvṛtter ākhyānam. ata eva ca svasambandhibhyo 'nyatrādarśanāt

between the word or inferential mark and X, as Dignāga sometimes seems to want to do,[42] they would never be observed applied to X,

tadvyavacchedānumānaṃ svārthābhidhānam ity ucyate. (Pind 2015: I.40,2–41,4)

> The relation of a word [with its meaning] is easily made, and it does not deviate [i.e., it is not ambiguous], because it is not observed [employed] for the referent of another word, and it is observed [employed] for part of its own extension as well. [34]

For positive and negative concomitance are the means of a word indicating a [certain] meaning, and those are the occurrence and non-occurrence [of the word] in regard to what is similar and what is not similar[, respectively]. In the case of what is similar [the word's] occurrence necessarily cannot be stated for each one, in some cases (*kvacit*) [namely, in the case of general terms], since, the extension [of the word] being infinite, it is impossible to state it. In the case of what is not similar, on the other hand, even though it is infinite [too], the statement of non-occurrence [of the word in regard to those things] is possible merely by non-observation. Just for this [reason] it is said that the inference of an exclusion from those [other things it does not refer to] due to not observing it used for something besides its own relata – that is a word's designation of its own meaning. (Cf. Pind 2015: II.116–125)

That is to say, Dignāga appears to believe that merely by *never observing* X in Y one can establish the universal negation, "There are no X in Y." Thus, simply by *never observing* that a particular word is used to refer to Y, e.g., non-cows – and of course it is not difficult *not* to observe something – one ascertains that it does not refer to Y, which is equivalent to its referring to what is not Y – in the case of "cow," to what is not non-cow. One could not, on the other hand, ascertain that the word "cow" refers to all cows by directly observing that it is used to refer to all cows, since cows are infinite. We cannot be sure, but Dignāga's belief that negative concomitance, which he of course understood to be equivalent to a positive concomitance, can be established by mere non-observation may be attributable to the widespread use of non-apprehension (*anupalabdhi*) as a means of establishing non-existence in general. See Kellner and Taber 2014. Kumārila rejects the use of *adarśana* as the only means of establishing the relation between the *hetu* and *sādhya* of an inference at ŚV *Anumāna* 131cd–132, simply referring the reader to his discussion in *Apohavāda*. He does so more fully, arguing that non-observation cannot establish non-existence, at ŚV *Arthāpatti* 36–38. See also ŚV *Apohavāda* 158–159ab, below; Katsura 1992: 222–231; Kataoka 2012.

[42] Thus, PSV 5.34: *yatas tu vṛkṣaśabdo 'pārthivādiṣu na dṛṣṭaḥ, ato vyati-*

either. Hence, everything, even X, would be excluded and the word or inferential mark would not indicate anything at all.

76 If one postulated an *apoha* even though there is no similarity [of those things on which it is based], why isn't it postulated that there is this exclusion of non-cow for both cows and horses?

It was previously stated (v. 71) that various cows, etc., could not be known as the bases of an *apoha* if one did not know them to be similar. Kumārila now returns to this idea, pointing out that if one postulated an *apoha* even without a similarity of the things it is based on, there is no reason why the exclusion of non-cow could not reside in horses as well as cows, so that a horse would be called "cow." The idea seems to be that such a similarity is not possible without the continuity of a single universal, whether it is apprehended by positive or negative concomitance.[43]

77 And if there is no other universal [with regard to which the exclusion of non-cow might occur, then] the difference

---

rekamukhenaivānumānam (Pind 2015: I.41,6–42,1). "But since the word'tree' is not observed when there are things that are not earthen, etc., there is an inference [from the word, of its referents] *only* by means of negative concomitance." However, PS 5.34b: *svārthasyāṃśe 'pi darśanāt*, "and it is observed [employed] for part of its own extension as well," seems to indicate that Dignāga thought that positive concomitance is at least minimally involved. Kumārila will assume this when developing the "non-generalization problem," vv. 81–82, below. It would indeed seem that *not* observing the word "cow" being applied to non-cows would require *observing* it being applied to at least one cow. Cf., however, n. 291 below.

[43] ŚVŚar 46,24–26: *asaty api sārūpye*[1] *yadi yatkiṃcidvyavacchedena yatkiṃcit pratyāyyam ity ucyate tato 'yam ago 'poho yasya kasyacid ekasyāpi piṇḍasya vyavacchedaṃ kṛtvā yaṃ kaṃcit piṇḍaṃ pratipādayann aviśeṣād aśvapiṇḍam api*[2] *pratipādayed ity āha* [...] /. [1]*asaty api sārūpye* em. : *saty api* ed. [2]*api* em. : *vā* ed. "If it is claimed that even though there is no similarity, any X can be made known [arbitrarily] by excluding any Y (i.e., non-X), then this exclusion of non-cow – because there is no difference in making known any X by excluding any Y (i.e., non-X) – would make known even a horse. Thus, he says [...]."

from a spotted cow is the same for [both] a black cow and a horse. In regard to what does the exclusion of non-cow occur?

If there is no class of similar things or universal that is the basis of the *apoha* referred to by "cow," then its basis can only be a certain type of cow, spotted, black, etc.[44] So taking a spotted cow as the example of a cow, black cows as well as horses would not fall under the meaning of "cow," the exclusion of non-cow, for both are different from a spotted cow (hence both would be non-cows). Thus, one obtains the absurd consequence that "cow" would not make a black cow known any more than a horse.

78 The exclusion of non-cow is not at first ascertained by the senses. Nor does the word ["cow"] occur in regard to something else [i.e., the particular]. On the condition of perceiving what is it to be used?

79 Nor, by the previously stated sequence [of reasoning, vv. 73–75], is there an inference of it. Nor, for that [reason], is an [original] experience [whether by perception or inference] of the relation of this [word with an *apoha*] at all possible.

When employing a word, one first determines that "this particular word is to be used in regard to this thing." How could one do that if the *apoha* were the meaning? For the Buddhist says that an *apoha* is known only by language or inference, not by the senses. And a word is not employed to refer to a particular; words can only refer to universals (real or imagined). Nor can the *apoha* be known by inference, as was explained before. Thus, for the Apohavādin it would seem that there is nothing that can serve as the occasion for the use of a word. These considerations also imply that, if an *apoha* were the meaning, the relation between word and meaning could never be learned in the first place.

---

[44] Jayamiśra, however, says that the basis of the exclusion would be an *individual* cow of a certain type, ŚVŚar 47,3–4: *tadā piṇḍāpekṣayā vyavacchedaḥ kalpanīyaḥ*.

80 And for those [language learners] for whom words [in particular, the negative particle "non-"] are not [yet] known to express negations, for them, since non-cow is not established, there can be no rejection of a [positive] universal.

81 And how, furthermore, would one know that [non-cow] is expressed by the word "non-cow"? [If one were to say,] that in regard to which the word "cow" is not observed when the relation is [initially] learned [is what is expressed by "non-cow"],

82 then everything other than a single individual would be what is to be excluded. In this way, a universal would not be the meaning.

Kumārila now takes up another problem relating to how one comes to know an *apoha*. Doesn't the exclusion of non-cow, which is supposedly the meaning of the word "cow," already presuppose an understanding of cow? First of all, one can know the exclusion of non-cow only if one knows what a non-cow is in advance. But how can it be known that something is a non-cow? If a child who is learning the language does not know what the negative particle "non-" means, namely, the negation of cow, then non-cow cannot be what is excluded by the *apoha* and one would have to accept a positive universal as the meaning instead. If it were held that one knows that non-cow is everything other than the individual cow which is pointed out when one is taught the meaning of the word "cow" – that is to say, one knows the meaning through *vyatireka*, negative concomitance, combined with one instance of positive concomitance[45] – then everything besides that individual cow would be a non-cow, and all of those things would be excluded by the meaning of "cow," so that "cow" would end up referring just to that one individual![46]

---

[45] That is to say, here Kumārila seems to be assuming that for the Apohavādin, at least one cow is pointed out when one learns the meaning of "cow." Cf. ŚV *Apohavāda* 75 and notes 41 and 42.

[46] Hugon 2011: 111 refers to this as the "non-generalization problem."

83 And [only] a non-cow which is known would be excluded, and that has the nature of the negation of cow. In that regard, one must state that it is the cow which is negated by "non-."

84 If it has the nature of exclusion of non-cow, then there would be mutual dependence. If for the sake of something to be excluded [i.e., non-cow, you say that] cow is known, then it is useless to postulate an *apoha.*

85ab On the other hand, if cow is not established, there is no non-cow, and in the absence of that [non-cow] how is there a cow?

It would seem that in order to understand the negation "non-cow" one must know the meaning of "cow." If that is explained as the exclusion of non-cow, then the meaning of "cow" will presuppose that of "non-cow" and vice versa, which would be absurd. If one held that the meaning of "cow" is already known, so that it does not presuppose that of "non-cow," then contrary to what the *apoha* theory implies, one would not have to understand what a non-cow is in order to grasp the meaning of "cow." But if we simply do not know what a cow is, then we cannot understand what a non-cow is, either, and so cannot understand the meaning of "cow" as the exclusion of non-cow.[47]

4 A word does not express something qualified by an *apoha.*

85cd And for two absences there are no relations such as the relation of the occurrence (*vṛtti*) of the contained in the container.

86 And a unique, real thing is not understood [from the use of the word "cow"] to be possessed of an *apoha.* Moreover,

---

[47] This is perhaps the most famous objection against the Apohavāda, known as the Circularity Argument. As mentioned (n. 35) it is anticipated by the Sāṃkhya Mādhava and the Naiyāyika Uddyotakara. Dharmakīrti responds to it at PV(SV) 1.113ab–121. See Hugon 2011 for an analysis of the debate.

how would one imagine a relation between a real thing and something unreal?

Up to this point, starting from verse 1, Kumārila has been challenging the idea that the meaning of a word can be an *apoha*. Now he seems to have shifted to considering another view, namely, that a word refers to something *possessing* an *apoha* (*apohavat*). Dignāga, at PS(V) 5.4–11c, after previously refuting the theories that (1) words refer to individuals, (2) that they refer just to universals, and (3) that they refer to the connection with the universal, attacks the theory (4) that a word refers to something possessing a genus (*jātimat*). Kumārila may well wish to show here that the idea that a word refers to something possessing an *apoha* is just as problematic as the theory that it refers to something possessing a universal. He will raise further objections against this view later, in vv. 120 ff., specifically with respect to the problems of coreference and qualification. For now, he questions whether it is possible for an *apoha* to have a relation with anything, so that the latter could be said to possess it.[48] The various subtypes of a thing – a spotted cow, etc.

---

[48] This comes closest to the interpretations of Pārthasārathimiśra and Sucaritamiśra. Jayamiśra, on the other hand, takes 85cd to be attacking the idea that a word could refer to the *relation* with the *apoha*, analogous to theory (3), which Dignāga attacks at PS(V) 5.2. Kamalaśīla, meanwhile, relates 85cd (= TSś 944cd) to Dignāga's oft-quoted statement, PSV 5.36d: *śabdo 'rthāntaranivṛttiviśiṣṭān eva bhāvān āha* (Pind 2015: I.45,2–3), which he paraphrases, TSPś I.371,11: *nīlotpalādiśabdā arthāntaranivṛttiviśiṣṭān arthān āhuḥ* /. "Words such as 'blue lotus,' etc., express [their] referents precisely insofar as they are qualified by the negation of other referents." Apparently misunderstanding Dignāga's intent, he thinks the problem being raised with 85cd is whether one *apoha* can qualify another, as for instance in the expression "blue lotus" – which, however, Kumārila will address more directly at ŚV *Apohavāda* 115–116cd. If two *apoha*s cannot have any relation to each other, whether that of container and contained or any other relation, that would be impossible (TSPś I.371,12–17).

In his commentary on ŚV *Apohavāda* 130cd, ŚVKāśK 294(27),7–293(28),1, Sucaritamiśra concisely gives his understanding of the progression of topics from v. 88 through 130cd. It is only with v. 130cd that Kumārila rejects the idea that a word expresses the connection (*sambandhavācyatā*) (on the same grounds that the Buddhists reject it). With vv. 88 ff. the idea that a word expresses what is explicitly

– could not "have" the exclusion of non-cow; for being types, they are as unreal as that exclusion, and it is inconceivable that there could be a relation of any kind between two unreal things.[49] Nor could an individual possessed of an *apoha* be the meaning of a word; for individuals are believed to be inexpressible.[50] Moreover, a relation between something real, the individual cow, and something unreal, the *apoha*, would be just as problematic as a relation between two unreal things. Thus, the meaning of a word could not be something possessing an *apoha*.

87 And something is not a qualifier simply because it exists. That which "colors" the qualified thing through a cognition of itself (*svabuddhyā*) is a qualifier.

88 And awareness of an *apoha* does not arise from words like "horse," etc. And the cognition of something to be qualified whose qualifier is not known, is not accepted here [i.e., normally].

---

qualified by an *apoha* (*apohaviśiṣṭavācyatā*) – i.e., that one is *aware* of it as qualified by an *apoha* – is refuted (though it would seem that this discussion begins at least with v. 87) ; with vv. 115 ff. the idea that it expresses the *apoha* by itself (*kevalāpohābhidhāna*); and with vv. 120 ff. the view that a word expresses a "qualifed entity" (*viśiṣṭābhidhāna*), i.e., an individual thing which possesses an *apoha*. He, unfortunately, does not explain there what Kumārila is doing in vv. 85cd–86 and how it might differ from these other topics.

[49] The expression in 85c, "the relation of the occurrence (*vṛtti*) of the contained (*ādheya*) in the container (*ādhāra*)" (*ādhārādheyavṛttisambandha*) might allude to PS 2.19: *sambandho yady api dviṣṭhaḥ sahabhāvyaṅgaliṅginoḥ / ādhārādheyavad vṛttis tasya saṃyogivan na tu //* (Pind 2015: II.4–5, n. 16). "Although the relation of the inferential mark and the term coexistent with it resides in both, it occurs in the manner of container and contained, not like [two] things in contact." Here, Dignāga wants to say that *liṅga-liṅgi-sambandha* is not like *saṃyogi-saṃyogi-sambandha* in which the two relata are interchangeable. Rather, it should be regarded as an asymmetrical relationship, like that of container and contained. In other words, there is only a one-way direction in the case of *liṅga-liṅgi-sambandha*. See Hayes 1989: 247–248.

[50] See above, n. 7.

Kumārila continues to attack the idea that a word may refer to a thing possessing an *apoha*, now conceived, specifically, as a qualifier (*viśeṣaṇa*). In the background of the discussion could well be Dignāga's remark, PSV 5.36d, that "a word expresses entities precisely insofar as they are qualified by the negation of other referents."[51] For an *apoha* could only qualify something if it were cognized as qualifying it, and when someone utters a word such as "horse," there is no awareness of an *apoha* at all. So the meaning of the word could not be a thing qualified by the *apoha* of non-horse.

89 It is not the case that a qualifier that has a particular form could produce a cognition that has another form. And how could that [*apoha*, which is unreal] be called the qualifier when the cognition has a different form?

90 If there were a postulation of a qualifier even though something is qualified differently then it would follow that anything could be a qualifier [of that].

91 And if the thing qualified is understood to have the nature of non-existence, then it is not real. So there is not for you a real thing qualified by an *apoha* that is the meaning.

Moreover, if an *apoha* qualified a particular, since the *apoha* has the nature of a non-existence it would produce a cognition of the particular as something non-existent; it could not, qualifying it, produce a cognition of it as a real, existing thing. Indeed, if a qualifier produced a cognition of something as having a different nature from that of the qualifier, then anything could qualify anything without affecting how we perceive it. In light of all these considerations, the meaning of a word cannot be some real thing, even a particular, qualified by an *apoha*, and Dignāga's statement, PSV 5.36d, that "a word expresses entities precisely insofar as they are qualified by the negation of other referents" is refuted.

---

[51] *śabdo 'rthāntaranivṛttiviśiṣṭān eva bhāvān āha* (Pind 2015: I.45,2–3). See n. 48 above. See Pind 1999. The commentators do not, however, quote Dignāga's statement.

Kumārila continues to reflect on exactly what it is that is presented in a verbal cognition.

92 Even though the use of a word or inferential mark in regard to something devoid of an exclusion is not admissible, nevertheless,[52] the awareness of the knower has for its object a real thing.

93 Nor does a unique thing occur noticeably (*viparivartate*)[53] in [a verbal] cognition. Nor, since that [unique thing] is devoid of conceptualization, could it be what is designated.[54]

94 And it is rash to say that something not comprehended by a word [i.e., the unique individual] is the thing qualified [by an *apoha*]. Therefore, a [real] universal should be sought as the referent of the cognition and the word.

It is true that a word or inferential mark can never be applied to something devoid of an *apoha*, since all things have discrete, unmixed natures that exclude each other. Even the awareness of cowness, from the word "cow," is the awareness of something that excludes horses, elephants, and so forth. Nevertheless, the awareness of the knower that

---

[52] *tu* in 92c seems pleonastic together with *tathāpi*, so "nevertheless" could translate both. At the same time, the function of *tu* seems to be to highlight the contrast between reasoning (*yukti*), that is to say, arguments to the effect that words *must* refer to *apoha*s, and our actual awareness (*bodha*).

[53] Sucaritamiśra, ŚVKāś$_{K}$ 401(104),11, glosses: *ābhāsate*, "appears," Pārthasārathimiśra, ŚVN 417,29: *bhāsate*. The original meaning of *vi pari √vṛt* is "to roll (on the ground)." Cf. Manu 6.22a: *bhūmau viparivarteta* [...] /. "He [an ascetic] should roll on the ground." *buddhau vi pari √vṛt*, literally, something is "rolling" in a cognition, is often used in the sense "it appears/occurs/exists in cognition." The word "rolling" emphasizes the feeling that something does actually appear in our cognition.

[54] Note that Sucaritamiśra, ŚVKāś$_{K}$ 401(104),14, seems to favor *yuktā viśeṣyatā* in 93d. Perhaps this reading was suggested by *viśeṣyam iti* in 94b. All manuscripts have the reading *yuktābhidheyatā*. Thus, *abhidheyatā*, or possibly TS$_{Ś}$ 952d/TS$_{K}$ 953d, *adhigamyatā*, seems to be the original reading which Sucaritamiśra changed to *viśeṣyatā* to suit the context. It is the *lectio difficilior*.

arises from a word or inferential mark is of some real thing (*vastu*). This thing may indeed be distinct from other things, but it is something positive, not a negation. Moreover, the real thing in question cannot be just the particular; for what appears in a verbal cognition is an aspect of a real thing that it has in common with others, not something unique. Particulars, in fact, are said to be inexpressible, so how could a particular be apprehended as qualified by an *apoha* in a verbal cognition at all? And, as Kumārila has already explained, vv. 88–90, it would be ridiculous to suggest that a particular could be presented as qualified by an *apoha* in such a cognition without one being aware of it. Thus, it would seem that in a verbal cognition the real thing that is the object is a universal.[55]

---

[55] We have more or less followed Sucaritamiśra's interpretation. Both Pārthasārathimiśra and Jayamiśra (though not Sucarita) allude to PV 1.43 in their explanation of the position v. 92 is rejecting: *ekasyārthasvabhāvasya pratyakṣasya sataḥ svayam / ko 'nyo na dṛṣṭo bhāgaḥ syād yaḥ pramāṇaiḥ parīkṣyate //*. "If a thing's undivided (*eka*) nature is perceptible of itself, what other unperceived part would there be which [could] be examined by [other] valid cognitions?" Pārthasārathimiśra actually quotes the verse, ŚVN 417,18–19; Jayamiśra paraphrases the idea, ŚVŚar 52,7–9. Dharmakīrti is making the point here that perception already reveals the object completely in a positive way. Therefore, there is nothing left to be apprehended by language or inference than the exclusion of certain aspects of it from other things. Indeed, failing to ascertain that the object is distinct from other things, thinking it rather to be similar to them, one could easily be tempted to superimpose upon the object a common property it does not have. Thus, inference and language serve the purpose, in the first instance, of removing possible superimpositions of false predicates (PV 1.44). See PVSV 25,26–27,5.

Pārthaśārathimiśra and Jayamiśra interpret ŚV *Apohavāda* 92 to be responding to this idea by maintaining that, even though words and inferential marks may indicate objects that are excluded from others in different ways, the cognitions [of things possessing certain properties] that arise from them either *present* a real thing (Jayamiśra, ŚVŚar 52,10: *vastumātraṃ ca śabdaliṅgajñāne pratibhāsate*) that is, presumably, something positive, or else at least depend on one (Pārthaśārathimiśra, ŚVN 417,24: *vastv evālambate*) – despite the Buddhist avowal that that would not be suitable because the object has already been perceived in all of its aspects. In other words, *apohas* – *negative* entities – simply do not present themselves in verbal

5 What is excluded (*apohya*) must be something real.

Kumārila now turns his attention again to the *apohya*, what is excluded. Above, vv. 47–72, he focused on the *apohya* in discussing whether a difference of *apoha*s could be based on a difference of *apohya*s. Then, vv. 80–85ab, he focused on the logical relation between *apoha* and *apohya* – that is, cow and non-cow – arguing that one cannot be established without the other. Now he considers what it would mean for the *apohya* to be excluded by the *apoha*. He will emphasize that something real would have to be excluded, and since it could not be individuals it would have to be a real universal. If unreal things – that is, non-existences like *apoha*s – are what is excluded, then insuperable difficulties arise, which are particularly evident in the case of the word "existing."

95 And when individuals cannot be what is excluded because they are inexpressible by words, then a universal would be excluded. And because of its exclusion it is a real thing.

96 Nor are non-existences [i.e., unreal universals = *apoha*s] what is excluded, because then non-existences would give up being non-existent (*abhāvābhāvavarjanāt*).[56] Therefore, it is clear that this *apoha* [of cow, etc.] in another *apoha* [i.e., in

---

cognition. Thus, our experience contradicts the Buddhist reasoning that language and inference could apprehend only *apoha*s.

[56] Kamalaśīla records two interpretations of *abhāvābhāvavarjanāt*: (1) *abhāvānām abhāvarūpatyāgāt*, TSPś I.375,6, "because non-existences would abandon the nature of a non-existence," or (2) *abhāvānām abhāvābhāvāt*, TSPś I.375,9, "because non-existences are not non-existent" – that is to say, because it is not possible for *apoha*s, which have the nature of non-existences, to be the *apohya*, since what is negated must be a real thing (TSPś I.375,9–10: *na hy abhāvasvabhāvā apohā apohyā yujyante / vastuviṣayatvāt pratiṣedhasyeti yāvat /*).

what is considered the exclusion of non-horse = horse] is [the exclusion] of a real universal.[57]

Since individuals are inexpressible, they cannot be what is being excluded when one refers to "the exclusion of non-cow." Only some universal could be what is excluded, e.g., horseness. Since it is the object of the action of excluding, it must be a *real* universal, not an imaginary one (i.e., an *apoha*). If unreal universals, i.e., *apoha*s, were what is excluded, they would no longer be non-entities. Alternatively, considering the exclusion of non-horse = horse as the example, it must be a real universal such as cowness, etc., that is excluded as non-horse. Kumārila has already mentioned this problem in discussing whether *apoha*s could be differentiated on the basis of their *apohya*s, v. 64.

97 And the non-existence$_2$ of a non-existence$_1$ [i.e., the exclusion of something unreal$_1$] – if that [non-existence$_2$ = exclusion] were different from that [non-existence$_1$], then it would be something existing. If not, then for you it would follow that a cow is a non-cow!

Here is another argument for why what is excluded must be a real universal: If what is excluded were an imaginary universal and the exclusion of it were different from it, then the latter exclusion would be something real; for that which is different from what is unreal must be

---

[57] Sucaritamiśra explains, ŚVKāśK 316(5),3–4: *ataḥ siddham apohāntare 'naśvāpohābhimate sāmānyavastuna evāpohyatvaṃ na vyaktīnām, na cābhāvātmano 'pohasya* /. "Therefore it is established that in another *apoha*, which is thought to be the exclusion of non-horse, it is a real universal [cowness] that is to be excluded, not individuals, nor an *apoha*, which has the nature of non-existence." This agrees with Kamalaśīla's explanation, TSPś I.375,11–12: *tasmād vyaktaḥ sphuṭo 'pohāntare 'śvādāv apohāntarasya gavāder apoho bhavan sāmānyabhūtasyaiveti niścīyate* /. "Therefore, the *apoha* of cow, etc., which [in turn] is [supposedly] an *apoha*, existing in another *apoha*, namely, horse, and so forth, is ascertained clearly as [being the exclusion] of what has the status of a [real] universal." We believe that *apohyāntare* at ŚVŚar 53,16 should be emended to read *apohāntare*. This would yield the same interpretation: *tasmād avaśyaṃ yo 'yam apohāntare 'śvādirūpe parasmād vyāvṛttirūpo 'pohaḥ sa sāmānyasya vasturūpasyaivāṅgīkartavyaḥ* [...], ŚVŚar 53,16–17.

real. But the Buddhist wants to consider an exclusion a non-existence. If, on the other hand, the unreal universal to be excluded were not different from the exclusion, then non-cow would be the same as the exclusion of non-cow, which is the same as cow; so a non-cow would be the same as a cow!

98 Even if a real thing were the *apohya* in the case of other words, for the word "existing," on the other hand, that which is excluded is not considered distinct from what is called non-existence.

99 [If the opponent says that] in that case what is non-existent, too, is something existing, there would be a lot of trouble. [On the other hand] that [non-existent thing] not being established [as the *apohya* of the word "existing," insofar as it is nothing at all], there is no existence; and [existence not being established], non-existence is not established.

Even if one went along with the idea that for words like "cow" real things (like horse, etc.) are excluded, something real could not be excluded in the case of the word *sat*, "existing." The meaning of *sat*, according to the *apoha* theory, would be the exclusion of *non-existent* things. Hence, what is to be excluded, for *sat*, is something non-existent, and this gives rise to the following problem. If non-existent things somehow existed, insofar as they are *apohya*s (*objects* of exclusion; for being an object implies reality), then there would be no distinction between what exists and what doesn't. If on the other hand the non-existent things excluded by *sat* did not exist, then existence – that is, the exclusion of non-existent things – would be nothing, too! In that case, one would land in the situation of not being able to predicate either existence or non-existence of things. Sucarita continues: in that case – if there is no being or non-being – even the self, Īśvara, or *pradhāna*, which are the primary existents, could not be said to exist.[58]

[58] ŚVKāś$_K$ 315(6),13–15.

6 Further problems

Kumārila now returns to consider other problems having to do with *apoha*s themselves, including both meaning-*apoha*s and, as we shall see, word-*apoha*s. Here, he seems concerned with bringing out some of the more far-reaching implications of the Apohavāda.

One of the main objections Kumārila has developed up to this point is that there is no way to distinguish *apoha*s, since they are not real things; hence on the Apohavāda all words would be synonymous (see vv. 44-46). Perhaps, however, the distinguishing of *apoha*s and *apohya*s, exclusions and things excluded, from each other is grounded on beginningless impressions (*vāsanā*s). That is to say, differences among *apoha*s and among *apohya*s are *imagined* due to *vāsanā*s. Therefore, the problem that all words mean the same thing because their *apoha*s cannot be distinguished would be dispelled. *vāsanā*s could also be the reason why *apoha*s, which are in fact non-entities, are mistakenly apprehended as the real aspects of things in verbal and inferential awareness.[59]

---

[59] Sucaritamiśra gives the Buddhist *pūrvapakṣa in extenso*, ŚVKāśK 314(7),1–313(8),2:

atra bauddhā vadanti / kim idaṃ vāstavam ivāpohāpohyabhedaṃ vyavahāra-bhedaṃ manvānair dūṣaṇam abhidhīyate / vāsanāmātranirmitaḥ khalv ayam apohānām apohyānāṃ ca bhedaḥ / asti hy anādikālapravṛttā śabdārtheṣv eva bhedavāsanā / sodbhūtā satī teṣāṃ bhedam ivādarśayati / ata eva paryāyatvādi-prasaṅgaparihāro 'pi, vāsanaiva śabdārthānām avastubhūtānām api bhedam āpādayati yataḥ / yadā hi vyāvṛttasvabhāveṣu svalakṣaṇeṣu parasparam asaṃkīrṇāny anugatāni sāmānyāni na pramāṇabalopapannāni, tadā kathaṃ nāmānyathā śabdārthānāṃ bhedam abhidhāsyāmo 'nyato vasanābhedād / ata evāsadrūpāviśeṣe 'py apohyāpohabhedapratyayaḥ / so 'pi hi vāsanāmātrakārita eva, na vastulakṣaṇaḥ / vāstavas tu svalakṣaṇānām eva bhedaḥ / sa ca sajātīya-vijātīyānām aviśiṣṭa eveti na śabdārthavyūhabhedam āpādāyitum alam /

yat tūktaṃ bodhas tu jñātur vastv avalambata iti, tatrāpi vāsanaiva ni-bandhanam / saiva hy asadrūpān apy apohān vasturūpān iva darśayati, tathaivānādikālapravṛtteḥ / ato yad eva kiṃcid iha siddhānte durghaṭaṃ, tad eva vāsanānusāreṇa śakyasamādhānam /.

Kumārila will now reject *vāsanā*s as the solution to the problem of the distinction of both meaning-*apoha*s and word-*apoha*s, principally on the grounds that even a *vāsanā* presupposes an original experience of a real thing. As he goes on to present other arguments against the distinction of *apoha*s, the disastrous consequences of the Apohavāda become evident. Not only would it entail that all words are synonymous; it would entail that one word could not be distinguished from another. Nor would there even be a distinction between words and meanings. Thus, a particular word could not be the indicator of a particular meaning. The entire system of words, meanings, and things excluded would collapse.

To this, Buddhists say: What is this criticism which is stated by those who consider a [merely] practical distinction of exclusions and of what are excluded to be a real distinction? For this difference of exclusions and of what are excluded is brought about merely by a *vāsanā*. For there is a *vāsanā* of difference for words and meanings which has functioned since beginningless time. Once it arises it reveals them as if they have a difference. Precisely for this [reason], the unwanted consequence of synonymy, and so forth, is refuted, too, since that very *vāsanā* brings about a difference of words and of meanings, even though they are unreal; for when, in particulars which have natures that are excluded [from each other], common universals which are not intermingled (*asamkīrṇa*) with each other are not justified by a *pramāṇa*, then how indeed will we indicate a difference of words and of meanings otherwise than due to a difference of *vāsanā*? Precisely for this [reason], even though they have the same non-existent nature, there is a cognition of the difference of exclusions and of what are excluded; for that [difference], too, is caused just by the *vāsanā*; it does not have the character of something real. But the difference of particulars is real. And since that [difference] is the same [both] for particulars that are similar and dissimilar, it cannot bring about a difference of a multitude of words and of meanings.

As for what is said, "The awareness of the knower has for its object a real thing" (ŚV *Apohavāda* 92c'd) – a *vāsanā* is the cause of that, too; for it reveals exclusions, even though they are unreal, as real, since it has functioned that way since beginningless time. Thus, whatever is difficult to establish regarding this *siddhānta* [of ours] can be answered by appeal to *vāsanā*.

6.1 Ideas of distinct *apoha*s could not be produced by *vāsanā*s.

100 Nor could a difference of *apoha*s or their having a real nature be conceived as being due to a difference of *vāsanā*s; for there cannot be a *vāsanā* in regard to something unreal.

101 And [a *vāsanā*] does not have the capacity for another action besides memory. Therefore, that does not produce a cognition of one type in regard to a thing of another type.

A *vāsanā* of the difference of *apoha*s would have to be deposited by some previous experience. But there are no real, distinct *apoha*s, experiences of which could have produced it. Nor could experiences of real, distinct particulars somehow give rise to a *vāsanā* that causes one to think that *unreal apoha*s are different from each other. In general, a *vāsanā* produces just a memory of something previously experienced.[60] If it were somehow based on an *unreal apoha*, how could it present it as something real? And how could it derive from the experience of a *real* universal, since according to the Buddhist there is no such thing?[61]

6.2 If words are *apoha*s, then like meanings they could not be distinct from each other; consequently, there could be no relation between word and meaning.

Now Kumārila takes up the problem of word-universals. Not only must the meaning of a word be some kind of universal, the word itself must

---

[60] ŚVŚar 55,6–7: [...] *pūrvavijñānaviṣayākārabuddhijanitā hi vāsanā nāpratipannākārabuddhijanitā* /. "[...] For an impression is the producer of a cognition that has as its content the object of a previous cognition; it does not produce a cognition whose content was not [previously] cognized."

[61] The idea of the reality of *apoha*s and their distinctions being based on *vāsanā*s seems to anticipate the role Dharmakīrti assigns to *vāsānā*s in the arising of conceptual awareness (*vikalpa*). Dharmakīrti, however, sees a *vāsānā* chiefly as responsible for the conceptual awareness apprehending its object as non-different from other particulars and as external. See, e.g., PVSV 42,13–22; 38,17–39, 4. He does not appeal to *vāsānā*s to explain differences among *apoha*s.

also be a universal. For we recognize the same word "cow" everytime "cow" is uttered.[62] First, continuing his critique of *vāsanā*s, he argues that cognitions of word-universals could not be caused by *vāsanā*s.

102 You [Buddhists] do not obtain a difference among words[63] based on that [*vāsanā*], either. For a unique word is not expressive, because it has not been seen before.

The cognition of a particular word, e.g. "cow"$_1$, can deposit only the *vāsanā* that will later give rise to the idea of only that same word, i.e., "cow"$_1$. Therefore, another token word-utterance "cow"$_2$ will not be expressive of any meaning, since, not having been experienced before, no relation between it and a meaning has been established;[64] for what was experienced before was "cow"$_1$ and not "cow"$_2$.

103 Moreover, because [individual words] are distinct, a single *vāsanā* certainly cannot be produced (*prakalpyate*) by them. And [for you Buddhists] there is not a single real word [i.e., a word-universal "cow"] that will produce a *vāsanā*.

Since all word-particulars are different, the words we group together under the same word-type – different tokens of the word "cow," for instance – could not produce a *vāsanā* that will give rise to a cognition that has one form. Such a *vāsanā* could derive from a real word-

---

[62] This was already understood by the ancient grammarians. See Pind 1991: 176.

[63] Kamalaśīla, Sucaritamiśra, and Jayamiśra understand *śabdabheda* as the mutual difference of words. Pārthasārathimiśra, however, understands it to mean the difference of words from the meaning. ŚVN 419,19: *vācyād vācakānām api na vāsanānimitto bhedaḥ sidhyati* /. "Nor is a difference of expressions from the meaning caused by *vāsanā*s, either." Perhaps *vācyād* should emended to *vācyavad*? ŚV *Apohavāda* 104 in any case (specifically, *śabdāntarāpoha* in 104a) supports the former reading.

[64] ŚVŚar 55,17–18: *na ca nirvikalpakagrāhyeṇa rūpeṇa śabdo 'rthaṃ pratipādayati tasya sambandhādarśanāt* /. "And a word does not cause one to cognize a meaning by means of the form [of the word] that is grasped by a non-conceptual [perception], because the connection of that [form with the meaning] has not been observed."

universal, but the Buddhist does not believe in such a thing.

104 In that case, the [word-]universal [in the form of] an exclusion of other words being imagined, a difference of words will not be obtained, because [that universal] is not real, in precisely the same way [as for meanings].[65]

If a distinction between words cannot be based on *vāsanā*s produced by individual words, one might assume that there are distinct word-universals in the form of *apoha*s, as in fact Dignāga argues PS(V) 5.33ab.[66] But *unreal* word-universals could not account for distinctions among words any more than unreal meaning-universals could account for distinctions among meanings.

105 And as [there is no difference] for words, so [there is no difference] of a word and a meaning from each other. And it has been proven [in vv. 47 ff.] that there is no difference [of *apoha*s] due to a difference of *apohya*s.

Just as unreal word-universals cannot be distinguished from each other, unreal word-universals and unreal meaning-universals cannot be distinguished from each other. Kumārila proceeds to point out that this threatens the very possibility of communication.

106-107a And a word-*apoha* that is not apprehended [when the word is used][67] does not in any way make [a meaning]

---

[65] ŚVŚar 56,6–7: *arthasāmānyānām iva.*

[66] Pind 2015: I.38,5–39,2. For discussion see Pind 1991.

[67] We follow Sucaritamiśra's interpretation. Jayamiśra interprets *agṛhīta* in 106a as referring to the time of learning the relationship (**saṃbandhagrahaṇakāle* – he does not use this expression, however). He states, ŚVŚar 56,16–17: *yathā cāpohasya pūrvam agṛhītasya śabdena pratyāyyatvaṃ nāstīty uktam evaṃ śabdāpohasyāpi vācakatvam api vācyam* /. "Just as it was said that an *apoha* which has not been apprehended previously cannot be made known by a word, so is it to be said of the expressiveness of a *śabda-apoha*, too." Jayamiśra, in other words, thinks *agṛhīta* is applicable to both *artha-apoha* and *śabda-apoha*. But there is no

known. And perception is not capable of that, nor is there an inferential mark or a word due to which there would be an apprehension of it.

107bcd And if an inferential mark, etc. [i.e., a word] is postulated [as the means of apprehending a word-*apoha*], then in this way, without perception [of a real universal] as a basis, it is to be said that there is no stopping.[68]

If the word is a word-*apoha*, there would be no means of knowing it; and in that case it would not convey its meaning. First of all, an *apoha* cannot be known by perception. If one, then, maintained that a word-*apoha* could be recognized by a word or inferential mark, then since that word or inferential mark is also an *apoha*, which would have to be apprehended through another word or inferential mark, one would be off on a regress.

108 On your view there would not be a relation of that which makes something known and the thing that is known for two *apoha*s [namely, a word-*apoha* and a meaning-*apoha*], because they are not real, like a sky-flower and a rabbit's horn in the world.

Kumārila shows again, now by means of a formal proof (*prayoga*), that on the *apoha* view communication would be impossible. On the *apoha* view, there cannot be a relation of indicator and thing-indicated

---

hint of such a parallelism by Kumārila here in vv. 106–107. (Jayamiśra may, however, have in mind Kumārila's argument in vv. 73–74 that a meaning-*apoha* cannot be grasped by language or inference, contrary to what Buddhists allege.) Rather it seems that Kumārila is pointing out a unique problem about *śabda-apoha*. Also the usage *agṛhīta* and not some other expression equivalent to *agṛhītasaṃbandha* suggests that this refers to the time of application and not the time of learning.

[68] 107c: *na vyavastheti vācyaivam*. *vācyā* agrees with *vyavasthā* inside the *iti* clause. Thus, Sucaritamisra suggests, ŚVKāśK 309(12),1–2: *vyavasthā "na" ity anena prakāreṇa vācyety arthaḥ* /. "The meaning is: a stopping is to be described in the manner of 'not.'" Jayamiśra also construes the phrase in this way, ŚVŚar 57,3: *vyavasthā nety anvayaḥ kāryaḥ* /. It is difficult to replicate this syntax in English. Kumārila's Sanskrit here, in fact, seems awkward.

(*gamya-gamaka-bhāva*), which is supposed to be exhibited by words and their meanings and inferential marks and what is inferred from them, because both that which is to be indicated and that which indicates it, being *apoha*s, are unreal.

109 If one were to say [the reason given, "because they are not real"] is inconclusive because of the observation of [the relation of] the absences of rain and clouds, [then] in this case, too, [each absence] is indeed a real thing, according to my view. On your view, how is even that [relation of revealer and revealed between the absence of clouds and the absence of rain] possible?

The opponent might object to the above proof by maintaining that it is possible for the absence of one thing to indicate the absence of another: the absence of clouds indicates the absence of rain. Kumārila points out, however, that on his view absences or non-existences are real entities; for instance, the absence of clouds is the existence of the surface of the sky and the absence of rain a property of the ground upon which no rain is falling.

6.3 An *apoha* presupposes some support (*āśraya*) which is real.

Kumārila now raises another objection against the view that word-universals are *apoha*s.

110 And for someone who does not assume a meaning of a word that is positive (*vidhirūpa*), there would not be a difference [of the word "horse" from the word "cow"],[69] either; for that [difference] is dependent on that.

If word-universals were *apoha*s, they would be defined by their

[69] ŚVKāśK 308(13),10–11: *na cāyaṃ gośabdavyatireko 'gośabda ityevamātmā vidhirūpaṃ gośabdam antareṇa sidhyati* /. "And this distinction from the word cow consisting in [a recognition] of the sort, 'It is not the word cow,' is not established without a word 'cow' which is positive in nature."

difference from other words. Now if the word "cow," e.g., is determined as being different from words that are not "cow," the latter words must be ascertained as "not the word 'cow'." But if "the word 'cow'" has no positive meaning of its own, the expression "not the word 'cow'" will have no meaning either. Or else, there will be mutual presupposition: "the word 'cow'" presupposes "not the word 'cow'" and *vice versa*. This verse essentially applies the argument of 85ab, which targets meaning-*apoha*s, to word-*apoha*s.

111 The non-existence of a non-existent thing which is due to a connection with two negations [and which pertains to the word "cow," insofar as one thinks: "The word 'cow' is not what is not the word 'cow,'"] – that, too, would pertain to something real (*savastuka*), not something empty (*tuccha*), because of the impossibility of a cognition of it.

As Kumārila has explained (vv. 1-2), a non-existence or absence must have a support (*āśraya*). Thus, even the non-existence of a non-existence must belong to something real.[70] In general, anything capable of causing a cognition must be in some sense real.

112 [Objection:] But isn't it the case that by this very argument [namely, that unreal *apoha*s do not differ from each other] this [*apoha*] does not differ from something real, either; thus the previously stated mistake [of there not being any difference between *apoha*s] will not arise?

113ab [Reply:] In this way, what is believed by me would be established, for there is no other possibility.

An opponent might argue that if one *apoha* does not differ from another because it is not real, then it would not differ from what is real, either!

---

[70] ŚVN 421,4-5: [...] *nirāśrayasyābhāvasya buddhyasambhavāt* /. "[...] For the cognition of a non-existence without a support is impossible." He refers back (loc. cit.) to ŚV *Apohavāda* 64cd: *apohyamāne cābhāve bhāva evāviśiṣyate* /.

In that case, *apoha*s, being real, could differ from each other after all![71] This tactic, however, would be tantamount to accepting the Mīmāṃsā view that an *apoha* is indeed an absence, and an absence is a property of an existing thing, so that it is not completely different from something real.

113cd [And if an *apoha* does not really differ from something real,] there is either a[n erroneous] cognition of something real [namely, a universal extending over many things] with respect to a non-existence, or else a cognition of non-existence with respect to something real.

114 In regard to that, if it has the nature of a non-existence, then the idea of a real thing is completely baseless. On the other hand, the awareness of non-existence in regard to something real is established [in *Abhāvapariccheda*], but it is dependent on another.

If the opponent identifies the *apoha* with a real thing (*vastu*) (Dharmakīrti for instance will say that the *svalakṣaṇa* is the basis of the *apoha* and the latter is not really distinct from it), then we have to consider how best to describe the situation. In cognizing the meaning of a word, is one grasping an absence as a real universal (*abhāve vastubuddhiḥ*), or is one grasping a real universal as an absence, that is, an *apoha* (*vastuny abhāvadhīḥ*) – since universals, after all, do differ from each other? Of these two alternatives, the second is more reasonable; for an error must have a real basis.[72]

---

[71] The theory that exclusion (*vyāvṛtti*) and the thing excluded (*vyāvṛtta*) are the same thing is developed by Dharmakīrti, PV(SV) 1.59–63. See Hugon 2017.

[72] Pārthasārathi explains ad loc., since an *apoha* cannot have a unique thing as its *āśraya*, the dispute amounts to this: whether there is erroneously the idea of a real thing in regard to a universal that has the nature of an *abhāva*, or whether there is the idea of a non-existence in regard to a *real* universal (ŚVN 421,24–26: *kim abhāvātmake sāmānye bhrāntyā vastubuddhiḥ, kiṃ vā vasturūpe sāmānye 'śvo na bhavatīty abhāvabuddhir iti |*). Now an *apoha*, which is a non-existence, cannot be

7 A word does not refer to an *apoha* by itself (*apohamātra*).

Now Kumārila considers various options how an *apoha* could be referred to by a word. Could a word refer just to the *apoha* itself? Could it refer to the object possessing the *apoha*? Or the connection with it? By eliminating all of these options – as Dignāga did for the universal in PS 5 – Kumārila proves that *apoha* cannot be the meaning.

V. 115 marks the beginning of Kumārila's detailed critique of the fifth chapter of Dignāga's *Pramāṇasamuccaya*, which continues up to v. 164.

115-116c' But if it is assumed that the *apoha* alone is the meaning, then the relation of qualifier and qualificand and coreference are not established for [words] like "blue lotus,"[73] which express complex things (*śabalārthābhidhāyin*),

116c'-117ab for it is not the case there is the abandonment of non-lotus in the exclusion of non-blue. Nor is the other [i.e., the exclusion of non-blue] in that [abandonment of non-lotus]. Therefore, they are not qualifier and qualificand.

In the fifth chapter of his *Pramāṇasamuccaya*, beginning with PS 5.2cd,[74] Dignāga rejects the view that general terms refer to "genera"

---

the basis of a cognition; it has been shown, moreover, that a *vāsanā* cannot be its cause (*nimitta*), either. The cognition of a non-existence in regard to a real universal is possible, however, because real universals do in fact differ from each other; for real things have the nature of being the non-existence of each other (*vastūnām itaretarābhāvātmakatvāt*, ŚVN 422,1).

[73] The expression "blue lotus" in Sanskrit is the single compound word *nīlotpalam*.

[74] PS(V) 5.2cd: *na*(PSV) ... *vācako yogajātyor vā bhedārthair apṛthakśruteḥ* / (Pind 2015: I.3,6). "[Nor] does [the word *sat*] denote the connection or the genus, either, because it is heard together with [words] that have differences as their meanings." A "difference" is a particular kind of existing thing, such as a substance (e.g., a pot), a quality, etc.

(*jāti*) or universals[75] on the grounds that, if they did, coreference (*sāmānādhikaraṇya*) and qualification (*viśeṣaṇaviśeṣyabhāva*) would be impossible. In PSV 5.2cd he points out that a genus like existence (*sattā*) is neither a substance nor a quality, but rather *is possessed* by a substance or a quality.[76] Hence, if the word "existing" referred to existence, it could not be used coreferentially with words that refer to substances, qualities, or motions in expressions such as "an existing substance" (or "an existing pot," Dignāga's usual example), "an existing quality," or "an existing motion."[77] Later, at PS 5.19abc, he points out that the property blue and the genus "lotus" cannot relate to each other as qualifier and qualificand, either. Even if both occurred in the same substratum, so that the words "blue" and "lotus" could actually be coreferential, blueness and lotusness still would not be related to each other;[78] for, as Dignāga has said earlier (PS 5.11b), "a genus does not

---

[75] When discussing Dignāga's theory in PS 5 we shall, as a rule, render *jāti* as "genus"; elsewhere, especially in the translation of Kumārila's text, we have consistently used "universal" (see, e.g., ŚV *Apohavāda* 19b, 59d, 60cd, and 130a). *jāti*, however, appears to be roughly synonymous with the terms Kumārila uses for a (real) universal: *sāmānya* and *ākṛti*. Cf. ŚV *Ākṛtivāda* 18: *tenātmadharmo bhedānām ekadhīviṣayo 'sti naḥ / sāmānyam ākṛtir jātiḥ śaktir vā so 'bhidhīyatām //*. "Therefore, there is according to us [Mīmāṃsakas] a property of the nature of [diverse] individuals which is the object of a cognition of one thing (*eka*); let it be called *sāmānya*, *ākṛti*, *jāti*, or *śakti*."

[76] PSV 5.2cd: *na hi sattā* [...] *dravyaṃ guṇo vā bhavati, kiṃ tarhi dravyasya guṇasya vā* (Pind 2015: I.4,1–3). "For existence [...] is neither a substance nor a quality; rather it is *of* a substance or quality."

[77] Dignāga quotes VP 3.14.8 in this context, which states that the words that denote *guṇa* and *guṇin* are not grammatically coordinate, like *sad dravyam*, but rather should have different case-endings: *vyaktibhedo niyamād guṇaguṇyabhidhāyinoḥ / sāmānādhikaraṇyasya prasiddhir dravyaśabdayoḥ //*. "[Words] expressing a quality and the bearer of the quality have different case endings, due to a restriction [of function]. Coreference [i.e., having the same case ending] of words for substances is commonly acknowledged." (Cf. Pind 2015: II.16–17.)

[78] PSV 5.19abc: *yady api hi nīlaguṇotpalajātyor ekatra dravye vṛtteḥ sāmānādhikaraṇyaṃ syāt, na viśeṣaṇaviśeṣyabhāvaḥ* (Pind 2015: I.22,10–23,1).

possess [another] genus."[79] Hence, if words referred just to genera a compound like "blue lotus," which implies a qualifier-qualificand relationship, would not be possible.

Here, Kumārila is simply turning this same reasoning against the *apoha* theory. Specifically for the qualifier-qualificand relation, just as blueness does not exist in lotusness, so the exclusion of non-blue things does not exist in the exclusion of non-lotuses and vice versa. Thus, on the *apoha* theory as well, by Dignāga's own reasoning, words like "blue" and "lotus" could not be used to qualify each other.

117cd Nor would those [being qualifier and qualificand] exist for two words independently of what they designate.

After having pointed out that both coreference and qualification are impossible for *meanings* (*artha*) if they are taken to be genera, Dignāga states PS(V) 5.20ab that both are impossible for words (*śabda*) as well: "Similarly [both are impossible] for two words which denote just the genus of a substance and its property, respectively."[80] Here Kumārila

---

"Even if there were coreference because the quality blue and the genus 'lotus' reside in the same substance [there would] not [be] a qualifier-qualificand relation." Pind translates the continuation of the *Vṛtti*, based on his own reconstruction of the text, as follows: "For the quality blue (**nīlaguṇasya*) has no relation to the general property lotusness (**utpalajātiyogaḥ*), nor has the general property lotusness (**utpalajāteḥ*) any relation to the quality blue (**nīlaguṇayogaḥ*)" (Pind 2015: II.73; see n. 258 for Jinendrabuddhi's explanation). As Jayamiśra says, the genus "existing" does not exist in the genus "pot" (*ghaṭādijātau sadādijātir nāsti*, ŚVŚar 59,7); similarly, Sucaritamiśra says that the genus "blue" does not inhere in the genus "lotus" (*notpalajātau nīlajātiḥ samavaiti*, ŚVKāś$_K$ 304[17],9–10).

[79] PS 5.11b: [...] *jāter ajātitaḥ* (Pind 2015: I.13,7). Cf. Pind 2015: II.50-51: "[...] because a general property is without general properties." See Pind 2015: II.51, n. 168.

[80] Pind translates PS 5.20ab as follows: "So also with respect to the two words that denote the mere general property and the mere quality" (Pind 2015: II.75). He has not attempted to restore the Sanskrit. Our own tentative restoration, based on the Tibetan translations, is: **tathā dravyajātiguṇamātravācakaśabdayoḥ*. Jinendrabuddhi explains ad PSV 5.20ab: *viśeṣaṇaviśeṣyabhāvo 'pi jātiguṇavācinoḥ*

makes the same point against the *apoha* view. The words "blue" and "lotus" could not be used as qualifier and qualificand independently of their meanings standing in such a relation to each other.[81]

118 And there would not be coreference [of the two words "blue" and "lotus"], because the two *apoha*s are different. If [coreference] were believed to be due to the thing [i.e., the concrete particular which is the locus of both *apoha*s], of what sort would be their status as predicates?

Having explained how two words such as "blue" and "lotus" cannot be used as qualifier and qualificand if a word refers just to the *apoha*, Kumārila now argues that they could not even be used coreferentially. For if two words like "blue" and "lotus" refer to *apoha*s, they will have different meanings, as Dignāga himself admits at PS 5.14a.[82] "Blue"

śabdayor nopapadyate. arthadvārako hi tayor viśeṣaṇaviśeṣyabhāvaḥ. tadarthayoś ca jātiguṇayor na kaścanābhisambandhaḥ (Pind 2015: II.75, n. 269). "A qualifier-qualificand relation between two words that denote a genus and a quality is not justified. For the qualifier-qualificand relation of the two [words] is caused by [their] referents. And there is no relation between their two referents, namely, the genus and the quality" (cf. Pind 2015 loc. cit.).

[81] As Jayamiśra explains, a qualifier-qualificand relation among meanings could not be caused by concepts engendered just by the use of certain words, for a cognition without an object is impossible, ŚVŚar 59,9–10: *na ca śabdaviśeṣajanitavikalpanimitta evāyam ity parituṣya sthātavyam nirālambanabuddhyanupapatter ity āha* [...] /. "Nor can one be content that this [qualifier-qualificand relation] is caused by concepts produced just by certain words, because a cognition without an object is unjustified. Thus, he says [...]."

Although it is clear from his *Vṛtti* that Dignāga understands PS 5.20ab to be denying the possibility of coreference and qualification for words that indicate mere universals, the commentators concur in construing the dual form (*nāpi te syātām*, "nor would those two exist") in 117c as referring back to qualifier and qualificand (*viśeṣyaviśeṣaṇe*) in 117b, with the minor difference that Jayamiśra takes *te* as the genitive second person personal pronoun (*te na viśeṣaṇaviśeṣyabhāva ity arthaḥ*, ŚVŚar 59,9).

[82] PS 5.14a: *apohyabhedād bhinnārthāḥ* [...] (Pind 2015: I.16,7), "[Even though words] have different meanings because they exclude different things [...]." This,

will refer to the exclusion of non-blue things, and "lotus" will refer to the exclusion of non-lotuses.[83]

At PSV 5.14, however, Dignāga states, plausibly enough, that "words like 'blue' and 'lotus,' even though the things they exclude are different [so that they have different meanings], become coreferential by bringing together each of their meanings, i.e., *apoha*s, into one referent (*ekatra*) in order to specify their meanings, like height and a crow's nest."[84] That is to say, it is not by virtue of their meanings being the same, but by virtue of their meanings being located in the same thing that the two words are coreferential. Yet, Kumārila continues, how could those meanings have the same locus (*adhikaraṇa*) – say, some particular that is a blue lotus – if they are *apoha*s? For *apoha*s are non-entities, which cannot be located anywhere or inhere in anything; hence,

---

of course, overlooks the problems with basing a distinction of *apoha*s on their *apohya*s that Kumārila has brought out above, vv. 47 ff.

[83] This is Kamalaśīla's interpretation. Jayamiśra understands coreference to be impossible because one *apoha* cannot *inhere* in the other, ŚVŚar 59,12–13: *paras-parasamavāyitvābhāvenaiva nīlotpalāpohayor jātyor iva sāmānādhikaraṇyam api pratikṣiptam ity āha* [...] /. "Coreference of the exclusions of blue and lotus, too, like universals, is rejected, because one does not inhere in the other. Thus, he says [...] ."

[84] PSV 5.14: *nīlotpalādiśabdā hi saty apy apohyabhede svārthaviśeṣa-vyañjanārtham ūrdhvatākākanilayavat svam apohārtham ekatropasaṃharantaḥ samānādhikaraṇā bhavanti* (Pind 2015: I.16,9–17,2). Although two items cognized separately are the cause of doubt, they can become the cause of ascertainment when cognized together. In darkness, when one perceives mere uprightness (*ūrdhvatā*), one doubts whether it is a post or a man. Similarly, the idea of a crow's nest by itself is cause of the doubt whether it is on the ground or on top of a post. When the two items are combined, however, they cause an ascertainment that the thing being perceived is a post on top of which there is a bird's nest. NĀA 722,25–26: *yatho-rdhvatvaṃ sāmānyaṃ sthāṇuḥ syāt puruṣaḥ syād iti saṃśayahetuḥ, śakuninilaya-naṃ sthāṇur eva iti niścayahetur viśiṣṭatvāt* /. "Just as the universal uprightness is the cause of doubt, 'It could be a post, it could be a man,' a bird's nest is cause of the ascertainment, 'It is a post,' because [uprightness] is specified." Cf. Pind 2015: II.61 for a similar explanation by Jinendrabuddhi. Cf. also ŚV *Anumāna* 94cd–95ab: *kvacit saṃśayahetū yau pratyekatvena lakṣitau // saṃghāte nirṇayas tābhyām ūrdhvatākākavattvavat* /, and ŚV *Vākya* 363: *padārthā gamayanty etaṃ pratyekaṃ saṃśaye sati / sāmastye nirṇayotpādāt sthāṇum ūrdhvasthakākavat* //.

they cannot be predicates.[85] The realist, on the other hand, thinks that it is two real universals inhering in the same individual that allows one to predicate both "blue" and "lotus" of it, so this is not a problem for him.[86]

119 And a unique, real thing [which might serve as the locus of both *apoha*s] is not comprehended [in a conceptual cognition, so that both *apoha*s being known to be situated in that individual, both words could be used coreferentially]. And there is not something else for you [i.e., a real universal that could serve as the locus of the two *apoha*s]. With regard to what can two words having the same reference be useful, if it is not known?

If in fact the meanings of two words are located in the same object, but the object is not known because, being a particular, it cannot appear in a conceptual cognition, how could that explain both words being used coreferentially?

8 A word does not refer to a real thing possessing an *apoha* (*apohavad vastu*).

Having refuted the view that the *apoha* alone is the meaning, Kumārila now turns to the idea that it is the thing possessing the *apoha*. This in fact seems to have been Dignāga's preferred view.[87]

---

[85] ŚVŚar 59,16: *samavāyāsambhavāt*. That is to say, it is not just because one *apoha* cannot inhere in another that words indicating *apoha*s could not be coreferential, but because *apoha*s could not inhere in anything at all, not even the same individual.

[86] At PS(V) 5.14 Dignāga is concerned with how both coreference and qualification are possible if words refer to *apoha*s. While Kumārila appears to be addressing PS 5.14 here in vv. 118–119, he is focusing just on the problem of coreference, having dealt with the issue of qualification (for the *apohamātra* view) already in vv. 116c'd–117.

[87] As implied, e.g., at PS(V) 5.36cd. After arguing that the *apoha*-possessor view does not fall prey to the same objections as the universal-possessor view,

120 Or else, it is stated that a real thing possessing an *apoha* (*apohavad vastu*) is the meaning. In that case, too, inclusion (*vyāpti*) by a word is difficult to obtain because it is dependent on something else.

At PS 5.4a, after dispatching the theories that a word refers just to the genus or the connection with the genus, Dignāga criticizes the idea that a word refers to something possessing the genus or universal (*jātimat*/*tadvat*): "[A word does not denote] the possessor of that [genus], because it is dependent."[88] That is to say, if a word like "existing" (*sat*) referred, not just to existence itself, but to a substance possessing existence, then it would not refer just to the substance "directly" or "independently"; rather its use would be mediated by reference to the genus, which by itself does not imply any differences. "Existing," then, would not imply something possessing other more specific genera such as potness, cowness, and so on; that is to say, it would not imply or "include" a pot (something possessing potness). Similarly for the word "pot." Hence, the two words "existing" and "pot," on such a theory, could not be used coreferentially.[89]

Dignāga concludes: *evaṃ pūrvoktadoṣābhāvād guṇotkarṣāc ca śabdo 'rthāntaranivṛttiviśiṣṭān eva bhāvān āha* (Pind 2015: I.45,1–3). "In this way, since the mentioned problems do not exist and the merits [of a word denoting an exclusion] are superior, a word expresses entities precisely insofar as they are qualified by the negation of other referents." That this was Dignāga's preferred interpretation of the *apohavāda* is also suggested by Siṃhasūri; see Pind 2015: II.150, n.465. Tillemans 2011b, however, seems to think that it was Bhāviveka who came up with the *tadvadvāda* (i.e., *apohavadvāda*) that Dharmakīrti would later defend at PV(SV) 1.64 (see also Hugon 2017). The fact that Kumārila devotes a whole section here to refuting this theory, in any case, implies that *he* believed it was an alternative entertained by Dignāga, even if it was not his preferred view. A more precise understanding of how Dignāga thought the two views, *apohamātravāda* and *apohavadvāda*, relate to each other requires further investigation of PS 5 based on a critical edition of Jinendrabuddhi's commentary.

[88] PS 5.4a: *tadvato nāsvatantratvāt* (Pind 2015: I.5,6).

[89] Thus, PSV 5.4a: *evam api hi sacchabdo jātisvarūpamātropasarjanaṃ dra-*

Here, Kumārila develops a critique of the *apohavat* view that parallels Dignāga's refutation of the *jātimat/tadvat* view. In fact, his move from criticism of the *apohamātra* theory (vv. 115 ff.) to criticism of the *apohavat* theory (vv. 120 ff.) mimics Dignāga's move from a critique of the *jātimātra* theory (PS 5.2cd) to a refutation of the *tad*[=*jāti*]*vat* theory (5.4a). In his commentary on PS 5.4a Dignāga refers to the case of the words *śukla* "white" and *madhura* "sweet." On the *jātimat/tadvat* view, he argues, "white" means whatever is white but does not necessarily imply sweet – since it would indicate a white thing only insofar as it is qualified by whiteness – and vice versa; so one term would not include the meaning of the other. Thus, one could not use them coreferentially, say, to refer to sugar as "sweet [and] white." But the Apohavādin, or more precisely the Apohavadvādin, will have a similar problem. The next two verses state the argument.

121-122 Just as by "sweet" [and "white"] used in regard to sugar, there is no implication or qualification [of one by the other], due to the absence of the inclusion of white, etc., because they have different *apohya*s – so when there is ascertainment of a thing delimited by the aspect of exclusion of non-existent things (*asadvyudāsāṃśavicchinnārthāva-*

---

vyam āha, na sākṣād iti tadgataghaṭādibhedānākṣepād atadbhedatve sāmānādhikaraṇyābhāvaḥ (Pind 2015: I.6,1–3). "In this way, too, the word 'existing' expresses a substance to which merely the genus and the form of the [word itself] are subordinate; [it does] not express it directly. Hence, because it does not imply the differences pot, and so forth, that belong to that [thing possessing the genus, they] would not be its differences, in which case there would be no coreference [with the word 'pot', etc.]" (cf. Pind 2015: II.22–24). (For Jinendrabuddhi's explanation of why the form of the word is mentioned, see Pind 2015: II.22, n. 55.) Cf. ŚVŚar 60, 8–9: *paratantro hy asau sattāṃ nimittīkṛtya dravye pravartate na tu svatantraḥ / sarvaviśeṣaṇaviśiṣṭaṃ dravyaṃ vakti / tataś ca ghaṭādes tena sacchabdenānākṣepān nāsti tadvācinā sāmānādhikaraṇyam /*. "For that [word 'existing'] refers to a substance dependently, i.e., insofar as existence is the occasion for its use, not independently. It expresses the substance qualified by *all* of its qualifiers; and for that [reason] there is no coreference [of the word 'pot', and so forth] with [the word 'existing'] expressing that, since the word 'existing' does not imply pot, and so forth."

dhāraṇe), an inclusion of the aspect of the exclusion of non-pot, etc. is not cognized from the word ["existing"].

The word "sweet," according to the *apohavat* theory, expresses whatever is not non-sweet, i.e., something possessing the exclusion of non-sweet things. The word "sweet," when used in reference to sugar, does not include or necessarily imply its white aspect. Likewise, "white" when used in reference to sugar expresses something possessing the exclusion of non-white things and does not imply sweet. Therefore, the expression "sweet [and] white" (*madhuraṃ śuklam*) as a description of sugar, on the *apohavat* view, would be impossible. Similarly for an expression like "existing pot" (see below, v. 124).

123 If there were inclusion by that which has the nature of an object [that is, because "existing" indicates the object as qualified by the exclusion of non-existent things, and the object is a pot, then due to the connection with that object, something possessing the exclusion of non-pot is covered by "existing" after all – indirectly through the object, then we would reply:] that [inclusion of pot in fact] could be due just to [a real universal, namely,] existence. There is no object possessing potness, etc., that is not included by that.

The Buddhist might resort to the object itself to account for how existence could include a pot. Kumārila considered a similar proposal when discussing the *apohamātra* view above, v. 118cd. Through the *object* qualified by the exclusion of non-existent things there would be the inclusion of the object as qualified by the exclusion of non-pot, etc. But there is no reason to think that this kind of solution particularly favors the *apoha* theory. The object qualified by the *universal* existence could serve just as well serve to account for the inclusion of the object qualified by potness.

124 Nor does the fact that [existence] is a real thing prevent the inclusion [of pot] by that [existence] for the word ["existing"]. On the other hand, both a real and an unreal thing have the same operation in regard to cognition.

Whether existence represents a real universal or an unreal exclusion, either one will function either to make known the inclusion of the pot aspect *via* the object, or not. Pārthasārathimiśra suggests that neither would make known the inclusion of the pot aspect. Sucaritamiśra suggests that if an *apoha* made it known, so would real existence.[90] Dignāga, on the other hand, appears to have held that if a word denoted the thing possessing a real universal such as existence (*sattā*), the universal would, so to speak, interfere with the word's denotation of its meaning – namely, a *specific* kind of thing *possessing* that universal. On the other hand, an unreal *sattā*, i.e., the exclusion of non-existent things (*asadvyāvṛtti*), would not do that. That is to say, it would not cause a lack of independence (*asvatantratva/paratantratva*) or lack of directness of the word.[91]

125 And the nature of a real thing, even if it lacks parts, is [nevertheless] comprehended partially by words. For from the cognition of the word "existing" a thing such as a pot is not cognized.

Here, Kumārila seems to be attributing to Dignāga the view that an

---

[90] ŚVN 424,16–18; ŚVKāśK 299(22),5–11.

[91] See PS 5.4a and the explanation to v. 120, above. Dignāga says, PSV 5.36c, "For a word does not refer to its own particulars/differences while being dependent on another referent." *na hy arthāntaram upādāya śabdaḥ svabhedeṣu vartate* (Pind 2015: I.44,2). That is to say, on the *apohavat* view, a word does not refer to the object mediated by another thing (i.e., a real universal), so that it is actually separated from its referent. See Jinendrabuddhi's explanation ad loc.: *na hi tadvatpakṣa iva guṇarūpopakṛtaṃ vastu śabdenābhidhīyate. tatra hi guṇāntaropakārasya virodhāt tyāgaḥ. iha tu sattvādikaṃ guṇāntaram anapekṣyāsadvyudaste vastuni śabdo vartate* (Pind 2015: II,132, n. 446). "For it is not, as for the possessor-of-that-[genus]-theory, a thing influenced by the nature of a property (*guṇa*) that is denoted by the word. For on that [view], there is abandonment [of other properties] due to the opposition of the influence of another property. Here [on the *apohavat* view], on the other hand, without dependence on another property like existence, the word refers to a thing from which what is non-existent has been removed." Dignāga goes on to claim, PSV 5.36c, that an *apoha* can reside in many particulars, hence in effect function as a sort of universal, also, "because it is not substantial/not a substance" (*adravyatvāt*, Pind 2015: I.44,5).

entity lacks distinct parts. While such a position is not fully explicit in Dignāga, it was emphasized by his commentator Dharmakīrti.[92] Someone who held such a position might conceivably argue as follows: If an object is unified in nature, possessing different aspects which are united as one entity, then when one apprehends one aspect one will apprehend all of them. Thus, from comprehending *asadapoha*, the exclusion of non-existent things, one would comprehend *aghaṭāpoha*, the exclusion of non-pots; there would be covering of one property by another. But that would not be the case for the Mīmāṃsaka, who believes that existence and potness are *distinct* aspects of an object. That is to say, he does not believe that the nature of an object is unified. It would not be true, then, that a real and an unreal universal would operate in the same way in regard to cognition, as Kumārila has just maintained in v. 124.

Here, Kumārila points out that even if one believes entities to be without distinct parts, one accepts that they are nevertheless cognized partially in *verbal* cognition. In fact, this was Dignāga's stated position. At PS 5.12 he says, "[A referent] is not cognized by a word completely, even though it can be indicated in many ways. Rather, that [word] performs its purpose, which is exclusion, in accordance with its own relation."[93] Dharmakīrti adopted the same view, maintaining that while all aspects of an object are apprehended perceptually, its various properties are cognized distinctly by language and inference.[94] In that

---

[92] See, e.g., PV 1.43, 58; PVSV 26,4: *eko hy arthātmā* /. "A thing's nature is indeed undivided"; PVSV 27,1-2: *anaṃśasya caikadeśena darśanāyogāt* /. "For it is not possible to see something partially that is without parts," etc. Cf. PS 1.5ab: *dharmiṇo 'nekarūpasya nendriyāt sarvathā gatiḥ* /.

[93] PS 5.12: *bahudhāpy abhidheyasya na śabdāt sarvathā gatiḥ / svasambandhānurūpyāt tu vyavacchedārthakāry asau //* (Pind 2015: I.15,9–10). Cf. PS 2.13, restored by Pind 2015: II.56, n. 186, in which the same idea is expressed for inference. See further Pind 2015: II.231–233 (Appendix 7).

[94] See, e.g., PV 1.50–51: *yāvanto 'ṃśasamāropās tannirāse viniścayāḥ / tāvanta eva śabdāś ca tena te bhinnagocarāḥ // anyathaikena śabdena vyāpta ekatra vastuni / buddhyā vā nānyaviṣaya iti paryāyatā bhavet //*. "However many superimpositions of [extraneous] elements [there might be], there are just that many ascertainments and words to remove them; thus, these [ascertainments and words] have distinct

case, however, the problem of one word including the meaning of another remains, as Kumārila proceeds to say.

126a Therefore, there is the defect [for the Apohavādin as well] that there is no implication [of the thing the other word refers to, when two words are used coreferentially].

Thus, the view that a word indicates something possessing an *apoha* has the same problem as the view that a word indicates something possessing a real genus, which Dignāga has criticized at PS 5.4a – namely, that a particular substance such as a pot is not implied by the word "existing" in the phrase "existing pot" (*ghaṭādibhedānākṣepāt*, PSV 5.4a). Kumārila is, in effect, responding to Dignāga's explicit assertion, PSV 5.36c, that the *apohavāda* is *not* vulnerable to this objection.[95] So this way of understanding *apoha* as the meaning does not work.

Kumārila still raises another objection, mirroring Dignāga's objection, PS 5.4b', against the *jātimat*/*tadvat* view that it would make general terms figurative.[96] At PSV 5.36c Dignāga further maintains that the *apohavāda* is not susceptible to this problem, either.[97]

---

objects. Otherwise [i.e., if cognitions and words revealed the nature of a real thing without depending on an exclusion,] insofar as an undivided [real] thing [is completely] covered by a single word or a [single ascertaining] cognition, [there would be] no other object [for another word or cognition]. Consequently [all words and ascertaining cognitions used subsequently in regard to this object] would be synonymous" (Eltschinger et al. 2018: 45).

[95] See n. 91 above.

[96] PS 5.4b': *upacārāt* (Pind 2015: I.6,8). "[A word cannot refer to the possessor of that genus] because it would be metaphorical." Note that this is a *prasaṅga* of a Nyāya position for Dignāga. The Buddhist epistemologists did not subscribe to the view, defended by Sthiramati, that all language is figurative (see Tzohar 2018:153–177), nor is Dignāga addressing that view here.

[97] PSV 5.36c: *bhāktadoṣo 'pi nāsti* (Pind 2015: 44,3). "Nor is there the defect that [the word would be] used in a secondary sense."

126bcd And there is the defect that [the word would be] figurative. For the *apoha* would be primary, like the universal, because it would be a qualifier.

127 Therefore, since the possessor of that [*apoha*] is secondary, it cannot be what is directly indicated. If [the *apoha*] were not primary because it is not a real thing, then in this way it would not be a qualifier [either].

If the referent of a word is something possessing an *apoha*, then it is something qualified by an *apoha*. Generally, when a qualified thing is mentioned its qualifying property must be indicated first. In that case, the *apoha* itself being what is first, directly indicated, the word would refer to what possesses the *apoha* only secondarily or figuratively.

At PSV 5.36c, after claiming that on the *apohavat* view words would not indicate their referents dependently (*asvatantra*/*paratantra*), Dignāga states that there would also not be the defect of their being figurative, but he does not explain why. Presumably, however, the reason is the same: on the Apohavāda a word does not *first* refer to a genus and *then* to a thing possessing it. The word "existing" does not refer to the genus existence as its primary meaning, but merely *excludes* its referent from non-existent things. Here, Kumārila interprets Dignāga to be saying that a word that indicates a thing possessing an *apoha* would not be figurative because an *apoha* is a nonentity.[98] If a qualifier is real, then it is primary (*mukhya*, *abhidheya*) and the thing qualified by it or possessing it is secondary (*gauṇa*). If a qualifier is unreal, on the other hand, the thing possessing it can be regarded as primary, because there exists nothing that it possesses which would be primary. Here, Kumārila simply points out the incoherence of saying that an unreal thing can be a qualifier. Cf. v. 118, above.

128 And particulars would be what possess *apoha*s; and it has been stated that they are not the meaning, due to being

[98] Thus, ŚVŚar 62,4–5: *nāyaṃ mama doṣo bhavati yenāpoho nāma na kiṃcit / kutas tasya mukhyatvam iti /*. "[The Buddhist opponent says,] 'This is not a fault of mine, because an *apoha* is nothing at all. How could it be a primary meaning?'"

infinite and deviating. But there is nothing else that possesses an *apoha*.

At PS 5.8cd Dignāga states that the genus-possessor theory is unacceptable because the individual would become the referent, and it has already been explained at PS 5.2ab that individuals cannot be the referents of words because they are infinite.[99] Later, PSV 5.36c, however, he maintains that the *apoha*-possessor view does not have this defect.[100] Kumārila simply contradicts him. The *apoha*-possessor would be just as much an individual as the universal-possessor.

Could the meaning, then, be "being the possessor of the *apoha*" (*apohavattvam*)?

129ab There is not for you another "being the possessor of the *apoha*" (*apohavattva*) in another *apoha* of an individual.

Dignāga says, PS 5.9ab, that "merely the possessor of that [genus]" (*tadvanmātram*) or being the possessor of that genus in general cannot be the meaning of a word, as that has already been considered and rejected as either the relation or the genus existence (*sattā*).[101] Kumārila

---

[99] PS 5.8cd: *tadvāṃś ca bheda eveṣṭaḥ sa ca pūrvaṃ nirākṛtaḥ* // (Pind 2015: I.10,7). "Moreover, the possessor of that [genus] is considered just the individual, and that was previously refuted [as the meaning of a word]."

[100] PSV 5.36c: *nāpi bhedānavasthānād anabhidhānadoṣaḥ* (Pind 2015: I.44,4). "Nor is there the defect [that a word referring to the possessor of the *apoha*] does not indicate [its meaning] because individuals are infinite." The rationale is implied by what Dignāga says in PSV 5.34 (Pind 2015: I.40,6–42,1), namely, on the *apohavat* view the meaning of a word is ascertained by *vyatireka*; that is to say, the connection of the word with its meaning is determined simply by *not* observing that it is applied to other things. For the *jātimat*/*tadvat* view, on the other hand, the meaning would be ascertained by *anvaya* – by positively observing what it *is* applied to – in which case the infinity of individuals would become a problem; for it is impossible to observe positively that the word is applied to countless individuals. See n. 41.

[101] PS 5.9ab: *tadvanmātraṃ tu sambandhaḥ sattā veti vicāritam* / (Pind 2015: I.11,1). "The possessor of that [genus] in general (*tadvadmātra*) has already been considered [and rejected] as [either] the relation or existence." *tadvadmātra* is

is arguing here that considering the meaning to be being the possessor of the *apoha* in general would not be an option for the Buddhist, either, if that itself is conceived as a universal.[102] A Buddhist surely would not think that in the *apoha* of an individual (for instance, in the *apoha* of non-cows in a cow) there is another genus, "being the possessor of the *apoha* of non-cows" - which of course would also be an *apoha*![103]

129cd-130ab And that [being the possessor of the *apoha*], moreover, must be chosen from among two options: either it is an existing entity or a non-existence. If it is a real thing, then that is just a universal (*jāti*). Even if it is not something real,

---

equivalent to *tadvattva* (see the reconstruction of PSV ad loc., Pind 2015: II.41). The idea that existence (*sattā*) is specifically denoted by the abstract suffixes *-tva* and *-tā* is expressed by Bhartṛhari at VP 3.1.33–34. In PSV 5.9ab, however, Dignāga quotes a different statement, also attributed to Bhartṛhari by some, that the *bhāva* suffixes *-tva* and *-tā* indicate a relation in the case of compounds and words with *kṛt* and *taddhita* suffixes: *samāsakṛttaddhiteṣu sambandhābhidhānam anyatra rūḍhyabhinnarūpāvyabhicāritasambandhebhyaḥ* (Pind 2015: I.11,2–3). "In the case of compounds, *kṛt*-derivatives, and *taddhita*-derivatives, [the endings *-tva* and *–tā*] indicate a relation – except for conventional words, derivatives whose form is not different [from the words they are derived from], and words whose connection is invariable." On the source of this quotation see Pind 2015: II.42, n. 130. For an explanation of it see ibid., n. 132.

[102] ŚVN 425,16: *yadi tv apohavattvasāmānyaṃ śabdārthaḥ* [...] /. "But if the universal being the possessor of the *apoha* were the meaning of a word [...]."

[103] Here we have followed Jayamiśra, ŚVŚar 63,2–3: *bhedāpohāntare – ity ekasmāt svalakṣaṇād aparasmin svalakṣaṇe yad aparam apohāntaraṃ tasminn ity arthaḥ* /. "The meaning of 'in another *apoha* of an individual' (*bhedāpohāntare*) is this: [there is] another, different *apoha* [i.e., different from being the possessor of the *apoha*!] in a particular which is different from another particular – in that one [i.e., in that other *apoha*]." According to Sucaritamiśra, ŚVKāś$_K$ 295(26),1–6, a Buddhist surely would not think that in the *apoha* which is one subtype (spotted cow) there is another universal, "being the possessor of the *apoha*" (which would be the referent of the word "cow"), which would also exist in the *apoha* which is another subtype (black cow); for the subtypes exclude each other. He refers to PS 5.28ab: *bhedo bhedāntarārthaṃ tu virodhitvād apohate* / (Pind 2015: I.31,5). "A particular [general term = *bhedaśabda*], however, excludes the meaning of another particular [general term], because it is opposed [to it]."

then [it is inadmissible] as before [because it would result in problems like the synonymy of all words, etc., as pointed out vv. 42 ff.].

130cd Or else this could be postulated as the relation, but that is not believed [by Buddhists] to be the meaning.

According to Dignāga at PS 5.9ab *tadvanmātra* might also be the *relation* (*sambandha*) between the genus and the individual possessing it, as we have seen.[104] Analogously, *apohavattvam* could be the *relation* between the *apoha* and the thing possessing it. At PS 5.2cd, however, Dignāga rejected the idea that the "connection" (*yoga*, i.e., the relation) could be the meaning of a word at the same time he ruled out the genus as the meaning: neither will allow for the coreference of a general term and words for particulars that fall under it.[105] That is to say, coreference with words like "pot" would be impossible if the word "existing" just indicated the relation. Kumārila is saying here that the Apohavādin would have the same problem if a word referred to *apohavattvam*, being the possessor of the *apoha*, and *apohavattvam* were understood as the relation between a particular and its *apoha*.

131 And a single thing possessing an *apoha* [such as a pot] does not exist in some other thing [such as a cloth]. For that reason, also, the meaning would not be a universal; nor would it be a qualifier.

If the meaning of "existing" were what possesses the *apoha* (of non-existent things), such as an individual pot, etc., then it would be a concrete thing that is not common with other individuals. Therefore, it could not function as a universal. Yet the meanings of general terms like "existing" must obviously extend over many things, since we use those words to refer to many different individuals – pots, cloths, and so forth; the meanings of general terms must function as universals – even if, for the Buddhist, they would not be *real* universals. Kumārila's argument here, once again, is analogous to an argument Dignāga makes

---

[104] See n. 101.

[105] See n. 74.

against the genus-possessor view (PS 5.9cd–10a), which is quoted by Kumārila's commentators.[106] Moreover, if the word "existing" referred just to some individual possessing the exclusion of non-existent things, it could not be a qualifier, since it could not reside in something else, for instance a cloth.[107]

132 And [the more general exclusion, such as the exclusion of non-existent things] does not imply the subtype-exclusion [such as the exclusion of non-pot] because [the latter] does not exist in it (*ātmani*) [i.e., the general exclusion]. Therefore, it is not qualified by those [specific *apoha*s, such as exclusion of non-pot], as blue is by intensity.[108]

---

[106] PS 5.9cd-10a: *tadvān artho ghaṭādiś cen na paṭādiṣu vartate / sāmānyam arthaḥ sa katham* [...] // (Pind 2015: I.11,6–7). "If the meaning is the possessor of that [genus], i.e., a[n individual] pot and so forth, [then it] does not reside in a cloth and so on, [so] how can the meaning be a universal [...]?"

[107] ŚVKāś$_K$ 293(28),15–292(29),1: *ata eva sacchabdena yatra kvacid ekasminn arthe sattāviśiṣṭa ukte tasyārthāntare vṛttyabhāvād viśeṣaṇatvānupapattir* [...] /. "For just this [reason], whatever object is expressed as being qualified by existence by the word 'existing' cannot be a qualifier, since it does not exist in something else [...]."

According to Sucaritamiśra, "for that reason, also" (*tasmād api*, 131c) means that, not only can the meaning of a word not be a universal because of the impossibility of coreference – here, he seems to be referring back to the argument ŚV *Apohavāda* 115–118, which was directed against the *apohamātra* view – "but also for the *apohavat*-view" it could not be a universal because, as explained, it would lack commonality. ŚVKāś$_K$ 293(28),11–13: *na kevalaṃ sāmānādhikaraṇyānupapattyāsāmānyavācyatvam / tadvadabhidhānapakṣe 'pi tadvatām anugamābhāvān na sāmānyavacanatā sidhyatīty apiśabdasyārthaḥ* /.

[108] The Chowkhamba edition published in 1898 has the reading *viśeṣo 'pohasūcakaḥ*, but the translation by G. Jhā accords with the reading *viśeṣāpohasūcanam*: "The *Apoha of 'Asan'* does not indicate the particular *Apoha* (of the non-jar, & c.), while these latter do not inhere in the former; consequently, the *Apoha of 'Asan'* cannot be qualified by these (*Apohas*), in the same manner as 'Blue' is (qualified) by the successive higher degrees of its shades" (Jhā 1907: 320).

Yet perhaps the thing possessing the exclusion of non-existent things need not exist *in* some other individual in order to qualify it. Perhaps, rather, the thing possessing the exclusion of non-existent things and the thing possessing some other exclusion could simply be the same individual. At PS 5.10d Dignāga considers the idea that the universal-possessor referred to by "existing" (that is, an existence-possessor) need not exist *in some other* individual universal-possessor referred to by "pot" (a potness-possessor), in order for there to be coreference and qualification of the words "existing" and "pot." Rather, when something possessing existence is indicated by the word "existing" an expectation that it is some specific kind of existing thing will arise, just as when someone says "blue" there is the expectation of some particular intensity of blue: very blue, extremely blue, etc. That expectation will then be satisfied by use of the word "pot." Thus, "existing" and "pot" may be used together, since "existing" also implies potness.[109] Dignāga, however, with PS 5.11a'b, rejects this attempt to save the genus-possessor theory simply on the grounds that a genus does not possess another genus.[110] Thus, existence cannot have potness as a subtype, and

---

Probably Jhā translated the verse in accordance with Pārthasārathimiśra's interpretation (ŚVN 426,22: *na hy asadapohaḥ svātmany avidyamānān aghaṭādyapohān sūcayati* /), so that his understanding conforms to the latter (correct) reading that Pārthasārathi must have known.

[109] PSV 5.10d, introduction: *atha punar ananyasmiṃ dravye vartate sadguṇam, sacchabdād ghaṭādyākāṅkṣāyāṃ viśeṣaṇaviśeṣyabhāvaḥ syāt nīlatarādivat* (Pind 2015: I.12,6–13,1). "Suppose on the other hand that something having the quality existence (*sadguṇam*, according to Jinendrabuddhi; see Pind 2015: II.48, n. 158) resides in the same substance. There being the expectation of a pot, and so forth, from [hearing] the word 'existing,' there could be a qualifier-qualificand relation, as in the case of 'bluer' and so forth." As Sucaritamiśra puts it, ŚVKāśK 292(29),3–5: *mā bhūd ekatra vṛttaḥ sacchabdo 'rthāntare viśeṣaṇam, tatraiva tu tadgatāparaviśeṣākāṅkṣāyām arthāntareṇa viśeṣaṇaṃ bhaviṣyati* /. "Let the word 'existing' referring to one thing not be the qualifier of another thing. Rather, precisely of that same thing [to which it refers], upon the arising of an expectation (*ākāṅkṣā*) of another difference that belongs to it, there will be qualification by another meaning."

[110] PS 5.11a'b: *upetyāpi naitaj jāter ajātitaḥ* (Pind 2015: I.13,7). "Even assuming [that the blue thing resides in the bluer thing,] this is not the case [for two genera such as existence and potness], because a genus does not possess [another] genus."

so cannot imply it. Blue, on the other hand, is a quality and not a universal; as a quality it could have different intensities.[111] Here, Kumārila once again is simply saying that an analogous problem would affect the *apohavat* theory.

133 There is, also, indeed not an implication [of the specific meaning, the exclusion of non-pot, etc.], as there is [implication] of the *liṅgin* by the *liṅga*, because there is doubt. And it is not the case that an unspecified (*sāmānyātmanā*) *apoha* cannot be established without those [qualifying *apoha*s].

A genus like existence might well give rise to the expectation of some subtype, some specific kind of existence, but it would not imply one subtype rather than another. Thus, "existing" would not in any way imply a pot. Dignāga raises this objection to the universal-possessor theory at PS(V) 5.11c.[112] The same objection, clearly, can be made against the *apohavat* theory: the exclusion of non-existent things occurs in many things besides pots. The Apohavādin, however, has an additional problem. As Sucaritamiśra explains, "For the *apoha* of non-existent things, which has the nature of something unreal, is void (*tuccha*), so it is not the case that it is not established without those subtype-*apohas*."[113] Hence, it would not imply them.

134 In just the same way, on the other hand, an *apoha* would not imply a real thing, since that [same] exclusion would be possible even in a rabbit's horn.

Not only would an *apoha* not imply any subtypes (which, if it did, would make it possible for a word to be used coreferentially with other words that qualify it). It would not even imply a real thing – the indi-

---

[111] Thus our provisional understanding of the difficult passage PS(V) 5.10d–11ab. Cf. the explanation of Jinendrabuddhi, Pind 2015: II.51, n. 169.

[112] PS 5.11c: *arthākṣepo 'py anekāntaḥ* (Pind 2015: I.14,5, emended; see loc. cit., n. 68). "An implication, also, [would be] uncertain."

[113] ŚVKāśK 289(32),1–2: *asadapoho hy avasturūpo tucchaḥ, nāsau viśeṣāpohair vinā na sidhyati yat tān ākṣiped iti bhāvaḥ* /.

vidual substratum that supposedly possesses it; for, since it is itself unreal, it could be located even in a rabbit's horn, a non-existing thing![114]

135 And an *apoha* is not related to gender, number, etc. And because [according to you] the individual is inexpressible, that [relation with gender, number, etc.] would not occur through that [individual], either.

136 For that [individual] is not comprehended through the *apoha*, either, as something unique. Nor could something real which is not comprehended [in a verbal cognition] be something to be qualified [by gender, number, etc.].

The Apohavādin cannot explain how a word could have gender or number, since the *apoha* itself cannot be related to gender or number. The realist about universals can at least say that a universal inheres in or is not different from a particular thing that has gender and number, so a word could have gender and number through the individual implied by it. But for the Apohavādin this route is not possible because the individual is inexpressible as something unique. Rather, insofar as the individual is somehow made known through the *apoha*, it would be its general nature, which it would have in common with other individuals, that is made known. And that cannot be related to gender or number.

137 There is no assisting by a gender-*apoha*, number-*apoha*, etc. by themselves. And how can a real thing being assisted [by them] be cognized by words?

At PS(V) 5.5cd Dignāga considers whether a genus could "influence" (*uparāga*) the thing that possesses it, so that it takes on its nature – in the same way a red piece of lac "influences" a crystal next to it by making it red. If so, then a word such as "existing," which in the first

---

[114] ŚVN 427,7–8: *vastumātraṃ tāvaj jātir ākṣipati, tucchas tu apohas tad api nākṣipati, śaśaviṣāne 'pi saṃbhavāt* /. "For a genus implies a real thing in general, but an unreal *apoha* doesn't imply even that, since it can exist even in a rabbit's horn."

instance refers to existence, as we have seen above (vv. 126bcd–127), directly (and not just figuratively) can refer to an *existing thing* (the possessor of existence), which has taken on the nature of existence. This rather subtle theory is supposed to support the genus-possessor view. Dignāga rejects it for equally subtle reasons that we needn't go into.[115] Here, Kumārila seems to be considering an analogous theory that the Apohavādin (or more precisely, the Apohavadvādin) might put forward to solve the problem of how words can have gender and number. The individual thing – the *apoha*-possessor – could be referred to by words that indicate a gender-*apoha* and a number-*apoha* insofar as the latter *apoha*s "assist" it by influencing it, so that it takes on, as it were, the aspects of gender and number. Kumārila heads off this (rather desperate) solution simply by saying that *apoha*s, being unreal, cannot assist anything. Therefore, words cannot make known some real individual thing as assisted (that is, influenced) by such *apoha*s (nor, for that matter, any other *apoha*s) – in the way a crystal is influenced by a piece of lac.[116]

138 And there cannot ever be a cognition of the non-existence of something without non-apprehension (*anupa-labdhi*). And it is not understood here [in this world] that

[115] PS 5.5cd: *guṇopakārāt tādrūpye prakarṣaḥ syād vinā dhiyā* / (Pind 2015: I.8,4). "If [the property-possessor] were similar to [the property] because of the influence of the property, there would be [a perception of the] degree of intensity [of the property] without its perception" (cf. Pind 2015: II.31). When a crystal appears colored red by a red flower placed next to it, it does not require another cognition of a red flower in order to be cognized as red. Without cognizing a red flower separately, one cognizes the crystal as red – even as being a certain intensity of red – because it appears to have acquired that color. But this is not the case when apprehending something as qualified by a qualifier (*viśeṣaṇa*): the qualifier and its degree or intensity must both be cognized in order for something to be qualified by it. Similarly for something possessing a genus: one cannot apprehend a genus-possessor without apprehending the genus separately. See Pind 2015: II.32, nn. 85–88.

[116] We believe our interpretation of this verse follows Jayamiśra's explanation, ŚVŚar 65,22–66,5. Sucaritamiśra and Pārthasārathimiśra do not make any reference to PS 5.5cd.

cowness, etc., are known by [the *pramāṇa*] *abhāva*.

Cowness, etc., cannot be *apoha*s, because an *apoha* is a non-existence, an *abhāva*, and for the Mīmāṃsaka an *abhāva* is known only by means of the *pramāṇa abhāva*, which consists in the non-existence of other *pramāṇa*s. But there is no non-apprehension of cowness, since in fact it is accessible to perception. As Jayamiśra explains, whatever negation there is in regard to something, that is always due to non-apprehension. So, there should be a cognition of an *apoha*, which has the nature of a negation, in that way. That, however, is not the case because it is cognized, *qua* the meaning of a word, as an existing thing [whether erroneously or not].[117] Essentially, what Kumārila is saying is that the Buddhist view of *apoha* contradicts our experience: our cognition of the meaning "cow" is of something positive, and that can only be the case if it is *not* a negation, an *apoha*.

9 *apoha*s cannot be the meanings of words that are not general terms.

Having shown that the meanings of substantives and adjectives – general terms – cannot be *apoha*s, Kumārila now turns to other parts of speech.

139 And in the case of verbs, the negation of something else is not cognized. For there is not something to be negated which has the nature of a *paryudāsa* in their case.

Dignāga's theory of *apoha*, as presented in PS 5, concerns only general terms: words for genera (like "cow"), qualities, motions, and individual

[117] ŚVŚar 66,8–9: *yāvān kvacit pratiṣedhaḥ sa sarvo 'nupalabdheḥ – iti / tataś cāpohasyāpy anyaniṣedharūpasya tathaiva pratītyā bhāvyam / na caitad asty bhāvarūpapratīter ity āha* [...] /. "Every negation of something is due to non-apprehension. Therefore, there should be a cognition of that sort [i.e., a non-apprehension] of an *apoha*, which has the nature of the negation of something else. But that is not the case, because [even an *apoha* according to the Buddhist] is apprehended as existing. Thus, he says [...]."

substances (like "the man with a stick").[118] With this verse Kumārila

[118] Dignāga holds the *apoha* theory to be applicable to all *naimittikaśabda*s, that is, words having a specific cause of application. PSV 5.50a: *yuktaṃ tāvan naimittikeṣu śabdeṣv anyāpohenārthābhidhānam, yādṛcchikeṣu tu katham* (Pind 2015: I.58,6–7, emended). "[Objection:] It is indeed (*tāvat*) correct that [a word] indicates its referent by excluding others in the case of *naimittikaśabda*s, but how [is that the case] for proper names?" He accepts the following as *naimittikaśabda*s, as shown in PSV 1.3d (2,10–12):

a. *jātiśabda*, such as *go*
b. *guṇaśabda*, such as *śukla*
c. *kriyāśabda*, such as *pācaka*
d. *dravyaśabda*, such as *daṇḍin* and *viṣāṇin*.

In addition he regards *yadṛcchāśabda*s, proper names, such as *ḍittha*, as also explained by the *apoha* theory.

As shown in this section of ŚV *Apohavāda* (cf. TV 1.3.30; Harikai 61,2–3) Kumārila considers in addition to the categories mentioned by Dignāga the following categories and specific types of words:

ākhyāta (vv. 139–142ab)
nañ (v. 142cd)
cādi (v. 143ab)
vākya (v. 143cd)
anyāpoha (v. 144ab)
prameya, *jñeya* (vv. 144cd–146ab)
evam, etc. (v. 146cd).

Jayanta in his discussion of the Apohavāda explicitly states that he will focus only on *jātiśabda*s. That is to say, when *jātimat* is claimed to be the meaning of a word, the "word" is understood as a *jātiśabda*. In general, however, Jayanta accepts the following typology of language. (See Kataoka 2011b: 619[18]–618[19].)

śabda
- 1. *pada*
  - 1.1. *nāman (subanta)*, including *upasarga, nipāta, karmapravacanīya*
    - 1.1.1. ***jātiśabda***
    - 1.1.2. *dravyaśabda*
    - 1.1.3. *guṇaśabda*
    - 1.1.4. *kriyāśabda*
    - 1.1.5 *upasarga*
    - 1.1.6 *nipāta, karmapravacanīya*
  - 1.2. *ākhyāta (tiṅanta)*
- 2. *vākya*.

points out that the theory cannot be extended to verbs. In the case of the word "cow" the *apoha* can be understood as the exclusion of non-cow (*ago*), where "non-cow" refers to a nominally bound negation (*paryudāsa*) (see fn. 18) which is the complement of the class of cows. Such an understanding is not possible, however, in the case of a verb, such as "cooks." The expression "non-cooks" (**apacati*) would not refer to a nominally bound negation that is the complement of the act of cooking – in fact, it would have no meaning at all – so that "cooks" could refer to the exclusion of what it refers to.

140 For even if "not not" is stated [so that the *apoha* of a finite verb is, "He is not not cooking"] there is [only] a negating of a negation. "He cooks," which is not negated, on the other hand, remains in its own [original, positive] form.

One might take "non-cooks," however, simply to refer to the negation of cooking (rather than the complement of the act of cooking). On this interpretation of the *apoha* of the verb "He cooks," however, it would be equivalent to, "It is not the case that he does not cook." This double negation is equivalent to the positive assertion "He cooks," so that the verb "cooks" would still express something positive and not a negation at all.

141 And it would follow [for the Apohavādin] in regard to these [finite verbs] that a cognition of something to be done and the ascertainment (*rūpaṇa*) of the past, etc., would be without basis, due to an *apoha* being something accomplished.

An action is understood as something to be carried out or performed (*sādhya*) which can belong to the past, present, or future, etc., as in "He cooked," "He cooks," and "He will cook." But an *apoha*, being something accomplished (*niṣpanna*, *siddha*) and always belonging to the present (*pratyutpanna*), could not be understood in those ways.

142 And there would be no ascertainment of the exclusion of another in the case of a multitude of meanings such as injunction. And what kind of *apoha* would there be from [the word] "not" joined with "not"?

In the case of the various meanings of the optative ending – commanding or directing (*vidhi*), granting permission, and so forth[119] – it is also unclear how there could be complements to be excluded, since such meanings function to motivate the hearer to act and so are not "accomplished" (*pariniṣpanna*) entities. Similarly, it is not clear what the word "not" would mean according to the *apoha* theory. Presumably, it would be the exclusion of non-not. But we have no idea what non-not might be.

143 For "and" (*ca*) and so forth as well there is no joining at all with "non," so there is no exclusion [that could be their meaning]. And in the case of the sentence meaning, the elimination of another cannot be designated.

While the expression "non-pot" has a meaning, we can attach no meaning at all to an expression such as "not and" or "non-and." Thus, the word "and" also lacks a complement, the exclusion of which could be its meaning. Similarly for the other particles (such as *vā*, "or," and *tu*, "but"), verbal prefixes, and prepositions of Sanskrit (such as *anu*, "after," and *abhi*, "toward").[120]

---

[119] The different meanings of *liṅ*, the optative ending, are given at P 3.3.161: *vidhinimantraṇāmantraṇādhīṣṭasampraśnaprārthaneṣu liṅ*. Kamalaśīla alludes to this *sūtra* (*ādiśabdena nimantraṇāmantraṇādīnāṃ grahaṇam*, TSPś I.383,24). Jayamiśra does not, but nevertheless says that Kumārila has the various meanings of the *liṅ-pratyaya* in mind, ŚVŚar 67,8–9: *anenaiva nyāyena liṅpratyaya-pratipādye vidhyādyarthe paryudasanīyasya darśayitum aśakyatvāt tatprati-ṣedharūpo 'poho na sambhavati* [...] /. "By this same reasoning, in the case of the meaning to be conveyed by the optative ending, i.e., commanding and so forth, because one cannot show the object of nominally bound negation (*paryuda-sanīyasya*), an *apoha* that has the nature of the negation of that is not possible [...]." Sucaritamiśra, ŚVKāśK 285(36),6–8, takes 142a, *vidhyādāv artharāśau*, to be referring to the various functions of a verb: assertion (*vidhi*), repetition (*anuvāda*) (that is, referencing something previously mentioned), and even the syntactic functions expressed by the various case endings. Clearly, it would be difficult to explain such things in terms of *apoha*.

[120] These classes of words are referred to by Sanskrit grammarians as *nipāta*s,

Sentence meaning is complex – variegated, as one commentator says[121] – so there would not be one accomplished thing that could be combined with the word "non." Through its verb, a sentence also expresses an action, which is something to be brought about and not fixed. And if one were to attach the particle "non" to a sentence such as "Bring the cow," only the meaning of the word with which "non" is connected would be negated, not the entire sentence meaning. Thus, the sentence as a whole lacks an accomplished complement, the exclusion of which could be its meaning.

144 And a meaning in the case of words such as *an-anyāpoha*, "non-exclusion of another," is not ascertained. For the words "knowable," "cognizable," etc., on the other hand, from what is [its meaning] excluded?

According to the Apohavādin the meaning of every word is just *anyāpoha*, exclusion of another. The word "non-exclusion of another," therefore, would have to mean the negation of exclusion of another. That, however, would contradict the thesis that the meaning of every word is the exclusion of another. And since there is nothing that is not knowable, cognizable, etc., there would not be something to be excluded in the case of the words "knowable" (*prameya*), "cognizable" (*jñeya*), and so forth.[122]

145 Or if an *apohya* is imagined,[123] it is better to imagine

---

upasargas, and *karmapravacanīyas*, respectively. The class of particles that include *anu* and *abhi* can function as prefixes (*upasargas*) when conjoined with a verb and as prepositions (*karmapravacanīyas*) when not.

[121] TSPś I.384,15: *vākyārthaḥ kalmāṣavarṇavac chabalaikarūpa iṣyate* /. "Sentence-meaning, like a variegated color, is accepted as [both] variegated and [yet] one." Cf. ŚVŚar 67,20: *viśiṣṭārthabuddhijanakaṃ hi vākyam* /. "For a sentence produces a cognition of a qualified meaning."

[122] Uddyotakara makes a similar argument for the word "all" (*sarva*), NV 314,13–22.

[123] Jayamiśra's gloss (*yat kalpitākāraniṣedhena kalpitarūpaṃ vācyam iti tato*

something real. And because of the denial of a form of the cognition something internal cannot be what is designated.

If the Buddhist were to say, in all of these cases, that the *apohya* (e.g., *aprameya*, non-knowable) is something imagined – as Dignāga may have suggested in his *Hetumukha*[124] – then it would be better to imagine a real universal (i.e., *prameyatva*, knowableness). Or, as Jayamiśra puts it, a meaning that is imagined as a real thing (i.e., the universal *prameyatva*) in a positive way is preferable to a meaning that is imagined (i.e., the *apoha* of *aprameya*) on the basis of the negation of another imagined entity (i.e., *aprameya*).[125]

If the Buddhist accepted an imagined universal as the meaning, then

---

varam uktaṃ syāt [...], ŚVŚar 68,8–9, emended; see below n. 125) supports the ablative (*apohyakalpanāyāḥ*) in 145a rather than the locative. Kamalaśīla's gloss (*yadi jñeyam api sarvaṃ jñeyatvenāpohyam asya kalpyate tadā varam* [...], TSPś I.385,13), on the other hand, if we accept that his presupposed text is the same as that of the ŚV, supports the locative rather than the ablative. From the text-critical point of view, we prefer the locative as the *lectio difficilior*. The change from locative to ablative (by a scribe) is conceivable due to the occurrence of *varam*, whereas that from ablative to locative is less likely.

[124] Sucaritamiśra, ŚVKāśK 283(38),7, cites a half-verse, *ajñeyaṃ kalpitaṃ kṛtvā jñeyaśabdo 'bhivartate* /, "The word 'knowable' occurs insofar as one imagines the non-knowable," but does not identify its source. Kamalaśīla, in the introduction to his commentary on TSś 979 (≈ ŚV *Apohavāda* 145) quotes a statement similar to this in wording – which now, however, refers to inference instead of language – and attributes it to Dignāga's *Hetumukha*. TSPś I.385,11–12: *ajñeyaṃ kalpitaṃ kṛtvā tadvyavacchedena jñeye 'numānam* /. "Imagining the non-knowable, one infers the knowable by excluding that." Cf. Pind 2015: II.161, n. 539.

[125] ŚVŚar 68,8–9: *yat kalpitākāraniṣedhena kalpitarūpaṃ*[1] *vācyam iti tato varam evam uktaṃ syāt – vidhimukhenaiva kalpitarūpaṃ vastv abhidhīyate – iti* /. [1]*-niṣedhena kalpitarūpam* em: *-niṣedhenākalpitarūpam* ed. "Instead of a meaning whose nature is imagined by means of the negation of an imagined aspect, it would be better to say that a real thing is indicated whose nature is imagined in a positive way." Sucaritamiśra's explanation, ŚVKāśK 283(38),9–11, is slightly different: It would be a "big defect" (*mahān ayaṃ kleśaḥ*) to try to explain the meaning of a word which one does not cognize in any other way (and so in effect itself is postulated), that is, an *apoha*, through the negation of an *imagined apohya* when one can posit directly, according to our experience, a real universal as the meaning.

the meaning would be an internal form in the cognition, and that a cognition cognizes its own form is denied in the *Śūnyavāda* chapter.[126]

146 Nor could [something internal] be what is excluded. [For that has been refuted previously; see 41ab.] Therefore, an *apoha* is not established in these [cases, namely, "knowable," etc.]. Nor can an *apohya* be ascertained for the words "thus," etc.

Finally, words such as "thus" (*evam*) and "this," which are called indexicals in modern linguistics, point to something present – according to Sucaritamiśra they indicate "the manner of something that is merely proximate"[127] – and so they potentially apply to everything. Thus, just like *jñeya*, *prameya*, and so forth, they lack defined *apohya*s, and so cannot be explained as referring to *apoha*s.

10 The theory of *apoha* cannot explain why some words cannot be used coreferentially.

Now Kumārila considers how the Apohavāda can explain why words for subtypes of a genus *cannot* be used coreferentially, e.g., *śiṃśapā* and *palāśa*. This is a problem Dignāga discusses at PS(V) 5.28. A theory of meaning has to be able to explain not only why coreference is possible when it occurs, but also why it is not possible in other circumstances.

147 If it is postulated that there is [mutual] exclusion of [words for] subtypes because they conflict [with each other], [then] in that case conflict is due to exclusion and excluding is due to conflict.

That is to say, you would have mutual presupposition. If two words for subtypes are not used coreferentially – for example, one does not say **palāśaḥ śiṃśapā* (or "birch elm") – because, as Dignāga maintains at

---

[126] See Taber 2010.

[127] ŚVKāśK 282(39),10: *saṃnihitamātraprakāravacanatvāt.*

PS 5.28ab, each "excludes" the other by virtue of "conflicting" with it[128] – then what is this conflict of the words other than the fact that they exclude each other? It would seem that they are in conflict with each other because they exclude each other, and they exclude each other because they conflict – hence, *anyonyāśraya*, mutual presupposition!

148 According to you those [words for subtypes] (*tatra*) do not appropriate the universal positively. [For you, only] after having excluded *palāśa* and so forth, does *śiṃśapā* take tree away [from them].

Explaining further the idea of a mutual presupposition, Kumārila alludes to the theory Dignāga offers at PSV 5.28ab. A word for a subtype, Dignāga proposes there, is in conflict with another word for a subtype by "appropriating the common property" (*sāmānyāpahāritvāt*), in the way each of the sons of a king, upon his death, attempts to claim for himself his father's entire kingdom. As he says, "When the word *śiṃśapā* is used together with the word 'tree' in [the statement], 'This tree is a *śiṃśapā*,' it confines treeness to its own object by cutting it off from *khadira*, etc."[129] Since both *śiṃśapā* and *khadira* function in this way (presumably, even when "tree" is not mentioned) they cannot be used together (in a sentence such as **śiṃśapā khadiraḥ*). To this, Kumārila's response is that for the Buddhist subtype-words do not appropriate the common universal "positively" (*vidhirūpeṇa*).[130] That is

---

[128] PS 5.28ab: *bhedo bhedāntarārthaṃ tu virodhitvād apohate* / (Pind 2015: I.31,5). "A [word for a] subtype excludes [a word] having as its meaning another subtype because they are opposed [to each other]." Sucaritamiśra quotes this statement and explains it as follows, ŚVKāś$_K$ 281(40),2–3: *yo 'yaṃ vṛkṣatvasya bhedaśabdaḥ palāśādiḥ, ayaṃ śiṃśapādibhedāntarārthaṃ śabdam apohate, virodhitvāt* /. "A word for a subtype of treeness, *palāśa*, etc., excludes a word which means another subtype, *śiṃśapā*, etc., because [those words] are opposed."

[129] PSV 5.28ab: *tadyathāyaṃ vṛkṣaḥ śiṃśapeti śiṃśapāśabdo vṛkṣaśabdena saha prayujyamānaḥ khadirādibhyo vṛkṣatvaṃ vyavacchidya svaviṣaye vyavasthāpayati* (Pind 2015: I.31,7–32,3). Translation adapted from Pind 2015: II.97.

[130] Despite some imprecision in the commentaries, we understand Kumārila to

to say, they do not appropriate the universal for themselves merely by indicating their own meanings; for according to the Apohavāda, they can indicate their own meanings only by excluding each other's meanings![131] If, however, the exclusion of subtype-words from other subtype-words is to be explained by their appropriating the common property (which allegedly explains why they are in conflict), then we would have a situation of mutual presupposition: they would appropriate the common property by excluding each other's meanings, and they would exclude each other's meanings by appropriating the common property.[132]

But if words for subtypes cannot be used together – indeed, if words in general refer to their meanings by excluding other meanings – how is it possible for words to be used together at all? Dignāga addresses this question at PS 5.25cd, "[A word] does not exclude the meanings of universal [terms], subtype [terms], and synonyms, even though it is

---

be talking about the exclusion of one *word* by another – so that they cannot be used coreferentially – due to the *word* appropriating the universal for itself by excluding the meanings of other subtype-words, as is clear from Dignāga. Sometimes Sucaritamiśra, for instance, talks about the *subtype śiṃśapā* appropriating the universal, not the subtype-*word*, e.g., at ŚVKāśK 281(40),14–280(41),2.

[131] As Sucaritamiśra puts it, the word *śiṃśapā* does not appropriate the universal treeness insofar as it conveys, "This tree is a *śiṃśapā*." Rather, it does so by conveying, "This is *not* a tree that is not a *śiṃśapā*," that is to say, by excluding *palāśa* etc. – hence negatively. ŚVKāśK 279(42),1–4: *na tvanmate vidhirūpeṇa sāmānyāpahāraḥ "śiṃśapāyaṃ vṛkṣa" iti / kiṃ tarhy aśiṃśapārūpān palāśādīn apohya paścād ataḥ palāśāder vṛkṣatvasāmānyam apaharati, ātmasātkaroti śiṃśapā "nāyam aśiṃśapā vṛkṣa" iti /*. "On your view, there is not a positive appropriation of the universal [when one says,] 'This tree is a *śiṃśapā*.' Rather, after having excluded non-*śiṃśapā*s, i.e., *palāśa*s, etc., [the word] *śiṃśapā* subsequently appropriates the universal treeness from *palāśa*, etc., i.e., makes it its own [insofar as it conveys,] 'This not a tree that is not a *śiṃśapā*.'" Cf. also the explanation of Pārthasārathimiśra ŚVN 429,25–30.

[132] Our interpretation of 148cd follows the second explanations of Sucaritamiśra (cited above, n. 131) and Jayamiśra, ŚVŚar 69,20–27.

different [from them]."[133] Thus, one can say, "The tree is earthen" (*vṛkṣaḥ pārthivaḥ*); "The tree is a *śiṃśapā*" (*vṛkṣaḥ śiṃśapā*) "A tree [, that is,] a tall perennial plant..." (*vṛkṣaḥ taruḥ*). But Kumārila now argues that the Apohavādin cannot explain how coreference is possible in these cases, either.

149-150ab And the non-exclusion of universals, etc. [by words indicating subtypes, or of subtypes by words indicating universals, or of synonyms by other synonyms] is not possible by virtue of [their] not conflicting. For there would not be conflict or non-conflict of the words themselves, nor [will there be a conflict] by virtue of the nature of real things, since that is not related to words.

Only meanings can conflict or not conflict; a word will exclude or not exclude another word only if their *meanings* are in conflict or not. But we have just seen how, on the Apohavāda – that is, the view that meanings are exclusions – a conflict of meanings cannot be explained without circularity; hence, the *absence* of conflict would not make sense on that theory, either. And of course, the Buddhist cannot appeal to the conflict or absence of conflict among the "real things" (*vastu*), either, since for him words only refer to *apoha*s and not real things.

150cd Nor is [that conflict or non-conflict, on the basis of which two words can be used together or not] cognized for *apoha*s prior to the functioning of words.

One also cannot argue that the conflict or non-conflict of two words is based on their *apoha*s, since their *apoha*s are not evident prior to the functioning of language or inference; they are inaccessible to other

---

[133] PS 5.24cd: *anyatve 'pi na sāmānyabhedaparyāyavācyanut* / (Pind 2015: I.7). Sucaritamiśra quotes a verse from an unidentified source, probably a work of Dignaga, ŚVKāśK 279(42),12–13: *anyatve 'pi na sāmānyabhedaparyāyavācinām / avirodhād bhavet tyāgo bhedānām iva bhedataḥ //*. "Even though they are different, [a word] would not reject [the meanings] of [other] words expressing its universals, subtypes, and synonyms, because they do not conflict, like [a subtype-word rejects the meanings of other] subtype[-word]s due to its difference [from them]."

pramāṇas.[134] So one could not know whether two words conflict or not prior to their employment, and one can't employ them without knowing that. For the universal-theory, on the other hand, it is possible to know the universals treeness and *śiṃśapā*-ness independently, by perception. Thus, prior to employing the words "tree" and *śiṃśapā* one can know that their meanings do not conflict. Hence, one can know that it is permissible to use them together in a sentence such as, "The tree is a *śiṃśapā*."

151 When a word [such as "tree"] is used in regard to a meaning that is not known by another [*pramāṇa*], how (*kena rūpeṇa*) will it be comprehended that the [meaning] has the nature of a universal?

152 If one said that exclusion of another [word] would be ascertained in accordance with [the difference of] the word [itself],[135] then what rules out the [mutual] exclusion of [syn-

[134] ŚVŚar 70,9–10: *na ca śabdavyāpārāt pūrvam anyena kenacit pramāṇena sā viruddhāviruddhatā pratipannā pratyakṣasya vastumātragrāhitvād apohagata-viruddhāviruddhatāgrahaṇāsāmarthyāt* /. "And that conflict or absence of conflict is not cognized by any other *pramāṇa* prior to the functioning of language; for since it grasps just the thing, perception is incapable of apprehending that the *apoha* is opposed or not opposed." Cf. ŚV *Apohavāda* 73c: "And without those two [language and inference] an *apoha* is not [cognized]."

[135] That the exclusion of words (as opposed to meanings) is the concern here is evident from ŚVKāśK 277(44),7–9: *yadi tv arthagatavirodhāvirodhāvadhāraṇam antareṇa śabdānurūpeṇaivānyāpohanirūpaṇam iṣyate, tataḥ śabdāpohānām anyonyaparihāreṇa vyavasthiteḥ paryāye 'pi virodhād anyonyāpohāpattiḥ* /. "But if the determination of exclusion of another is considered merely according to [the form of] the word [itself] without ascertaining the opposition or non-opposition of its meaning, then since the exclusions of words are fixed by their setting each other aside (*anyonyaparihāra*), in the case of a synonym, too, there would be the mutual exclusion [of synonymous words] due to opposition." Cf. ŚVŚar 70,18: *yadi punar artham anādṛtya svarūpabhinno gośabdo 'śvaśabdam apohata ity ucyate* [...] /. "If it is said, on the other hand, that the word 'cow,' which is distinct [just] due to its form, excludes the word 'horse,' regardless of its meaning [...]."

onymous words] like *vṛkṣa* and *taru*, due to [their] being distinct?

If the meaning of a word is not cognized independently by another *pramāṇa*, how will one even know that it refers to a universal, let alone that it is a universal that does or does not conflict with a certain subtype (so that it can or cannot be used together with the word for that subtype)? If on the other hand one maintained that the mutual exclusion or non-exclusion of words is ascertained on the basis of their phonetic forms – without any ascertainment of a conflict or absence of conflict of their meanings – then synonymous expressions like "tree" and "tall perennial plant" could not be used coreferentially, for they have different phonetic shapes.[136]

153 And without a connection (*spṛṣṭi*) with a word an *apoha* is not comprehended by an inferential mark. And [hence] its conflict or non-conflict is not established by a *liṅga*, either.

Nor could one argue that the conflict or absence of conflict of *apoha*s is determined inferentially prior to the employment of words; for inference being a conceptual activity which apprehends universals, one cannot infer the *apoha*s of words without already availing oneself of language.

154ab That their exclusion is due to not being seen, on the other hand, has been rejected previously.

At PS 5.31a Dignāga suggests that one word can be understood to exclude the meaning of another, not because it conflicts with it, but simply because it is not seen used for the referent of the other.[137] At ŚV

[136] In Sanskrit *vṛkṣa* and *taru* are synonymous words. In English there is no single word synonym for "tree"; therefore we have used the common definition "tall perennial plant."

[137] PS 5.31a: *adṛṣṭatvād vyudāso vā* (Pind 2015: I.35,6). "Or, rather, the exclusion is due to [the word for the subtype] not being observed [used for something of the other subtype]." See Pind's explanation of the passage as introducing an alternative to *virodhitva* to explain the impossibility of coreference, Pind 2015: II.105,

Apohavāda 75, however, Kumārila has already rejected the view that an *apoha* can be known by non-observation of the application of the word to other things.

154cd-155a And a universal-word is not considered to be expressive of a subtype (*bheda*). In that case, exclusion [of the subtype] is not ruled out.

At PS(V) 5.31b Dignāga considers an objection to the view that a word would be known to exclude another by *not* observing it to be applied to the same things. According to such a view, a universal-word, such as "tree," which is not synonymous with a word for one of its subtypes, such as "birch," because it is not used when one wants to indicate the subtype, would *exclude* the word for the subtype, so that "tree" and "birch" could not be used coreferentially.[138] Kumārila repeats this objection here, and now will reject Dignāga's response to it.

155bcd [Objection:] But there is somehow the observation [of the universal-word in regard to a subtype, due to context, etc., so that it does not exclude the subtype]. [Reply:] Even [the word] *kṣatriya* [is used] in some cases for a Brahmin [e.g., insofar as one refers to a courageous Brahmin as a "Kṣatriya"], so that non-exclusion [of Brahmin by *kṣatriya*] would follow.

In response to the stated objection Dignāga argues that "a universal-word makes known a difference [that is, a subtype] when it is observed

n. 378. This, according to Pind, is Dignāga's *siddhānta* for why two words cannot be employed together.

[138] PS(V) 5.31b: *evaṃ tarhi* ***sāmānyaṃ syāt svabhedanut***. [31b] *yady adarśanenāpohate, sāmānyaśabdasyāpi svabhedeṣu adarśanād apohaprasaṅgaḥ syāt* (Pind 2015: I.35,10–36,1). "[Objection:] If that is so, then **a universal [word] would exclude its own subtypes**. [31b] If [a word for a subtype] excludes [the referents of other subtype-words] because of not being observed [used for them], then a universal-word, too, insofar as it is not observed [used] for its own subtypes, would exclude [them]" (cf. Pind 2015: II.107–108).

together with purpose, context, etc."[139] That is to say, it is well known that various factors such as purpose, context, employment together with other words, and so forth, can disambiguate words or make their meanings more specific.[140] For instance, the word *saindhava*, which can mean either salt or horse, is determined to mean the former and not the latter when used in the sentence *saindhavam ānaya*, "Pass the *saindhava*," in the context of a meal. And the word *deva*, "god," which can refer to any god or lord, specifically refers to Śiva when used together with an appropriate word, e.g., when one says *devasya purārateḥ*, "of the god, the enemy of the Puras."[141] Thus, Dignāga implies, it is not the case that a universal-word cannot be used coreferentially with a word for one of its subtypes; indeed, the word for the subtype would help specify the meaning of the universal-word.

Kumārila, however, responds that if one follows this principle that merely the use of one word for another in a certain context can establish that their meanings do not exclude each other, then the word *kṣatriya* would not be opposed to the word *brahmin*, since we can imagine contexts where a Brahmin might be called a Kṣatriya! If we go by whether a word is or is not used in regard to something to determine whether its meaning excludes that of the other or not, we could get into lots of trouble.

156 If one said there is not a rejection [of a subtype by a general term] due to expectation, then it is the same for substances and actions, etc. Thus, there would undoubtedly be

---

[139] PS(V) 5.31c: ***nānyayuktasya dṛṣṭatvāt***. [31c] *dṛṣṭo hy arthaprakaraṇādibhiḥ sāmānyaśabdo viśeṣaṃ pratipādayati* (Pind 2015: I.36,2–4). "[Reply:] [That is] not [the case,] because [a universal-word] is observed connected with other [factors]. [31c] A universal-word makes known a difference [that is, a subtype] when it is observed together with purpose and context."

[140] This principle is stated by Bhartṛhari, VP 2.251: *yaugapadyam atikramya paryāye vyavatiṣṭhate / arthaprakaraṇābhyāṃ vā yogāc chabdāntareṇa vā //*. "Due to purpose or context or connection with another word, [a word] gives up simultaneity [that is, its power to convey more than one meaning at the same time] and is restricted to a sequence [indicating now one meaning, now another]."

[141] See Kunjunni Raja 1969: 55.

the same non-exclusion of standing, etc., by "tree."

Dignāga has also suggested that a subtype would not be rejected by a universal-word because the subtype is expected as what specifies the universal.[142] Kumārila points out, however, that in a sentence such as, "It stands/is located in the tree," *vṛkṣe tiṣṭhati*, the substance-word "tree" (*vṛkṣa*) as a *kāraka*-word (for the locus) expects an action. Thus, if due to "expectation" two words did not exclude each other, then "tree" and "stands" could be used coreferentially in a sentence such as, "The tree stands/is located," **vṛkṣaḥ tiṣṭhati*, which of course does not occur.

157 Similarly, [there would not be an exclusion] of *puruṣa* ["man"] by *rājan* ["king," in the expression *rājñaḥ puruṣaḥ*, "the king's man"]. And if there were exclusion (*vyudāsa*) [of *puruṣa* by the word *rājan*], then [*puruṣa*] would not be something to be qualified. But on the view that they do not exclude each other, they would be the same as "blue" and "lotus."

The word *rājan* being in the genitive in the phrase *rājñaḥ puruṣaḥ*, "the king's man," is in syntactic need of a counterpart, which is satisfied by the word *puruṣa*. So if syntactic expectation determines that words do not exclude each other, the word *rājan* would not exclude *puruṣa* and the words *rājan* and *puruṣa* would refer to the same thing. Conversely, if one accepted that the word *rājan* excluded *puruṣa*, then since that exclusion would not be possible if there were syntactic expectation, the words *rājan* and *puruṣa* could not stand in syntactic need of each other. Thus, *puruṣa* would not be qualified by the word *rājan* in the genitive case; nor, in the sentence, "It stands in the tree," *vṛkṣe tiṣṭhati*, would *tiṣṭhati*, "stands," be qualified by *vṛkṣa*, "tree," in the seventh case.[143]

---

[142] PS 5.26ab: *tanmātrākāṅkṣaṇād bhedaḥ svasāmānyena nojjhitaḥ* / (Pind 2015: I.30,9). "A subtype[-term] is not rejected by its own universal[-term], because just that is expected." See Pind 2015: II.94, n. 351.

[143] As Sucaritamiśra puts it, "standing," which is not syntactically expected

If, once again, one accepted that the words *rājan* and *puruṣa* do not exclude each other,[144] so that there could be expectation, hence a relation of qualifier and qualified, they would occur coreferentially, like "blue" and "lotus," which however is not the case. One never says, "king man" or "The tree stands."

11 The Apohavāda does not explain the hierarchy of concepts.

158-159ab As for what is said [at PS 5.35], that if [a word were learned and used] positively, it would make all meanings known, in [both] reverse and direct order, of treeness, earthen, substance, existing, and knowable (*vṛkṣatva-pārthiva-dravya-saj-jñeyeṣu*), that is incorrect. For it is not the case that every word is observed [used] for everything.

Dignāga argues at PSV 5.34 that a word is ascertained as indicating a

---

(*anākāṅkṣita*), cannot be qualified by a word in the seventh case: *saptamyantena ca tiṣṭhater anākāṅkṣitasya viśeṣyatvāyogād iti*, ŚVKāśK 273(48),3–4.

Jayamiśra, however – perhaps thinking that the discussion of the problem of syntactic expectation was concluded with v. 156 – construes 157ab (*puruṣasya tathā rājñā vyudāse na viśeṣyatā* /) differently, reading it as, "If *puruṣa* is excluded by *rājan* in that way (*tathā*), [i.e., because of non-observation], then [*puruṣa*] is not a *viśeṣya*." (Or else: "If *puruṣa* is excluded in that way, [i.e., because of non-observation], then [*puruṣa*] is not to be qualified by *rājan*.") That is, the word *puruṣa* not being employed for kings, *puruṣa* and *rājan* would exclude each other, just like "cow" and "horse." Therefore, one could not qualify the other (that is, *rājan* could not qualify *puruṣa* in the expression "the king's man"). See ŚVŚar 72,10–12: *kiṃca yo yatra na dṛṣṭaḥ sa cet tatparyudāsena pravartate tataḥ puruṣaśabdo rājani na dṛṣṭa iti so 'pi tatparyudāsena pravartamāno gaur aśva itivan na tena saha viśeṣaṇaviśeṣyabhāvaṃ yāyāt – rājapuruṣaḥ – ity atra* /. "Moreover, if a [word] which is not seen [used] for something occurs by excluding it, then since the word 'man' is not seen [used] for a king, it too would occur by excluding that [i.e., king, and] like 'cow horse' it would not enter into a qualifier-qualificand relation with that [other word 'king'] in [the expression] 'the king's man.'"

[144] Again, Jayamiśra takes *avyudāsatvapakṣe*, 157c, to mean: if one believes that one word is "somehow" (*kathaṃcit*; cf. ŚV *Apohavāda* 155b) seen used for the other kind of thing, ŚVŚar 72,14.

certain meaning primarily by *vyatireka*, that is, by its not being employed for things other than what it means. The designation of the word "tree," for example, is primarily determined by the fact that it does not occur in regard to non-trees. This can be ascertained, maintains Dignāga, simply by *not* observing its being used for non-trees (*adarśana*).[145] If, on the other hand, the meaning of a word were determined positively, by observing (when one is taught the meaning of the word by an elder) what it is used *for* – that is to say, by "positive concomitance" (*anvaya*) – then, like perception, it would reveal *all* aspects of its meaning – in the case of the word "tree," not just that it is a tree but also what specific kind of tree it is, e.g., a *śiṃśapā*.[146] But that

---

[145] See above, ŚV *Apohavāda* 75 and n. 41; see also Katsura 1991: 139–141.

[146] The idea seems to be that, if one establishes the relation of a word to what it means by negative concomitance (ascertained just by non-observation), *then one is not directly presented with its referent*, except perhaps on one or two occasions. If, on the other hand, one were to do so by positive concomitance, then one would be directly presented with its referent – and not with just one isolated property of it but all of its properties. This idea was already stated by Dignāga in PS 2.15: *dṛṣṭavad vidhirūpeṇa yadi liṅgaṃ prakāśayet / sarvatrādarśanān na syāt sarvathā vā gatir bhavet //*. "If an inferential mark revealed [the *liṅgin*, that is, the thing that has the inferential mark] positively [i.e., by positive concomitance], in the way it was [previously] perceived, then there would not be [any comprehension of it], due to [the inferential mark] not being observed for every instance [of the *liṅgin*], or else there would be total comprehension [of the *liṅgin*]." Cf. Hayes 1988: 245. This seems to presuppose the theory, articulated more clearly by Dharmakīrti, that perception apprehends the particular *in its entirety*, since its nature is cohesive, united. See Pind's discussion of PS(V) 2.15, which includes the restoration of the Sanskrit verse above based on Jinendrabuddhi's *Ṭīkā*, Pind 2015: II.225–229.

Sucaritamiśra presents the Buddhist view at some length, ŚVKāś$_{K}$ 272(49),3–271(50),4. If words like "tree," "earthen," and so on indicated universals positively (*vidhimukhena*) (that is to say, not by exclusion), then each word would make its entire meaning known (*sarvātmakārthāvabodhanam*). A word that relates to a real thing would indicate that thing as it really is. Since a tree has an earthen nature, is a substance, an existing entity, and something knowable, the word "tree" would indicate not just treeness but all of those other natures. Conversely, since existence, substancehood, earthenness, and treeness are all natures of something that is knowable, the word "knowable" would indicate, besides knowableness, all of those

is contrary to our experience. When someone says "tree," the hearer does not thereby comprehend that a specific type of tree is being referred to.[147] And this is true of all nominal expressions. They make known all the higher categories that include their meanings, but they do not specify the lower categories that are included by their meanings. Thus, if something is called a "tree" one also knows that it is earthen, a substance, an existing thing, and a knowable thing. On the other hand, if something is called "knowable," one does not know whether it is existing or non-existent, a substance or a non-substance, and so on. Dignāga summarizes this idea in PS 5.35.[148] His point is that this

---

things, too. Thus, if words indicated their meanings "positively," a word would indicate not just a certain universal but also the entire series of higher universals that include it, as well as all the lower universals it includes – for all those belong to the nature of the thing indicated. Thus, it is preferable to adopt the *apoha* theory, which implies that words do not indicate their meanings positively but rather give rise to notions that do not "touch" things (*arthāsaṃsparśinaḥ*). The other commentators also understand the Buddhist point in this way, probably under the influence of Dharmakīrti, e.g., PV 1.52–53ab.

[147] Dignāga continues at PSV 5.34: if one thinks there will be doubt because, on different occasions, the word "tree" is used to refer to different types of trees – now a *śiṃśapā*, now a *palāśa*, and so forth – then there will also be doubt when it is observed that it is used to refer to something that is earthen, something that is a substance, something existent, and so forth; that is, there will be doubt as to which of these things it refers to in addition to treeness. *anvayadvāreṇa cānumāne vṛkṣaśabdād ekasmin vastuni śiṃśapādyābhāsaḥ saṃśayo na syāt. tatsaṃśayavat pārthivatvadravyatvādyābhāso 'pi saṃśayaḥ syāt. yatas tu vṛkṣaśabdo 'pārthivādiṣu na dṛṣṭaḥ, ato vyatirekamukhenaivānumānam* (Pind 2015: I.41,4–42,1). "But if there were an inference by means of positive concomitance, [then] from the word 'tree' there would not be doubt, in regard to the same real thing, that presents a *śiṃśapā*, etc. [i.e., doubt whether it is a *śiṃśapā* or not]. [Or, if there were a doubt as to what specific type of tree is meant then] like that doubt there would be doubt that presents 'earthenness,' 'substancehood,' and so forth. But since the word 'tree' is not observed when there are things that are not earthen, etc., there is an inference [from the word, of its referents] just by means of negative concomitance." See Pind 2015: II.125, n. 428.

[148] PS 5.35: *vṛkṣatvapārthivadravyasajjñeyāḥ prātilomyataḥ / catustridvyeka-*

asymmetry is possible if the denotation of a word is based on *vyatireka*, but not if it is based on *anvaya*. If one learns the meaning of "tree" by *not* observing that it is used for a non-tree, it will leave unspecified the type of tree that is meant. But since one also does *not* observe that it is used for something that is not earthen, not a substance, and so forth, it will include those exclusions as parts of its meaning as well.

With 158–159ab Kumārila, after repeating Dignāga's idea, rejects it on the grounds that although, strictly, some real thing that is a knowable, e.g., will also be, more specifically, either an existing thing or a non-existent thing, either a substance or not a substance, either earthen or not earthen, and either a tree or not a tree, nevertheless the word "knowable" will not indicate *all* of those categories. It will only designate that aspect of it that is its proper meaning, for which a positive as well as a negative concomitance has been observed – namely, knowableness. Kumārila means by, "It is not the case that every word is observed [used] for everything," that it is not the case that, when a word is learned, it is seen to apply to all aspects of a thing. The word *jñeya*, "knowable," thus refers to knowableness, but not to any of the lower categories, existence, substanceness, etc. Therefore, by hearing *jñeya* one does not cognize all aspects of a thing, such as existing, non-existent, etc.[149]

When Kumārila says "when a word is used positively" (*vidhau*) he means: when a word is employed against the background of learning its meaning through positive concomitance (*anvaya*). In other words, using

---

sandehe nimittaṃ niścaye 'nyathā // (Pind 2015: I.42,2–3). "Treeness, earthen, substance, existent, and knowable are the cause of doubt in regard to four things, three things, two things, and one thing[, respectively,] in reverse order. Otherwise, [i.e., in direct order, they are the cause] of certainty" (cf. Pind 2015: II.125).

[149] ŚVKāśK 271(50),9–11: *ayam abhiprāyaḥ / nātyantam abhinnā vṛkṣatvādayo yenaikātmāvadhāraṇe sarvātmakāvadhāraṇaṃ bhavet / sabhāgaṃ hi tad vastu / bhāgāvalambinaś ca vicitraśaktayaḥ śabdā iti* /. "This is [his] intention: [The universals] treeness and so forth are not completely identical, so that if there is the ascertainment of one nature there would be the ascertainment of [the thing] possessing [this nature] in its entirety. For a real thing is possessed of parts, and words of diverse capacities [used to refer to it] depend on [its] parts." ŚVŚar 73,8–9 is similar.

the word, one thinks of what it is used *for*, not of what it is not used for.[150]

159cd [If one claimed that a word like “knowable” would indicate existence] due to the non-separation of their location [then there would be] a functioning of the eye in regard to taste, etc., also.

160 [Objection:] But [something’s] functioning as an agent of apprehension is fixed according to its type. [Reply:] In just the same way as in the case of [the perceptual faculties] such as vision, here [in the case of the functioning of words] there will not be a confusion.

One might, however, object that where there is one aspect of a thing, e.g., treeness, there will also be its other higher and lower aspects, e.g., substancehood, *śiṃśapā*-ness, and so forth, for they are all located in the same thing. So, if a word functioned in a positive way, how could it indicate just one aspect without indicating all the others?[151] In response, one could say that by the same reasoning one would apprehend all the sensible qualities of an object by means of just one sense, because they are all present together in the same object. Moreover, just as a sense faculty, by virtue of its type (whether vision, hearing, etc.) is restricted to apprehending an object by possessing a specific capacity for doing so, so a word is restricted to indicating a certain universal due to the possession of a specific capacity. And so, as in the case of a sense

[150] Kumārila’s *vidhau* in 158d echoes Dignāga’s *anvayadvāreṇa cānumāne* at PSV 5.35 (Pind 2015: I.41,4) and therefore should be understood as primarily related to the learning of language. The commentators, however, seem to construe it as related to the use of language. ŚV *Apohavāda* 158d, *vidhau sarvārthabodhanam*, is glossed at ŚVŚar 72,20-21 by *vidhimukhena śabde pravartamāne sarvātmakārthagrahaṇaṃ prāpnoti* and at ŚVKāśK 272(49),3–4 by *vidhimukhena jātivacanatve ... sarvātmakārthāvabodhanam āpāditam.*

[151] Jayamiśra, ŚVŚar 73,9–10, sees the problem to be that a word would include lower categories as part of its meaning. Sucaritamiśra, ŚVKāśK 271(50),15–270(51),1, explains the problem as being that a word would include all the higher categories as part of its meaning.

faculty which apprehends only one sensible quality of an object endowed with multiple qualities, when a word apprehends one universal all the others will not be apprehended.

161 But when the [designative] activity of a word has ceased, there would be the making known of existence, etc. – in some cases fewer [universals], in some cases more – due to pervasion and non-pervasion.

One might object, however, that if a word is restricted to designating only one universal in this way, then from the word "tree" one would not also acquire the idea that the object is earthen, a substance, and so forth, which one in fact does. To this, Kumārila responds in effect by saying that such knowledge will arise, but it will not be verbal knowledge; rather, it will be, essentially, inferential, that is, it will arise from the meaning itself. From the awareness that something is a tree – having heard it referred to by "tree" – one will be able to infer, on the basis of the inclusion of treeness by earthenness, substancehood, existence, and knowability, that it is earthen and so forth as well. From the fact that something is earthen – having heard it referred to by the word "earthen" – one will understand that it is a substance, existent, and so forth – but not that it is a tree, for earthenness is *not* included by treeness.

162 This fault [that a word would convey all aspects of a thing] would really (*eva*) be *yours*, because you hold the view that a general word applies [also] to a subtype (*viśeṣa*). Nor [if one takes *apoha*s as different from each other] is there really a difference of meanings [for you], either.

Only the Buddhist has the problem that the word *jñeya* denotes not only the exclusion of unknowable things but also the exclusion of non-existent things, and so forth, due to the non-separation of their location (i.e., due to the fact that both general and subtype exclusions are located in the same thing). For he believes, as Dignāga himself states PS(V) 5.18, that a general word like *jñeya* indicates the subtype exclusion (i.e., exclusion of non-existent things) as well as the exclusion of unknowable things, insofar as it includes (does not exclude) its subtype.[152] In other words, there is inclusion (*antarbhāva*) of a subtype by a general word. This idea lies at the heart of Dignāga's solution to the problem of coreference: the words "blue" and "lotus," for instance, can be used coreferentially because each indicates the differences or subtypes of the universal as well as the universal itself. "Blue" indicates not just blueness, but also specific blue things – eyes, lotuses, whales, etc. – insofar as they, too, are not excluded by it; it indicates whatever it does not exclude.[153] In that case, however, the ontological system of ordering meanings hierarchically by different degrees of pervasion (*vyāpti-avyāpti*) of the realist is not possible for the Buddhist, since all the differences that fall under the word *jñeya*, for instance – existence, non-existence, and so forth – are indicated by it.

Nor can the Buddhist claim that just like universals, exclusions can be different from each other even though they reside in the same locus; for Kumārila has already shown above (vv. 42–46) that exclusions, being non-existences, are really not distinct.[154]

---

[152] See PSV 5.17d: *dvāv api viśeṣārthau, sāmānye viśeṣāntarbhāvāt* (Pind 2015: I.19,8). "Both [words 'blue' and 'lotus'] mean the difference/subtype, because the subtype is included in the universal." This is Dignāga's answer to the question how "blue" and "lotus" can be coreferential if each in fact indicates a different universal. Each word indicates the differences or subtypes of the universal as well the universal itself just *insofar as they do not exclude them* (PS 5.18b': *anapohanāt*).

[153] While Dignāga considers this type of solution – namely, that there is inclusion of the subtype by a general word – possible for the Apohavāda, he clearly rejects it, PS 5.11a'b, for the *jātimat/tadvat* theory. See the explanation to ŚV *Apohavāda* 132 above. In response Kumārila, ŚV *Apohavāda* 132–134, once again using Dignāga's own argument against him, argues that for the *apohavat* theory, too, there could not be an implication of the subtype exclusion by the general word.

[154] The commentators interpret v. 162 rather differently from what we propose. Taking *viśeṣe* in 162b to mean the individual particular (rather than the difference or subtype, as we do), they construe Kumārila to be saying that since the Buddhist thinks that a word refers to the particular (*svalakṣaṇa*), say, a particular tree, it will make known all of its aspects, from knowableness down to the specific type of tree. ŚVŚar 74,3–4: *ekavyāvṛttiviśiṣṭe vastuni gṛhyamāṇe samastavyāvṛttiviśiṣṭagrahaṇaṃ prāpnoty eva* /. "When a real entity qualified by one exclusion is grasped,

163 Moreover, for the one who places (*kurvataḥ*) [properties of universals such as] oneness, eternality, [and] inherence in each [individual of the genus] in unreal (*nirupākhya*) *apoha*s, [for him] there is a cloth without threads!

At PS(V) 5.9cd–10a Dignāga states, as his final criticism of the *jātimat/tadvat* view, that it would imply that the meaning of a word is not something universal in nature, hence a word could not refer to many

---

grasping of a thing qualified by all exclusions would indeed follow." ŚVKāśK 269(52),10–12: *bauddhasya hi pakṣe ye 'smākaṃ sāmānyaśabdāḥ, te viśeṣe svalakṣaṇe vartante, arthāntarābhāvāt / tac ca nirbhāgam eveti ya eva kaścit tadvacanas, tenaiva sarvātmakapratītiprasaṅga iti /*. "For on the Buddhist's view, what are for us [Mīmāṃsakas] words for universals occur in regard to a difference, that is, a particular, because there is not another meaning [it *could* refer to, such as a real universal]. And since that [particular] is without parts, one would cognize it possessing all its natures by means of whatever [word] expresses it." This interpretation seems mistaken, first of all, because Dignāga does not hold the view that a general word denotes a *svalakṣaṇa*. Second, it misses the context of Kumārila's statement, namely, Dignāga's claim at PSV 5.35, that if the meanings of words were learned "positively," a universal-word (*sāmānyaśabda*), e.g., *jñeya*, would make known a subtype (*viśeṣa*), e.g., existence (*sattā*), determinately without leaving any doubt (*saṃśaya*) (see ŚV *Apohavāda* 158–159ab). As we construe Kumārila's response, he is turning the tables on the Buddhist, charging that *he* (the Buddhist) is the one with the problem (of all aspects of a thing being comprehended from a word) because *he* in fact is the one who thinks that the universal-word also indicates the difference or subtype.

For 162 c'd Sucaritamiśra then suggests, ŚVKāśK 269(52),14–268(53),3, as the first of two alternative interpretations, that it would do no good for the Buddhist to insist that words refer, not to particulars but to exclusions, and exclusions can be distinct from each other; for he (the Buddhist) actually holds that the exclusion is not different from the real (excluded) particular. Here he cites (imprecisely) PVSV 32,17: *tasmād yaiva vyāvṛttiḥ sa eva vyāvṛttaḥ*. Pārthasārathimiśra, ŚVN 433,2, even reads *vastunaḥ*, "from the real thing," for *vastutaḥ* in 162d, reinforcing the (mistaken) impression that *viśeṣe* in 162b means the particular. Sucaritamiśra's second interpretation of 162c'd conforms to ours: there is, for the Buddhist, in fact no real (*tāttvika*) difference of meanings if they are *apoha*s, ŚVKāśK 268(53),8–10.

things; for the thing possessing the genus is an individual[155] (see above, v. 128). Later, at PS(V) 5.36d, concluding an extended argument that the Apohavāda is vulnerable to *none* of the objections that affect other theories, Dignāga claims that *apoha*s do have some of the attributes of universals – without of course being *real* universals. Specifically, and rather extraordinarily, Dignāga claims that *apoha*s are one, eternal, and exist completely (not partially) in each individual.[156] Particularly because of the last characteristic it would seem that they would be able to extend over many things at once.[157] Kumārila here simply ridicules the idea that *apoha*s, which are non-existences, could possibly have the properties of real universals. Someone who thinks so would be like someone who thinks there could be a cloth without threads.[158]

Now, summarizing his critique of the Apohavāda, Kumārila says:

164 Therefore, for just those words for which there is a connection with "non-" – only for them would the portion that

---

[155] PS(V) 5.9cd-10a: *tadvān artho ghaṭādiś cen na paṭādiṣu vartate // sāmānyam arthaḥ sa katham* (Pind 2015: I.11,6–7). "If the meaning, the possessor of that [genus 'existence'], i.e., a pot and so forth, does not exist in a cloth and so forth, how can this meaning be a universal?"

[156] PS(V) 5.36d: *atra ca* ***jātidharmavyavasthiteḥ*** [36d]. *jātidharmāś caikatvanityatvapratyekaparisamāptilakṣaṇā atraiva vyavatiṣṭhante, abhedād āśrayāvicchedāt kṛtsnārthapratīteḥ* (Pind 2015: I:44,9–45,1). "And because the attributes of a genus are valid for it. [36d] Moreover, the attributes of a genus, which are characterized by oneness, permanence, and complete [not partial] existence in each individual, are valid only for it, because [an exclusion] is not a particular, because its substratum is not destroyed, and because its referent is cognized completely." According to Jinendrabuddhi *vyavatiṣṭhante* simply means *yujyante*; see Pind 2015: II.272, n. 460. "Only for it" (*atraiva*) could refer to the fact that none of these characteristics could be true of *real* universals, since the latter are impossible.

[157] Cf. PSV 5.36c: *avyāpakatvāc cāsāmānyadoṣo 'pi nāsti, arthāntarāpohamātrasyābhinnatvād adravyatvāc ca* (Pind 2015: 1,44,4–5). "And the defect of not being a universal because it does not pervade [all the individuals] does not exist [for an *apoha*], because the mere exclusion of other meanings is without division and because it is not a substance."

[158] Or, as one might say in American English, "I have a bridge I'd like to sell him."

is the exclusion of another [be the meaning]. In the case of any other word (*anyatra*) just the thing itself is comprehended.

"The portion that is the exclusion of another" expresses the idea that non-being is an aspect – a *real* aspect – of an existing thing.

12 One cannot prove by inference that words *do not* refer to *apoha*s.

Now Kumārila criticizes a Nyāya refutation of the Apohavāda.

165 By whom it is said that there is non-exclusion of things other than the thing to be known [by a word] (*jñeyārthānyānapohatva*) because it is a factor of valid cognition (*pramāṅgatvāt*) like [a sense faculty] such as touch, for him there would be inconclusiveness [of his reason] on account of words connected with "non-."

Some Naiyāyikas[159] rejected the Apohavāda on the basis of the following inference (*anumāna*): A word does not indicate its meaning by excluding another, because it is a factor or means of valid cognition (*pramāṅgatvāt*), like a sense faculty.[160] The *vyāpti* (major premise) of this inference, however – whatever is a factor of valid cognition does not function by exclusion – admits of counterexamples. Words like "non-Brahmin" are factors of valid cognition, yet they make something known – Brahmins – by excluding other things that are not Brahmins. So the reason of the Nyāya argument ("because it is a factor of valid cognition") is inconclusive.

---

[159] We have been unable to trace this argument to any Nyāya text. Jayamiśra says simply that it is what is put forward by "the knower of the subject of logic" (*nyāyavistaravidā*, ŚVŚar 74,18), which probably does not refer to a specific author.

[160] ŚVKāśK 267(54),9–11: *yo 'rthaḥ śabdāj jñāyate sa tadanyaṃ nāpohate, pramāsādhanatvāt / yat pramāṅgaṃ tan nānyāpohavṛtti tvagādīndriyavad iti /.* "The meaning which is known from a word does not exclude something else, because it produces a valid cognition. That which is a means of valid cognition does not function by exclusion of another, like the faculties of touch and so forth."

166 If one were to take all [words, even those prefixed by "non-"] as the subject [of the inference], then there would be non-conclusiveness due to indirect reasons (*āvītahetu*) and contradiction by what is established for ordinary people.

One might, however, consider words like "non-Brahmin" to fall within the subject of the inference, for they are words after all. Thus, they could not be counterexamples to the *vyāpti* and the reason would not be inconclusive. There are other counterexamples, however, in particular indirect (*āvīta-*) logical reasons[161] that are related to the property-to-be-proved merely by negative concomitance (*vyatireka*), that is, so-called *kevalavyatirekihetu*s. For instance "breath," or the fact that something is breathing, proves that it has a self, effectively by ruling out things that lack a self. The *vyāpti* of such an inference is established solely by negative concomitance: it is never observed that something that has breath lacks a self.[162] Because of such indirect logical reasons, then, the major premise of the Naiyāyika's argument against the Apohavāda, namely, that whatever is a factor of valid cognition does not function by exclusion, is still inconclusive.

---

[161] See Franco 1999, which establishes that *āvīta* is the original form of this expression (as opposed to *avīta*, which occurs in some texts) and that in Nyāya it was interpreted as a *kevalavyatirekihetu*.

[162] One must rely on a *kevalavyatirekihetu* for proving the existence of a self, because, selves being unobservable, one cannot establish a positive concomitance between them and other things. On the *kevalavyatirekihetu* argument for the existence of a self from the body's possession of breath see Eltschinger/Ratié 2013: 116–138. Note, however, that the example Uddyotakara gives of an argument with a *kevalavyatirekihetu* is formulated rather differently: "This living body is not without a self, because [if it were] it would follow that it would not have breath, etc." *nedaṃ jīvaccharīraṃ nirātmakam aprāṇādimattvaprasaṅgād iti*, NV 43,12. In other words, if something is without a self, then it is without breath; the body has breath, therefore, it has a self. The major premise of this argument ("if something is without a self then it is without breath") is a *vyatireka*, a statement of co-absence, which is based merely on non-observation: one *never observes* that something that lacks a self has breath. Dharmakīrti objects, in essence, that precisely because a self is *not* observable, talk about non-observation is meaningless: one cannot *tell* whether something has a self or not. Therefore, one cannot say that something that *lacks* a self is without breath (see Eltschinger/Ratié 2013: 126–129).

Moreover, by bringing negative expressions such as "non-Brahmin" into the subject of the inference, the thesis of the inference would be refuted by experience: ordinary people are all aware that the prefix "non-" has the meaning of negation.[163]

167 And if "it does not exclude" means does not exclude physically (*kārakatvena*) or [does not cause] an awareness of just the *apoha*, then that would be proving what is already proven.

What could the Naiyāyika mean when he says, "A word does not exclude another," anyway? He could not mean that a word does not function as a causal factor, a *kāraka*, that physically excludes what is other; for the Buddhist certainly does not believe that. The Buddhist, like others, holds that a word is not a *kāraka*, something which causes something, but a *jñāpaka*, something which makes something known. And the Naiyāyika could not mean that a word, even if it were a *jñāpaka*, does not produce an awareness of just the *apoha* without a substratum; for the Buddhist would also agree with that. For the Buddhist, a word produces an awareness of a thing qualified by an *apoha*.

168 [Objection:] What is proved [by the *anumāna* of the Naiyāyika] is that [the word] does not apply to a thing possessing an *apoha*. [Reply:] Then it would be negated by a previous thesis due to the fact that there is [actually] the absence of horse, etc., in cowness, too.

If the Naiyāyika maintains that his inference serves to prove that a word like "cow" does not even apply to a thing that *possesses* an exclusion – i.e., the exclusion of non-cow – then that would be contradicted by the Naiyāyika's acceptance of mutual non-existence: a cow is not a horse and a horse is not a cow. Even for the Naiyāyika the word "cow" refers to something qualified by the absence of horse, namely, cowness.

---

[163] That is to say, the inference would have the fault of the thesis (*pratijñābhāsa*) called *sarvalokaprasiddhivirodha*. See ŚV *Anumāna* 64cd–65ab.

169 And the example lacks the property to be proved. For his [i.e., the observer's] vision, etc., also function towards an object which has an *apoha*, even though he does not notice (*budhyate*) it.

Moreover, if one interpreted the inference as proving that a word does not make known something possessing an *apoha*, then the example would lack the property to be proved. Even for the Naiyāyika, as for the Buddhist, *all* things have discrete natures (*asaṅkīrṇasvabhāva*); everything is excluded from everything else. So whatever particular object a sense faculty applies to, it too is excluded from all other things. Touch, vision, etc., in other words, do make something possessing an *apoha* known, even though the knower may not be aware of the *apoha* as such.[164]

170 [Objection: What we claim is that] there is no cognition that presents exclusion of another [itself]. [Reply:] That is proving what is already proven [for the Buddhist]. For even if

---

[164] We note that the commentators construe *budhyate* as causative, i.e. equivalent to *bodhayati*, perhaps because they are uncomfortable with Kumārila's syntax in which the subject evidently changes from 169bc to 169d. Kumārila's original intention, however, is this: his (*tasya*, i.e. an observer's) eye, etc. function towards an object which has an *apoha*, though he (the observer) does not notice it (*tam*, i.e., the *apoha*).

169bc: *cakṣurādy api tasya$_1$ hi vartate 'pohavaty arthe*

169d: *taṃ (apohaṃ) yady api (sa$_1$) na budhyate*

Here – as we understand the verse – the subject of *budhyate* ("notices"), the observer, is not expressed by any noun (pronoun) in 169d but is referred to by *tasya* in 169b. The commentators, on the other hand, consider the eye, etc. to be the subject in both, thus in effect construing v. 169 as follows:

169bc: *cakṣurādy api tasya$_1$ hi vartate 'pohavaty arthe*

169d: *taṃ (apohaṃ) yady api na budhyate (= bodhayati)*

Cf. ŚVŚar 76,2: *yadi param evaṃ te na pratipādayanti* [...] /. "Although they do not make [it] known in this way [...]." ŚVKāś$_K$ 264(57),2: *apohaṃ tu na pratipādayanti, tasya [apohasya] pramāṇābhāvagamyatvāt* /. "But they do not make the exclusion known, because it is to be known by means of the absence of *pramāṇa*s." Construing the verse in this way may have led them to neglect to explain *tasya* in 169b.

this [meaning] has the nature of an *apoha*, it is comprehended as a real thing.

The Naiyāyika might, however, come back and insist that what his inference is intended to prove is that a word does not give rise to a cognition that *presents* the exclusion of another. The Buddhist, however, would readily agree to this, too. Due to beginningless mental impressions *apoha*s are indeed apprehended – erroneously – as real universals common to many particulars. They, too, therefore would agree that a cognition does not *present* an *apoha*.

171 [Objection:] [When it is said that a word does not exclude another] it is denied that [the word's] application to [its] meaning is caused by an exclusion. [Reply:] Again, since it is accepted [by the Naiyāyika] that negative concomitance [also] is the means [of a word indicating its meaning], there is negation by a previous thesis

The Naiyāyika might hold that "a word does not indicate its meaning by excluding another" just means that it is not *caused* by an exclusion. That is to say, the meaning of a word is not learned just by ascertaining a negative concomitance, i.e., that it does *not* apply to other things. But in fact the Naiyāyika believes that *both* positive and negative concomitance, *anvaya* and *vyatireka*, are the means of ascertaining the meaning of a word. So if he denies that negative concomitance (e.g., ascertaining that the word "cow" does not apply to non-cows) is a cause of its use, he contradicts his own thesis.

172 And since it is that way in the case of inference, [the Naiyāyika's reason "because it is a factor of valid cognition"] would be inconclusive; [and it would be inconclusive] on account of a perceptual cognition that arises by setting aside doubt, too.

The Naiyāyika admits that valid logical reasons are generally ascertained by *both* negative and positive concomitance. So, if he interprets his inference against *apoha* as proving that exclusion is not the cause of the application of a word, then the major premise that *pramāṅgas* in general do not function by exclusion would be false and the reason, "because it is a factor of valid cognition," inconclusive. Moreover, when one cognizes perceptually, "That is a person, not a post," after having doubted whether it is a post – this too is a means of veridical awareness that functions by excluding something else, and so would be a counterexample to the major premise. Thus, once again, the logical reason of the inference, "because it is a factor of valid cognition," must be seen as inconclusive.

173 And (*ca*) the reason is contradictory, because a word, like [the sense faculties] the ear, etc., [which are factors of veridical cognition], also (*ca*) abandons being expressive of the self, the mind (*antaḥkaraṇa*), space, and heaven.

Moreover, the reason "because it is a factor of valid cognition, like a sense faculty," could actually be used to prove the opposite of what the Naiyāyika intends. One could formulate the inference: "The words 'self,' 'mind,' 'space,' and 'heaven' do *not* indicate the self, etc., because they are factors of valid cognition, like hearing, etc." Since sense perception is a factor of valid cognition that does *not* apprehend supersensible things like the self, the mind, etc., words would not indicate such things, as well, insofar as they are factors of valid cognition too.

174 Or [for the Naiyāyika attempting to refute *apoha* in this way, there is a counterproof, namely:] A word which [allegedly] functions positively [actually] functions by means of *apoha*, because it is a factor of inference, like [the word indicating the negative example] that negates.

One can construct a counterproof just on the basis of a word being a factor of inference, parallel to the word being a factor of veridical cognition. For the word indicating the negative example in an inference, e.g., "space" in the inference of the non-eternality of sound, which is certainly a factor in the arising of a correct inferential cognition,[165] functions to exclude it from the class of things to which the *hetu* applies.

175 Moreover, this [word] does not express (*bravīti*) either a universal, nor an individual qualified by that [universal], because it serves as a factor of valid cognition, like the sense of touch, hearing, etc.

If one takes as one's reason *pramāṅgatvāt*, "because it is a factor of valid cognition," and the sense of touch or hearing as the example, then a word doesn't even express a universal or something qualified by one; for these other faculties do not "speak" (*bravīti*) at all![166] Thus, *pramāṅgatvāt* becomes in this way, too, a *viruddhahetu*.

So much for the Naiyāyikas' attempt to refute the Apohavāda by means of a simple *anumāna*!

176 Thus, the determination of what is the meaning and what is not the meaning is not settled by means of proof [that is, a formal inference]. Therefore, here, it is taught according to [the understanding of] ordinary people.

---

[165] As in the stock example of an inference, "Sound is not eternal, because it is produced, like a pot, unlike space." The negative example "space" serves to illustrate that the reason is not found in what lacks the property to be proved.

[166] This objection is based on taking "expresses" or "speaks" literally, in a way no doubt unintended by the Naiyāyika, and thus would fall under the category of cavilling (*chala*), specifically, cavilling about a word used in a secondary sense (*upacārachala*). See NS 1.2.14.

Part Three

Interpretive Essays

John Taber

The Place of the *Apohavāda* Chapter in the Early Debate about *apoha*: Dignāga, Uddyotakara, Kumārila, and Dharmakīrti

1 The situation of the *Apohavāda* chapter in Kumārila's system

In order to understand the *Apohavāda* chapter of Kumārila's *Ślokavārttika* one must, first of all, understand how it fits into his system. Three chapters of the *Ślokavārttika* are dedicated to presenting the Mīmāṃsā view of universals, expanding and elaborating Śabara's interpretation of MS 1.1.5, which states that the "original" or "natural" relation of word and meaning is the (means of) knowledge of Dharma.[167] The word "original" or "natural" (*autpattika*) is glossed variously by Śabara as "authorless" (*apauruṣeya*), "unfabricated" (*akṛtaka*), and "eternal" (*nitya*). With the first two verses of ŚV *Ākṛtivāda*, the first of the three chapters concerned with universals, Kumārila seems to be laying out a strategy for defending MS 1.1.5. In order for the relation of word and meaning to be eternal – hence in order for language to be eternal, which is required for the Veda to be an eternal, infallible means of knowing Dharma – not only must words be eternal, but also their meanings. If the meaning of a word were something other than a universal – if, say, a word directly indicated all the individuals it can be used for – "the relation [of the word with its meaning] and its eternality could not be established" (ŚV *Ākṛtivāda*

---

[167] *autpattikas tu śabdasyārthena sambandhas tasya jñānam* [...] (Frauwallner 1968: 34,13–14). "The natural connection of a word with [its] meaning [in a Vedic sentence] is, rather, the [instrument of] knowledge of that [i.e., of Dharma, and not perception or any other means of knowledge] [...]."

1).[168] One could not possibly learn the relation of a word with countless individuals, and even if one could, since individuals are perishable, the relation would not be permanent. The *Ākṛtivāda*, therefore, will be concerned with proving the existence of universals. The demonstration that universals are in fact the meanings of words, however, will come later, Kumārila tells us, when considering MS 1.3.30–33, the *Ākṛtyadhikaraṇa*, which Kumārila will take up in his *Tantravārttika* (ŚV *Ākṛtivāda* 2).[169]

Both Śabara and Kumārila clarify that the word *ākṛti* used in MS 1.3.33 – "The *ākṛti*, rather, [is the word-meaning,] because [an injunction] is for the purpose of action"[170] – does not mean shape or configuration, as it does in Nyāya, but genus (*jāti*) or commonality (*sāmānya*).[171] Śabara, for his part, does not think it necessary to prove the existence of universals since, as he believes, they are perceptible. Even Kumārila's proof in his *Ākṛtivāda* is based mainly on an appeal to experience: we cognize things as being both distinct and common in nature. A particular cow is apprehended as distinct from other kinds of animals as well as other individual cows, but also as the same as other cows.[172] We should take such cognitions at face

[168] ŚV *Ākṛtivāda* 1: *ākṛtivyatirikte 'rthe sambandho nityatāsya ca / na sidhyetām iti jñātvā tadvācyatvam ihocyate //*. "If the meaning were distinct from the *ākṛti*, then a relation and its eternality could not be established. Realizing this, it is stated here [in this treatise, or more generally, in Mīmāṃsā] that that is what is meant."

[169] ŚV *Ākṛtivāda* 2: *tatsadbhāvaprasiddhyartham atra tāvat prayatyate / vācyatve vakṣyate yuktir vyaktyā saha balābale //*. "Here, first of all, an effort is made to prove the existence of that [universal]. The reasoning in regard to its being what is expressed will be stated [later], with respect to [its relative] strength or weakness [in comparison] with the individual." Cf. TV 308,3–14/Harikai 2012: 77,12–24.

[170] MS 1.3.33: *ākṛtis tu kriyārthatvāt /*.

[171] MSBh 294, 2-3: *dravyaguṇakarmaṇāṃ sāmānyamātram ākṛtiḥ /*. "*ākṛti* is the mere commonality of substances, qualities, and actions." ŚV *Ākṛtivāda* 3: *jātim evākṛtiṃ prāhur*[1] *vyaktir ākriyate 'nayā / sāmānyaṃ tac ca piṇḍānām ekabuddhinibandhanam //*. [1]*prāhur* ŚVś : *prāha* ŚVK. "They call the genus *ākṛti* [with the following derivation in mind:] The individual is formed (*ākriyate*) by this. And that is the commonality of individuals which is the cause of a cognition of one thing."

[172] ŚV *Ākṛtivāda* 5: *sarvavastuṣu buddhiś ca vyāvṛttyanugamātimikā / jāyate*

value, insists Kumārila; there is no valid reason to think that they are mistaken.

The *Apohavāda* chapter then, the second in the series of chapters concerned with universals, refutes the Buddhist view that the meanings of words are exclusions, though Śabara does not mention *apoha*. The *Vanavāda* chapter, the last in the series, answers various objections to the reality and perceptibility of universals, one of which Śabara discusses at some length, namely, that the idea of a universal distinct from individuals is a kind of delusion (*vyāmoha*), like the notion of a forest distinct from its trees.[173]

This brief overview of the organization of Kumārila's treatment of universals, I believe, will make one of most of the most striking features of the *Apohavāda* chapter of the ŚV a little less mysterious, namely, that it is almost entirely negative in its intent. Its purpose, that is to say, is only to *refute* the *apoha* view, not to prove the Mīmāṃsā position that universals are the meanings of words, nor even to defend the latter against Dignāga's criticisms of it. For, as has just been mentioned, the demonstration that universals are word-meanings is postponed until the exegesis of the *Ākṛtyadhikaraṇa* (MS 1.3.30–33). At most, the theory that universals are word-meanings receives indirect support in ŚV *Apohavāda*, insofar as it is shown that the *apoha* theory, in one way or another, entails that meanings are real universals. Hence, Kumārila's opening statement (ŚV *Apohavāda* 1): "It is obvious that those who imagine the general entity which is the negation of non-cow as the denotation [of words], speak of cowness, which is indeed a real thing, by means of the expression 'exclusion of non-cow.'"[174]

This primarily negative orientation of the *Apohavāda* chapter stands in marked contrast to the approach taken by Uddyotakara in his critique of Dignāga's Apohavāda in *Nyāyavārttika* ad NBh 2.2.66, which must have

---

dvyātmakatvena vināsau[1] *ca na sidhyati* //. [1]*vināsau* ŚV$_K$: *vinā sā* ŚV$_Ś$. "Moreover, in regard to all things a cognition arises which has the nature of exclusion and inclusion; and that is not admissible without [those things] having a dual nature."

[173] Frauwallner 1968: 40,14–42,9.

[174] ŚV *Apohavāda* 1: *agonivṛttiḥ sāmānyaṃ vācyaṃ yaiḥ parikalpitam / gotvaṃ vastv eva tair uktam ago'pohagirā sphuṭam* //.

influenced Kumārila. An initial grasp of Kumārila's undertaking in the *Apohavāda* chapter can be gained by comparing it with Uddyotakara's discussion. This will also provide an opportunity to offer a preliminary characterization of Dignāga's Apohavāda, the target theory, at least as seen through Uddyotakara's eyes, and thereby to begin to acquaint ourselves with some of the philosophical issues at the heart of the debate.[175]

2 Dignāga and Uddyotakara

According to Uddyotakara, Dignāga – whom he quotes and paraphrases but never mentions by name – establishes that *apoha*s are the meanings of words by process of elimination. Having shown that all the theories of word-meaning put forth by other teachers are beset with insuperable difficulties, the view that they are *apoha*s is the only viable option.[176] Uddyotakara's critique, thus, in effect, considers only the beginning of Dignāga's presentation of his Apohavāda in *Pramāṇasamuccaya* 5, up to verse 11. The rest of PS 5, which goes into many subleties of the theory and also explains how it escapes the difficulties that plague other theories, is ignored by him. This is, certainly, one of the main differences between Uddyotakara's and Kumārila's discussions of *apoha*. Kumārila examines PS 5 much more comprehensively and in depth, with a much better understanding of the technical issues, than Uddyotakara. Kumārila's treatment represents a significant advance in the critique of Dignāga's theory.

NS 2.2.66 states the final Nyāya view (*siddhānta*) concerning the meanings of words. A word denotes all three of the entities that were considered and rejected, one by one, in the preceding *sūtra*s as exclusively the meaning of a word: the individual (*vyakti*), the genus (*jāti*), and the

[175] Previous discussions of Uddyotakara's refutation of the *apohavāda* in NV 2.2.66 are to be found in Matilal 2002: 230–254, Sen 2011: 180–183, and Much 1994.

[176] NV 308, 4–5: *na cānyā gatir asti / tasmād anyārthāpohakṛc chrutir iti /.* "And there is no other alternative. Therefore, a word causes the exclusion of other meanings." Cf. PS 5.11d: *tenānyāpohakṛc chrutiḥ* (Pind 2015: I.15,4).

shape or configuration (*ākṛti*).[177] I shall refer to this view as the combination theory. Uddyotakara begins his exposition of Dignāga's view with the assertion: "Some say that individual, configuration, and genus are not the meaning of a word. Why? Because these alternatives are not possible."[178] First, the genus or universal[179] cannot be the meaning. Taking the word "existing" as the example, it could not refer to the genus existence, because it is used in grammatical coordination with words that express "differences," that is, specific kinds of existing things, as in the phrase "an existing substance." A genus is one thing, a substance a completely different thing. Coreferential words, however, must refer to the same thing. Nor can coreference be accounted for in this case by the genus existence being located in the substance; for a genus located in a substance is said to be possessed by the substance, not to *be* the substance. For this same reason – that coreference would be impossible – the relation of an individual substance, quality, or motion with the genus, that is, the inherence of the genus in the individual, could not be the meaning, either.[180] This initial argument of Uddyotakara's *pūrvapakṣa* corresponds to PS(V) 5.2cd.[181]

Next, the Apohavādin argues that all individual existing things could not be the meaning of "existing," either. First of all, the number of existing

---

[177] NS 2.2.66: *vyaktyākṛtijātayas tu padārthaḥ* /. "The individual, configuration, and genus are the meaning of a word."

[178] NV 307,5: *na vyaktyākṛtijātayaḥ padārtha iti kecit / kutaḥ / vikalpānupapatteḥ* /.

[179] NS, NBh, and NV prefer to use the expression *jāti* when talking about universals, as do Dignāga and Dharmakīrti. I shall translate *jāti* as "genus," taking it however to be synonymous with the expressions typically used by Mīmāṃsakas, *ākṛti* and *sāmānya*, which I shall normally translate as "universal" (the term used in modern philosophical discourse); see n. 75 above. In other words, as far as I am able to tell, *jāti*, *ākṛti*, and *sāmānya* all mean the same thing in the texts I shall be discussing: a universal. Nevertheless, out of respect for the fact that different authors preferred different expressions (but at the risk of causing some confusion in the reader), I shall render them with distinct terms that are, at the same time, essentially synonymous. There is only a slight difference in meaning between "genus" and "universal" in philosophical English, if any.

[180] NV 307,7–13.

[181] Pind 2015: I.3,3–4,3.

things is countless if not infinite.[182] In that case, one could never apprehend the relation between a word and all the things it supposedly refers to, and a word whose relation with its meaning is unknown cannot give rise to a cognition of its meaning when it is heard. Second, even if a relation between a word and infinitely many existing things could be established, one would not know which kind of existing thing is being referred to when the word is used. The mind would be uncertain as to whether it is a substance, a quality, or an action. Thus, "existing," and by analogy any other word, would be ambiguous.[183] This argument corresponds to PS(V) 5.2ab.[184]

One should note that, absurd as the idea may seem that a word directly denotes infinitely many individuals (and not *via* some kind of universal), certain participants in the debate about word-meaning in early Indian philosophy defended the view that a word must refer to an individual when it is used.[185] It is represented, for instance, by the *pūrvapakṣin* of Śabara's commentary on MS 1.3.30–33. His *pūrvapakṣin*, who may well represent a certain tendency within Mīmāṃsā, argues that if words did not indicate individuals, there could be no injunctions of actions; for an action can only be carried out in relation to a concrete individual – a cake to be offered, an animal to be sacrificed and dismembered, and so on.[186] Moreover, the

---

[182] Uddyotakara, following Dignāga PS 5.2b, uses the expression "infinity." NV 307,14: *piṇḍānām ānantyāt*, "due to an infinity of individuals."

[183] NV 307,13–18.

[184] Pind 2015: I.2,3–3,3.

[185] The idea goes back to the ancient grammarian Vyāḍi, whose arguments are preserved by Patañjali in the debate about the meaning of general terms ad P 1.2.64 (Vyāḍi's view being represented in *vārttika*s 45–52). See Scharf 1996: 52–56.

[186] Śabara takes MS 1.1.30, *prayogacodanābhāvād arthaikatvam avibhāgāt* /, "Because there would not be the injunction of the performance [of actions otherwise], there is sameness of meaning [of Vedic and ordinary words], because of non-distinction," in two ways.[1] First, MSBh 291,9–12, he interprets it as asserting the *siddhānta* that the meanings of ordinary words and Vedic words are the same, due to the impossibility of enjoining actions otherwise (i.e., as the *siddhānta* of the *Lokavedaśabdaikyādhikaraṇa*).[2] Second, MSBh 296,2–301,2, he interprets it as stating the *pūrvapakṣa* of the topic concerning whether the meaning of a word is the universal or the individual (i.e., as the *pūrvapakṣa* of the *Ākṛtyadhikaraṇa*). It must

pūrvapakṣin continues in MS 1.3.31, if a word did not denote individuals – if, that is to say, it denoted a universal – then "it could not be a word for a substance."[187] That is to say, as Kumārila explains, there could be no

---

be the individual, the *pūrvapakṣin* holds, because of the impossibility of enjoining actions otherwise; for actions such as the slaughtering of a sacrificial victim can be performed only on individuals.[3]

[1] Cf. different translations of the *sūtra*, Jhā 1933: I.116 and 118. Kumārila notes that *prayogacodanābhāvād* can also be construed positively, namely, as "because of the existence of the injunction of the performance [of actions]." TV 291,27/Harikai 2012: 62,34: *ekatve sati sadbhāvād iti vā hetuvarṇanā* /. "Or [the *sūtra*] is a stating of the reason [why Vedic and ordinary words and their meanings are identical, namely,] because there is [the injunction of the performance of actions] when there is identity."

[2] Śabara notes, however, MSBh 291,13–14, that this only states the purpose (*prayojana*) of the identity of meanings – *and* words; for both Śabara and Kumārila interpret the *sūtra* to be asserting the identity of both words and meanings. The reason (MSBh 291,13: *hetu*; TV 292,11/ Harikai 2012: 63,8: *pramāṇa*) is given by the second ablative of the *sūtra*, "because of non-distinction" (*avibhāgāt*). Kumārila explains various ways of understanding this reason at TV 292,11–14/ Harikai 2012: 63,10–14, e.g., because of the non-distinction of recollective cognitions [when one or the other word is uttered?] (*pratyabhijñārūpapratyayāvibhāgāt*; emended according to Harikai). Some of the alternatives are rather obscure, however; it is possible the text of the TV here is corrupt.

[3] Kumārila suggests the following reading of MS 1.3.30 along these lines, TV 300,14–15/Harikai 2012: 71,14–15: *prayogacodanābhāvād vyaktir vācyā na tūbhayam / arthaikatvaṃ yato yuktam avibhāgād dvayor gatiḥ //*. "Because there would not be the injunction of the performance [of actions otherwise], the individual is expressed [by a word], not both [universal and individual]. Due to this, there is the identity of meaning [of Vedic and ordinary words]. There is comprehension of both [the universal and individual from the word, however], because they are not distinct."

[187] MS 1.3.31: *adravyaśabdatvāt* /. Śabara analyses *dravyaśabda* as *dravyāśrayasya* (= *guṇasya*) *śabdo dravyaśabdaḥ* (MSBh 301,7). Thus, for him, the *sūtra* means that a word expressing a quality, such as number, could not be used together with a word for a substance, as in the phrase, "Six cows are to be given." That is to say, *adravyaśabdatvāt* means, "Because [if words like "cow" indicated universals] there would not be words [expressive of] what have substances [as their support, i.e., qualities, occurring with them]" (cf. Jhā 1933: I.119). Kumārila criticizes this

coreference of a word like "cow" with a word for a quality, like "red," or with a word for a number, like "six"; for a universal has nothing to do with color or number.[188] We have also seen that, while the Naiyāyika's final position, stated in NS 2.2.66, is that the individual is *part* of the meaning of a word, along with the genus and the configuration, the view that a word refers exclusively to an individual is considered and rejected under NS 2.2.60–61.

Uddyotakara's Apohavādin next considers the possibility that a word refers to a thing possessing a genus (*jātimat*);[189] that is to say, "existing" refers to an individual (that is, a substance, quality, or motion) possessing the genus existence. This proposal, too, seems specifically related to the Nyāya position. Both Vātsyāyana and Uddyotakara will say that a word, insofar as it indicates both genus and individual, indicates the individual *as qualified* by the genus.[190] This seems very close, if not equivalent, to saying

---

interpretation as "far-fetched" (*atikliṣṭa*; see TV 302,16–21/Harikai 2012: 73,5–12), preferring to take *dravya* in its usual sense as "substance." Hence, the *sūtra* means, if general terms referred to universals, then they would not refer to individual substances, and so could not be used coreferentially with words indicating qualities (i.e., adjectives).

[188] See TV 301,21–302,16/Harikai 2012: 72,22–73,4. Cf. Jhā 1983: I.340.

[189] Literally, to "the possessor of the genus in general" (*jātimanmātra*). NV 307,18–19: *jātimanmātrābhidhāyako 'pi sacchabdo na bhavati /*. "Nor does the word 'existing' indicate the possessor of the genus in general." Although Dignāga himself introduces the view in question in this way – PSV 5.4a: *ye tv āhuḥ viśeṣaśabdaiḥ sāmānādhikaraṇyāt sambandhasaukaryād avyabhicārāc ca jātimanmātraṃ vivakṣitam iti* (Pind 2015: I.5,4–5) – he later, PS(V) 5.9ab, allows his opponent to object that it would not fall prey to the problems Dignāga raises if it were properly interpreted to mean that a word refers to "the possessor of the genus *in general*" (*jātimanmātra*). Dignāga, however, swiftly points out, loc. cit., that it would then be vitiated by other problems.

[190] NBh 130,3–4: *nātra dravyamātram aviśiṣṭaṃ jātyā vinābhidhīyate / kiṃ tarhi / jātiviśiṣṭam / tasmān na vyaktiḥ padārthaḥ /*. "In these cases ['The cow which is standing,' 'The cow which is sitting'], the mere, unqualified substance is not indicated without the genus. What, then? [The substance] qualified by the genus. Therefore, the individual is not the word-meaning." NV 309,19–20: *asmākaṃ tu dravyaguṇakarmāṇi sattāviśeṣaṇāny* [*sacchabdena*] *abhidhīyante /*. "For us, on the

that it indicates an individual possessing a genus – *jātimat*. Śabarasvāmin, meanwhile, refutes the view that the individual qualified by the universal (*ākṛti*) is the meaning of a word in his commentary on MS 1.1.33.[191]

The Apohavādin rejects the *jātimat* view on the grounds that it, too, fails to provide for coreference. Indeed, the criterion of coreference is beginning to appear as the crucial test any theory of word-meaning must pass. If a word referred to an individual possessing the genus, maintains the Apohavādin, then it would not refer to it directly or independently. Rather, its use would be mediated by reference to the genus, which by itself does not imply any differences. Thus, a word such as "existing" could not be used coreferentially with a word for a "difference," that is, a particular kind of existing thing, such as "pot," which *directly* indicates its referent, the pot.[192] Moreover, the word "existing" on the *jātimat* view would primarily

---

other hand, a substance, quality, and motion are indicated [by the word 'existing'] as having the qualifier existence."

[191] MSBh 304,5–317,3. The *pūrvapakṣin* falls back on this position after the individual view has been refuted, in order to explain how a word can be applied to more than one individual of a certain type (e.g., different individual cows) but not other individuals of other types (e.g., horses).

The *ākṛtiviśiṣṭavāda* is one of the eight main possible theories Kumārila enumerates at the beginning of his discussion of MS 1.3.30, which he goes on to show can be combined recursively to yield a plethora of theories (TV 293,13–294,8/ Harikai 2012: 64,16–65,16). The eight main possibilities are that the meaning is: just the *ākṛti*, just the *vyakti*, either the *ākṛti* or the *vyakti*, both *ākṛti* and *vyakti*, their relation (*sambandha*), their collection (*samudāya*), the *vyakti* qualified by the *ākṛti*, and the *ākṛti* qualified by the *vyakti* (TV 293,13–15/ Harikai 2012: 64,16–19). Countless other theories can be generated by combining these possibilities, which can be even further multiplied by bringing in considerations such as gender, number, and factor of action (*kāraka*). (Cf. TV 311,7–20/Harikai 2012: 80,21–28.) However, the theory that just the *ākṛti* is the meaning stands apart from all the others, which involve the *vyakti* in some way. Once it is shown that the individual cannot be the meaning, all the other theories are eliminated. Therefore, the Bhāṣyakāra has chosen not to discuss all of them (TV 294,18–20/ Harikai 2012: 65,24–27).

[192] NV 307, 19-20: *na hi sacchabdāt tadbhedā ghaṭādayo gamyanta iti tadgata-ghaṭādibhedānākṣepāt sāmānādhikaraṇyābhāvaḥ* /. "For from the word 'existing'

refer to existence, according to the Apohavādin; it would only secondarily or figuratively indicate what possesses it. Yet it seems it could not do even that, since there is no resemblance between the genus and the individual possessing it, or some other mechanism that would explain the transference of the idea of one to the other. Moreover, a word would actually give rise to a *false* cognition if the genus-possessor appeared as if colored by the genus in the same way a (normally transparent) crystal appears blue when a blue flower is placed next to it.[193] This part of Uddyotakara's presentation of the Apohavāda corresponds to PS(V) 5.4–6ab.[194]

The Apohavādin's critique of other theories culminates in the claim that "because there is no other alternative" *apoha*s must be the meanings of words.[195] In response, Uddyotakara mounts his defense of the Nyāya understanding of word-meaning. He begins by pointing out that the various criticisms of other theories raised by the Apohavādin really do not apply to the Nyāya view. The Naiyāyika holds that all three entities, individual, genus, and configuration, comprise the meaning of a word. Any of these can be the primary referent, depending on one's intention, the others becoming secondary referents. The Apohavādin's criticisms are valid only against those who hold that one or the other of these items exclusively is the meaning of a word.

After arguing (rather unhelpfully, in my opinion) that the Apohavādin cannot even say something like, "The word 'existence' does not indicate

---

its differences pot and so forth are not understood; hence, there is no coreference [with the word 'pot'], because [the word 'existing'] does not imply the differences pot, and so forth, that belong to it." Cf. PSV 5.4a: *evam api hi sacchabdo jāti-svarūpamātropasarjanaṃ dravyam āha, na sākṣād iti tadgataghaṭādibhedānā-kṣepād atadbhedatve sāmānādhikaraṇyābhāvaḥ* (Pind 2015: 1.6,1–3). "In this way, too, the word 'existing' expresses a substance to which merely the genus and the form of the [word itself] are subordinate; [it does] not express it directly. Hence, because it does not imply the differences pot, and so forth, that belong to that [thing possessing the genus, they] would not be its differences, in which case there would be no coreference [with the word 'pot']."

[193] NV 307,18–308,4.

[194] Pind 2015: I.5,4–9,1.

[195] See n. 176 above.

existence," without self-contradiction,[196] Uddyotakara returns to a more substantive response, namely, that the Nyāya view of a composite meaning avoids the kinds of problems the Apohavādin raises for other theories. Thus, when the Apohavādin alleges that the word "existing," referring to the genus existence, could not be used coreferentially with words referring to "differences," it is because he "fails to grasp the common meaning [of both words]."[197] The word "existing," while it includes existence as part of its meaning,[198] primarily indicates a means (*sādhana*) of existence, that is, a substance, quality, or motion. Therefore, it can be used coreferentially with the word "substance." It is the word "existence," rather, not "existing," that cannot be coreferential with "substance"; one never says "existence substance." That is because, as normally employed, the word "existence" refers primarily to existence itself, not a means thereof, though it also indicates the means of existence, substance and so forth, as something secondary.[199]

---

[196] NV 308,8–22. See Much 1994: 356–357; Matilal 2002: 238–240.

[197] NV 309,1: *yat punar etad bhedārthair abhinnavibhaktitvād iti, tan na, samānārthāparijñānāt* /. "On the other hand, as for the [opponent's statement], 'because [the word 'existing'] has the same ending as words that mean differences[, which would not be possible if words referred just to genera]' – that is not the case, because he fails to grasp the common meaning [of both words]."

[198] For, as noted above, Uddyotakara will say that by the word "existing" substance, etc., are denoted *as having the qualifier existence*: *asmākaṃ tu dravyaguṇakarmāṇi sattāviśeṣaṇāny* [*sacchabdena*] *abhidhīyante* (NV 309, 19–20). See n. 190.

[199] NV 309,1–7: *na brūmaḥ sattādiśabdena dravyaśabdasya sāmānādhikaraṇyam, api tu sattāyāḥ pradhānasādhanavācinā sacchabdena dravyaguṇakarmāṇy abhidhīyante dravyaguṇakarmaśabdair apītaretaraviśeṣaṇaviśeṣyabhāvāpannais tāny eva / evaṃ sati yuktam sāmānādhikaraṇyam, ubhayoḥ saddravyaśabdayor ekaviṣayatvāt / yadā punar ayaṃ sattāśabdaḥ sattāpradhāna evāṅgabhūtaṃ sādhanam abhidhatte, na tadā sāmānādhikaraṇyam, dravyasya satteti bhavati / tasmāt sāmānādhikaraṇyānupapattir adoṣaḥ* /. "We do not say that there is coreference of the word 'substance' with the word 'existence.' Rather, by the word 'existing,' insofar as it expresses a means of existence as its primary element, a substance, a quality, or a motion is denoted; while by the words 'substance,' 'qual-

In short, coreference is possible because the individual can be primarily indicated by a word. The word "existing," Uddyotakara says, is not really a "genus-word" (*jātiśabda*) but an "individual-word" (*bhedaśabda*).[200] How, then, does the Naiyāyika avoid the problems pointed out by the Apohavādin for the view that a word denotes individuals, namely, that one could never learn the relation of the word with its meaning because the individuals are innumerable, and the word would be ambiguous because one would never know which individual is meant? Because, Uddyotakara explains, although words indicate individuals, they do not indicate individuals by themselves (*kevalānām*, NV 309,18). Rather, the individuals indicated by a word are qualified by the genus that is also (secondarily) indicated. "For us, on the other hand," he says, "a substance, quality, and motion are indicated as having the qualifier existence. Wherever one sees existence, there one employs the word 'existing,' and existence is one because there is the continuity of its cognition (*tatpratyayasyānuvṛtteḥ*)."[201] Therefore, the fact that the individuals are innumerable is not a problem. Nor is there ambiguity. The word "existence" occurs consistently in regard to some individual qualified by existence. The composite theory of meaning, in effect, allows the Naiyāyika to have his cake and eat it, too. When necessary, for instance, in order to claim that the meaning of a word in its various uses is one, one can emphasize that the word refers to a genus; on the other hand, when necessary, for instance, in order to account for coreference, one can stress that the word also refers to an individual.

---

ity,' and 'motion,' which have entered into a relation of mutual qualifier and qualificand [with 'existence'?], precisely those [same things are denoted]. In that case, coreference is admissible, since both the words 'existing' and 'substance' have the same object. But when this word 'existence,' having indeed as its primary element existence, denotes a means of existence as what is subordinate, then there is no coreference, as in 'the existence of the substance.' Therefore, [the charge] that coreference is impossible is not a problem."

[200] NV 309, 14–15: *nāyaṃ bhoḥ sacchabdo jātiśabdaḥ, api tu bhedaśabda evāyam* /. "Alas! this word 'existence' is not a genus-word, rather it is an individual-word!"

[201] NV 309,19–21: *asmākaṃ tu dravyaguṇakarmāṇi sattāviśeṣaṇāny abhidhīyante / yatra yatra sattāṃ paśyati tatra tatra sacchabdaṃ prayuṅkte / ekā ca sattā tatpratyayasyānuvṛtteḥ.*

Finally, Uddyotakara even defends the *jātimat* view against the charge that it does not allow for coreference because then the word would refer to something in reliance on or subodinate to the universal and would not imply any differences. Uddyotakara pursues the same line of reasoning in answering this criticism. While the word "existence" may not imply any differences, the word "existing" surely does, for as Uddyotakara has said, it indicates the means of existence, which will be either a substance, quality, or motion. Yet these entities are also made known by the word "existence," as well, however now as subordinate factors. The word "existing," in other words, has a composite meaning, which Uddyotakara now explains as consisting of existence, connection with existence, and "another thing," that is, the individual. One or the other becomes primary or secondary depending on the intention according to which it is used or understood. [202] Certainly, "existing" does not indicate the means of

[202] NV 310, 13–21: *yat punar etan na tadvato 'svatantratvād iti / na kila sacchabdena tadbhedā ghaṭādayo gamyante, tadgataghaṭādibhedānākṣepāt sāmānādhikaraṇyābhāva iti / tan na, uktottaratvāt / uktottaram etat, saddravyaśabdayor ekaviṣayatvāt sāmānādhikaraṇyam iti, tadgataghaṭādibhedānākṣepa iti ca na yuktaṃ śacchabdena sattāsādhanānāṃ dravyaguṇakarmaṇām ākṣepāt / sattāśabdena dravyaguṇakarmāṇi nākṣipyante na punaḥ sacchabdena śakyaṃ vaktum sattāśabdenāpi guṇabhūtāni gamyanta iti / sad iti cāyam abhidhānaśabdaḥ, kas tasyābhidheyaḥ / yo 'smāt pratīyate, sa tasyārtha iti / ko 'syārthaḥ / sa vibhajyate / sattā tadyogo 'rthāntaram iti trayo 'rthāḥ / tat pradhānopasarjanabhāvasyāniyamena vivakṣāyāṃ pradhānaṃ sādhanaṃ gamyate, aṅgaṃ sattā tadyogaś ca /*. "When again it is said: '[A word is not indicative] of the possessor of that [genus], because it would not be independent'; for they say that from the word 'existing' its differences, pot and so forth, are not comprehended, so that due to not implying the differences pot and so forth that pertain to it [i.e., the possessor of the genus], there is no coreference – that is not the case, for its refutation has already been stated. [Namely,] this refutation has been stated: Since the words 'existing' and 'substance' have the same object, they are coreferential. And it is not correct that there is no implication of the differences, since by the word 'existing' there is implication of substance, quality, or motion, which are the means [of manifestation] of existence. [True,] by the word 'existence' there is no implication of substance, quality, or motion, but it cannot be said [that they are not implied] by the word 'existing.' [And] even by the word 'existence' they are understood as subordinate factors. And this word 'existing' is a word which denotes; what is denoted by it? That which is

existence figuratively, by some transference of the notion of existence onto the individual.[203]

If we compare just this much of Uddyotakara's discussion of Dignāga's Apohavāda to Kumārila's treatment of it in the *Apohavāda* chapter of his *Ślokavārttika* a significant difference between them is immediately obvious. Kumārila is much less concerned with defending the view of word-meaning of his own tradition, the Mīmāṃsā, than Uddyotakara is with defending the view of his, the Nyāya. This is, then, one way in which the primarily negative purpose of the *Apohavāda* chapter, simply to refute the Apohavāda and not to prove the Mīmāṃsā position, comes out. Indeed, Kumārila's response to the problems Dignāga raises against other theories, specifically, that they cannot account for coreference or the qualifier-qualificand relationship, is simply to say that the same problems affect the Apohavāda as well, however one interprets it.[204] The detailed critique of Dignāga's PS 5 that begins with v. 115 consists mostly of *tu quoque* arguments; Kumārila says very little about how the Mīmāṃsā theory that the word-meaning is a universal can meet Dignāga's objections. One might think that this is because Mīmāṃsā in fact lacks the resources to address them. We have seen that the Nyāya composite theory of meaning is versatile enough to offer a solution for at least the coreference problem: the word "existing" can be used with the word "substance" because it refers to *both* the individual and the universal. Kumārila, however, will deny in his discussion of the *Ākṛtyadhikaraṇa* in the *Tantravārttika* that the word can refer to an individual at all.

Nevertheless, it becomes clear from Kumārila's later discussion of word-meaning in his *Tantravārttika* what his solution to the problems of coreference and qualification would be. Although no longer concerned

---

cognized from it is its meaning. And what is its meaning? It is divided into parts. Existence, connection with it, and another thing [besides those two, namely, the individual] – there are [these] three meanings. Thus, without restriction as to whether it is primary or subordinate, when there is an intention, it is comprehended that the means is primary, while existence and their connection are subordinate."

[203] NV 311, 4–21.

[204] That is, whether the meaning of a word is to be taken as *apohamātra*, just the *apoha*, or *apohavat*, the possessor of the *apoha*.

with Dignāga there, or even the Apohavāda, for that matter,[205] Kumārila addresses a version of the coreference problem raised by the *pūrvapakṣin*, who holds that the word refers to the individual. If a word referred to a universal, the *pūrvapakṣin* argues, it could not be used coreferentially with a word for a quality.[206] This problem is associated with another problem,

---

[205] The only reference to the idea of exclusion in TV *Ākṛtyadhikaraṇa* occurs at 315,17–316,4/ Harikai 2012: 85,25–86,13, where – to paraphrase the debate – the *pūrvapakṣin* is defending the position that a word such as "cow," when used, refers to a single, unique *vyakti*, not to all individuals, nor a collection of them. Kumārila argues that in that case the word could not be used to refer to other individuals of the same type on other occasions. Individuals are "completely devoid of commonalities and differences" (*sāmānyaviśeṣavinirmukta*), so that one would be completely unlike another; there would be no basis for the application of the same word to all. The *pūrvapakṣin* proposes that it is the fact that individuals of the same type (e.g., all cows) are devoid of commonalities and differences that makes it possible to use the same word for them – to which Kumārila replies: in that case, the universal "being devoid of commonalities and differences" (*sāmānyaviśeṣavinirmuktatva*) would be the meaning of the word. The *pūrvapakṣin*, now evidently an Apohavādin, then articulates his position more clearly, TV 315,27–28/Harikai 2012: 86,3–5: *naivaṃ mayocyate sāmānyaviśeṣanirmuktatvād vyaktau śabdo vartate vyaktantare ceti, kiṃ tu sāmānyaviśeṣavyatirekeṇānyāpohavadvyaktiḥ kathyate.* "It is not said by me in this way that a word refers to one *vyakti* or another due to their both being devoid of commonalities and differences. Rather, an individual possessing an exclusion from others due to a difference from universal and difference is expressed." But Kumārila simply responds, TV 316.1–4/Harikai 2012: 86,10–13: *yadi tāvat sāmānyaviśeṣavinirmuktatvāc chabdo vartate. tataḥ sāmānyam eva vācyam. atha samānaṃ nimittaṃ nāsti tadā vyaktyantare vṛttir na prāpnoti. tadabhāve 'pi ced varteta ato 'śvavyaktāv api vṛttiprasakter atiprasaṅgaḥ syād iti.* "If, to begin with, a word occurs due to [the universal] 'being devoid of commonalities and differences,' then a universal is the meaning. Or, if there is not a common occasion for [its] employment, then it would not occur in regard to another individual. If it did occur even in the absence of that [i.e., a common occasion for employment], then [the word 'cow'] would occur also in regard to an individual horse, so that there would be absurd consequences." Apparently, by the time he wrote the *Tantravārttika*, Kumārila did not see much point in going to a lot of trouble to refute the Apohavāda.

[206] MS 1.3.31. See above n. 187. Cf. TV 312,30–313,6/Harikai 2012: 82,18–25. If a noun referred to a universal, it could not take endings indicating number and

namely, that if a word referred to a universal there could be no injunctions of actions, since actions can only be performed using things that are perishable and possessed of form, whereas universals are eternal and incorporeal.[207] Both problems can be dealt with, Kumārila suggests, if it is understood that universal and individual are not absolutely distinct – a claim he believes he has already established in the *Ākṛtivāda* of his *Ślokavārttika*.[208] If universal and individual are not completely distinct, then when it is enjoined that the sacrificial victim should be cut up, one will know that it is the individual that is to be cut up.[209]

In summary, what might appear to the reader as a dialectical flaw in the *Apohavāda* chapter, namely, that it relies too heavily on negative argumentation and does not establish the universalist view as a counterbalance to the *apoha* theory, is explained by the fact that Kumārila, having proved

---

case. Moreover, it would only indicate an individual indirectly, hence the coreference of words in a sentence such as "Devadatta is a man" would also be indirect.

[207] TV 300,22–23/Harikai 2012: 71,22–23: *amūrtā hy ākṛtir nityā nāvaghātādibhājanī / tadvidhiḥ pratiṣedho vā tenāsyā nāvakalpate //*. "For an incorporeal, eternal universal does not partake of threshing, etc. Therefore, the injunction of that or a prohibition is not appropriate for it." See the continuation of the discussion, TV 300,24–301,10/Harikai 2012: 71,24–72,5.

[208] ŚV *Ākṛtivāda* 54–65ab.

[209] TV 304,28–305,6/Harikai 2012: 74,13–18: *anatyantavyatirekāc cākṛter amūrtatvādyāśrayadoṣāprasaṅgaḥ. sā hi pratīyate niṣkṛṣṭarūpā, kriyāyoginī tu nityaṃ vyaktyupetā bhavaty eveti prokṣaṇāvekṣaṇādy tu na kathaṃcin na saṃbhavati. viśasanādy api tu vyaktyavyatirekāpekṣayā saṃbhavaty eva. tathā hi paśvādiṣv apanītāṅgeṣu viśeṣabuddhyabhāvāt sāmānyarūpaiva viśasanādiviśiṣṭā buddhir dṛṣṭā*. "And the defects due to the universal being incorporeal, and so forth, do not result, because it is not completely distinct [from the individual]. For it is cognized separately [by the word itself], but united with an action [as expressed by a sentence such as, 'Bring the cow'] it is accompanied by an individual indeed. [Such ritual acts as] sprinkling and regarding, however, are not in any way impossible [if words refer to universals]. Even cutting up the victim, and so forth, are possible taking into account that [the universal] is not distinct from the individual. Thus, in the case of dismembered sacrificial animals, since there is no cognition of the specific nature [of the animal], one observes a cognition having the form of a universal which is qualified by cutting up, and so forth." See the (rather challenging) continuation of the discussion, TV 305,6–16/Harikai 2012: 74,19–31.

to his satisfaction the existence of universals already in the *Ākṛtivāda* (the chapter immediately preceding the *Apohavāda* chapter), will not attempt to establish that they are the meanings of words until the topic of words and meanings actually comes up in the *Mīmāṃsāsūtra*. By that point, however – MS 1.3.30–33 – the urgency of addressing threats from outside seems to have faded for Kumārila and he is more concerned with canvassing all the positions that really came into consideration for Mīmāṃsakas.

Of course, I have not done full justice to Uddyotakara's critique of the Apohavāda. He, too, devises numerous negative arguments against the theory, some of which anticipate arguments Kumārila will develop. We shall return to some of these after gaining an overview of Kumārila's critique.

3 Kumārila

Let us now turn to the central themes of Kumārila's critique of the *apoha* theory in his *Apohavāda* chapter.

According to the Apohavāda, as Kumārila sees it, the meaning of "cow" is a negation, that is, an absence or non-existence. If you exclude all the things that are not cows, that is what the word "cow" refers to. The meaning of "cow" is what is not non-cow or the non-existence or absence of non-cows. As Kei Kataoka shows in his essay, the double negation reflects how the meaning of a word is learned – primarily, by ascertaining what it is not used for. All the things the word "cow" is not used for are non-cows; the meaning of "cow," then, is what is other than all those things.

Now, for Kumārila, the non-existence of something is a property of something else that exists. He believes he has already shown this in the *Nirālambanavāda* and *Abhāvapariccheda* chapters of the ŚV. The non-existence of a chair in a room is a property of that room, insofar as the room is not the chair; the non-existence of yoghurt is a property of milk, insofar as the milk is not yoghurt. According to Kumārila things have not only positive properties but also negative ones. Everything both is what it is and is not what it is not. So if there is a non-existence or absence of something, there must be some real, existing thing that that non-existence or absence is a property or aspect of. Kumārila refers to the real thing that bears the non-existence as the "support" (*āśraya*) of non-existence. Given this analysis of non-existence, one can ask the Apohavādin, What is the real thing of which an *apoha* is the property or aspect? In other words, when one employs the word “cow” and refers thereby to the non-existence of non-cows, what is it that is not non-cow?

Presumably, it is not the universal cowness, for the point of the Apohavāda is to explain the meanings of words without bringing in real universals! But could anything else serve as the support of the non-existence of non-cows that is the *apoha*? Kumārila goes through all the possibilities. It could not be the individual, because individuals, for the Buddhist, are not objects of conceptual awareness; we could not, in the case of the word “cow,” conceive of an individual cow as the non-existence of what is non-cow, i.e., of horse, and so forth (3ab). Nor, in the case of the word “cow,” could it be some subtype of cow, say, spotted cows; for a particular subtype of cow does not include cows of all subtypes, yet the word “cow” refers to all cows (3cd–8ab). Finally, it could not be the collection of all individual cows, because then the word “cow” could be applied only if one takes in the entire collection. Each individual, then, would only be “partially” a cow (8cd–9). Kumārila concludes that the “cause” of the cognition “cow” must be some nature that is “complete” in all cows – presumably, a (real) universal, cowness (10). But of course, that is the last thing the Apohavādin wants to accept.

This is Kumārila’s first main criticism of the Apohavāda based on his interpretation of *apoha*s as non-existences.

His second is that, insofar as *apoha*s are non-existences, they cannot be distinguished from each other. If *Apoha*s were the meanings of words yet indistinguishable from each other, all words would refer to the same thing – they would be synonymous (42). Insofar as they are non-existences *apoha*s are in effect non-entities. Thus, they could hardly be distinguished from each other intrinsically (44–45, 47). But could they be distinguished extrinsically, on the basis of the things they exclude, their *apohya*s? This proposal seems plausible enough. The exclusion referred to by “cow” and the exclusion referred to by “horse” differ by virtue of the fact that they exclude different things; for the class of non-cows is different from the class of non-horses.

In fact, Kumārila argues, they are barely different from each other. The class of non-cows differs from that of non-horses only in that horses are among the things that are non-cows and cows among the things that are non-horses. Otherwise, the class of non-cows and the class of non-horses have all the same members: elephants, lions, humans, coffee grinders, laptops, etc., etc. If the meanings of "cow" and "horse" – both exclusions – are defined only by what is excluded, then they are indeed practically the same, and the synonymy objection retains its force (52–55). Kumārila also asks, how would all of the things excluded by the word "cow" be excluded? If they were excluded one-by-one, then there would be a separate *apoha* for each thing that is excluded and the word "cow" would thus refer to infinitely many things (58–60). If all the things to be excluded by "cow," on the other hand, were excluded all together, as a collection, then they would all have to share some property that unites them as a collection, and it seems that that could be nothing other than a real universal (an unreal universal is not something that could be excluded) (61–64). Even if one maintained that all the different *types* of things that are excluded by "cow" – horses, lions, elephants, etc. – define a different exclusion from that of "horse" (which would exclude other *types* of things), still these types are in effect universals in relation to their own subtypes, and so must be considered nonentities by the Buddhist. Therefore, they could not account for any differences. Indeed, taking the Buddhist view to its extreme, even an individual thing has the nature of a nonentity with respect to its ultimate constituents; for it is what is common to those constituents, hence also a kind of universal (67–68ab).

Can two *apoha*s, then, be distinguished from each other on the basis of the things that fall under them, their "bases" (*ādhāra*)? In the case of the word "cow" this would be all cows, in the case of the word "horse," all horses. The proposal, in other words, is that the meaning of "cow" is different from that of "horse" in that the class of cows is distinct from the class of horses.

This idea, however, is also vulnerable to the last problem raised against the proposal that the difference of *apoha*s is due to the difference of their *apohya*s, namely, even individual things, if one takes the Buddhist position to its extreme, are nonentities. How could one collection of nonentities be different from another (67–68ab)? Indeed, Kumārila suggests at one point, it would seem that the Apohavāda ultimately just amounts to the doctrine of Emptiness: nothing real is referred to by words at all (35cd–36)! On the other hand, if what is to be excluded and the bases of exclusion came down to the atoms that horses and cows are made of – well, in fact, they are all made out of the same kinds of atoms (69cd–70cd), so from that perspective there would be no difference of their meanings, either! If all cows, collectively, and all horses, collectively, are the respective bases of "cow" and "horse," then, once again, each collection would have to have some similarity, i.e., something all its members have in common (71–72). Even if individual cows were real and the *apoha* of "cow" were based on them, then since each cow is in fact distinct from every other cow, there would be as many exclusions as there are cows (51).

In sum, the status of *apoha*s, indeed, any universals, as non-existences, hence nonentities, makes it impossible to distinguish meanings from each other. This has the absurd consequence that on the Apohavāda all words would be synonyms. This absurdity is compounded by the fact that there would not be any way to distinguish words from each other, either (104). For words are universals; Indian philosophers and grammarians generally recognized the fact often mentioned in modern linguistics, that a word is a type. It is the same word "cow" that is uttered on different occasions; the utterances are tokens of the same type.[210] The Mīmāṃsaka, in particular, makes the point that if the word were not a permanent type that transcends its token, then one could never learn a fixed relation between it and its meaning so that it could be used to communicate something to other people.[211] With words being no more distinguishable from each other than meanings if one held the Apohavāda, communication would become im-

---

[210] See MSBh ad MS 1.1.20: *saṃkhyābhāvāt* /. "[A word must be eternal] because there is no number [in connection with a word]." That is to say, there is only one word "cow." One recognizes the same word "cow" every time it is uttered.

[211] Kataoka 2007: 541(68),5–540(69),2 (Śabara ad MS 1.1.18): *uccaritamātre hi vinaṣṭe śabde navo 'nyo nārthaṃ pratyāyituṃ śaknuyāt / ato na parārtham uccāryeta / athāvinaṣṭaḥ, tato bahuśa upalabdhatvād arthāvagama iti yuktam* /. "If a word has ceased to exist as soon as it is uttered, another new [word] could not cause someone to cognize the meaning, and so it would not be uttered for the sake of others. If, on the other hand, it has not ceased to exist [as soon as it is uttered], then having been perceived many times, it is proper that there is comprehension of its meaning."

possible. And just as words are not different from other words and meanings are not different from other meanings, words and meanings would not even be different from each other (105)! Moreover, both being nonentities, there could be no relation between them, so that a particular word could indicate a particular meaning. As Kumārila puts it, "On your view there would not be a relation of that which makes something known and the thing that is known for two *apoha*s [namely, the word-*apoha* and the meaning-*apoha*], because they would not be real, like a sky-flower and a rabbit's horn in the world" (108).

All of these consequences would follow, Kumārila believes, if one correctly understands an *apoha* as a non-existence. An equally serious problem for the Apohavāda arises when one asks how it is possible to learn which *apoha* a word refers to. According to Dignāga an *apoha* is known only by a word or an inferential mark (*liṅga*).[212] Indeed, it seems obvious that, being a nonentity, an *apoha* could not be accessible to perception. But in order to be indicated by a word or inferential mark there would already have to be a relation established between the word or inferential mark and the *apoha*. How could that be established in the first place if the *apoha* cannot be cognized by any other means than a word or an inferential mark (73–74)?

Could the *apoha* corresponding to a word be learned, however, just by observing that the word is *not* used to refer to other things, or more precisely, following Dignāga's idea, *by not observing* that it is used for

---

[212] See PV 1.47ab: *tasmād apohaviṣayam iti liṅgaṃ prakīrtitam* /. "Therefore, it is declared that an inferential mark has an exclusion for its object." In other words, it is known by an inferential mark. Manorathanandin ad loc., PVV 305,6, attributes this statement to Dignāga: *tasmād ācāryeṇāpohaviṣayaṃ liṅgam iti prakīrtitam*. He may have in mind the statement he will attribute to Dignāga later in his comment on PV 1.133cd–134ab, PVV 334,7: *apohaḥ śabdaliṅgābhyāṃ pratipādyate* /, "An exclusion is made known by a word and an inferential mark," which is echoed by Dharmakīrti at PVSV 25, 26–28: *kathaṃ punar etad gamyate vyavacchedaḥ śabdaliṅgābhyāṃ pratipādyate vidhinā na vasturūpam eveti* /. "But how do we understand that an exclusion (*vyavaccheda*) is made known by a word and an inferential mark, and not the nature of the [real] thing in a positive way?"

other things?[213] No, says Kumārila. If the relation between a word and its meaning were just established by negative concomitance, by not observing that the word is applied to certain things, and one never observed what it is applied to, then it simply would have no meaning at all (75)! For Dignāga, an *apoha* is like a clearing surrounded by all the things the word does not apply to.[214] Kumārila's point is that, if we do not also know, in a positive way, what is in the clearing, then the word has no meaning for us.

It is in this connection that Kumārila develops his most well-known objection to the Apohavāda, the mutual presupposition or Circularity Argument – which however had already been anticipated by Uddyotakara and apparently others as well (see below). If someone is taught the meaning of the word "cow" by being told, "The word 'cow' refers to what is not non-cow," then one must know what a non-cow is. But how can one comprehend what a non-cow is if one does not already know what "cow" means (or, for that matter, what "non-" means; see 80–82). The meaning of "cow," it seems, presupposes the meaning of "non-cow," while the meaning of "non-cow" presupposes the meaning of "cow" (83–85ab).

It is quite possible that Kumārila's mutual presupposition objection is based on a misunderstanding of Dignāga's theory; Kataoka addresses this question in his essay. Be that as it may, the reader will hopefully be able to appreciate that this objection is just one of many directed by Kumārila against the Apohavāda, and perhaps not even the most serious one. His critique does not stand or fall with just this one objection – as Dharmakīrti was well aware.

Several of the criticisms of the Apohavāda considered so far have been what might be called ontological objections. They stem from the idea that an *apoha* is an absence or non-existence and Kumārila's understanding of a non-existence as a property of a real thing that is its "support." Well aware that this view would not be obvious to everyone, Kumārila, in one of the more difficult sections of the treatise, vv. 11–35ab, takes the trouble to set aside some obvious counterexamples to it. What about the word "non-

[213] See PS(V) 5.34, discussed in nn. 41 and 42, and Kataoka's essay in this volume.

[214] This is my own, not any classical author's, analogy.

Brahmin," for instance? What would be "the other entity" that is not a Brahmin, that is, the "support" of non-existence, in this case? Kumārila in the end suggests that it is the universal humanity, common to all the *varṇa*s, that is apprehended as "non-Brahmin" in the case of Kṣatriyas, Vaiśyas, and Śūdras. Several other alleged counterexamples to Kumārila's view – such as the words *adharma*, "impermanence," and even the words for the various kinds of non-existence recognized by the Mīmāṃsakas, "previous non-existence" (*prāgabhāva*), and so forth – are explained away in this section.[215]

In the last part of the *Apohavāda* chapter, starting from v. 115 and continuing through v. 164, Kumārila turns from epistemology and metaphysics to linguistics, arguing that the Apohavāda cannot account for generally observed linguistic phenomena.[216] His procedure in much of this section is to go through the fifth chapter of Dignāga's *Pramāṇasamuccaya* point by point, showing that the criticisms Dignāga directs against other theories apply equally to his own. This final section of the work does not consist entirely of *tu quoque* arguments, however. There are a number of other criticisms Kumārila raises against specific features of Dignāga's theory. Yet, although Kumārila occasionally suggests how the theory that words refer to real universals could do a better job handling the various linguistic phenomena Dignāga draws attention to, his approach in this section is still mainly critical.

As we saw when discussing Uddyotakara's critique of *apoha*, the main problem Dignāga sees in other theories is that they are unable to account for coreference. At PS 5.2cd, for instance, he claims that if words referred to genera (i.e., universals) they could not be coreferential, because a genus like existence is not a substance or a quality, but rather belongs to a

[215] Vv. 11–35ab do not correspond at all to any of the verses found in the Mīmāṃsā *pūrvapakṣa* of TS *Śabdārthaparīkṣā*. Assuming that Śāntarakṣita, in that *pūrvapakṣa*, was quoting from Kumārila's lost *Bṛhaṭṭīkā* – for many of the verses that do correspond to verses of ŚV *Apohavāda* do not match them exactly – are we to conclude that these points simply were not covered in the *Bṛhaṭṭīkā*?

[216] Again, much of this discussion is missing in TS *Śabdārthaparīkṣā*. From TS *Śabdārthaparīkṣā* 967–981 we find verses more or less matching only ŚV *Apohavāda* 115–120, 135, and 139–146 – presumably, however, cited from the *Bṛhaṭṭīkā*.

substance or a quality. Thus, the word "existing" could not be coreferential with a word for a substance, like "pot." Later, PS 5.19abc, he also points out that two genera such as blueness and lotusness cannot relate to each other as qualifier and qualificand, since, as he has said, a genus does not possess another genus (PS 5.11b). Thus, an expression such as "blue lotus" (*nīlotpala*) on the genus-theory would be impossible. At *Apohavāda* 115–118 Kumārila argues that the same problems would arise for the Apohavāda. Just as a genus does not possess another, so one *apoha* does not inhere in another (116c'–117ab); hence, "blue" and "lotus" could not be qualifier and qualificand. And since "blue" and "lotus" on the Apohavāda would also refer to quite different things – the exclusion of non-blue things and the exclusion of non-lotuses, respectively – they could not, on the Apohavāda, even be coreferential.

Kumārila goes on to argue that if the Apohavāda is interpreted as claiming that the word does not refer merely to an *apoha*, but refers to something *possessing* an *apoha*, analogous to the so-called genus-possessor (*jātimat/tadvat*) theory, then it would be susceptible to the same kinds of objections that Dignāga levels against the latter. First of all, a word would not refer to the individual directly or independently, but only as mediated by the *apoha*, as it were, so that "differences," such as being a pot would not be implied; hence, the word "existing" could not be used coreferentially together with the word "pot" (120–122). Dignāga's confidence that this problem arises only if one believes that a word refers to something possessing a real genus, but not if it refers to something possessing an (unreal) exclusion (PS[V] 5.36c), is dismissed by Kumārila. If the exclusion of non-existing things could somehow "cover" the exclusion of non-pots, why couldn't the universal existence cover the universal pot (124–126a)? Second, all words would become figurative on the *apoha*-possessor view, just as Dignāga claimed they would on the universal-possessor view (126bcd–127). Third, just as something possessing a genus would actually be an individual and so lack a general nature, which is required of meanings – the meaning of a word must somehow extend over many individuals – so would something possessing an *apoha* (128, 131). Fourth, just as, according to Dignāga, a genus possessed by an individual would not imply another, more specific genus (i.e., a "difference," *viśeṣa*) in the way the quality blue implies some particular intensity of blue, thereby making possible the qualifier-qualificand relation – for, again, as all Indian philosophers acknowledged, universals/genera do not possess other universals/genera – so an *apoha* possessed by something would not imply another more specific *apoha* (132). Indeed, just as, in general, a broader genus does not imply a narrower one, as Dignāga also points out – the opposite, rather, is the case – so a more general *apoha* (such as the exclusion of non-existent things) could not imply a more specific one (such as the exclusion of non-pots) (133).

Kumārila moves beyond *tu quoque* arguments in the next part of the treatise, extending from vv. 135–146, in order to draw attention to various aspects of language he believes the Apohavāda is simply unable to account for. Here, his critique is no longer specifically tied to Dignāga's presentation, since the point of it is that there are many things Dignāga has overlooked. In vv. 135–137 Kumārila argues that it does not seem that an *apoha* could in any way be connected with gender or number. In vv. 139–146 he calls attention to various expressions for which it is difficult to see what the *apohya* could be – that is, the complement non-X that is being excluded – or even absurd to suggest that there is one at all: verbs, which do not designate something fixed but rather something to be done, that is, an action; conjunctions like "and," "or," and "but" (is there a non-and which is excluded by "and"?) and the negative particle "not"; verbal prefixes and prepositions; certain adjectives like "knowable" (*prameya*) and "cognizable" (*jñeya*) (since everything that exists, at least according to some philosophers, is cognizable, there is nothing to be excluded in the case of "cognizable"); and so on.

In vv. 147–157 Kumārila returns to PS 5, delving deeper into the intricacies of Dignāga's explanation, PS(V) 5.28–32, of why sometimes words *cannot* be used coreferentially. For example, while it is permissible to say "blue lotus," it is not permissible to say "birch elm." Kumārila argues, in effect, that Dignāga's account is incoherent. Kumārila's final attack on PS 5 comes in vv. 158–162, where he refutes Dignāga's argument, PS(V) 5.34–35, that if the meaning of a word were learned "positively," i.e., by means of positive concomitance (*anvaya*) and not primarily negative concomitance (*vyatireka*), as Dignāga believes – that is to say, if the meaning of a word were learned by observing what it is used *for* and not by *not* observing what it is *not* used for – then a word would convey knowledge of not only all the higher categories that include its meaning but also of all the subtypes that fall under it. For instance, in the case of the word "tree," the word would make known not only, besides treeness, earthenness, substanceness, existence, and knowableness – i.e., the higher categories that include treeness – but also birchness, elmness, oakness, and so forth, the lower subtypes that treeness includes. In fact, however, Dignāga points out, when the word "tree" is employed one is in doubt as to which specific type of tree is meant. Dignāga wants to argue that this phenomenon that, when a word is used, one comprehends all of the higher, more inclusive categories but is in doubt about the subtype, is explicable only if words refer to *apoha*s. Kumārila argues, to the contrary, that this would be equally intelligible if words refer to universals.

No doubt believing himself by this point to have completely demolished the Apohavāda, using first general metaphysical and epistemological arguments that would seem to apply to any version of the theory and then attacking Dignāga's exposition of it point by point, Kumārila, in the last passage of the treatise, vv. 165–175, sets aside a Nyāya argument against the Apohavāda he believes is not up to the task of refuting it. This argument is couched formally as an *anumāna*, which can be paraphrased as follows: "A word does not indicate its meaning by excluding another, because it is a factor (or means) of valid cognition (*pramāṅgatvāt*), like a sense faculty such as touch." Interestingly, this argument does not derive from Uddyotakara. Indeed, its source is unknown.

There are many ways in which Kumārila's critique of the Apohavāda extends beyond Uddyotakara's. Clearly, Kumārila offers a much more detailed treatment of Dignāga's arguments in PS 5 which, especially when read together with the commentaries of Sucaritamiśra and Jayamiśra, sheds much light on what Dignāga is up to. Overall, it seems that Kumārila has reached a much deeper understanding of Dignāga's Apohavāda than Uddyotakara. Meanwhile, the lead argument of the first section of Kumārila's critique, that one cannot give a plausible account of *apoha* as a kind of non-existence, as well as the synonymy objection, that, given that *apoha*s are non-existences, all words would be synonyms – these are not to be found in Uddyotakara at all. Nor is the argument that, since the

Apohavādin holds that *apoha*s cannot be known independently of language or inference, there would be no way to establish a relation between a word or inferential mark and an *apoha*, hence a word or inferential mark could not make an *apoha* known after all.

Nevertheless, several of Kumārila's points are anticipated, and were possibly even inspired, by Uddyotakara's discussion. Thus, while Uddyotakara does not stress that an *apoha* is an absence or non-existence in the way Kumārila does, he poses a dilemma: Is this exclusion an existing thing or not?[217] This question might have moved Kumārila to ask seriously, exactly what is the metaphysical status of an *apoha*? It is also well known that Uddyotakara already articulates the mutual presupposition objection, though he does not use the term *anyonyāśraya*. Rather, he says that if it is not possible to know the meaning of a word in a positive way (*vidhānataḥ*), then "there would not be a first cognition" of the meaning (i.e., the *apoha*).[218] He states the idea of mutual presupposition plainly enough, however, when he says, "As long as one does not know a non-cow, a knowing of cow is not possible, and as long as one does not know cow, [a

[217] See NV 314, 8–9: *yaś cāyam anyāpohaḥ agaur na bhavatīti gośabdasyārthaḥ sa kiṃ bhāvo 'thābhava iti* /. "And this exclusion of another which is the meaning of the word cow, [namely,] 'It is not non-cow,' is it an [existing] entity or a non-existence?" Uddyotakara continues: If it is an existing entity, is it, in the case of the word "cow," a non-cow or a cow? If it is a cow, then there is no dispute. [We, too, agree that the meaning of "cow" is a cow!] If it is a non-cow, then one arrives at the absurd position that the meaning of "cow" is non-cow! If, on the other hand, it is a non-existence, then ordering and agreeing (*praiṣasampratipatti*) would not be possible. One does not issue a command, or agree to a command, with respect to some non-existent thing when the word "cow" is uttered. And in fact, "the meaning of a word is what is cognized by the listener, and no one cognizes a non-existence from the word 'cow.'" *śabdārthaś ca pratipattrā pratīyate / na ca gośabdād abhāvam kaścit pratipadyata iti*, NV 314, 11–12. Cf. ŚV *Apohavāda* 138.

[218] NV 314,1–2: *yat punar etad anyaśabdārthāpohaḥ śabdārtha iti / tad apy ayuktaṃ vidhānataḥ śabdārthāsambhave saty ādyāpratipatteḥ* /. "And when it is said that the meaning of a word is the exclusion of other word-meanings, that too is incorrect, because if it is not possible for the word-meaning to exist positively, there would be no first cognition." The objection in this formulation was already known to Dignāga, voiced by the Sāṃkhya philosopher Mādhava. He contends with it at PS(V) 5.43a. See ŚV *Apohavāda* translation, n. 35.

knowing of] non-cow [would not be possible], so that there would be non-cognition of both."[219] The objection that the Apohavāda is too narrow, in that it does not account for the meanings of most words that are not substantives – verbs of various kinds, conjunctions, prepositions, and so forth – is also anticipated by Uddyotakara: "When there is a dichotomy (*dvairāśya*), there could be the cognition of one by the negation of the other,"[220] but this is not the case for the word "all." That is to say, there is no such thing as non-all, the negation of which could be the meaning of "all."[221] Kumārila's contribution here is essentially to multiply examples. Finally, one could even think that most of Kumārila's *tu quoque* arguments are suggested, in essence, by Uddyotakara's final point that the Apohavādin still owes us an explanation of what the coreference of two expressions would mean on his theory.[222] Undoubtedly there are other passages in Uddyotakara's long disquisition on *apoha* that could be seen as preparing the ground for Kumārila's critique.[223]

---

[219] NV 314, 5–7: *yāvac cāgāṃ na pratipadyate, na tāvad gavi pratipattir yuktā yāvac ca gāṃ na pratipadyate, na tāvad agavīty ubhayapratipattyabhāvaḥ* /. Cf. ŚV *Apohavāda* 85ab: *gavy asiddhe tv agaur nāsti tadabhāve ca gauḥ kutaḥ* /.

[220] NV 314, 13–14: *yatra dvairāśyaṃ bhavati, tatretarapratiṣedhād itarat pratīyate* /. See the continuation of the passage through NV 314, 22.

[221] See Sen 2011: 182–183.

[222] NV 316, 4–8: *samānādhikaraṇārthaś cānyāpohavādinā vācyaḥ / yasya cānyāpohaḥ śabdārthaḥ, tenānīlānutpalavyudāsau kathaṃ samānādhikaraṇāv iti vācyam / yasya punar vidhīyamānaḥ śabdārthaḥ tasya jātiguṇaviśiṣṭaṃ nīlotpalaśabdābhyāṃ dravyam ucyate, jātiguṇau ca dravye vartete, na punar anīlānutpalavyudāsau* /. "And a coreferential meaning has to be explained by the Apohavādin. [That is to say,] someone for whom the meaning of a word is exclusion of another has to explain how the exclusions of non-blue and non-lotus are coreferential. But for whom the meaning of a word is indicated positively, for him, by the words 'blue' and 'lotus,' a substance qualified by a genus and a quality is expressed. And the genus and quality exist in the substance, not the exclusions of non-blue and non-lotus."

[223] The dilemma posed at NV 315, 12–14, whether an *apoha* is "one or many for each thing" – that is, is it different from cow to cow (for the word "cow") or the same? – reminds one of Kumārila's discussion ŚV *Apohavāda* 58–62. If it is one,

Of course, there are many points of Uddyotakara's critique that Kumārila does not make use of. A prominent difference between their approaches is that Kumārila, though arguing mostly negatively, eschews the kinds of charges of self-refutation and incoherence that Uddyotakara is wont to make. For instance, how can the Apohavādin, when denying that individuals can be the meaning of a word, say, "A genus-word (*jātiśabda*) does not express individuals,"[224] since he (as a Buddhist) does not think that any word expresses individuals, nor for that matter that anything is expressed by a genus-word? The predicate that is being denied ("expresses individuals") is, therefore, meaningless. It would, moreover, be a contradiction to suggest that a genus-word might express individuals. If it expressed individuals, after all, it would not be a genus-word! Who in his right mind would think that a genus-word could express individuals, anyway?[225] If, on the other hand, individuals are not expressed by genus-words, as the Buddhist maintains, then they must necessarily be expressed by other kinds of words; for if they are not expressed either by genus-words or other kinds of words, they would not be expressed at all, and it would, once again, make no sense to deny that they are expressed by genus-words![226] Continuing in this vein, Uddyotakara eventually foists upon his opponent the position that "words are not expressive [of anything] and things are not expressed" – which of course could not be asserted without contradiction, since it would have to be stated in words! It would, moreover, nullify the meaning of the opponent's claim that "a genus-word does not express individuals" and the reason he gives for it ("because they are infinite"), or for that matter any other claim he might try to make.[227]

---

continues Uddyotakara, and it is connected with many cows, it is just cowness. If it is many, then because of being infinite in number like individuals, there could be no cognition of it. And so on. See Sen 2011: 183.

[224] NV 312, 1: *na jātiśabdo bhedānāṃ vācaka iti* /. This is PS(V) 5.2ab, the beginning of Dignāga's refutation of other theories of meaning.

[225] Recall that, as we have noted above, n. 200, Uddyotakara thinks that when one uses the word "existing" in the phrase "existing pot," it is an *individual*-word (*bhedaśabda*).

[226] NV 312, 1–12.

[227] NV 312, 20–24.

There are several other passages of this nature in Uddyotakara's discussion. Their general thrust is that the thesis that *apoha*s are expressed by words contradicts itself,[228] and that various arguments employed in support of it are nonsensical; in most cases they, too, are self-contradictory in that they refer to, hence imply the existence of, things they are intended to refute.[229] Kumārila eschews this kind of reasoning in his *Apohavāda* chapter. He may have found such arguments tedious and unconvincing. Indeed, to a non-logician's ear they sound sophistical.

We can see from the comparison of Kumārila's and Uddyotakara's critiques of the Apohavāda that there was already a well-developed, sophisticated discussion of *apoha* prior to Kumārila, which he was undoubtedly informed by and probably drew on. Uddyotakara gives us a glimpse into what was going on in Nyāya, but there was almost certainly a search for ways to counter the theory being carried on in Mīmāṃsā as well, which must also have been accompanied by continued study of Dignāga's writings. In short, Kumārila's critique, brilliant as it is, certainly did not appear out of nowhere. For all we know, some of its main points had already been worked out by unknown predecessors, though we lack the evidence to say this with any confidence.

Buddhists reading Kumārila's critique of Apohavāda must have been alarmed. He seems to have pointed out major flaws in the theory. In order to respond to his critique it could not just be patched up here and there, but would have to be completely overhauled. This is what Dharmakīrti accomplished.

Dharmakīrti[230]

I can only indicate briefly here some of the ways in which Dharmakīrti responds to Kumārila's critique of Dignāga in his presentation of the

---

[228] See NV 315, 16–22.

[229] Uddyotakara adopts similar strategies on other occasions, for instance when critiquing the Buddhist denial of the existence of a self. See Taber 2012b.

[230] An earlier version of this section was presented as a talk on the occasion of the celebration of Prof. Ernst Steinkellner's eightieth birthday, held at the University of Vienna, 30 June, 2017, sponsored by the Austrian Academy of Sciences.

Apohavāda at PV(SV) 1.40–185 (the "Apoha Section"). What is perhaps most striking about Dharmakīrti's discussion is how he revises the Apohavāda from the ground up, apparently in order to solve what he must have thought were real problems with the theory that were pointed out by Kumārila. There has been some controversy about the chronological relation of Dharmakīrti to Kumārila. Most scholars have held the view that, as Ernst Steinkellner once felicitously put it, Dharmakīrti "was in dialogue with Kumārila."[231] That is to say, when discussing not only points directly related to known Mīmāṃsā teachings such as the eternality and authority of the Veda, but also more general issues of logic and philosophy of language, Dharmakīrti often had in mind, not some generic representative of Mīmāṃsā, nor even some specific Mīmāṃsaka or Mīmāṃsakas whose names and works are lost to us, but the only Mīmāṃsaka of the same period whose name we know and some of whose works we have, namely, Kumārila. Kei Kataoka, among others, has also tenaciously defended this position. [232] I have expressed reservations about it in some of my publications,[233] but have now come round to believing that, at least when discussing the Apohavāda, Dharmakīrti is systematically referencing Kumārila. Although some caveats still need to be made, having to do with other elements of Kumārila's philosophy that Dharmakīrti neglects (these will be mentioned below), the evidence, with a better understanding of the early debate about *apoha*, seems to be converging on the view that Dharmakīrti presupposes Kumārila.

Of all the objections raised against the Apohavāda in Kumārila's *Ślokavārttika*, two in particular stand out. The first is that, if *apoha*s were the meanings of words, then all words would be synonymous. We have seen that this objection turns on viewing an *apoha* as an absence. Being an absence, it cannot have a distinct nature; hence, it cannot differ intrinsically from another *apoha*. Nor could it differ extrinsically, either due to what it is based on (its so-called *ādhāra*, substratum, e.g., in the case of the *apoha* "cow," individual spotted cows, black cows, etc.) or the things it excludes

[231] Steinkellner 1997. Frauwallner 1962 was the first articulation of this position.

[232] See Kataoka 2011a: 27–34. See also Kellner 1997 and Eltschinger 2007.

[233] See Taber 1991, 2001, and 2012a.

(for "cow," horses, lions, elephants, etc.). The second is that *apoha*s cannot be known. The Buddhist seems to suggest that they are made known by words and inferential marks. Dharmakīrti himself will say, PV 1.47ab, "Therefore, it is declared that an inferential mark has an exclusion for its object." [234] Yet *apoha*s, being absences, are certainly not objects of perception. In that case, however, it seems that there would be no way of knowing them at all. For a word or inferential mark can indicate something for someone only if one knows the connection between that thing and the word or inferential mark, and if it is not available independently of language and inference, that is, perceptually, one could never ascertain the connection between it and the word or inferential mark in the first place, so that it could be indicated by them.[235]

Someone responding to Kumārila on behalf of the Apohavāda, then, would have to show

(1) that, if *apoha*s are the meanings of words, then all words are not synonymous, and

(2) that *apoha*s do not have a purely conceptual nature unrelated to perceptual states of affairs, and so can be cognized in some sense independently of the words and thoughts that refer to them.

Dharmakīrti's argument for the second point will perhaps be more familiar to those who already have some acquaintance with his views on *apoha*, so I shall begin with that.

The demonstration of (2) appears to be a prominent part of what Dharmakīrti is attempting to do in the first part of his discussion of *apoha* in PV 1, from verses 40 to 91. That is, he is attempting to show how conceptual cognitions (*vikalpa*), which present us with universals, that is, present multiple particulars as one thing (e.g., multiple trees as "tree"), are caused by perceptual experiences of distinct particulars. The universals presented in these conceptual cognitions are in fact only exclusions or *apoha*s based on the differences of certain particulars from others that do not have the same effects; they are, however, mistaken by us to be real,

---

[234] *tasmād apohaviṣayam iti liṅgaṃ prakīrtitam* /. See n. 212 above.

[235] Taber 2017 argues that this is the principal reason why the Mīmāṃsaka adopts the unusual thesis that universals are perceptible.

external things, i.e., real properties of those particulars, due to the inherently erroneous character of conceptual cognitions. These imagined universals are conventionally assigned as the meanings of words. Thus, word-meanings, *apoha*s, are ultimately grounded on perceptual experiences – not of course experiences of *apoha*s themselves, which are themselves partly conceptual constructions based on certain judgments of "sameness," but of distinct particulars, which however naturally give rise, through the awareness of *apoha*s, to the formation of conceptual cognitions that ascertain them as being the same in various ways.[236] Once again, Dharmakīrti is not claiming that *apoha*s are perceptible. Rather, he is explaining how the meaning of a word, this difference (*apoha*) that distinct particulars of a certain type, e.g., all individual cows, share is ultimately derived from perceptual experiences of those distinct particulars. Thus, one is able to ascertain *apoha*s, the differences of things from others that do not have the same effects, independently of language and inference and assign them as the referents of words and inferential marks.

As discussed in the Preface to this volume, some scholars have been tempted to characterize this aspect of Dharmakīrti's exposition of *apoha* in a broader philosophical way that brings it into relation with contemporary philosophy: he is giving a causal account of intentionality[237]; he is explaining how our thought is anchored in extra-mental reality; he is proposing how to "bridge the scheme-content gap"[238] or offering a "naturalistic explanation of reference,"[239] and so on. All of these interpretations, I believe, agree in essence with what I am proposing, namely, that Dharmakīrti is attempting to show how the awareness of an

---

[236] I cannot go further into the complicated and confusing details of this process here. Those who are familiar with the treatments of Dharmakīrti's theory by Dunne, Tillemans, and others will be able to recognize the description I have just given of what seems to be one of its main objectives. See Dunne 2004: 116–126; Dunne 2011: 90–99; Tillemans 2011a: 54–58; Arnold 2012: 133–141. One of Dharmakīrti's clearest statements of the theory is PVSV 38,17–39,4 (Eltschinger et al. 2018: 76–78).

[237] Arnold 2012: 133–157.

[238] Tillemans 2011a: 53.

[239] Tillemans 2011a: 57.

apoha is grounded in perceptual experience. Given the stage that had been reached in the debate about *apoha* by the time of Dharmakīrti, however, the purpose of this would be to answer Kumārila's challenge, that if meanings are *apoha*s, and *apoha*s are known only through language and inference, then it is difficult to see how we could ever learn the meanings of words.[240]

In order to see how Dharmakīrti demonstrates point (1) it is necessary to understand more about the logical background of Dharmakīrti's discussion of *apoha* in PV(SV) 1.40–185. Dharmakīrti, ostensibly, introduces the idea that words indicate *apoha*s, not in order to solve a problem about language, but a problem about inference. He has been discussing the *svabhāvahetu*, the essence reason. This is the kind of reason that figures in inferences such as, "That is a tree, because it is a birch," and, "Joe is unmarried, because he is a bachelor." According to Dharmakīrti, this type of reason is invariably connected with the consequent of the inference – e.g., being a birch is invariably connected with being a tree – because the two terms (that is, the reason and the consequent) are not different from each other; something cannot be the one without being the other (PV 1.39cd).

But explaining the *svabhāvahetu* in this way gives rise to a problem. If indeed, in the case of the essence-reason (as opposed to other kinds of reasons, such as the effect-reason) the reason is of the essence of the consequent, then the reason itself falls in the domain of what the inference is supposed to prove. As Dharmakīrti puts it, the reason becomes part of the content of the thesis of the inference (*pratijñārthaikadeśa*), namely (in

---

[240] I believe there are special difficulties, however, with the interpretation that Dharmakīrti is giving a "causal," i.e., non-intentional, account of intentionality. The formation of *apoha*s appears, in Dharmakīrti's discussion, to take place on the "personal" level and involves obviously intentional mental states such as judgments of the sameness of distinct particulars (*ekapratyavamarśa*). Arnold notes this, and takes it as a *problem* for Dharmakīrti's account, since it would presuppose what he is trying to explain (Arnold 2012: 140–141). But it is a problem only if one sees him as attempting to provide a causal (i.e., non-intentional) explanation of intentionality.

the case of the example we have been considering), "That is a tree."[241] In that case, the reason ("being a birch") could not be used to prove that something is a tree. If a birch just is a tree, saying that something is a tree because it is a birch would be like saying that something is a tree because it is a tree!

It is ostensibly in order to solve this problem about the use of a specific type of reason in inference that Dharmakīrti launches into a discussion of the meanings of predicates. Only if words refer to *apoha*s, he will argue, is it possible for two words to refer to the same thing without actually being synonymous. For *apoha*s are not real properties. Rather, they are differences, contrasts, that distinct individuals share by differing from the same (more exactly, similar) other things. They are not commonalities that things of a certain type have in themselves (e.g., all cows) independently of those contrasts. A certain individual, then – say, a tree – will have one property (that of being a tree) insofar as it is viewed, together with certain other individuals, as different from one set of things (i.e., non-trees), and another property – say, being a birch – insofar as it is viewed, together with certain other individuals (other birches), as different from a set of other things (non-birches, some of which are trees). Different words that are applied to the same object – "birch" and "tree" – will have different meanings depending on the different properties they indicate, which correspond to different differences or exclusions from other things. This is stated already in the first three verses of the Apoha Section:

> All entities, due to being established in their own natures, naturally partake of exclusions from homogeneous [i.e., similar] as well as heterogeneous [i.e., dissimilar things]. Therefore, from whatever things objects are excluded, different types (*jāti*) are conceived, based on those [exclusions], which reveal the [various] differences of these [objects]. Hence, the difference that is known through a [certain] property [or word] cannot [be understood] through another [word]. And so, the

---

[241] PVSV 24,16–17: *pratijñārthaikadeśo hetuḥ syāt* /.

> [semantic] delimitation [of words and concepts] is not the same." (PV 1.40–42)[242]

Explaining these verses in his *Svavṛtti* Dharmakīrti says,

> Therefore, although the nature [of a particular, which might serve as the subject of an inference] is undivided, the "difference" (*viśeṣa*)[, that is,] distinction that is known through any "property" (*dharma*)[, that is,] name whatsoever cannot be imparted by another [property or word – because that other word would exclude other things]. Thus, all words do not have the same meaning. (PVSV 25,24–25)[243]

Rather, only if words indicated real properties of things would they become synonymous when applied to the same object. According to Dharmakīrti, as he has said in the passage just quoted, the nature of a particular is one, without parts. It is a basic principle of his metaphysics that for something to be real it must be cohesive, unified. If one were to apprehend the nature of a particular, i.e., a real property of it, one would necessarily apprehend it completely, that is, with all of its properties (which however cannot really be distinct from one another). Indeed, this is what happens in perception – the nature of the particular is grasped completely.[244] If, indeed, after perceiving something one employed a word or an inferential mark to ascertain "conceptually" an aspect of the *nature* of the thing, one would necessarily ascertain all of its aspects; for, once again, its nature must be one. Only the fact that, by means of words and inferential marks, we ascertain *apoha*s, which are not intrinsic properties of things or aspects of their natures – despite being derived from the natures of objects insofar as the latter are distinct from other things in different ways, as we have seen

---

[242] *sarve bhāvāḥ svabhāvena svasvabhāvavyavasthiteḥ / sabhāvaparabhāvābhyāṃ yasmād vyāvṛttibhāginaḥ // tasmād yato yato 'rthānāṃ vyāvṛttis tannibandhanāḥ / jātibhedāḥ prakalpyante tadviśeṣāvagāhinaḥ // tasmād yo yena dharmeṇa viśeṣaḥ saṃpratīyate / na śakyas tato 'nyena tena bhinnā vyavasthitiḥ //.* Translation by Eltschinger et al. 2018: 29–30.

[243] *tasmāt svabhāvabhede 'pi yena yena dharmeṇa nāmnā yo viśeṣo bhedaḥ pratīyate na sa śakyo 'nyena pratyāyayitum iti naikārthāḥ sarvaśabdāḥ /.* Translation by Eltschinger et al. 2018: 36.

[244] See PV(SV) 1.43; see Kellner 2004. This unusual idea is perhaps already implied by Dignāga at PS 2.15. See Pind 2015: II.225–229.

– only this fact can save the distinct meaningfulness of distinct expressions applied to the same object.

Summarizing his discussion of this point Dharmakīrti says,

> However many [potential] superimpositions of [extraneous] elements there are, there are just that many ascertainments and words to remove them; thus, these [ascertainments and words] have distinct objects. Otherwise [i.e., if cognitions and words revealed the nature of a real thing without depending on an exclusion,] insofar as an undivided real thing [is completely] covered by a single word or a [single] cognition, [there would be] no other object [for another word or cognition]. Consequently [all words and ascertaining cognitions used in regard to this object] would be synonymous. (PV 1.50–51)[245]

Dharmakīrti, then, appears to be trying to turn the tables on Kumārila. Kumārila argued: if words indicated *apoha*s, then all words would be synonyms. Dharmakīrti is saying: on the contrary, if words did not indicate *apoha*s, then at least all words referring to the same object would be synonyms. In this way, he appears to have answered Kumārila's alarming synonymy objection against Dignāga's Apohavāda.

Other objections raised by Kumārila against the Apohavāda are answered in the Apoha Section of PV 1 as well. Some of them, however, were also raised by Uddyotakara, or at least anticipated by him, so it is not entirely clear in their case that Dharmakīrti is specifically directing himself against Kumārila. The Circularity Argument, for instance, is addressed at PV(SV) 113cd–121.[246] Given that a related argument was put forward by Uddyotakara (namely: without an initial positive denotation of something one cannot understand its negation) and that Dignāga himself tries to address the argument in a version similar to Uddyotakara's (at PS[V] 5.43a), which Jinendrabuddhi attributes to the Sāṃkhya philosopher Mādhava, we cannot be sure that Dharmakīrti is responding specifically to Kumārila on this occasion – though his use of the term "mutual

[245] *yāvanto 'ṃśasamāropās tannirāse viniścayāḥ / tāvanta eva śabdāś ca tena te bhinnagocarāḥ // anyathaikena śabdena vyāpta ekatra vastuni / buddhyā vā nānya-viṣaya iti paryāyatā bhavet //*. Translation by Eltschinger et al. 2018: 45.

[246] See Hugon 2011.

presupposition" (*anyonyāśraya*, PV 1.114a) points to that.[247] The same can be said for his answer to the problem of the word *jñeya*, "knowable." How can it refer to an *apoha* when there does not seem to be any *apohya*, thing to be excluded, since all things are allegedly knowable? Although Dharmakīrti mentions Kumārila's example, Uddyotakara had already essentially raised this same problem with respect to the word "all," as has been mentioned.

Moreover, Dharmakīrti does not discuss the other problematic expressions Kumārila calls attention to at ŚV *Apohavāda* 139–146: verbs, conjunctions, verbal prefixes, and conjunctions. Nevertheless, at PV(SV) 1.122–123 he offers what appears to be a clever, universal solution to problems of this type. All words must, of necessity, he argues, refer to exclusions; otherwise their use would be pointless. "For if this [speaker] did not turn away the thought of some [hearer] from something [not desired] or direct it [towards something desired, then] he would not utter any [word at all] in any practical situations (*sarvavyavahāreṣu*), since it would authorize [a meaning] such as it is [for the hearer prior to its utterance, i.e., in any way whatsoever]; for an utterance is inseparably bound up with delimitation."[248] Dharmakīrti illustrates his point by considering various kinds of commands.[249] If one desired only water and it did not matter how it is delivered, whether by means of a pot or one's hands, one would just say, "Bring water," and not, "Bring water with a pot." One mentions a pot in order to rule out other means of bringing the water. If it did not matter what is brought and one's purpose could be accomplished

---

[247] Uddyotakara, on the other hand, does not use this term. See Hugon 2011: 110.

[248] PVSV 61,17–19: *yadi hy ayaṃ na kasyacit kutaścin nivartayet pravartayet vā buddhiṃ yathābhūtānujñānāt sarvavyavahāreṣu na kiṃcid vyāharet / vyāhārasyāvadhāraṇanāntarīyakatvāt /*. Karṇakagomin explains the difficult expression *yathābhūtānujñānāt* as follows, PVSVṬ 244,18-19: *śabdaprayogāt pūrvaṃ pratipattur yathā sampramugdharūpo 'rthas tathābhūtasya śabdenānujñānāt / yathākiṃcid yādṛśasya tādṛśasyānujñānād ity arthaḥ /*. "Due to the authorization of the meaning by the word just as it was for the hearer prior to the use of the word, i.e., completely confused. That is to say: the authorizing of any kind of [meaning] in any way whatsoever."

[249] PVSV 61,20–26.

by water, dirt, or some other substance, one would simply say "Bring." One mentions water in order to rule out other substances. Finally, if simply some action or other were desired, not necessarily the action of bringing, one wouldn't even say "Bring." One mentions bringing in order to rule out other actions. Thus, a word is uttered only when certain things are to be excluded by uttering it, not otherwise, and presumably this would be true of all parts of speech. Moreover, words are uttered only when there is some doubt.[250] One might say that sound is "knowable" as impermanent, for instance, when one's interlocutor wonders if it is *un*knowable as impermanent, or that all things are "knowable" when the topic is whether all things are "knowable" as far as an omniscient person goes.[251] In general, a word is rarely uttered in isolation, but almost always in a sentence in a certain situation where its excluding function is specified by the context and its relation to the other words of the sentence. The word "knowable" by itself does not mean anything, but neither does the word "pot."[252]

Dharmakīrti's solutions to the problems of coreference and qualification, however, reflect deeper disagreements with parts of Kumārila's system. The key to Dharmakīrti's solutions is his claim that the exclusion (*vyāvṛtti*) and that which is excluded (*vyāvṛtta*) are not really different;[253]

[250] PVSV 62,1–4: [...] *ananyāśaṅkāyāṃ prayogāyogāt / tatra hi yad eva mūḍhamater āśaṅkāsthānaṃ tad eva nivartyam / anāśaṅkamāno vā kiṃ parasmād upadeśam apekṣate /*. "[...] since the use [of words such as 'knowable'] is not possible when there is no doubt about another. Indeed, in regard to that, precisely that which is the object of doubt (*āśaṅkāsthānam*; PVSVṬ 245,29–30: *āśaṅkāviṣayaḥ*) for a confused person is excluded. For why would someone who lacks doubt need instruction from someone else?"

[251] The examples are Karṇakagomin's, PVSVṬ 245,13–16.

[252] PVSV 62,5–10.

[253] PV 1.59: *tatrāpi cānyavyāvṛttir anyavyāvṛtta ity api / śabdāś ca niścayāś caiva saṅketam anurundhate //*. "In the case of the [exclusion from another as the meaning of a word], as well, both the expressions and ascertainments 'exclusion from another' and 'excluded from another,' [which refer to the property and the property-bearer, respectively,] are merely a matter of convention" (Eltschinger et al. 2018: 55). See Hugon 2017.

they are, namely, simply the particular excluded from other particulars.[254] However, we use, merely as a matter of convention, different words to refer to it that express different ways in which it is excluded from others. When one wishes to express that, let us say, a particular cow is excluded from non-cows, without acknowledging that it is also excluded from many other things – it may, for instance, also be excluded from non-white things and from non-pregnant things – we use the word for the property, "cowness." When, on the other hand, one wishes to refer to the cow without disregarding those other exclusions, one uses the word "cow." In the former case, where the word "cowness" refers just to the exclusion of non-cows without implying other exclusions, coreference and qualification are not possible. One cannot say, "Cowness is white." In the latter case, on the other hand, both are possible, since "cow" refers to the exclusion of non-cows without disregarding other exclusions. Hence, one may say, "The cow is white."[255]

Dharmakīrti emphasizes that the use of these different expressions, with these connotations, for the same thing is purely a matter of convention, just as convention allows one to indicate a wife, which is one thing, by means of an expression that is grammatically plural (*dārāḥ*).[256] That is to say, there is nothing about a particular cow itself that justifies the use of either expression. A cow is neither one thing common to other cows, which would justify the use of "cowness"; for a particular cow is completely unique, distinct from everything else, even other cows. Nor is it many things, that is, a property-bearer with many properties, which would justify the use of "cow"; for everything that is real is one and not many. Similarly, the use of the genitive in sentences such as, "The cowness of the cow," which suggests a distinction between property and property-bearer, is purely

---

[254] PVSV 32,17: *tasmād yaiva vyāvṛttiḥ sa eva vyāvṛttaḥ* /. Dharmakīrti offers a quick (and rather dodgy) metaphysical argument in support of this claim, PVSV 32,15–16. If the exclusion were different from the thing excluded, then the excluded thing (*vyāvṛtta*) x would be non-x; for what is different from the exclusion of non-x, i.e., what is not not non-x, is just non-x. A cow, for instance, being other than the exclusion of non-horse, would be a horse. Cf. Hugon 2017: 166.

[255] PVSV 33,7–34,4, Eltschinger et al. 2018: 57–60.

[256] PVSV 36,18–26, Eltschinger et al. 2018: 68–69.

conventional. It is not determined by the nature of the cow; for, once again, everything that is real is completely unified, not divided. It is, then, only by virtue of the imagining of diverse exclusions and the designation of those exclusions by diverse expressions that allows for the possibility of coreference and qualification. Neither would be possible if "cow," in the sense of property-bearer, and "cowness," in the sense of a separate universal, referred to real features of things, since things do not really have such features.[257]

Without going further into details, we are able to see how Dharmakīrti has again turned the tables on Kumārila. Kumārila had argued that, if words referred to mere *apoha*s, they could neither be coreferential nor qualify each other, since *apoha*s would have the same features that, Dignāga argued, would prevent words from being coreferential or qualifying each other if they referred to universals. Now Dharmakīrti comes back and insists that Dignāga was right all along: universals are indeed very problematic, but for deeper, metaphysical reasons than Dignāga stated in PS 5.[258] The fact is that universals simply do not exist – Dharmakīrti will argue for this throughout the Apoha Section, and in many other passages elsewhere in his corpus, in a variety of ways. Moreover, there is no such thing as a property-bearer, since it would be a completely fragmented entity: there would be a basic distinction between the property-bearer and its properties, on the one hand, and distinctions between its various properties, on the other.

Even if the meaning of a word is conceived of as an individual possessing an *apoha* (*apohavat*), analogous to an individual possessing a genus (*jātimat*/*tadvat*), the Apohavāda can easily account for coreference and qualification, Dharmakīrti suggests. We saw that Kumārila claimed that the *apoha*-possessor theory would have a problem analogous to what Dignāga attributed to the universal-possessor theory, namely, a word would indicate its meaning "dependently." That is to say, a word would indicate an individual possessing an *apoha* mediated by the *apoha*, which

---

[257] PVSV 43,14–44,12, Eltschinger et al. 2018: 93–97.

[258] Dignāga's critique of universals, the *Sāmānyaparīkṣā* or *Sāmānyaparīkṣāvyāsa*, is lost. See Pind 2015: I.xii.

no more implies any differences than a universal does. Thus, it could not be used coreferentially with another word that indicates a difference, in a phrase such as "existing pot." This problem vanishes if the exclusion and the thing excluded are the same, as Dharmakīrti believes. In that case, since the *apoha* and the *apoha*-possessor are the same, by indicating the latter through the *apoha* a word is in fact indicating it directly. In effect, the *apoha* and *apoha*-possessor collapse into one.[259]

This will have to suffice as an overview of the various ways in which Dharmakīrti responds to Kumārila's critique of the Apohavāda. Dharmakīrti seems to have realized that criticisms such as Kumārila's required a complete revision of the theory. For one thing, one had to explain in greater detail the psychological mechanism that produces the conceptual awarenesses that ascertain *apoha*s, and in particular how they are grounded on perceptual experiences of concrete particulars. In this way Dharmakīrti is able to answer, if only implicitly, the objection that if an *apoha* is not somehow knowable independently of language and inference, then the connection between a word or inferential mark and an *apoha* could never be learned so that the former could indicate the latter. As other scholars have indeed pointed out, Dharmakīrti's psychological theory shows how words and inferential marks ultimately relate to perceptible particulars.

Dharmakīrti also makes explicit the metaphysical foundations of the Apohavāda, which Dignāga neglected to do (in his *Pramāṇasamuccaya*, at least). The world, according to Dharmakīrti, is populated by entities that "do not mix their natures with one another,"[260] that is, discrete particulars. There are no common natures, no universals. These entities, moreover, are one in the sense that the nature of each is unified, undivided. Thus, if its nature is known at all, it is known entirely. Entities, therefore, do not have real, diverse properties, and certainly there is no real distinction between a thing and its properties. All this entails that the properties (*dharma*) that we do predicate of things, and which are the objects of words and inferential marks, cannot be real. They are based merely on the differences things share with other things, *from* certain other things, by virtue of having

---

[259] See PVSV 34,17–23, Eltschinger et al. 2018: 62–63.

[260] PVSV 24,24–25: *te nātmānaṃ pareṇa miśrayanti* /.

certain effects that the latter lack. These are "exclusions." Depending on which "other" entities a thing is taken to be excluded from – usually, there are multiple possibilities – it partakes of different exclusions. Thus, contrary to Kumārila's contention, only on the Apohavāda can words (referring to the same thing) *not* be synonymous.

In defining these metaphysical principles Dharmakīrti, at the same time that he is providing a new foundation for the Apohavāda, is also calling into question some of the basic metaphysical teachings of the realist Brahmanical traditions of Mīmāṃsā, Nyāya, and Sāṃkhya. All of these traditions accepted, in their own ways, the existence of real universals, as well as a real distinction between property-bearer and property. Indeed, just as he aggressively attacks the existence of universals, he also explicitly argues against the notion of a substance possessing distinct properties.[261] Yet he also calls into question a fundamental Mīmāṃsā idea when he insists that the relation between a word and its meaning is strictly conventional. It is the arbitrariness of the assignment of words to certain meanings that allows one to call the same thing a "cow" or "cowness" as one wishes, just as one may refer to a wife by means of either a word in the singular or one in the plural. This supports the denial of any real distinction between property-bearer and property. It is the Mīmāṃsā tradition, of course, that maintains that the relation between word and meaning is "natural" (*autpattika*). Kumārila vigorously attacks the view that the relation is conventional in ŚV *Sambandhākṣepaparihāra* 13–41.

Thus, Dharmakīrti's discussion of the Apohavāda in *Pramāṇavārttika* 1 is much more than a defense of the Apohavāda. It represents a rejection of the entire way of thinking about reality of those traditions that insisted that the meanings of words are real entities.

To return, finally, to the issue of the chronological relation of Dharmakīrti to Kumārila that was mentioned at the beginning of this section, we have seen that Dharmakīrti is answering specific criticisms Kumārila makes of Dignāga's Apohavāda in a comprehensive way, moreover, that some of the positions he develops imply criticisms in turn of more fundamental aspects

---

[261] PVSV 43,19–30; Eltschinger et al. 2018: 94–95.

of the Mīmāṃsā system as we know it from the writings of Kumārila. It is difficult to imagine that Dharmakīrti could have had anyone besides Kumārila in mind when he mounted his defense of *apoha*. One would have to postulate some other great Mīmāṃsaka, whose name has been entirely forgotten, who devised a philosophical system that neatly maps onto Kumārila's. That Kumārila was Dharmakīrti's opponent in the debate about *apoha* in PV 1 is, thus, certainly the more parsimonious hypothesis. Dharmakīrti, indeed, appears to have been "in dialogue with Kumārila."

That does not mean, however, that Kumārila was the only Mīmāṃsaka Dharmakīrti knew. On other occasions, when refuting Mīmāṃsā positions, Dharmakīrti is considering formulations of arguments that are not found in Kumārila.[262] Meanwhile, there are important theories and arguments of Kumārila he does not address, at least not explicitly. Most prominent among these is the theory of intrinsic validity (*svataḥ prāmāṇyam*), which Kumārila employs in attempting to demonstrate some of the most central Mīmāṃsā teachings: the authority of the Veda, the existence of universals, and the existence of a self. Dharmakīrti may have refrained from launching an all-out attack on the Mīmāṃsā theory of intrinsic validity, in the way some of his successors did (in particular, Śāntarakṣita), because he considered it to be essentially compatible with the Buddhist idea that the mind is luminous by nature: cognition apprehends objects as they are so long as it is not impaired by impurities.[263] However, he seems to have failed to appreciate how pervasive the notion of *svataḥ prāmāṇyam* is in Kumārila's thought, specifically, how Kumārila resorts to it in supporting the above-mentioned, central teachings. Finally, the possibility that Kumārila had a predecessor or predecessors who worked out many of the theories and arguments he presents in his works in a more forceful, definitive way – who could have been targeted by Dharmakīrti – cannot be completely ruled out until we have thoroughly examined Kumārila's writings with a view to determining what other significant Mīmāṃsā

[262] See Taber 2019: 85–86. Taber 2012 argues more broadly that, when it comes to his critique of Mīmāṃsā practices of Vedic exegesis at the end of PV 1, Dharmakīrti appears to be attacking either a straw man or else much less sophisticated Mīmāṃsakas than Śabara and Kumārila.

[263] Taber 2019.

sources he might have had besides Śabara.

Thus, in the end, perhaps the safest hypothesis to adopt at this time is the following. Dharmakīrti almost certainly had Kumārila's critique of Dignāga in front of him when he set out to defend and elaborate the Apohavāda. He may, however, not have known Kumārila's system – as vast, difficult, and complex as his own – thoroughly and in detail. Rather, when it came to other Mīmāṃsā doctrines, such as the infallibility of the Veda based on its authorlessness or the inherent imperfection of humans, he was more acquainted with the ideas of other teachers. Kumārila was a mountain on the landscape that Dharmakīrti, probably already educated in Mīmāṃsā in his youth, had neither the time nor desire to scale. But his critique of the Apohavāda, which was so pointedly directed against the revered preceptor Dignāga, and which attacked a theory Dharmakīrti wanted to place at the center of his own system, was something he could not ignore. He felt obligated to develop a thorough and decisive refutation of it. Some situation such as this could explain why, when it comes to his treatment of *apoha*, it seems very difficult to deny that Dharmakīrti is reacting to Kumārila, but less so when it comes to his polemical treatment of other Mīmāṃsā positions.

KEI KATAOKA

How Successful is Kumārila's Criticism of Dignāga?

0. Introduction

In the following I will first summarize the core issues that Kumārila addresses in his critique of Dignāga's Apohavāda in the order in which they appear in the *Ślokavārttika*. I will then elucidate the limitations and merits of Dignāga's theory to see to what extent he would have been able to defend his view, had he faced Kumārila's criticism.

1. Dignāga's *apoha* theory: a parallel between inference and verbal cognition

It should be remembered that Dignāga's main objective in the *apoha* section of the *Pramāṇasamuccaya* (PS 5) is to reject the status of verbal cognition (*śābda*) as an independent *pramāṇa*. He explicitly claims in the opening verse, PS 5.1, that verbal cognition is not a *pramāṇa* separate from inference. This claim implies that valid inference and valid verbal cognition are congruent in terms of the main features of their operation, including their application and their reliance on prior knowledge. Just as from its being produced (*kṛtakatva*) sound reveals its transience (*anityatva*) by excluding that which is intransient, a word such as "cow" indicates the nature of a cow by excluding non-cows. Furthermore, just as an inference functions solely on the basis of a previously grasped invariable concomitance (*vyāpti*) which is negative in nature, verbal cognition functions solely on the basis of a previously learned negative relationship between a word and its referent. The relation in both cases is, strictly speaking, an *avinābhāva* relationship ("without X never Y"), as exemplified in "Smoke has never been seen without fire." Similarly, the word "cow" is never used in the absence of a cow. The relationship is learned through a negative method called *vyatireka*, concurrent absence ("without X no Y"), which is confirmed by non-perception (*adarśana*).

2. *apoha*, *apohya*, and *apohavat*

In his theory of *apoha* Dignāga assumes the following framework: the word "cow," for example, makes known things qualified by the exclusion of non-cows (*ago'pohaviśiṣṭa*). Non-cows, such as horses and elephants, are the objects to be excluded (*apohya*). To this point Dignāga states, PSV ad 5.36d, that a word conveys things that are necessarily qualified by the negation of other things (*śabdo 'rthāntaranivṛttiviśiṣṭān eva bhāvān āha*).[264] The same principle is applied in the opening verse, which runs as follows: "A word expresses its own referent[265] by excluding other things, just as does an inferential mark such as being produced."[266] Altogether, there are four terms to be taken into consideration: *śabda*, *apoha*, *apohya*, and *apohavat*. A word (*śabda*) expresses things that "have exclusion" (*apohavat*), i.e., things qualified by exclusion (*apoha*) of the things to be excluded (*apohya*).

śabda → *apoha* <---> *apohya*
|
apohavat

3. Exclusion as non-existence

Kumārila criticizes the ontological status of *apoha*, which for Dignāga, is a type of non-existence/absence (*abhāva*). For example, the nature of a cow is the same as the exclusion of non-cows (*ago'poha*), which amounts to the

---

[264] See also Katsura 1991: 138 and Pind 1999 for this passage.

[265] This *svārtha* corresponds to *arthāntaranivṛttiviśiṣṭa* (Dignāga's term) and *apohavat* (Kumārila's term) (cf. also Hugon 2017: 172–174). Kumārila examines possible candidates of *apohavat* in ŚV *Apohavāda* 128 ff. and refutes each of them. Katsura 1991: 138 discusses the exact meaning of this *svārtha* and concludes, "I would like to take '*svārtha*' as referring to the perceptual object itself which is something real in our external world." Katsura's identification of this *svārtha* as something real seems inappropriate (cf. Hugon 2017: 174, n.56), considering that Dignāga probably intends the general remainder of exclusion, i.e., the sphere that has not been excluded, as the *svārtha* as discussed below.

[266] PS 5.1bcd: *saḥ / kṛtakatvādivat svārtham anyāpohena bhāṣate //* (Pind 2015: I,1,3–4).

absence of non-cows (*ago'bhāva*). The nature of X is simply the absence of non-X for Dignāga. Furthermore, the word "cow," too, being a general characteristic (*sāmānyalakṣaṇa*) and thus an *apoha* in reality, is precisely the absence of words (*śabdāntarābhāva*) other than "cow." Thus, for Dignāga, both relata, e.g., the word "cow" and its referent, are kinds of non-existence in reality.

4. Non-existence as an aspect of a positive entity

By contrast, for Kumārila non-existence is an aspect of another existent entity. For example, the (prior) non-existence of curds is precisely another existent thing, namely, milk. Viewed in terms of substratum (*āśraya*) and property (*ādheya*), we can easily regard the absence of curds as "residing in" milk. It is to be noted that in Kumārila's ontology, a property is not completely different from its substratum (*bhedābheda*). Therefore, Kumārila prefers an expression such as "the absence of curds is another existent thing, namely, milk." Kumārila states in the second verse, "For it was taught previously that non-existence is another entity."[267]

5. Non-existence of non-cows and the universal cowness

Moreover, the non-existence of non-cows is also a real entity for Kumārila. Or, it can be regarded as an aspect of a cow or a portion (*aṃśa*) of one. The positive entity that functions as the substratum of the non-existence of non-cows, i.e., the general characteristic, is for him the universal cowness. Therefore, in the opening verse of the *Ślokavārttika*, what Dignāga alleges to be the non-existence of non-cows is understood as the universal cowness: "It is obvious that those who imagine the general entity which is the negation of non-cow as the denotation [of words] speak of cowness, which is indeed a real thing, by means of the expression 'exclusion of non-cow'."[268]

---

[267] ŚV *Apohavāda* 2ab: *bhāvāntaram abhāvo hi purastāt pratipāditaḥ* //.

[268] ŚV *Apohavāda* 1: *agonivṛttiḥ sāmānyaṃ vācyaṃ yaiḥ parikalpitam / gotvaṃ vastv eva tair uktam ago'pohagirā sphuṭam* //.

6. Kumārila's critical strategy appears in the first part of ŚV *Apohavāda*.

Dignāga claims that the word "cow" conveys something that "has exclusion" of non-cows (*a-go-apoha-vat*). In the first part of ŚV *Apohavāda* Kumārila criticizes his view from several angles. The main points of his critique can be summarized in the form of questions, as follows.

(1) What is exclusion (*apoha*)? 1–46

(2) What are the non-cows that are to be excluded (*apohya*)? 47–72

(3) What is the relationship between the word "cow" and the exclusion of non-cows; in particular, how is it learned? 73–79

(4) What is the relationship between the exclusion of non-cows and non-cows, especially in regard to their mutual dependence? 80–85a

(5) What is the relationship between an exclusion and what possesses the exclusion, especially regarding the qualifier-qualificand relation? 85cd–94

(6) What is the nature of the exclusion (i.e., the non-existence) of non-cows (i.e., a non-existence)? 95–99

(7) What is the overall framework of the theory of exclusion, in particular with regard to the distinction of exclusions (especially between word-exclusions and meaning-exclusions)? 100–114[269]

In the diagram below numbers (1)–(7) correspond to the numbers of the questions above.

(=*śabdāntarāpohaḥ*) (=*apohāntarasya*$_2$ *apohaḥ*$_1$(6))

śabda(7) → (1)*apoha*(7) <---> (7)*apohya*(2)

(3) (5)| (4)

apohavat

(1) First of all, as stated above, the exclusion of non-cows is a kind of

[269] In the remaining parts (115–119, 120–138, 139–146, 147–157, 158–162, and 163–164) Kumārila criticizes Dignāga's discussions in detail from different perspectives. In the final part (165–176) he criticizes a Naiyāyika's criticism of Dignāga's theory.

non-existence. And for Kumārila, non-existence amounts to another existent entity. For Kumārila, this existent entity can only be cowness. He states in 10d, "And that is nothing other than cowness" (*gotvād anyac ca nāsti tat*); and in 35a, "Therefore, there would be exclusions only in respect to something real" (*tasmād vastuny apohāḥ syuḥ*).

(2) In vv. 47–72 Kumārila introduces the topic of *apohya*s with a discussion of the distinction of exclusions (i.e., the distinction of word-meanings). Kumārila refers to a Buddhist view – one that is in accord with Dignāga's – that the distinction of exclusions (*apoha-bheda*) is due to differences in the things to be excluded (*apohya-bheda*). Although any two exclusions are the same insofar as both are exclusions, they differ from each other in terms of what they exclude. For example, in the case of the exclusion of non-cows (which is the meaning of the word "cow") and the exclusion of non-horses (which is the meaning of the word "horse"), the things to be excluded (non-cows and non-horses) are different from each other. Therefore, the two exclusions can be distinguished from each other.

non-cows <---> exclusion$_1$ $\neq$ exclusion$_2$ <---> non-horses

Kumārila then rejects the following as possible candidates for the things to be excluded: individuals (*piṇḍa*, 58cd–60); a collection (*samudāya*, 61–63ab); some kind of universal, i.e., exclusion (63cd–66); horses, etc. (67–68ab); and atoms (68cd–70). He argues that none of these entities can properly bring about distinct exclusions because without identifying the non-cows to be excluded they cannot constitute one group. Thus, Kumārila concludes, "Nor can anyone discern horse, etc., [equally] as what is to be excluded without continuity of the same property. In that case exclusion is not established."[270]

(3) The Apohavāda is a semantic theory which intends to explain the phenomenon that one understands cows in general when hearing the word "cow." Naturally, how we understand the relationship between the word "cow" and the exclusion of non-cows requires an explanation.

---

[270] ŚV *Apohavāda* 72: *apohyān api cāśvādīn ekadharmānvayād vinā / na nirūpayituṃ śaktis, tatrāpoho na sidhyati //.*

For Dignāga, the semantic relationship between a word and its referent parallels the inferential relationship between being produced and transience. In other words, he regards learning the semantic relation as identical with learning invariable concomitance or *avinābhāva*. Kumārila attempts to refute the possibility of experiencing the relation between the word "cow" and the exclusion of non-cows. In particular, he tries to disprove Dignāga's idea of grasping the relation through concurrent absence (*vyatireka*). Kumārila concludes, "Nor, for that [reason], is an [original] experience [whether by perception or inference] of the relation of this [word with an *apoha*] at all possible."[271]

(4) Having discussed the relationship between the word "cow" and exclusion, Kumārila turns to the relationship between exclusion and the things to be excluded. As might be expected, he points out the mutual dependence between non-cows (i.e., the exclusion of cows) and the exclusion of non-cows (84b).

exclusion of non-cows <---> non-cows (exclusion of cows)

The fallacy of mutual dependence cannot be avoided without the assumption that non-cows are given as already established (*siddha*). As we will see, Dignāga himself regards non-cows as something established through non-perception (*adarśana*). Therefore, Dignāga would not accept Kumārila's criticism. Kumārila, for his part, denies (in 75) Dignāga's view that non-perception (*adarśanamātra*) is a basis for establishing non-cows. Kumārila has concurrently also rejected different possible candidates for the group "non-cows," as described under point (2) above. Thus, his criticism is cogent in that it considers every answer possible within Dignāga's system.

(5) After having discussed the relation between the word "cow" and exclusion, and the relation between exclusion and the things to be excluded, Kumārila addresses the question of the relation between *apoha* and *apohavat*, i.e., the relation between exclusion and the things that have exclusion. Dignāga had taken the theory of *jātimat* (things that have a universal) as the main target of his criticism. In its place, he

[271] ŚV *Apohavāda* 79cd: *saṃbandhānubhavo 'py asya tena naivopapadyate* //.

posited his own theory of *apohavat*.[272] Kumārila's main target here is the qualifier-qualificand relation between *apoha* and *apohavat*. First of all, he says, it is necessary to cognize the qualifier in advance in order to cognize the qualificand. Kumārila states in 87, "And something is not a qualifier simply because it exists. That which 'colors' the qualified thing through a cognition of itself is a qualifier."[273] He points out that, in an actual cognition upon hearing the word "horse," an exclusion, i.e., something negative, does not appear in the first place. In other words, it is not the case that one (directly) obtains a negative cognition of "not non-horse" by hearing the word "horse." Kumārila writes, "And awareness of an *apoha* does not arise from words like 'horse,' etc. And the cognition of something to be qualified whose qualifier is not known, is not accepted here [i.e., normally]."[274] Therefore, Kumārila finds it problematic to posit a thing qualified by exclusion (*apohaviśiṣṭa*) as a word-meaning. From his perspective, the problem originates with the assumption that *apohavat*, which does not appear in an actual cognition, is the qualified word-meaning of "cow." His conclusion runs as follows: "And it is rash to say that something not comprehended by a word [i.e., the unique individual] is the thing qualified [by an *apoha*]. Therefore, a [real] universal should be sought as the referent (*viṣaya*) of the cognition and the word."[275]

(6) In vv. 1–72, Kumārila discusses *apoha* (1) and *apohya* (2). He then addresses the relationship between a word and *apoha* (3) and the relationship between *apoha* and *apohya* (4); and finally he looks at the relationship between *apoha* and *apohavat* (5). Whereas in (1) and (2) exclusion and non-cows were separately discussed, in (6) Kumārila discusses them in combination, i.e., he looks at the exclusion of non-

---

[272] Dignāga himself uses the expression *arthāntaranivṛttiviśiṣṭa* and not the technical term *apohavat* used by Kumārila.

[273] ŚV *Apohavāda* 87: *svarūpasattvamātreṇa na ca kiṃcid viśeṣaṇam / svabuddhyā rajyate yena viśeṣyaṃ tad viśeṣaṇam //.*

[274] ŚV *Apohavāda* 88: *na cāpy aśvādiśabdebhyo jāyate 'pohabodhanam / viśeṣyabuddhir iṣṭeha na cājñātaviśeṣaṇā //.*

[275] ŚV *Apohavāda* 94: *śabdenāgamyamānaṃ ca viśeṣyam iti sāhasam / tena sāmānyam eṣṭavyaṃ viṣayo buddhiśabdayoḥ //.*

cows. First of all, he argues, the non-cow should be a real entity inasmuch as it is the object of exclusion, because absence cannot be excluded: "And because of its exclusion it is a real thing" (*tasyāpohāc ca vastutā*, 95d). He continues, "If, on the contrary, the non-cow were an absence, the exclusion of the non-cow, i.e., absence of absence, would be an existent" (97abc). Although he concedes that common examples such as the exclusion of non-cows might be acceptable because we can think of real entities such as horses, how, he asks, can we explain words such as "existing"? In the case of the exclusion of something not existing, how can we exclude a non-existent entity, which is clearly not a real entity and therefore cannot be an object of exclusion? "Even if a real thing were the *apohya* in the case of other words, for the word 'existing,' on the other hand, that which is excluded is not considered distinct from what is called non-existence."[276]

(7) Thus, to examine Dignāga's claim that a word expresses things qualified by exclusion, Kumārila discusses each relatum and its relations mainly from the ontological viewpoint of whether the relata are existent or non-existent. Ultimately, he argues that the entire framework of the theory of exclusion does not work. First, he intercepts a Buddhist who may try to evade his critique by resorting to the concept of residual impression (*vāsanā*). He points out that, because a residual impression is necessarily preceded by an original experience (*anubhava*) and because one has to accept something real as the object of the original experience, one cannot arbitrarily appeal to *vāsanā* in order to defend *apoha* and the difference between *apoha*s (100).

Kumārila then takes into consideration that a word, too, is said to be of the nature of *apoha*, although he has not focused much on this aspect so far. Dignāga himself stresses that a word, being a general characteristic, is a type of *apoha*.[277] If, however, one accepts that a word is an *apoha*, the same problem of a meaning-*apoha* will arise. That is to say, the problem that the difference between *apoha*s cannot be

[276] ŚV *Apohavāda* 98: *yady apy anyeṣu śabdeṣu vastunaḥ syād apohyatā / sacchabdasya tv abhāvākhyān nāpohyaṃ bhinnam iṣyate //.*

[277] For this aspect of *śabda*, see Pind 1991: 270 and Pind 2015: II.113, n. 401.

explained because *apoha*s are non-existent entities, applies also to word-*apoha*s. Consequently, the difference between "cow" and "horse" cannot be explained, because, being equally identified as exclusions and therefore essentially non-existent, no difference between them can be established. The Buddhist might then resort to the difference between *apohya*s in order to explain the difference between word-*apoha*s. But the difference between *apohya*s as a device to explain the difference of *apoha*s has already been denied by Kumārila in his discussion of meaning-*apoha*s. Therefore, the Buddhist cannot explain the difference between word-*apoha*s, e.g., the exclusion of non-"cow" and the exclusion of non-"horse." Consequently, the *apoha* theory cannot even account for the difference between words and meanings, because word-*apoha*s and meaning-*apoha*s, being exclusions by nature, are all the same. Kumārila states, "And as [there is no difference] for words, so [there is no difference] of a word and a meaning from each other. And it has been proven [at vv. 47 ff.] that there is no difference [of *apoha*s] due to a difference of *apohya*s".[278] Furthermore, he states, because *apoha* is unreal, the difference between *apoha* and *apohya*, e.g., between a cow and a non-cow as well as between "cow" and non-"cow," cannot be explained. Consequently, the holder of the Apohavāda has to accept that an unreal *apoha* is based on a real entity, which can be nothing other than cowness. The Apohavāda cannot explain how a non-existent *apoha* is understood by people in a positive way. Were it non-existent, the notion "cow" would be baseless (114ab). On the other hand, it is accepted in Mīmāṃsā that cowness can be understood as "the absence [of horses, etc.]" (114cd).

Kumārila's criticisms can, thus, be summarized as follows:

1. What is exclusion? Exclusion (*apoha*) is a type of absence (*abhāva*). However, the absence of a non-cow requires the existence of the universal cowness. Similarly, because exclusion is absence in reality,

[278] ŚV *Apohavāda* 105: *vācakānāṃ yathā caivaṃ vācyavācakayor mithaḥ / na cāpy apohyabhedena bhedo 'stīty upapāditam //.*

the difference of *apoha*s cannot be established without appealing to a positive entity.

2. The object to be excluded (*apohya*), such as non-cow, cannot be ascertained. Therefore, one cannot differentiate between *apoha*s on the basis of the difference between *apohya*s.

3. It is impossible to understand the relationship between the exclusion of non-cows and the word "cow."

4. If one does not accept that cowness is a universal, the fallacy of mutual dependence arises between the exclusion of non-cows and non-cows (the latter of which are the exclusion of cows).

5. Neither the exclusion of non-cows nor the things qualified by this exclusion appear in an actual cognition. Therefore, Dignāga's claim that the referent of the word "cow" is the thing qualified by the exclusion of non-cows cannot be accepted.

6. Absence, being an unreal entity, cannot be the object of exclusion. The thing to be excluded (*apohya*) has to be something real. If the non-cow were an absence, its exclusion, being the absence of absence, would be something existent.

7. Finally, Kumārila concludes that the ontological framework of the Apohavāda is flawed, primarily because the distinction between *apoha*s cannot be established inasmuch as words and meanings, being *apoha*s in reality, are all non-existent.

7. An evaluation of Kumārila's criticism

7.1. The non-ascertainment of the *apohya*

Dignāga would not agree with Kumārila's criticism with regard to the second point, that *apohya*s cannot be ascertained. For Dignāga, the *apohya* non-cow can be ascertained as something "in regard to which the word 'cow' is not observed when the relation is [initially] learned."[279] Thus, because the *apohya* can be ascertained, the fallacy of mutual dependence between the *apoha* and the *apohya* can be avoided. And because *apohyas* can be distinguished from each other, the difference of *apoha*s can be

[279] ŚV *Apohavāda* 81cd: *na dṛṣṭo yatra gośabdaḥ saṃbandhānubhavakṣane* //.

explained, at least from Dignāga's perspective.

7.2. The establishment of the relationship between word and meaning

However, Kumārila's fundamental criticism, that it is impossible to learn the relationship between the exclusion of non-cows and the word "cow," can be justified from a philosophical point of view. In this respect Dignāga's theory of *apoha* falls into a difficulty as will be explained in detail below.

8. Dignāga's notion of non-perception (*adarśana*)

8.1. *Adarśana* in the framework of *apoha*

The ultimate foundation for Dignāga's theory of *apoha* is the absence of perception (*adarśana*). Whereas the relation between "cow" and its real referent (such as the universal cowness or things that have cowness) is based on perception for the realists, who accept real universals, for Dignāga, the relation, which is determined through a negative method of co-absence (*vyatireka*), is based on an absence of perception (*adarśana*). To explain, in learning the word "cow," non-cows are things to which the word "cow" has never been seen applied. The learner recognizes that whenever there is no cow, "cow" is not used. Hence, the word "cow" is applied *only* to cows after learning the relation through concurrent absence. Thereafter, non-cows are excluded when hearing the word "cow." The complement or the remainder of the exclusion of non-cows is the referent of the word "cow." The steps presupposed by Dignāga can be summed up as follows:

1. The *apohya* (e.g. non-cows) is ascertained by means of non-perception: non-cows are ascertained as things to which the word "cow" has never been seen applied.
2. The relationship between a word and its referent is learned through concurrent absence (*vyatireka*).
3. Exclusion of non-cows is understood when hearing the word "cow."
4. The complement is understood in a general form, i.e., as the things qualified by the exclusion of non-cows.

8.2. Perception and inference: *Apoha* as the object of verbal cognition

In Dignāga's system, inference has as its object a general characteristic (*sāmānyalakṣaṇa*), whereas perception has as its object a particular characteristic (*svalakṣaṇa*). A particular tree has various aspects in common with others of the same type. For example, a particular tree may have rosewoodness (*śiṃśapātva*), and like other trees it has treeness (*vṛkṣatva*), earthenness (*pārthivatva*), substancehood (*dravyatva*), existence (*sattā*), knowability (*jñeyatva*), etc.[280] However, these general aspects of a tree are not real for Dignāga. That is to say, the referent of the word "tree" is not the real universal treeness, but merely the exclusion of non-trees. Each of these aspects is made manifest by a word not in a positive way, but in a negative way. For example, treeness is made manifest by the word "tree" because the word excludes other things such as non-trees. As Dignāga states in the opening verse of the fifth chapter of the *Pramāṇasamuccaya*, a word expresses its own referent by excluding other things, just as an inferential mark does.

8.3. Perception and non-perception

The objects of perception are real, individual particulars. To explain, perception_1 grasps cow_1 in a particular place, whereas perception_2 grasps cow_2 in another place. Likewise, perception_n grasps cow_n in yet another place. It is, however, impossible for perception_1 to grasp all instances of cow ($\text{cow}_{1...n}$) in all places. On the other hand, the non-perception "there is no cow here" tells us that $\text{cow}_{1...n}$ does not exist in this place. In other words, non-perception can confirm that no instance of cow whatsoever exists in this place at this moment. Non-perception can thus universally cover the absence of all cows ($\text{cow}_{1...n}$), at least with regard to the here and now. The denoted sphere of the word "cow" is every instance of a cow, namely, $\text{cow}_{1...n}$. In other words, "cow" is applied only to $\text{cow}_{1...n}$ and nothing else.

As to how the relation between the word "cow" and its denotation is learned, two possibilities are proposed: concurrent existence (*anvaya*) and

---

[280] For the hierarchy of universals and particulars, see Katsura 1991: 131.

concurrent absence (*vyatireka*). Dignāga argues that the method of concurrent existence does not work for learning the universal relationship between cow and "cow" because it does not cover all instances. One cannot perceive each and every case of their co-existence because cows are infinite in number.

Concurrent absence, on the other hand, can cover all possible cases (at least according to Dignāga). As noted above, the negative method of concurrent absence is based on non-perception. One has never seen the word "cow" applied to non-cows. Whenever there is no cow, "cow" is not used. The non-perception at stake presupposed by Dignāga in this context is an accumulation of non-perceptions and can be distinguished from a single instance of non-perception such as $adarśana_1$ or $adarśana_2$. I tentatively designate this cumulative non-perception as $adarśana_{\text{so far}}$ (this non-perception may also be thought of as cumulative non-perception or never-perception: one has *never* perceived the object in question as the referent of the word in question. No *gauḥ* has ever been seen applied to non-cow.)

According to Dignāga, it is not the case that the word "cow" covers all instances of cows on the basis of a positive, strong relationship learned through the positive method of concurrent existence ("cow" → $cow_{1...n}$). Rather, a negative, weak relationship is learned through the negative method of concurrent absence and is confirmed by cumulative non-perception ($adarśana_{\text{so far}}$) in such a way that whenever there is no cow, there is no use of the word "cow." As mentioned above, the universal relationship, negative and weak, learned through the negative method of concurrent absence is called *avinābhāva*, i.e., without X never Y. In other words, one learns, in a general form, the relationship between the absence of a cow and the absence of the word "cow." On the basis of this general relationship, thus learned, the word "cow" makes manifest (*dyotayati*) its own referent as a general remainder by excluding from the word's denoted domain non-cows that have never been seen. The denoted domain of "cow" is the complement that remains (and thus becomes manifest in a general form) after the exclusion of other things. It is not the case that the word "cow" positively denotes (*abhi-√dhā*) each and every case of a cow on the basis of a strong relationship positively learned for each case through perception. Rather, the learning of the general but negative relationship *avinābhāva*, i.e., without a cow "cow" is never applied, is the basis for understanding cows in general (i.e., cows qualified by the exclusion of non-cows) from hearing "cow."

8.4. Dignāga's non-perception (*adarśana*)

Generally speaking, later authors divided non-perception (*anupalabdhi, anupalambha, adarśana*) into four subtypes depending on the nature of the agent and the manner in which non-perception is qualified:[281]

anupalambha	1. *nirviśeṣaṇa*	2. *saviśeṣaṇa*
A. *sva-*	A1	A2
B. *sarvapuruṣa-*	B1	B2

Regarding the agent of non-perception, two possibilities are proposed by later authors: A. oneself, i.e., one has never seen the case personally; B. all people, i.e., nobody has ever seen the case. As for the qualification of non-perception, two types are proposed: 1. simple, non-qualified non-perception (later called *adarśanamātra*); 2. non-perception of a perceivable object (*dṛśya-anupalabdhi*), i.e., a perceivable thing that fulfills the conditions of perception is not perceived. Dharmakīrti introduces the latter distinction (between 1 and 2) by critically designating 1 as *adarśanamātra*, mere (non-qualified) non-perception.[282] This is the non-perception of an

[281] TSPś II.1030,20–22 ad TSś 3269: *kiṃ svopalambhanivṛttis tvayā sarvajñābhāvasiddhaye 'nupalambho 'bhipretaḥ, āhosvit sarvapuruṣopalambhanivṛttir vā / anupalambho 'pi kiṃ nirviśeṣaṇo 'bhīṣṭa upalabdhilakṣaṇaprāptasyety etasya viśeṣaṇasyānāśrayaṇāt, āhosvit saviśeṣaṇa iti /*. "I wonder whether you intend, in order to prove the absence of an omniscient being, non-perception to be the absence of your own perception, or the absence of perception on the part of all people. Furthermore, regarding non-perception, I wonder whether it is intended to be without a qualification, i.e., without resorting to a qualification 'which fulfills the condition for perception,' or with a qualification."

[282] For Dharmakīrti's criticism of *adarśanamātra*, see, e.g., Katsura 1991: 141 and Katsura 1992.

object without specifying as to whether it is perceivable (*dṛśya*) or not perceivable (*adṛśya*):[283]

A1. One has never seen the object oneself.

A2. One has never seen the object oneself though it is perceivable.

B1. Nobody has ever seen the object.

B2. Nobody has ever seen the object though it is perceivable.

One cannot claim that X does not exist just because one has not seen X for oneself. Śāntarakṣita points out that one's own non-perception (A1) is subject to deviation. Therefore, it does not guarantee the non-existence of X. On the other hand, ordinary people like us (who are not omniscient) cannot be sure that nobody else has ever seen X. Therefore, non-perception by all people, too, is doubtful as a witness to the non-existence of X. Hence, Śāntarakṣita states that both one's own non-perception and non-perception attributed to all people are problematic.[284]

It is to be noted that *dṛśya*- and *adṛśya-anupalabdhi* are used in an important argument against the Mīmāṃsakas. The Mīmāṃsakas want to prove the non-existence of an omniscient being, but an omniscient being is essentially unknowable in that his mind cannot be fully known by ordinary people. Therefore, his non-existence cannot be proven by means of non-perception, because non-perception with a qualification, i.e., non-perception of a perceptible object (*dṛśya-anupalabdhi*), does not work with regard to an unknowable, omniscient being. And the non-perception of an unknowable entity (*adṛśya-anupalabdhi*) only leaves doubt as to whether such a being exists.[285]

Dignāga tries to confirm the concurrent absence of "cow" and its

---

[283] See, e.g., Katsura 1992: 228 for *dṛśyānupalabdhi* and *adṛśyānupalabdhi*.

[284] TSś 122: *sarvādṛṣṭiś ca saṃdigdhā svādṛṣṭir vyabhicāriṇī / vindhyādriran-dhradūrvāder adṛṣṭāv api sattvataḥ //*. "Non-perception by all people is open to doubt; and non-perception by oneself is subject to deviation. For Dūrvā grass, and so on, in a cave in the Vindhya mountains exists although unseen."

[285] With the same critique of *adarśanamātra* that he uses (implicitly) against Dignāga and (explicitly) against Īśvarasena, Dharmakīrti criticizes Kumārila's proof of the non-existence of an omniscient being. Cf. Katsura 1992: 227–228.

referent by demonstrating that the word "cow" has never been seen applied to non-cows. If we look at Dignāga's notion of non-perception from the critical perspective of later followers of Dharmakīrti,[286] it can be identified precisely as type B1, i.e., mere (unqualified) non-perception by all people. It seems that Dignāga presupposes as common sense that the word "cow" has never been seen applied to non-cows. But, as Śāntarakṣita points out, there may be doubt, at least for ordinary people who are not omniscient, as to whether no one has ever seen this. Further, from the perspective of Dharmakīrti and later Buddhist epistemologists, confirmation of concurrent absence through mere non-perception is also not justifiable.

Thinkers before Dharmakīrti, however, simply presupposed that non-perception (of the kind we can identify as B1) was genuine evidence for the non-existence of X. In the case of Kumārila, *pramāṇābhāva*, i.e., the absence of the five positive *pramāṇa*s, functions as the sixth, independent *pramāṇa* for confirming the non-existence of X. If an object X is not confirmed by any of the five positive *pramāṇa*s, it is proved to be non-existent by means of *pramāṇābhāva*. Therefore, Dignāga's idea of non-perception is a device that is, on its own, acceptable for Kumārila. And because Kumārila takes a similar stance, he cannot criticize Dignāga's notion of non-perception.[287] The reasoning that the word "cow" has never been seen applied to non-cows is acceptable for Kumārila as a genuine application of non-perception, because Kumārila, as an empiricist,[288]

---

[286] For the grammatical aspect of Dignāga's theory of non-perception, see Ogawa 2017: 98–101.

[287] Cf. TSś 2870-2871 (quotation from the *Bṛhaṭṭīkā*): *evaṃ parīkṣakajñānatritayaṃ nātivartate / tataś cājātabādhena nāśaṅkyaṃ bādhakaṃ punaḥ // utprekṣeta hi yo mohād ajātam api bādhakam / sa sarvavyavahāreṣu saṃśayātmā kṣayaṃ vrajet //.*

[288] Kumārila can be regarded as a pure empiricist in that he accepts that repeated experiences (*bhūyodarśana*) are sufficient for the ascertainment of invariable concomitance.

himself presupposes that X does not exist if X has not been experienced by means of any *pramāṇa*.[289]

9. Concurrent absence (*vyatireka*) based on non-perception (*adarśana*)

9.1. *Anvaya* and *vyatireka*: the realists' method of grasping the semantic relationship

The grammatical tradition presupposes that the relationship between a word and its referent is learned through concurrent existence ("Hearing the word 'cow,' one understands its meaning") and concurrent absence ("When the word 'cow' disappears, the understanding of the meaning also disappears"). Kumārila presupposes the same method. Indeed, when Kumārila criticizes a realist view, probably ascribed to the Naiyāyikas, he points out that the Nyāya school requires concurrent absence in addition to concurrent existence as a means of explaining how the semantic relation is learned. Like Kumārila, Sucarita too presupposes that learning the semantic relationship requires both when he states, "It has already been explained that the extraction of a word's denotative capacity occurs through concurrent existence and concurrent absence."[290]

Dignāga, on the other hand, claims that the grasping of the universal relationship between a word and its referent is possible only through concurrent absence (*vyatirekamukhenaiva*) based on non-perception.[291]

---

[289] In this connection, see also Katsura 1991: 142: "Thus the first and foremost important difference between Dignāga and Dharmakīrti on the *apoha* doctrine is closely related to the fundamental difference of their systems of logic; namely, Dignāga's logic carries with itself the inductive approach of traditional Indian logic, while Dharmakīrti's system has a strong tendency towards deductive logic with his new theory of *svabhāvapratibandha*. Dignāga's theory of pervasion reveals a hypothetical nature, which is strongly criticized by Dharmakīrti."

[290] ŚVKāś$_K$ 271(50),11–12 ad 159ab: *anvayavyatirekābhyāṃ śabdaśaktiniṣkarṣo varṇita eva* /.

[291] His statement that at least a single case of concurrent existence is necessary (PS 5.34) should be understood as a statement on the necessity of excluding a

9.2. Kumārila's criticism of Dignāga's reliance on *vyatireka*

Kumārila does not accept Dignāga's view here. Suppose that one relies *solely* on concurrent absence when learning the invariable relation between a word and its meaning. It is true that one has never seen "cow" applied to non-cows, but it is also the case that one has never seen it applied to a cow. Therefore, nothing remains as the general referent conveyed by the word. This problem is parallel to what is known as Hempel's Raven Paradox.[292] Kumārila's criticism is justifiable in this regard.

If we posit an individual person as the agent of non-perception, we can say that the non-perception of X is in fact based on a limited number of non-perceptions. Take as an example a child who learns the semantic relationship through non-perception. When she sees the word "cow" applied to a particular cow_1, the situation might be described as follows: She does not see the word "cow" applied to things other than cow_1. When learning the word, there is a single case of $non\text{-}perception_1$ of the word "cow" with regard to $non\text{-}cow_1$. It is to be noted that the $non\text{-}cow_1$ includes other cows (cow_2 ... cow_n), besides other types such as horses, elephants, lions, and so on.

Essentially the problem remains the same, however much the number

---

pseudo-reason called *asādhāraṇānaikāntika* in the terminology of inference. In other words, at least a single case of *anvaya* is required to exclude *ad hoc* an undesirable case. It is not that *anvaya* contributes to the establishment of the universal relationship, as he clearly explains when denying its role in his *Vṛtti* to this passage. Dignāga's sticking to the old idea of *trairūpya* can be regarded as an attempt not to contradict the tradition. It is to be noted that for Dignāga *anvaya* is not substantially different from *vyatireka*, as he explicitly states in PSV 5.38d: *anvayavyatirekau na bhinnārthau*. Therefore, 'only through concurrent absence' is his logical stance, whereas 'primarily through concurrent absence' (cf. Pind 2015: I.lx; II.231–233 [Appendix 7]) can be regarded as a result of the exegetical (apologetic) attitude he adopts in his effort to somehow show the raison d'etre of *anvaya*. Logically speaking, for Dignāga, *vyatireka* alone is sufficient to establish the universal relationship. But then the *asādhāraṇānaikāntika*, which is traditionally regarded as a pseudo-reason, would be a correct reason. It is in this context that *anvaya* is required and not in the context of establishing the universal relationship.

[292] On the parallelism between the *asādhāraṇānaikāntika* and Hempel's Raven paradox, see Katsura 1998: 277–278.

of non-perceptions may increase. In vv. 81–82 Kumārila explains the difficulty as follows:[293]

[M] And how, furthermore, would one know that [non-cow] is expressed by the word "non-cow"? (81ab)

[B] That in regard to which the word "cow" is not observed when the connection is [initially] learned [is what is expressed by "non-cow"]. (81cd)

[M] Then everything other than a single individual [– even other cows!] would be what is to be excluded [as non-cow]. In this way, a universal would not be the meaning. (82)

The number of non-perceptions in the learning stage is limited. It can ultimately be reduced to one. If everything else other than cow_1 were to be learned as the domain of the *apohya*, the *apohya* would include other cows (cow_2 ... cow_n), too. Consequently, the word "cow," which has been seen applied only to cow_1, could not be applied to other cows.

9.3. Evaluation of Kumārila's criticism

Kumārila's criticism here is based on his tendentious interpretation of Dignāga's notion of non-perception. Kumārila accepts that the non-existence of X can be ascertained by the sixth *pramāṇa*, called *pramāṇābhāva*. In this regard, we can say that Dignāga and Kumārila share a similar epistemic view with respect to the ascertainment of non-existence. However, in his critique, Kumārila reduces non-perception to a single instance (non-perception_1), whereas Dignāga himself intends a universal type of non-perception ($\text{non-perception}_{\text{so far}}$). If Kumārila had criticized Dignāga's view of non-perception in a manner faithful to his intended meaning, he would be subject to the same criticism. We should pay attention to Kumārila's clause, v. 81d, "when the relation is learned" (*saṃbandhānubhavakṣaṇe*). It is likely that Kumārila intentionally attaches this qualification to Dignāga's argument in order to avoid a criticism that could turn back on himself. In any case, we can judge Kumārila's criticism here as not decisive.

---

[293] Cf. also Hugon 2011: 111–112.

As mentioned above, Dignāga probably intends social, universal non-perception$_{\text{so far}}$ of type B1 ("No one has ever seen the object") and not a limited number of private non-perceptions of type A1 ("One has not seen the object"), although he nowhere explicitly refers to this distinction. The agent of non-perception ultimately comprises all (appropriate) members of a society who standardly use the language in question. This is why Dignāga's general claim that "cow" has never been seen applied to non-cows is possible. Dignāga presupposes that the use of language is purely social. When discussing language, he has mundane usage in mind (*lokavad evānugamyante*, PSV ad 5.37b), although he thinks that language is essentially false with regard to external entities. Therefore, we should understand his claim that the word "cow" has never been seen applied to non-cows as a statement based on common practices.[294]

As pointed out by Śāntarakṣita and Kamalaśīla, the notion of non-perception is ambiguous. A private non-perception of X does not guarantee the absence of X. Nor is it certain, at least for ordinary (non-omniscient) human beings like us, that nobody has ever seen X. As previously noted, among the four types of non-perception explained above, Dignāga's non-perception can be identified as that of type B1. Dignāga takes for granted the social agreement that the word "cow" is never applied to non-cows. Of course, there is uncertainty as to whether "cow" has ever been seen applied to non-cows. Only an omniscient being can be sure. But we have to turn to Dharmakīrti's critique of non-perception to criticize Dignāga's view in this manner. His notion of *dṛśya-anupalabdhi* will add a difficulty for Dignāga.

10. Dignāga's ascertainment of the *apohya*

As we have already seen, Dignāga claims that it is possible to ascertain through non-perception that non-cows are not the domain denoted by the word "cow." In other words, the domain of non-cows (the *apohya*s) is claimed to be established. Therefore, it is not the case, quite contrary to Kumārila's claim, that the theory of *apoha* is vitiated by the fallacy of

---

[294] Cf. Katsura's remark regarding Dignāga's logic. Katsura 1992: 227: "I believe that his final recourse in determining the pervasion between two items was people's common sense or the way they used their own language (*lokavyavahāra* or *lokaprasiddhi*)."

mutual dependence between the absence of non-cows and the absence of cows (2).

10.1. Kumārila's allegation of mutual dependence

When criticizing Dignāga, Kumārila presupposes that the domain of the *apohya* is not yet established (*asiddha*). But Dignāga would not agree with this assertion. First, Kumārila's argument in vv. 83–85ab can be summarized as follows: Non-cows (*agauḥ*$_1$ ... *agauḥ*$_n$), which have never been seen as the denoted domain of the word "cow," are of the nature of the absence of cows (the negation of cows) inasmuch as non-cows are the object of non-perception. If the <cows> in the <absence of cows> were of the nature of the absence of non-cows, there would arise the fallacy of mutual dependence between the absence of cows and the absence of non-cows. If, on the other hand, the <cows> are claimed to be already established, it would be pointless to introduce the roundabout notion "exclusion of non-cows," because the <cows> in general, i.e., the universal cowness, functions as a general property. If the <cows> are not established, however, their negation, i.e., non-cows, will not be established. Consequently, the exclusion of non-cows will not be established either. In this way, Kumārila asserts that the fallacy of mutual dependence arises between the absence of cows and the absence of non-cows, or the exclusion of non-cows and non-cows (i.e., the negation of cows), on the basis that the non-cows are not yet established.

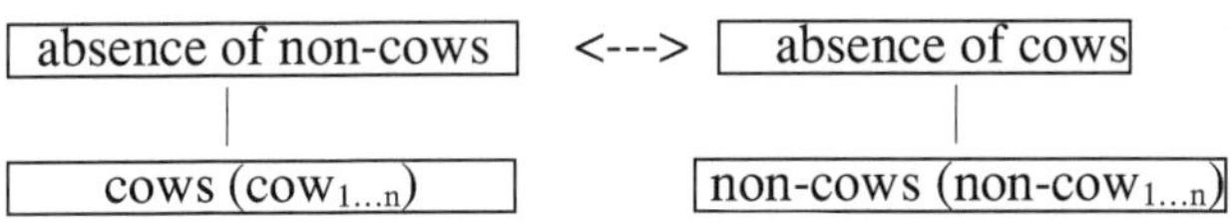

As explained above, however, for Dignāga non-cows are established as something with regard to which the word "cow" has never been seen applied. In other words, non-cows, that is, the absence of cows, are already given as the object of non-perception. On the basis of this, given that non-cows are already established as the *apohya*s, he can ensure, in a general (non-specific) form, the domain of the complement that remains after excluding non-cows.

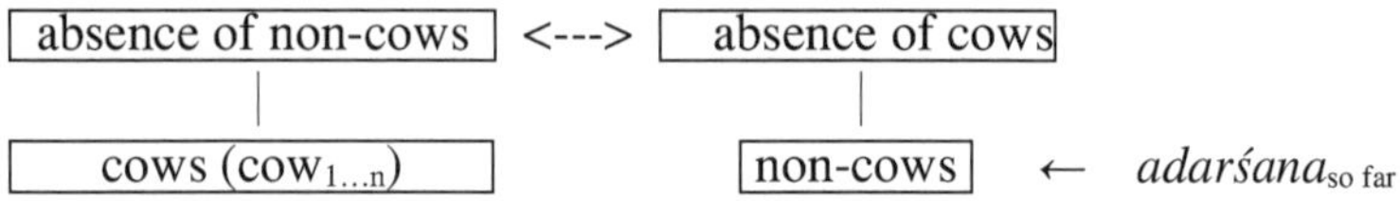

10.2. The exclusion of non-cows

To understand how Dignāga can posit non-cows as already established, we need to pay attention to the distinction between a single non-perception (non-perception$_{1}$) and universal non-perception (non-perception$_{\text{so far}}$). The former, non-perception$_{1}$, covers only one instance of non-cow$_{1}$, whereas the latter can cover the entire group of non-cows (non-cow$_{1...n}$). If a single non-perception were required for each case of non-cow, the number of non-perceptions required to cover the entire group would be infinite. Thus, as Kumārila points out, the exclusion of non-cows would be impossible. We can clarify his intended criticism by supplying the concrete example of "cow" in the following verses:

> **58** If it is believed that there is the exclusion of all [non-cows, then] it must be explained how that [is possible]. If [this exclusion of all non-cows were to be done] one-by-one, then it would not be possible because of the unlimited number of things to be excluded.
>
> **59ab** Furthermore, because of the difference of the things to be excluded the *apoha* would be divided.

The number of non-perceptions would be infinite if we posit an accumulation of single instances of non-perception for each case of non-cow. Correspondently, the exclusion of non-cows would be infinite. As such, the exclusion, divided into innumerable individual exclusions, could not fulfill the role of a general property. As noted above, we can confirm that in his critique Kumārila presupposes a single non-perception (non-perception$_{1}$) for each case of non-cow and not the non-perception (non-perception$_{\text{so far}}$) that can conveniently cover all cases at once.

Dignāga himself, however, presupposes that non-perception can cover all cases, because his non-perception covers all of space (known to the linguistic community) and time (up to the present moment), although there are an infinite number of non-cows.[295] He states,[296]

> PSV ad 5.34: *atulye tu saty apy ānantye śakyam adarśanamātreṇāvṛtter ākhyānam.*
>
> Non-application to a dissimilar case, on the other hand, can be stated merely by non-perception, in spite of infinitude.[297]

In this passage Dignāga refers to the non-application (*avṛtti*) of the word "cow" to non-cows. Although there is an infinite number of individual non-cows, Dignāga thinks that non-perception$_{\text{so far}}$ can cover all cases at once. The phrase *saty apy ānantye* gives us the impression that Dignāga indeed presupposes individual particular non-cows. The word *atulya*, however, should be interpreted as *tulya-abhāva* in Dignāga's system and thus can be interpreted as referring to the absence of cows. Therefore, it is not clear whether the present <non-cows>, i.e., the absence of cows, are conceived of as individual particulars, a collection of individuals, or an *apoha* as a universal (i.e., the negation of cows). Dignāga seems to make use of the ambiguity that *atulya* can refer both to the collection of individual non-cows and to the universal absence of cows.

In another context Dignāga explicitly accepts that the non-cows to be excluded are a universal *apoha* in reality. There, he states that the *apohya* is excluded generally (*sāmānyena nirākṛteḥ*, PS 5.43b) and not by means of its members one-by-one (*pratidravyam*). In the context of stressing the parallel operation between inference and verbal cognition, he states,

> PSV ad 5.43b: *na hi so 'nyāṃ jātiṃ pratidravyam apohate, kiṃ tarhi vyavacchedyavivakṣayaikena sāmānyadharmeṇa. uktaṃ cātra vijātīye 'darśanamātreṇānumānam* [...]. *tasmād yathā "viṣāṇitvād anaśvaḥ" iti vacane 'śve viṣāṇitvādarśanena tadvyavacchedānumānam, na tu karkādīn pratyekam apohate, nāpy ekaikeṣu gavādiṣu vartate.* (Pind 2012: I.53,4–54,5)

---

[295] Cf. also Pind 1991: 273 for Dignāga's idea of how the invariable concomitance can be established merely by non-perception.

[296] See also n. 41 above ad ŚV *Apohavāda* 75.

[297] See also Katsura 1991: 140 and Pind 2015: II.120–121.

Pind 2015: II.161–162: For the [word] does not exclude a different general property for each individual substance, but rather with the intention of denoting the things to be excluded by means of a single common property. And on this point it has been explained that the inference [of the referent] is from mere non-observation [of the word's application] to what belongs to the class of dissimilar things [...]. Therefore, like in the statement "it is a non-horse because it is horned," the inference is from its exclusion from this [namely a horse] because of not observing the general property of being horned in a horse, but the white horse, etc. are not excluded each separately, nor is every single cow, etc. apprehended.[298]

Dignāga explicitly states that the *apohya* is excluded collectively as non-cow in a general form and he denies the necessity of its exclusion for each and every particular. This passage confirms for us that Dignāga presupposes the *apohya* to be a universal *apoha* in reality, namely, the absence of cows. It implies that what Dignāga intended by *atulya* is the absence of cows and not the exclusion of individual non-cows. All things considered, we can say that his statement *saty apy ānantye* is carefully chosen, because it gives us the impression that non-perception can cover all individuals. But, in fact, non-perception ascertains only the absence of cows as a general *apoha*, and not the exclusion of each individual non-cow. Although there are an infinite number of non-cows, the absence of cows is a single quality.

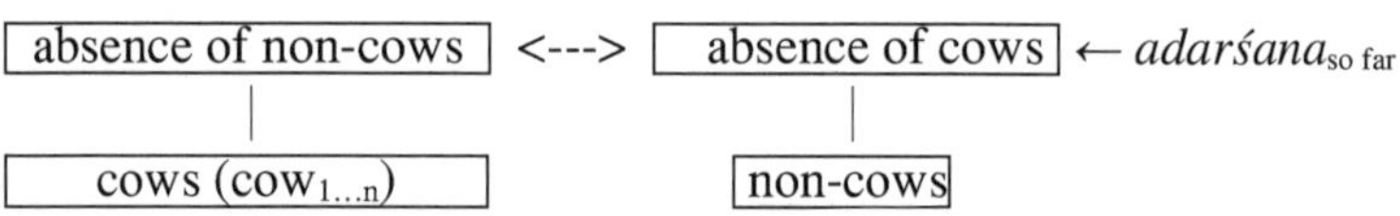

Nonetheless, we can judge Kumārila's criticism of non-perception for each individual as valid. Because of Dignāga's ambiguous usage of *atulya*, Kumārila is justified in considering all candidates in his evaluation.

After this, in v. 95, Kumārila convincingly rejects Dignāga's *apohya* as a general property:

95 And when individuals cannot be what is excluded because they are

[298] Cf. also Pind 2011: 76.

inexpressible by words, then the universal would be excluded. And because of its exclusion it is a real thing.

In this verse Kumārila identifies Dignāga's *apohya* as a general characteristic, i.e., *apoha* in reality, because it has to be so in order to be in the domain of word-referents. Considering Dignāga's own explanation in PS 5.43b, given above, Kumārila's interpretation appears justified. Then, of course, the *apohya* cannot be a general *apoha* in reality, as Kumārila finally points out, because if it were, it could not count as a real thing to be excluded. The object of exclusion has to be something real, that is to say, the non-cow has to be a real universal.

11. The merit of Dignāga's negative semantics

11.1. The remainder of the exclusion of non-cows is made manifest.

Dignāga's explanation of how to ascertain the universal relationship between words and their referents has an advantage which is absent from the realist theory. As we have seen, it is not the case, for Dignāga, that the word "cow" is positively connected with each and every cow ($cow_{1...n}$). In other words, the relation between the word and its referent is not a strong connection based on their co-existence (*anvaya*). Rather, the word "cow" is weakly connected with the complement that remains after the exclusion of non-cows, in the sense that the word has not been seen applied to non-cows. The general characteristic (*sāmānyalakṣaṇa*) for Dignāga is essentially a remainder left unexcluded in a learning process based on non-perception. Through this weak connection the word "cow" makes manifest the remainder in a general way. Dignāga glosses the phrase "[a word] expresses/tells" (*bhāṣate*) in PS 5.1 with the expression "makes manifest" (*dyotayati*) in his own *Vṛtti*, because for him the common expression "denotes" (*abhi-√dhā*) has too strong a connotation of positive denotation based on co-existence. He indeed refers to the strong denotation as *abhi-√dhā* when he distinguishes it from his own weak denotation based on non-exclusion (*anapohana*).[299] One can say that a higher/more general concept

[299] PSV 5.18b: *naitad uktam abhidheyatvāt, kiṃ tarhi,* ***anapohanāt*** (Pind 2015:

(such as "tree") includes lower/more particular concepts (such as *śiṃśapā*), not because the lower concepts are denoted (*abhidheyatvāt*) by a word expressive of the general concept (such as "tree"), but rather because they are not excluded (*anapohanāt*). Thus, the word "tree" can make manifest the exclusion-complement which includes lower concepts because they are not excluded. Hence the words "tree" and *śiṃśapā* can be used co-referentially, as in, "The tree is a *śiṃśapā*."

11.2. *Anapohana* and *vyāpti*

Dignāga's own view of the semantic relation should be distinguished from that of the realists because he posits a relation that is negative and weak, inasmuch as it is based on co-absence, whereas according to the latter the relation is positive and strong, inasmuch as it is based on co-existence. Non-exclusion (*anapohana*), as distinguished from strong denotation (*abhi-√dhā*), is the key for us to understand Dignāga's own view of verbal denotation and relation. This difference results in the theoretical disparity between the two camps. The realists cannot explain the linguistic phenomenon of co-reference (*sāmānādhikaraṇya*) such as we see in the phrase "an existing pot" (*san ghaṭaḥ*). Here, we know the word "existing" refers to the pot, because it is juxtaposed with "pot" and is in grammatical agreement with it. If one were to follow the *jātimat/tadvat* theory of the realists, however, the word "existing" could refer only to things that have the universal existence (*sattā*) and not to a pot. Thus, the word "existing" could not include (*vi-√āp*) or imply (*ā-√kṣip*) a pot. According to Dignāga's own view, on the other hand, the word "existing" can include a pot, because a pot is not excluded.

Similarly, according to Dignāga, the realists cannot coherently explain the linguistic phenomenon that the word "tree" produces an ascertainment (*niścaya*) with regard to higher concepts (such as its being earthen, a substance, and existing), whereas it causes doubt with regard to lower concepts, such as whether it is a Śiṃśapā tree or a Khadira tree, etc. Following the *tadvat* theory that the word "tree" denotes anything that has

---

I.21,4–6). "The statement is made not because it is denoted, but because **it is not excluded**."

the universal treeness, the word "tree" would denote only trees in general and thereby would not bring about any ascertainment or doubt with regard to higher or lower concepts, because it denotes neither its higher concepts nor its lower concepts. If they claim that the word denotes both higher and lower concepts, they cannot explain the fact that the word causes doubt in regard to the lower concepts. Only the theory of weak connection based on non-exclusion can explain the phenomenon in question: because neither concepts are excluded therefore they are included as referents. In this way, Dignāga's negative semantics based on non-perception functions well to explain various linguistic phenomena.

12. Concluding Remarks

Is non-perception pervasive? Dignāga believes in its universal application to *apohya*s, but Dharmakīrti later reveals its limitation by way of distinguishing mere non-perception (*adarśanamātra*) from legitimate *dṛśya-anupalabdhi*. Kumārila criticizes Dignāga's non-perception as being too broad, saying that it permits nothing to remain, i.e., neither non-cows nor cows. Therefore, cows, which are alleged to be the remainder after non-cows have been excluded, cannot be connected with the word "cow." According to Dignāga's own system, however, non-cows can be ascertained by non-perception in a general form. What remains after excluding non-cows is the denoted domain of the word "cow." Dignāga's peculiar claim that the universal relationship 'without X never Y' (*avinābhāva*) can be ascertained through concurrent absence alone (*vyatirekamukhenaiva*) has several merits not found in the realists' positive method of concurrent existence. Dignāga's theory of weak relationship and weak denotation can straightforwardly explain the linguistic phenomena of co-reference (*sāmānādhikaraṇya*) and it can explain the existence of doubt and ascertainment with regard to a referent's lower and higher concepts respectively, without resorting to figurative usage (*upacāra*). His Apohavāda, which theoretically starts from the foundational thesis that no real universal exists, is possible as a semantic theory if we accept the validity of non-perception in establishing the *apohya*. Furthermore, it has its own merits which, as Dignāga himself claims, are missing in the realist theory.

Abbreviations, Bibliography, and Indices

Akamatsu 1971 — Akihiko Akamatsu: *Evolution de la théorie de l'apoha (L'Apohaprakaraṇa de Jñānaśrīmitra).* Ph.D. Thesis, Université de la Sorbonne Nouvelle (Paris III).

Arnold 2012 — Dan Arnold: *Brains, Buddhas, and Believing: The Problem of Intentionality in Classical Buddhist and Cognitive-Scientific Philosophy of Mind.* New York 2012: Columbia University Press.

AKBh — P. Pradhan: *Abhidharmakośabhāṣyam of Vasubandhu.* Patna 1975: Jayaswal Research Institute.

Chakrabarti/Siderits 2011 — Arindam Chakrabarti and Mark Siderits: "Introduction." Pp. 1–49 in Siderits et al. 2011.

Doniger/Smith 1991 — Wendy Doniger and Brian K. Smith (trans.): *The Laws of Manu.* London 1991: Penguin Books.

Dreyfus 1997 — Georges B. J. Dreyfus: *Recognizing Reality: Dharmakīrti's Philosophy and Its Tibetan Interpretations.* Albany 1997: State University of New York Press.

Dreyfus 2011 — Georges Dreyfus: "Apoha as a Naturalized Account of Concept Formation." Pp. 207–227 in Siderits et al. 2011.

Dunne 2011 — John D. Dunne: "Key Features of Dharmakīrti's Apoha Theory." Pp. 84–108 in Siderits et al. 2011.

Edgerton 1929 — Franklyn Edgerton: *The Mīmāṇsā Nyāya Prakāśa or Āpadevī: A Treatise on the Mīmāṇsā System by Āpadeva, Translated into English, with an Introduction, Transliterated Sanskrit Text, and Glossarial Index.* New Haven 1929: Yale University Press.

Eltschinger 2007 — Vincent Eltschinger: *Penser l'autorité des Écritures.* Vienna 2007: Verlag der Österreichischen Akademie der Wissenschaften.

Eltschinger/Ratié 2013 — Vincent Eltschinger and Isabelle Ratié: *Self, No-Self, and Salvation.* Vienna 2013: Verlag der Österreichischen Akademie der Wissenschaften.

Eltschinger et al. 2018 — Vincent Eltschinger, John Taber, Michael Torsten Much, and Isabelle Ratié: *Dharmakīrti's Theory of Exclusion (apoha). Part I, On*

Concealing. An Annotated Translation of Pramāṇavārttikasvavṛtti 24,16–45,20, on verses 1.40–91. Tokyo 2018: International Institute for Buddhist Studies (*Studia Philological Buddhica* 36).

Franco 1999 — Eli Franco: "*Avīta* and *Āvīta*." *Études Asiatiques/Asiatische Studien* 53/3: 563–577.

Frauwallner 1932 — Erich Frauwallner: "Beiträge zur Apohalehre: I. Dharmakīrti. Übersetzung." *Wiener Zeitschrift für die Kunde des Morgenlandes* 39: 247–285.

Frauwallner 1933 — Erich Frauwallner: "Beiträge zur Apohalehre: I. Dharmakīrti. Übersetzung. (Fortsetzung)." *Wiener Zeitschrift für die Kunde des Morgenlandes* 40: 51–94.

Frauwallner 1935 — Erich Frauwallner: "Beiträge zur Apohalehre: I. Dharmakīrti. Übersetzung. (Zusammenfassung)." *Wiener Zeitschrift für die Kunde des Morgenlandes* 42: 93–102.

Frauwallner 1937 — Erich Frauwallner: "Beiträge zur Apohalehre: II. Dharmottara." *Wiener Zeitschrift für die Kunde des Morgenlandes* 44: 233–287.

Frauwallner 1959 — Erich Frauwallner: "Dignāga, sein Werk und seine Entwicklung." *Wiener Zeitschrift für die Kunde Süd- und Ostasiens* 3: 83–164.

Frauwallner 1962 — Erich Frauwallner: "Kumārila's Bṛhaṭṭīkā." *Wiener Zeitschrift für die Kunde Süd- und Ostasiens* 6: 78–90.

Frauwallner 1968 — Erich Frauwallner: *Materialien zur ältesten Erkenntnislehre der Karmamīmāṃsā*. Vienna 1968: Verlag der Österreichischen Akademie der Wissenschaften.

Freschi 2010 — Elisa Freschi: "Facing the Boundaries of Epistemology: Kumārila on Error and Negative Cognition." *Journal of Indian Philosophy* 38: 39–48.

Ganeri 2001 — Jonardon Ganeri: *Philosophy in Classical India: The Proper Work of Reason*. London 2001: Routledge.

Ganeri 2011 — Jonardon Ganeri: "Apoha, Feature-Placing, and Sensory Content." Pp. 228–246 in Siderits et al. 2011.

Halbfass 1991 — Wilhelm Halbfass: *Tradition and Reflection: Explorations in Indian Thought*. Albany 1991: State University of New York Press.

Harikai 2007 — Kunio Harikai: *Sanskrit Text of the* Tantravārttika, *Adhyāya 1, Pāda 2 (Chapters of Arthavāda and Mantra)*. Saga 2007: Saga Medical School (Annual Report of Medical Anthropology and Humanity 2).

Harikai 2012 — Kunio Harikai: *Sanskrit Text of the* Tantravārttika, *Adhyāya 1, Pāda 3, Adhikaraṇa 10, 11*. Fukuoka 2012: Kyushu University (South Asian Classical Studies 7).

Hattori 1968 — Masaaki Hattori: *Dignāga, On Perception* (trans.). Cambridge, Mass. 1968: Harvard University Press (Harvard Oriental Series 47).

Hattori 1973 — Masaaki Hattori: "Mīmāṃsāślokavārttika, Apohavāda shō no Kenkyū (Jō)." *Kyōto Daigaku Bungakubu Kenkyū Kiyō* (Kyoto University) 14: 1–44.

Hattori 1975 — Masaaki Hattori: "Mīmāṃsāślokavārttika, Apohavāda shō no Kenkyū (Ge)." *Kyōto Daigaku Bungakubu Kenkyū Kiyō* (Kyoto University) 15: 1–63.

Hattori 1977 — Masaaki Hattori: "The Sautrāntika Background of the *Apoha* Theory." Pp. 47–58 in Leslie S. Kawamura and Keith Scott. (eds.): *Buddhist Thought and Asian Civilization: Essays in Honour of Herbert V. Guenther on His Sixtieth Birthday*. Emeryville, California 1977: Dharma Publishing.

Hattori 1980 — Masaaki Hattori: "*Apoha* and *Pratibhā*." Pp. 61–73 in M. Nagatomi, B. K. Matilal, J. M. Masson, and E. C. Dimock Jr. (eds.): *Sanskrit and Indian Studies: Essays in Honour of Daniel H. H. Ingalls*. Dordrecht 1980: D. Reidel Publishing.

Hattori 1982 — Masaaki Hattori: "The Pramāṇasamuccayavṛtti of Dignāga. Chapter Five: Anyāpoha-parīkṣā. Tibetan text, with Jinendrabuddhi's commentary." *Memoirs of the Faculty of Letters* (Kyoto University) 21: 102–224.

Hattori 2000 — Masaaki Hattori: "Dignāga's Theory of Meaning: An Annotated Translation of the *Pramāṇasamuccayavṛtti*: Chapter V: *Anyāpoha-parīkṣā* (I)." Pp. 137–146 in Jonathan A. Silk (ed.): *Wisdom, Compassion, and the Search for Understanding*. Honolulu 2000: University of Hawaii Press.

Hayes 1988 — Richard P. Hayes: *Dignāga on the Interpretation of Signs*. Dordrecht 1988: Kluwer Academic Publishers (Studies of Classical India 9).

Herzberger 1975 — Hans G. Herzberger: "Double Negation in Buddhist Logic." *Journal of Indian Philosophy* 3: 3–16.

Hugon 2011 — Pascale Hugon: "Dharmakīrti's Discussion of Circularity." Pp. 109–124 in Siderits et al. 2011.

Hugon 2017 — Pascale Hugon: "On *vyāvṛtta*." Pp. 153–183 in McAllister 2017.

Iyer 1974 — K. A. Subramania Iyer: *The Vākyapadīya of Bhartṛhari, Chapter III. pt. ii, English Translation with Exegetical Notes*. Delhi 1974: Motilal Banarsidass.

Jhā 1907 — Ganganatha Jha: *Ślokavārttika* (trans.). Calcutta 1907: Asiatic Society of Bengal (Biblioteca Indica, NS 965, 986, 1017, 1055, 1091).

Jhā 1933-36 — Ganganatha Jha: *Shabara-Bhāsya* (trans.). 3 vols. Baroda 1933–1936: Oriental Insitute (Gaekwad's Oriental Series 66).

Jhā 1983 — Gaṅgānātha Jhā: *Tantravarttika* (trans.). 2 vols. Calcutta 1903–1924. Repr. Delhi 1983: Sri Satguru Publications (Sri Garib Das Oriental Series 9 and 10).

Jhā 1984 — Gaṅgānāṭha Jhā: *The Nyāya-Sūṭras of Gauṭama* (trans.). 4 vols. Allahabad 1912–1919. Repr. Delhi 1984: Motilal Banarsidass.

Kāś — Paṇḍit Bāla Śāstrī: *Kāśikā: A Commentary on Pāṇini's Grammatical Aphorisms, by Paṇḍit Vāmana and Jayāditya*. Benares 1898: Medical Hall Press.

Kataoka 2007 — Kei Kataoka: "A Critical Edition of *Śābarabhāṣya* ad 1.1.6–23: *Śabdanityatvādhikaraṇa*." *Memoirs of the Institute of Oriental Culture* 152: 580(29)–530(79).

Kataoka 2009 — Kei Kataoka: "A Critical Edition of Bhaṭṭa Jayanta's Nyāyamañjarī: The Buddhist Refutation of Kumārila's Criticism of Apoha." *Memoirs of the Institute of Oriental Culture* 156: 498(1)–458(41).

Kataoka 2011a — Kei Kataoka: *Kumārila on Truth, Omniscience, and Killing*. 2 pts. Vienna 2011: Verlag der Österreichischen Akademie der Wissenschaften.

Kataoka 2011b — Kei Kataoka: "A Critical Edition of Bhaṭṭa Jayanta's *Nyāyamañjarī*: The Buddhist Refutation of *jāti*." *The Memoirs of Institute for Advanced Studies on Asia* (Tokyo University) 160: 636(1)–594(43).

Kataoka 2012/forthcoming — Kei Kataoka, "*Adarśanamātra* and *Utprekṣā*: A Study of a *Bṛhaṭṭīkā* Fragment." A paper read at an international symposium "Transmission and Tradition: The Meaning and the Role of 'Fragments' in Indian Philosophy," held at Shinshu University, Matsumoto, August 20–24, 2012. Forthcoming in volume containing the proceedings of the conference.

Kataoka 2014a — Kei Kataoka: "Sucaritamiśra's Critique of *Apoha*: A Critical Edition of *Kāśikā* ad *Ślokavārttika apoha* v.1." *The Memoirs of Institute for Advanced Studies on Asia* (Tokyo University) 165: 362(1)–289(74).

Kataoka 2014b — Kei Kataoka: "Dharmottara's Theory of *Apoha*." *Journal of*

Indological Studies (Kyoto University) 24 and 25 (2012–2013; published 2014): 115–135.

Kataoka 2015 — Kei Kataoka: "A Critical Edition of *Kāśikā* ad *Ślokavārttika apoha* vv. 2–94." *The Memoirs of Institute for Advanced Studies on Asia* 167: 466(39)–400(105).

Kataoka 2017 — Kei Kataoka: "A Critical Edition of Bhaṭṭa Jayanta's *Nyāyamañjarī*: The Section on Kumārila's Refutation of the *Apoha* Theory and the Buddhist Refutation of Kumārila's Criticism of *Apoha*." Pp. 3–34 in McAllister 2017.

Kataoka 2019 — Kei Kataoka: "A Critical Edition of *Kāśikā* ad *Ślokavārttika apoha* vv. 95–176." *The Memoirs of Institute for Advanced Studies on Asia* 175: 320(1)–261(60).

Katsura 1979 — Shoryu Katsura: "The Apoha Theory of Dignāga." *Indogaku bukkyōgaku kenkyū* 28: 493(16)–489(20).

Katsura 1991 — Shoryu Katsura: "Dignāga and Dharmakīrti on *apoha*." Pp. 129–144 in Ernst Steinkellner (ed.): *Studies in the Buddhist Epistemological Tradition* (Proceedings of the Second International Dharmakīrti Conference, Vienna, June 11–16, 1989). Vienna 1991: Verlag der Österreichischen Akademie der Wissenschaften.

Katsura 1992 — Shoryu Katsura: "Dignāga and Dharmakīrti on *adarśana-mātra* and *anupalabdhi*." *Asiatische Studien/Études Asiatiques* 46/1: 222–231.

Katsura 1998 — Shoryu Katsura: *Indojin no Ronrigaku.* Tokyo 1998: Chuo Koronsha.

Katsura 1999 — Shoryu Katsura (ed.): *Dharmakīrti's Thought and Its Impact on Indian and Tibetan Philosophy* (Proceedings of the Third International Dharmakīrti Conference, Hiroshima, November 4–6, 1997). Vienna 1999: Verlag der Österreichischen Akademie der Wissenschaften.

Kellner 1997 — Birgit Kellner: *Nichts bleibt Nichts: die buddhistische Zurückweisung von Kumārila's Abhāvapramāṇa*. Vienna 1997: Arbeitskreis für tibetische und buddhistische Studien (Wiener Studien zur Tibetologie und Buddhismuskunde 39).

Kellner 1999 — Birgit Kellner: "There are no pots in the Ślokavārttika. ŚV *abhāvapariccheda* 11 and patterns of negative cognition in Indian philosophy."

Journal of the Oriental Institute (Baroda) 46/3–4 (1996; published 1999): 143–167.

Kellner 2004 — Birgit Kellner: "Why Infer and not just Look? Dharmakīrti on the Psychology of Inferential Processes" Pp. 1–51 in Shoryu Katsura (ed.): *The Role of the Example (dṛṣṭānta) in Classical Indian Logic*. Vienna 2004: Arbeitskreis für tibetische und buddhistische Studien (Wiener Studien zur Tibetologie und Buddhismuskunde 58).

Kunjunni Raja 1963 — K. Kunjunni Raja: *Indian Theories of Meaning*. Madras 1963: Adyar Library.

Lasic 2009 — Horst Lasic: "Dignāga's Description of a Logical Mark in *Pramāṇasamuccaya* 2.5cd." *International Journal of Buddhist Thought and Culture* 13: 7–22.

Manu — J. L. Shastri: *Manusmṛti, with the Sanskrit Commentary Manvartha-Muktāvalī of Kullūka Bhaṭṭa*. Delhi 1983: Motilal Banarsidass.

Matilal 2002 — B. K. Matilal: *Mind, Language and World* (*The Collected Essays of Bimal Krishna Matilal, Volume I*, ed. by Jonardon Ganeri). New Delhi 2002: Oxford University Press.

McAllister 2017 — Patrick McAllister (ed.): *Reading Bhaṭṭa Jayanta on Buddhist Nominalism*. Vienna 2017: Verlag der Österreichischen Akademie der Wissenschaften (Beiträge zur Kultur- und Geistesgeschichte Asiens 95).

McAllister 2020 — Patrick McAllister: *Ratnakīrti's Proof of Exclusion*. Vienna 2019: Verlag der Österreichischen Akademie der Wissenschaften (Beiträge zur Kultur- und Geistesgeschichte Asiens 98).

McCrea/Patil 2010 — Lawrence McCrea and Parimal Patil: *Buddhist Philosophy of Language in India: Jñānaśrīmitra on Exclusion*. New York 2010: Columbia University Press.

MBh — Franz Kielhorn: *The Vyākaraṇa-Mahābhāṣya of Patañjali*. 3 vols. Bombay 1880, 1883, 1885. Repr. Poona 1962: Bhandarkar Oriental Research Institute.

Mejor 2002 — Marek Mejor: "On the Sevenfold Classification of the Negative Particle (*nañ*)." Pp. 87–100 in *Early Buddhism and Abhidharma Thought; In Honor of Hajime Sakurabe on His Seventy-Fifth Birthday*. Kyoto 2002: Heirakuji Shoten.

MHK — Chr. Lindtner: *Madhyamakahṛdayam of Bhavya*. Chennai 2001: The Adyar Library and Research Centre.

MNP — *Mīmāṃsānyāyaprakāśa* of Āpadeva. See Edgerton 1929.

Mookerjee 1935— Satkari Mookerjee: *The Buddhist Philosophy of Universal Flux*. Calcutta 1935: University of Calcutta.

MS — *Mīmāṃsāsūtra*. See MSBh.

MSBh — Subbāśāstrī: *Śrīmajjaiminīyapraṇītaṃ Mīmāṃsādarśanam.* 1st edition. 7 pts. Poona 1929–1934: Ānandāśrama Press (Ānandāśrama Sanskrit Series 97).

Much (1994) — Michael Torsten Much: "Uddyotakaras Kritik der Apoha-Lehre (Nyāyavārttika *ad* NS II 2,66)," *Wiener Zeitschrift für die Kunde Südasiens* 38: 351–366.

NĀA — Muni Jambūvijayajī. *Dvādaśāraṃ Nayacakram of Ācārya Śrī Mallavādī Kṣamāśramaṇa, with the Commentary Nyāyāgamānusāriṇī of Śrī Siṃhasūri Gaṇi Vādi Kṣamāśramaṇa.* 3 vols. Bhavnagar 1966–1988: Sri Jain Atmanand Sabha.

NKand — Vindhyeśvarīprasāda Dvivedin: *The Bhāshya of Praśastapāda, together with the Nyāyakandalī of Śrīdhara*. Benares 1895: E. J. Lazarus and Co. (Vizianagram Sanskrit Series 6).

NB — Peter Peterson: *The Nyāyabindu-Ṭīkā of Dharmottara Āchārya, to which is added The Nyāyabindu*. Calcutta 1929: The Asiatic Society of Bengal (Biblioteca Indica 128).

NBh — Anantalal Thakur: *Gautamīyanyāyadarśana with Bhāṣya of Vātsyāyana.* New Delhi 1997: Indian Council of Philosophical Research.

NS — *Nyāyasūtra*. See NBh.

NV — Anantalal Thakur: *Nyāyabhāṣyavārttika of Bhāradvāja Uddyotakara*. New Delhi 1997: Indian Council of Philosophical Research.

Ogawa 1999 — Hideyo Ogawa: "Bhartṛhari on Representations (buddhyākāra)." Pp. 267–286 in Katsura 1999.

Ogawa 2017 — Hideyo Ogawa: "The Qualifier-Qualificand Relation and Coreferentiality." Pp. 83–151 in McAllister 2017.

Ōmae 1998 — Futoshi Ōmae: "Kumārila no sphoṭa setsu Hihan—Ślokavārttika Sphoṭavāda shō no Wayaku (1) —." *Shimane Kenritsu Kokusai Tanki Daigaku Kiyō* (The University of Shimane) 5: 21–50.

P — Pāṇini's *Aṣṭādhyāyī*

Patil 2011 — Parimal Patil: "Constructing the Content of Awareness Events."

Pp.149–169 in Siderits et al. 2011.

Pind 1991 — Ole H. Pind: "Dignāga on *śabdasāmānya* and *śabdaviśesa*." Pp. 269–280 in Ernst Steinkellner (ed.): *Studies in the Buddhist Epistemological Tradition* (Proceedings of the Second International Dharmakīrti Conference, Vienna, June 11–16, 1989). Vienna 1991: Verlag der Österreichischen Akademie der Wissenschaften.

Pind 1999 — Ole H. Pind: "Dharmakīrti's Interpretation of *Pramāṇasamuccayavṛtti* V 36: *śabdo 'rthāntaranivṛttiviśiṣtān eva bhāvān āha*." Pp. 317–332 in Katsura 1999

Pind 2015 — Ole Holten Pind: *Dignāga's Philosophy of Language: Pramāṇasamuccayavṛtti V on anyāpoha*. 2 pts. Vienna 2015: Verlag der Österreichischen Akademie der Wissenschaften (Beiträge zur Kultur- und Geistesgeschichte Asiens 92).

Pind 2011 — Ole Holten Pind: "Dignāga's Apoha Theory: Its Presuppositions and Main Theoretical Implications." Pp. 64–83 in Siderits et al. 2011.

PKM — Mahendra Kumar Shastri: *Prameyakamala-mārtaṇḍa by Shri Prabha Chandra.* Delhi 1990: Sri Satguru Publications.

PS(V) 1 — *Pramāṇasamuccaya(vṛtti)* of Dignāga, Chapter 1. Sanskrit reconstruction in Ernst Steinkellner: "Dignāga's Pramāṇasamuccaya, Chapter 1. A hypothetical reconstruction of the Sanskrit text with the help of the two Tibetan translations on the basis of the hitherto known Sanskrit fragments and the linguistic materials gained from Jinendrabuddhi's Ṭīkā." http://www.ikga.oeaw.ac.at/Mat/dignaga_PS_1.pdf (April 2005).

PS 5 — *Pramāṇasamuccaya* of Dignāga, Chapter 5. Restored text in Pind 2015: I.1–63.

PSV 5 — *Pramāṇasamuccayavṛtti* of Dignāga, Chapter 5. Restored text in Pind 2015: I.1–63.

PV — *Pramāṇavārttika* of Dharmakīrti. See PVSV.

PVSV — Raniero Gnoli: *The Pramāṇavārttikam of Dharmakīrti. The first chapter with the autocommentary*. Roma 1960: Istituto Italiano per il Medio ed Estremo Oriente (Serie Orientale Roma 23).

PVSVṬ — Rāhula Sāṅkṛtyāyana: *Ācāryadharmakīrteḥ Pramāṇavārttikam (Svārthānumānaparicchedaḥ) Svopajñavṛttyā, Karṇakagomiviracitayā Taṭṭīkayā ca Sahitam*. Ilāhābād 1943: Kitāb Mahal.

PVV — Rāhula Sāṅkṛtyāyana: *Dharmakīrti's Pramāṇavārttika with commentary by Manorathanandin*. Journal of the Bhandarkar Oriental Research Institute 24–26 (1938–1940): Appendix.

Sandal 1974 — Mohan Lal Sandal: *Introduction to the Mimamsa Sutras of Jaimini*. Allahabad 1925. Repr. New York 1974: AMS Press.

Scharf 1996 — Peter Scharf: *The Denotation of Generic Terms in Ancient Indian Philosophy: Grammar, Nyāya, and Mīmāṃsā*. Philadelphia 1996: American Philosophical Society.

Sen 2011 — Prabhal Kumar Sen: "The Apoha Theory of Meaning: A Critical Account." Pp. 170–206 in Siderits et al. 2011.

Shaw 1978 — J. L. Shaw: "Negation and the Buddhist Theory of Meaning." *Journal of Indian Philosophy* 6: 59–77.

Siderits 1982 — Mark Siderits: "More Things in Heaven and Earth." *Journal of Indian Philosophy* 10: 187–208.

Siderits 1985 — Mark Siderits: "Word Meaning, Sentence Meaning, and Apoha." *Journal of Indian Philosophy* 13: 133–151.

Siderits 1991 — Mark Siderits: *Indian Philosophy of Language: Studies in Selected Issues*. Dordrecht 1991: Kluwer Academic Publishers (Studies in Linguistics and Philosophy 46).

Siderits 1999 — Mark Siderits: "Apohavāda, Nominalism and Resemblance Theories." Pp. 341-348 in Katsura 1999.

Siderits 2011 — Mark Siderits: "Śrughna by Dusk." Pp. 283–304 in Siderits et al. 2011.

Siderits et al. 2011 — Mark Siderits, Tom Tillemans, and Arindam Chakrabarti (eds.): *Apoha: Buddhist Nominalism and Human Cognition*. New York 2011: Columbia University Press.

Steinkellner 1997 — Ernst Steinkellner: "Kumārila, Īśvarasena, and Dharmakīrti in Dialogue. A New Interpretation of Pramāṇavārttika I 33." Pp. 625–646 in P. Kieffer-Pülz, J.-U. Hartmann (eds.): *Bauddhavidyāsudhākaraḥ. Studies in Honour of Heinz Bechert on the Occasion of His 65th Birthday*. Swisttal-Odendorf 1997: Indica et Tibetica Verlag.

ŚV — *Ślokavārttika*. Citations from the ŚV are based on a comparison of the relevant editions given below.

ŚV$_{K}$ — See ŚVŚar.

ŚV$_{R}$ — See ŚVTṬ.

ŚV$_{Ś}$ — Svāmī Dvārikadāsa Śāstrī: *Ślokavārttika of Śrī Kumārila Bhaṭṭa, with the Commentary Nyāyaratnākara of Śrī Pārthasārathi Miśra.* Varanasi 1978: Tara Publications.

ŚVKāś$_{K}$ — *Ślokavārttikakāśikā* of Sucaritamiśra. See Kataoka 2015 and 2019.

ŚVKāś$_{M}$ — *Ślokavārttikakāśikā* ad ŚV *Apohavāda* of Sucaritamiśra. A manuscript preserved in the Adyar Library, Chennai, No. 63359 (TR 66–5). Paper. Devanāgarī. Pp. 2613–2800.

ŚVN — *Nyāyaratnākara* of Pārthasārathi Miśra. See ŚV$_{Ś}$.

ŚVŚar — C. Kunhan Raja: *Ślokavārtikaṭīkā (Śarkarikā) of Bhaṭṭa Jayamiśra.* Madras 1946: University of Madras.

ŚVTṬ — S. K. Ramanatha Sastri: *Ślokavārtikavyākhyā Tātparyaṭīkā of Uṃveka Bhaṭṭa.* Madras 1971: University of Madras (Madras University Sanskrit Series 13).

Taber 1991 — John Taber: "Further Observations on Kumārila's *Bṛhaṭṭīkā*." *Journal of Oriental Research* 62: 179–189.

Taber 2001 — John Taber: "Much Ado About Nothing: Kumārila, Śāntarakṣita, and Dharmakīrti on the Cognition of Non-Being." *Journal of the American Oriental Society* 121/1: 72–88.

Taber 2010 — John Taber, "Kumārila's Buddhist." *Journal of Indian Philosophy* 38: 279–296.

Taber 2012a — John Taber: "Dharmakīrti and the Mīmāṃsakas in Conflict." Pp. 119–149 in Vincent Eltschinger, Helmut Krasser, and John Taber: *Can the Veda Speak? Dharmakīrti Against Mīmāṃsā Exegetics and Vedic Authority: An Annotated Translation of PVSV 164,24–176,16.* Vienna 2012: Verlag der Österreichischen Akademie der Wissenschaften.

Taber 2012b — John Taber: "Uddyotakara's Defense of a Self." Pp. 97–114 in Irina Kuznetsova, Jonardon Ganeri, and Chakaravarthi Ram-Prasad (eds.): *Hindu and Buddhist Ideas in Dialogue*. Farnham 2012: Ashgate Publishing.

Taber 2017 — John Taber: "A Road Not Taken in Indian Epistemology: Kumārila's Defense of the Perceptibility of Universals." Pp. 243–269 in Joerg Tuske (ed.): *Indian Metaphysics and Epistemology*. London 2017: Bloomsbury.

Taber 2019 — John Taber: "Dharmakīrti, *svataḥ prāmāṇyam*, and Awakening," *Wiener Zeitschrift für die Kunde Südasiens* 56–57 (2015–2018): 77–98.

Tillemans 2011a — Tom Tillemans: "How to Talk About Ineffable Things." Pp.50–63 in Siderits et al. 2011.

Tillemans 2011b — Tom Tillemans: "Dignāga, Bhāviveka and Dharmakīrti on apoha." Pp. 449–458 in Helmut Krasser, Horst Lasic, Eli Franco, and Birgit Kellner (eds.): *Religion and Logic in Buddhist Philosophical Analysis: Proceedings of the Fourth International Dharmakīrti Conference*. Vienna 2011: Verlag der Österreichischen Akademie der Wissenschaften.

TSK — Embar Krishnamacharya: *Tattvasaṅgraha of Śāntarakṣita, with the commentary of Kamalaśīla*. 2 vols. Baroda 1926: Oriental Institute (Gaekwad's Oriental Series 30–31).

TSŚ — Swami Dwarikadas Shastri: *Tattvasaṅgraha of Ācārya Shāntarakṣita, with the Commentary 'Pañjikā' of Shri Kamalashīla*. 2 vols. Varanasi 1981: Bauddha Bharati (Bauddha Bharati Series 1).

TSPK — *Tattvasaṅgrahapañjikā* of Kamalaśīla. See TSK.

TSPŚ — *Tattvasaṅgrahapañjikā* of Kamalaśīla. See TSŚ.

ṬṬ — *Ṭupṭīkā* of Kumārila. See MSBh.

TV — *Tantravārttika* of Kumārila. See MSBh.

Tzohar 2018 — Roy Tzohar: *A Yogācāra Buddhist Theory of Metaphor*. Oxford 2018: Oxford University Press.

Vasu 1997 — Śriśa Chandra Vasu: *The Ashṭādhyāyī of Pāṇini* (trans.). 2 vols. Allahabad 1891. Repr. Delhi 1997: Motilal Banarsidass.

VP 2 — K.A. Subramania Iyer: *The Vākyapadīya of Bhartṛhari, containing the Ṭīkā of Puṇyarāja and the Ancient Vṛtti, Kāṇḍa II*. Delhi 1983: Motilal Banarsidass.

VP 3 — K.A. Subramania Iyer: *The Vākyapadīya of Bhartṛhari, with the Prakīrṇaprakāśa of Helārāja, Kāṇḍa III*. 2 vols. Poona 1963 (Deccan College Monograph Series 21) and 1973: Deccan College.

Watanabe 2008 — Toshikazu Watanabe: "On *asapakṣa*." *Journal of Indian and Buddhist Studies* 56/3: 1151(109)–1145(115).

Watson/Kataoka 2017 — Alex Watson and Kei Kataoka: "The Apoha Section of the Nyāyamañjarī." Pp. 35–79 in McAllister 2017.

Yoshimizu 2011 — Kiyotaka Yoshimizu: "How to Refer to a Thing by a Word:

Another Difference Between Dignāga's and Kumārila's Theories of Denotation." *Journal of Indian Philosophy* 39: 571–587.

Yoshimizu 2017 — Kiyotaka Yoshimizu: "How Can the Word 'cow' Exclude Non-cows? Description of Meaning in Dignāga's Theory of Apoha." *Journal of Indian Philosophy* 45: 973–1012

Indices

(for Preface, Translation, and Essays)

Index locorum

Index of Indian Names